SHORT OF GENERAL WAR:
PERSPECTIVES ON THE USE OF MILITARY POWER
IN THE 21ST CENTURY

Edited by
Harry R. Yarger

April 2010

*****

*****

This collection of Student Research Papers from students of Class of 2008 reflect their differing perspectives on the use of military power short of general war.

*****

Comments pertaining to this report are invited and should be forwarded to: Director, Strategic Studies Institute, U.S. Army War College, 122 Forbes Ave, Carlisle, PA 17013-5244.

CONTENTS

Preface iv

Foreword v

Summary vi

1. Introduction 1
   Dr. Harry R. Yarger

2. Legitimacy in the Conduct of Military Operations 9
   Commander Jonathan P. Wilcox, U.S. Navy

3. Al-Qaeda, the Revolution in Military Affairs, and the Future of Warfare 23
   Lieutenant Colonel Thomas C. Graves, U.S. Army

4. Africa Command and the Militarization of U.S. Foreign Policy 39
   Mr. Dennis R. Penn

5. Strategic Bridge Towards Community Building: The Military's Role 57
   Colonel Lorelei E. W. Coplen, U.S. Army

6. Defining Criteria for Handover to Civilian Officials in Relief Operations 75
   Colonel John Bessler, U.S. Army

7. Economic and Reconstruction Considerations in a Failed State 93
   Colonel Roger H. Westermeyer, U.S. Air Force

8. The Organization for Security and Cooperation in Europe:
   A Case Study for a Return to Multilateralism 99
   Lieutenant Colonel Gary D. Espinas, U.S. Army

9. Redefining Security Cooperation: New Limits on Phase Zero and
   "Shaping" 111
   Colonel Thomas M. Rhatican, U.S. Army Reserve

10. Know Before You Go: Improving Army Officer Sociocultural Knowledge..........131
    Lieutenant Colonel James C. Laughrey, U.S. Army

11. El Salvador, Iraq, and Strategic Considerations for Counterinsurgency 159
    Lieutenant Colonel James F. Glynn, U.S. Marine Corps

12. The Use of Security Professionals in Counterinsurgency Operations 177
    Lieutenant Colonel Marco E. Harris, U.S. Army National Guard

13. Influencing the Forgotten Half of the Population in Counterinsurgency
    Operations 191
    Colonel Laura C. Loftus, U.S. Army

14. The British Approach to Counterinsurgency: Myths, Realities, and
    Strategic Challenges 207
    Colonel I. A. Rigden OBE, British Army

15. Finding an Exit: Delineating Battle Handoff in Phase IV 231
    Colonel Roger S. Marin, U.S. Army

16. Transitioning from War to Enduring Peace 245
    Colonel Michael E. Culpepper, U.S. Army

17. Stability Operations and Government: An Inherently Military Function 261
    Lieutenant Colonel Russell R. Hula, U.S. Air Force

About the Contributors 279

PREFACE

The U.S. Army War College provides an excellent environment for selected military officers and government civilians to reflect on and use their career experience to explore a wide range of strategic issues. To assure that the research conducted by Army War College students is available to Army and Department of Defense leaders, the Strategic Studies Institute publishes selected papers in its "Carlisle Papers" Series.

ANTULIO J. ECHEVARRIA II
Director of Research
Strategic Studies Institute

FOREWORD

Success in the Cold War unleashed a myriad of threats and challenges to the stability of the emerging U.S. inspired global order. Instability portends no good for U.S. national interests or the values on which these interests are founded. Fundamentally, Americans believe in freedom, democracy, and human dignity, and that free enterprise, individual rights, and global security are essential to our pursuit of these basic beliefs. Based on these foundations, the United States and its allies pursued policies and strategies during the last half of the 20th century that exposed the fallacies of communism and created the globalized world order. Fortunately, most of the nations of the world agree with and support the major premises of the current world order; but not all subscribe to it, or support the underlying beliefs that sustain it. Regrettably, in the instability induced by the end of the Cold War and the rapid onslaught of globalism, nonstate actors have emerged to challenge the very fabric of the order. These actors have used the advantages and disadvantages of globalism to conduct asymmetric warfare against the United States and its supporters. Combined with unprecedented natural and manmade disasters, these circumstances challenged U.S. military doctrine and its basic assumptions about the use of military power.

Seemingly slow to recognize and respond to the changes in the strategic environment, the U.S. military profession has once again been criticized by media pundits for trying to fight the last war—suggesting that the military mind is trapped in the 20th century. However, nothing could be further from the truth. It would be more accurate to state that the defense establishment has been perplexed by the multitude of current and future threats and challenges with which it is confronted and the incompatible policies, strategies, and doctrine needed to deal with them. In the force structure and budget debates, arguments are made over the types of forces and technology that will best prepare us for future uncertainty. In the field, current operations have led to a vigorous reconsideration of doctrine and practice. Notwithstanding the sometimes egregious Service partisanship, most military professionals recognize that future demands will span the spectrum of conflict from a stable peace to general war. And, as the papers in this anthology on the use of military power short of general war suggest, the minds of military professionals are reaching out to embrace new ideas indispensable to the restoration and sustainment of stability—ideas that are consistent with the future that has arrived and the core beliefs essential to our existence as a people.

DOUGLAS C. LOVELACE, JR.
Director
Strategic Studies Institute

SUMMARY

Looking out to 2025, many see the potential for a prolonged period of instability as a result of competing economic models, demographics, the rise of new international actors and the resurgence of old ones, climate change, and the scarcity of resources. The range of stability challenges will stretch the capabilities of any military force structure and require innovative thinking on the part of policymakers and military professionals alike concerning the appropriate development and use of the military element of power. In this anthology, sixteen students of the United States Army War College Class of 2008 offer their perspectives on the use of military power across the spectrum of conflict in the 21st century, short of or following general war, and they provide insights into the necessary force structure, policy, strategy, and doctrinal approaches for future success.

The first chapter, written by the faculty editor, describes the security dilemma confronting the United States and the implications for military force structure and operations. It argues that full spectrum operations are an appropriate doctrinal response, and that stability operations will present new challenges for the use of military force. The subsequent chapters are a collection of edited student research papers from the U.S. Army War College Class of 2008 selected for their focus on operations short of general war. The editor cast a wide net in search of papers that grasp the implications of the emerging strategic environment, apply strategic level thinking, and offer new and useful ways for the application of military power. Consequently, each of these writings shares in common a worthwhile idea or set of ideas that can materially contribute to how the United States military can best conduct full spectrum operations.

Collectively, these essays reveal the innovative thinking, diversity, and depth of thought that is characteristic of the U.S. and foreign military and civilian agency personnel that comprise each class of the U.S. Army War College as they prepare themselves to become senior leaders of their militaries or agencies. The essays also offer key insights at the policy, strategy, planning, and doctrinal levels that can be applied in the current and future strategic environments confronting the United States and its security partners.

CHAPTER 1

INTRODUCTION

Dr. Harry R. Yarger

Nearing the end of the first decade of the 21st century, the United States is involved in two ongoing wars. It faces a significant international terrorist threat, and it is witnessing an escalation of international resistance to its leadership of the global world order. Looking out to 2025, many see the potential for a prolonged period of instability as a result of competing economic models, demographics, the rise of new international actors and the resurgence of old ones, climate change, and the scarcity of resources. Such instability suggests a greater probability of interstate and intrastate conflict. While in the near term the United States remains the single most powerful state, it will act most often as only one of a number of important powers in an increasingly multipolar international system. In such an environment, the U.S. role will logically be more constrained, but its national interests will continue to place a premium on a peaceful world order and its military will continue to be a key factor in sustaining acceptable levels of regional and global stability.[1] The range of stability challenges will stretch the capabilities of any military force structure and require innovative thinking on the part of policymakers and military professionals alike on the appropriate development and use of the military element of power. In light of the economic recession of 2009, this debate will intensify over the next several years as the rising deficit levels force a closer look at defense spending. Some question what appears to be an over reliance by the U.S. Government on military power.[2] Consequently, force structure, and how military forces are best used to advance stability interests, will be key components of this debate. National success will require innovative ways of thinking about the military instruments of power.

The national security or military professional reading the latest security literature may well be confused by the various outlooks expressed by authors discussing the nature of emerging challenges and the security environment. Some argue that U.S. military thinking has lingered too long in the Cold War past and has tried to create a new monolithic threat out of China to justify the retention of large conventional forces.[3] Members of this school of thought believe that the era of conventional warfare is over, and that the threats of the 21st century are only asymmetric or hybrid in nature and require all, or at least a significant part, of the U.S. military capability to be comprised of unconventional and counterinsurgency forces.[4] Others look at the future and conclude that conventional warfare is not only possible, but even likely.[5] These arguments get at the heart of the famous Clausewitzean dictum that: "The first, the supreme, the most far-reaching act of judgment that the statesman and commander have to make is to establish by that test the kind of war on which they are embarking; neither mistaking it for, nor trying to turn it into, something that is alien to its nature."[6] Most quote the master without ever considering the "test." For Clausewitz, war was never to be thought of as autonomous but to be understood as an instrument of policy. Consequently, the kinds of war are determined by ". . . the nature of their motives and the situations which give rise to them."[7] In the 21st century, both motives and situations will be abundant and diverse — and this makes determining force structure and doctrine for the future challenging.

1

This quandary is not new. Clausewitz also understood that war consists of two distinct activities, preparation for war, and conduct of war.[8] Preparation for war consists of "... the creation of fighting forces, their raising, armament, equipment, and training."[9] For Clausewitz's purposes in *On War*, he accepted armed and equipped fighting forces as a given, the means by which war is conducted, because he was interested in the conduct of war. In his reasoning, "... if the art of war was always to start with raising of armed forces and adapting them to the requirements of the particular case, it would be applicable only to those few instances where the forces available exactly matched the need."[10] Consequently, you always go to war with the forces you have on hand, using the effects that the force is capable of generating although it is rarely the ideal force as adversaries invariably seek asymmetry in force strength, capabilities, techniques, or environments. Yet, the force developer logically must consider the kinds of war the future portends as well as the current fight in order to be best prepared. Both Clausewitz's and the force developer's perspectives are correct. When war comes, you conduct it with the forces and their effects on hand; but the better you can judge the kind of future war, the more effective will be the means at hand. Art, flexibility, and adaptability can bridge the gap — but the smaller the gap, the better. However, while the modification of forces can occur during a long war, it will be at a greater cost of blood and treasure.

From the end of the Vietnam War until 2006, the U.S. advocates of small wars succumbed to the conventional mantra of prepare for the greater risk and adapt to the lesser requirements. The near-simultaneous successful conclusions of the Cold War (the dissolution of Soviet Union in 1991) and the Persian Gulf War (August 1990-February 1991) validated this thinking in the minds of a whole generation of military officers. The U.S. experiences in Iraq and Afghanistan have challenged the wisdom of this mantra, with a number of proponents now arguing that future wars will be small and that the forgotten lessons from Vietnam, if now remembered, would have made recent conflicts easier to conduct. For these proponents, the learning curve that accompanied the lesser requirement was too expensive, and many others even perceived this kind of war as the greater challenge. On the other hand, some national security professionals now fear that, at least in the Army, the pendulum may have swung too far toward counterinsurgency at the expense of being prepared for more conventional threats. Of course, this is exactly the rub in preparation for war — what kind of wars will you be confronted with in terms of the motives and situations that give rise to them?

This argument has been recently articulated by referring to the 21st century as being a century characterized by irregular warfare as opposed to traditional warfare. Traditional war is defined as war between nation states or coalitions/alliances of nation-states. "Traditional war typically involves small-scale to large-scale, force-on-force military operations in which adversaries employ a variety of conventional military capabilities against each other in the air, land, maritime, and space physical domains and the information environment (which includes cyberspace)."[11] Irregular warfare is defined as "a violent struggle among state and non-state actors for legitimacy and influence over the relevant population(s)."[12] Irregular warfare is typically conducted when "a less powerful adversary seeks to disrupt or negate the military capabilities and advantages of a more powerful, conventionally armed military force, which often represents the nation's established regime."[13] While conceptually useful for distinguishing current conflicts from past ones and for better understanding of nonstate war, irregular warfare concepts provide no inherent justification for ignoring the lesser probability of and potentially greater risks at stake in traditional war. Both definitions also ignore a wide range of operations that the U.S. military can reasonably expect to conduct in the 21st century – peace operations, peacetime military engagement, and humanitarian operations.

Stuck on the horns of this dilemma, the U.S. Army in particular, and the U.S. military more generally, has modified its force structure and rushed to update its doctrine. Army changes have kept an eye on both the current wars and the challenges that the potential reemergence of conventional conflict present. The resulting modular force structure is reflected in the adoption of the brigade combat team (BCT). The Army also reformed the nearly extinct Peacekeeping Institute as the U.S. Army Peacekeeping and Stability Operations Institute (PKSOI) with a mission to "Serve as the U.S. Military's Center of Excellence for Stability and Peace Operations at the strategic and operational levels in order to improve military, civilian agency, international and multinational capabilities and execution."[14] In large part, the Institute helped to reestablish an intellectual balance for the consideration of both conventional and unconventional war. PKSOI elevated the importance of what used to be called "operations other than war," and it renewed the focus on a whole of government approach. Over the same period, the Army began to review its doctrine. Key doctrinal manuals, such as *Field Manual (FM) 3-24, Counterinsurgency*, developed by a specially organized workgroup, also helped to bring a doctrinal counterbalance much needed in the ongoing struggle in Iraq.[15] In 2008, the Army published *FM 3-07, Stability Operations*, which brought these operations into doctrinal perspective with the threats and challenges of the 21st century. It acknowledged the definition of stability operations found in *Joint Publication (JP) 3-0, Stability Operations*:

> [Stability operations encompass] various military missions, tasks, and activities conducted outside the United States in coordination with other instruments of national power to maintain or reestablish a safe and secure environment, provide essential governmental services, emergency infrastructure reconstruction, and humanitarian relief. . . .[16]

In the face of ongoing operations, the doctrinal pendulum has swung back to the realities of the current strategic environment – but the anxiety that the arc is too great should remain a real concern.

Any comprehensive strategic consideration of the future global environment can make a case for both low intensity and high intensity combat and multiple operational scenarios, particularly if the time horizon is expanded to allow for the rise of regional and global competitors. After all, if the United States only develops a counterinsurgency or stability operations force structure, then state actors can achieve asymmetric advantage with competent conventional forces. Clearly, in force development and operational forces, the United States must pursue a hedging strategy, one that cannot assume either a total low intensity or total high intensity environment. A hedging strategy is particularly useful when confronted with uncertainty or when the consequences of being wrong could be catastrophic.[17] A capabilities-based strategy may be considered a hedging strategy if the capabilities are balanced across multiple potential threats – such as traditional, irregular, catastrophic, and disruptive – or across the spectrum of conflict.[18] Given the U.S. global strategic position over the next decade, clearly some form of balanced force is required. Any other approach to force planning would encourage adversaries and other actors to more aggressively seek asymmetric advantages as world power rebalances in the first quarter of the 21st century. A balanced force may not be ideal for a particular threat or challenge, but it can respond to any, be more rapidly adapted, and make others' consideration of asymmetric strategies more problematic—in strategies, forces, and costs.

In a recent *Army* magazine article, Army Chief of Staff General George W. Casey, Jr., describes such a strategy to deal with what he labels an era of persistent conflict in which state and nonstate actors may use unconventional and conventional operations, or a hybrid of the two.[19] In the latter case, the traditional concept of a linear spectrum of conflict may be better visualized as a multidimensional graphic in which various kinds of war occur simultaneously. U.S. Army *Field Manual (FM) 3-0, Operations*, envisions this and counteracts the inherent complexity of future conflict by incorporating offensive, defensive, and stability operations across its defined spectrum of conflict, advocating full spectrum operations.[20] (See Figure 1.)

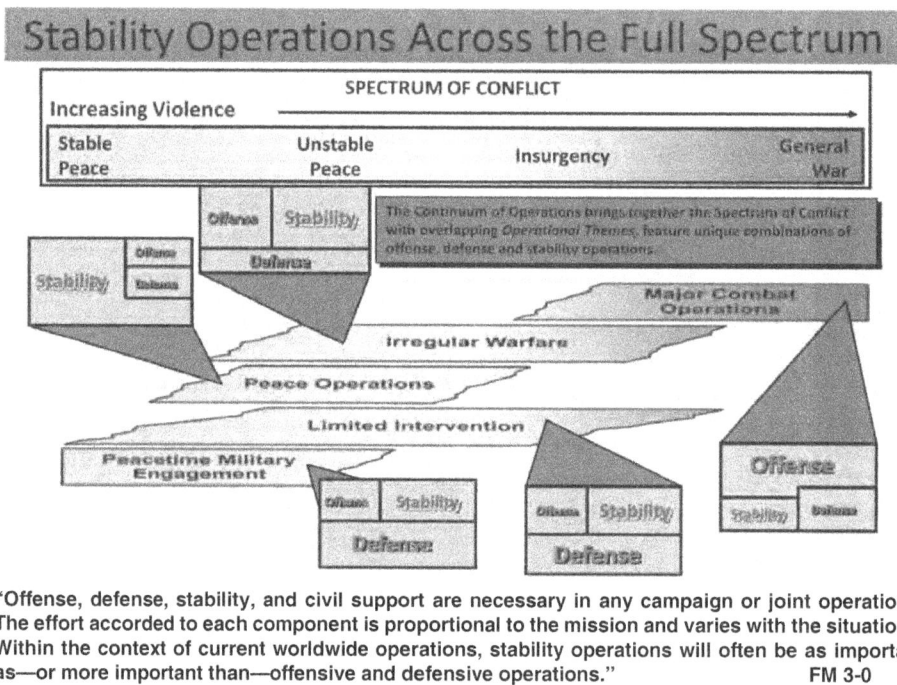

Stability Operations Across the Full Spectrum

"Offense, defense, stability, and civil support are necessary in any campaign or joint operation... The effort accorded to each component is proportional to the mission and varies with the situation... Within the context of current worldwide operations, stability operations will often be as important as—or more important than—offensive and defensive operations."   FM 3-0

Figure 1. Stability Operations across the Full Spectrum.

The meaning of offensive and defensive operations is reasonably understood within the defense community, but stability operations and full spectrum operations less so. Stability operations are more fully described in FM 3-0 as:

> Stability operations encompass the various military missions, tasks, and activities conducted outside the United States in coordination with other instruments of national power to maintain or reestablish a safe and secure environment, provide essential governmental services, emergency infrastructure reconstruction, and humanitarian relief (JP 3-0). Stability

operations can be conducted in support of a host-nation or interim government or as part of an occupation when no government exists. Stability operations involve both coercive and constructive military actions. They help to establish a safe and secure environment and facilitate reconciliation among local or regional adversaries. Stability operations can also help establish political, legal, social, and economic institutions and support the transition to legitimate local governance. Stability operations must maintain the initiative by pursing objectives that resolve the causes of instability.[21]

Full spectrum operations are defined as:

The Army's operational concept: Army forces combine offensive, defensive, and stability or civil support operations simultaneously as part of an interdependent joint force to seize, retain, and exploit the initiative, accepting prudent risk to create opportunities to achieve decisive results. They employ synchronized action—lethal and nonlethal—proportional to the mission and informed by a thorough understanding of all variables of the operational environment. Mission command that conveys intent and an appreciation of all aspects of the situation guides the adaptive use of Army forces.[22]

A strategic appraisal of the potential challenges and threats of the 21st century reveals nothing that negates the validity of the spectrum of conflict or full spectrum operations. Such analysis confirms, as FM 3-0 reflects, that stability operations apply across the spectrum of conflict from a stable peace to general war. As guidance, FM 3-0 and the supporting FM 3-07 provide purpose, tasks, processes, and tools that constitute valid doctrine. They answer most questions of how Army capabilities are to be operationally and tactically employed. Yet, large questions remain to be considered. How and when can military force be used without creating anti-Americanism—the question of legitimacy? Who, ourselves or our adversaries, will make best use of the purported revolution in military affairs (RMA)? How should the United States structure the force for the 21st century? How should the U.S. military interrelate with the whole of the U.S. Government and with other governments and actors is another key question? If it is an era of persistent conflict, and one in which insurgency is a major problem, is our counterinsurgency doctrine adequate—what further should we understand about this form of warfare? How does transition to nonmilitary support occur and how do you know when to transition from a military to a civil organizational lead?

In this anthology, students of the U.S. Army War College (USAWC) Class of 2008 offer their perspectives on the use of military power across the spectrum of conflict in the 21st century short of or following general war, and provide insights into the questions outlined above and other larger policy, strategy, and doctrinal issues. Beyond a focus on operations short of general war, these writings share in common a worthwhile idea or set of ideas that can materially contribute to how the U. S. military can best conduct full spectrum operations. Collectively, these papers reveal the innovative thinking, diversity, and depth of thought that is characteristic of the military and civilian agency personnel that comprise each class of the USAWC as they prepare themselves to become senior leaders and to fulfill their role in support of the College's mission "... not to promote war, but to preserve the peace by intelligent and adequate preparation to repel aggression."[23]

ENDNOTES - CHAPTER 1

1. National Intelligence Council, *Global Trends 2025: A World Transformed*, Washington, DC: U.S. Government Printing Office, November 2008, pp. 1-vi-xii, 61-74, 81-88.

2. Thom Shanker, "Top Officer Urges Limit On Mission Of Military," *New York Times*, January 13, 2009.

3. Nick Macfie and Dean Yates, eds., "China Tells U.S. to Drop 'Cold War' Mindset on Military," March 26, 2009, available from *www.reuters.com/article/politicsNews/idUSTRE52P1XM20090326*. Even China has picked up this refrain in a response to a Pentagon Report released under the Obama Administration criticizing China's lack of transparency in military spending.

4. Colonel Thomas X. Hammes, *The Sling and the Stone: On War in the 21st Century*, St. Paul, MN: Zenith Press, 2004. Hammes' work is one articulation of this argument.

5. United States Joint Forces Command, "The JOE 2008, Joint Operating Environment: Challenges and Implications for the Future Joint Force," November 21, 2008, available from *www.jfcom.mil/newslink/storyarchive/2008/JOE2008.pdf*.

6. Carl von Clausewitz, *On War*, Michael Howard and Peter Paret, eds. and trans., Princeton, NJ: Princeton University Press, 1976, p. 88.

7. *Ibid.*

8. *Ibid.*, pp. 127-128.

9. *Ibid.*, p. 127.

10. *Ibid.*, pp. 127-28.

11. *Joint Publication, (JP) 1, Doctrine for the Armed Forces of the United States*, Washington, DC: Joint Chiefs of Staff, May 2, 2007; w/change 1, March 20, 2009, p. x, available from *www.dtic.mil/doctrine/jel/new_pubs/jp1.pdf*.

12. *Ibid.*, p. GL-8.

13. *Ibid.*

14. U.S. Army Peacekeeping and Stability Operations Homepage, "Mission Brief," available from *https://pksoi.army.mil/PKSOI_Blogs.cfm*. Originally established as the Peacekeeping Institute by Chief of Staff of the Army, General Gordon Sullivan, in 1993, the Institute was nearly disbanded in 2003. In that year it was reinvigorated with new purpose and resources in acceptance of emerging trends in military operations.

15. *Field Manual (FM) 3-24, Counterinsurgency*, Washington, DC: U.S. Department of the Army, December 2006.

16. *Field Manual (FM) 3-07, Stability Operations*, Washington, DC: U.S. Department of the Army, October 2008, p. vi. See also *Joint Publication (JP) 3-0, Joint Operations*, Washington, DC: U.S. Joint Chiefs of Staff, September 17, 2006; w/change 1, February 13, 2008, p. GL 25, available from *www.dtic.mil/doctrine/jel/new_pubs/jp3_0.pdf*.

17. Henry C. Bartlett, "Approaches to Force Planning," *Naval War College Review*, No. 38, May-June 1985, pp. 37-48.

18. *Quadrennial Defense Review Report,* Washington, DC: U.S. Department of Defense, February 6, 2006, p. 19, *www.defenselink.mil/qdr/report/Report20060203.pdf.*

19. General George W. Casey, Jr., "America's Army In an Era of Persistent Conflict," *Army: 2008-09 Green Book,* Washington, DC: Association of United States Army, October 2008, pp. 19-28.

20. *Field Manual (FM) 3-0, Operations,* Washington, DC: U.S. Department of the Army, June 14, 2001. pp. 3-20.

21. *Ibid.,* pp. 3-12.

22. *Ibid.,* Glossary, p. 7.

23. U.S. Army War College Homepage, Registrar's Office, *AY 09 Resident and AY 10 [USAWC Curriculum] Catalog,* available from *www.carlisle.army.mil/students/registrar/pdf/catalogue.pdf.*

CHAPTER 2

LEGITIMACY IN THE CONDUCT OF MILITARY OPERATIONS

Commander Jonathan P. Wilcox
U.S. Navy

> If a national decision [to use force] is made without sufficient regard to whether its use of force has legitimacy in the eyes of the international community, the result can be a setback to the cause of peace and to the interests of the nation that has gone to war.[1]

— Ivo Daalder

INTRODUCTION

Since the end of the Cold War and the emergence of the United States as the world's only hegemonic power, public interest on questions of legitimacy in the use of military power has increased. U.S. interventions in Kosovo and Bosnia, the terrorist attacks of September 11, 2001 (9/11), and the wars in Afghanistan and Iraq are seminal events which call into question common guidelines on when, where, and how it is appropriate to use military elements of national power.[2] U. S. emphasis on the preemptive use of force as a means for dealing with emerging threats also calls into question the importance of international bodies for determining when the use of force is legal and legitimate.

Modern international rules which govern the use of force were originally drafted into the Charter of the United Nations (UN) at the end of World War II, specifically to prevent another global scale conflict. The world has changed dramatically since 1945, but the rules of governance have not kept pace with the changing times, causing the old paradigms to be challenged. According to Michael Glennon, "After Kosovo, Iraq, and over 200 additional instances in which force has been used in violation of the United Nations Charter, no consensus can any longer be said to exist within the international community as to when the use of force is either lawful or legitimate."[3] It is clear that a review of the old rules governing the use of force is desperately needed. Also requiring review is the concept of legitimacy, and whether it still has bearing on the decision to use military force. This chapter will examine the relevance of legitimacy, the issues surrounding legitimacy and the use of military power, and how the United States can ensure that future conflicts will be considered legitimate by the international community.

NEW SECURITY ENVIRONMENT

The world has changed dramatically since the founding of the UN. Today's strategic thinkers and policymakers face tremendous challenges as they struggle to adapt to an ever more fluid and dangerous security situation. The greatest challenge for the 21st century may be determining when to use force, how that force can be legitimately used, and the role that international institutions or coalitions play in making those decisions.

The presence of failed states, the proliferation of weapons of mass destruction (WMD), and the requirement for humanitarian assistance in war torn areas all coalesce to force a new consideration on how force can legally and legitimately be applied. In a March 2004 speech on the threat of global terrorism, British Prime Minister Tony Blair discussed the concepts of preemption and legitimacy in the face of a changing world environment.

> Already, before September 11th the world's view of the justification of military action had been changing. The only clear case in international relations for armed intervention had been self-defense, response to aggression. But the notion of intervening on humanitarian grounds had been gaining currency. I set this out, following the Kosovo war, in a speech in Chicago in 1999, where I called for a doctrine of international community, where in certain clear circumstances, we do intervene, even though we are not directly threatened.

> . . . Containment will not work in the face of the global threat that confronts us. The terrorists have no intention of being contained. Emphatically I am not saying that every situation leads to military action. But we surely have a right to prevent the threat materializing, and we surely have a responsibility to act when a nation's people are subjected to a regime such as Saddam's.[4]

Brookings Institute scholar James Steinberg outlines four justifiable circumstances for the legitimate use of force: operations against terrorists, preventing the spread of WMD, humanitarian crises, and actions to deal with failing states.[5] In the interest of clarity, it would be beneficial to review some of the factors which define the new security environment, and examine their relevance within the debate on the use of force.

Failed or Failing States.

During the Cold War, both the United States and the Soviet Union sought to gain an advantage and spread influence by liberally using aid and resources. As the Soviet Union slipped further into decline and its influence waned, neither state was inclined to apply wealth and material support as a balancing mechanism in international affairs. As external resources were removed, a shift in wealth and power occurred, and some states began to fail. The International Red Cross defines failing states as ones ". . . in which institutions and law and order have totally or partially collapsed under the pressure and amidst the confusion of erupting violence. . . ."[6]

Failed or failing states create problems which complicate the matter of enforcement of international law, and render traditional tools of deterrence ineffective. According to Seyom Brown, "Failed or failing states . . . could catalyze dangerous regional instabilities. Moreover, the entire system can be destabilized, and wars initiated and conducted by non-government actors: violent political movements, terrorist networks, and criminal syndicates."[7] Without the support, control, and oversight of the major powers, the problems of failed or failing states can alter regional balances of power and make it easier for terrorist or criminal elements to operate. Without governments or organizations upon which to focus its power, outside states have few options for deterrence or to ensure appropriate behavior from those elements.

Weapons of Mass Destruction.

WMD comprise the most dangerous threat to international peace and security. Their proliferation and the resulting threat is one of the most frequently used arguments justifying the preemptive use of force. According to James Steinberg, using force preventively against WMD capabilities has strong appeal because of the ". . . potentially devastating consequences of either failure of warning or inadequacy of defense. . . ."[8] Strategic decisionmakers must consider not only the local consequences of a successful nuclear or biological attack on a large metropolitan area, but also the effect that such an attack would have on the global economy. A single WMD could not only kill tens or hundreds of thousands of innocent civilians, but it could shift the global balance of power in an instant.

State and Nonstate Actors.

The tools of deterrence and the threat of mutually assured destruction which helped to contain the Soviet Union during the Cold War may not be effective against terrorists and other nonstate actors, especially those with religious apocalyptic or ideological underpinnings.[9] The changing nature of the enemy, the inefficacy of traditional deterrence, and the terrible consequences that accompany considerations of failure require new strategies specifically designed to deal with a new and nontraditional threat.

Future Warfare Challenges.

Conflict in the 21st century is likely to be asymmetric, low intensity, and will require greater levels of involvement of unconventional military power. Sir Rupert Smith calls these conflicts "wars amongst the people," and predicts that future enemies will appear ". . . in small groups operating at the tactical level, against which the maneuvers and mass firepower of industrial war are ineffective. . . ."[10] Gone are the days of conventional wars where great powers met on battlefields to decide issues with clear boundaries and concise start and end points. Today's threats come in the form of small, dissociated terrorist cells whose goals are to destabilize without direct confrontation and whose tools take the form of WMD and asymmetric warfare.

Nonstate actors and small terrorist cells do not warrant the full use of national power, and according to Jeffrey Record, the application of that power may not even be possible. "Massive, rapid, and decisive use of force is virtually impossible in a world of limited and politically messy wars, in a global environment in which non-state enemies practice protracted irregular warfare as a means of negating the potential effectiveness of America's conventional military supremacy."[11] Instead, the United States must focus its efforts and resources toward developing asymmetric capabilities. Richard Betts writes that ". . . with rare exceptions, the war against terrorists cannot be fought with army tank battalions, air force wings, or naval fleets. . . . The main challenge is not killing the terrorists but finding them, and the capabilities most applicable to this task are intelligence and special operations forces."[12] The challenge for modern military power is maintaining the ability to deal with both the conventional and asymmetric threat.

Humanitarian Assistance.

The need to provide relief for war-torn areas in the form of humanitarian assistance is increasingly accepted as one of the established and accepted reasons that a great power may resort to force without the approval of the international community. Because of political considerations, it is often difficult to gain UN Security Council approval for intervention.

Yet on occasion, the major powers have intervened without international approval, and have met with some success. With regards to the North Atlantic Treaty Organization (NATO)-led intervention in the Balkans, Chris Abbott writes "Kosovo is understood by many to have established the norm of resort to force without the authorization of the UN Security Council (although in fact most humanitarian interventions have taken place without prior endorsement by the UN)."[13] Furthermore, the United Kingdom (UK) Parliament's Foreign Affairs Committee report on NATO's action in Kosovo states that ". . . NATO's military action, if of dubious legality in the current state of international law, was justified on moral grounds."[14]

In 2001, the International Commission on Intervention and State Sovereignty released a report entitled *The Responsibility to Protect* to help outline the problem and identify solutions. The report concluded that national sovereignty was an important principle of international law, but that it was ". . . neither inviolable nor a legitimate justification for inaction by the international community when sovereign governments are unwilling or unable to protect their citizens from large-scale violations of human rights, crimes against humanity, ethnic cleansing, or genocide."[15] When governments cannot, or choose not to, protect their citizenry, the international community has a responsibility to act forcefully.

UNILATERALISM AND PREEMPTION

According to Colin Gray, "The strategic theory, the policy, the strategy, and the plans for the 21st century need to be radically different from those suitable from the Cold War."[16] He differentiates between the doctrine of preemption and the concept of preventive war, stating that "Preemption refers to the first use of military force when an attack already is underway or, at the least, is very credibly imminent."[17] The difference between preemptive war and preventive war is that preemptive war ". . . uniquely is exercised in or for a war that is certain, the timing of which has not been chosen by the preemptor."[18] Prevention, on the other hand, is an act of choice, requiring that the nation taking the action, ". . . must express a guess that war, or at least a major negative power shift, is probable in the future."[19]

A new U.S. unilateralism first appeared in statements of public policy in the Clinton Administration's 1998 National Security Strategy, which stated: "We will do what we must to defend these (vital) interests, including—when necessary—using our military might unilaterally and decisively."[20] The George W. Bush administration added preemption as a key point in its national security strategy:

> It is an enduring American principle that this duty obligates the government to anticipate and counter threats, using all elements of national power, before the threats can do grave damage. The greater the threat, the greater is the risk of inaction — and the more compelling the case for taking anticipatory action to defend ourselves, even if uncertainty remains as to the time and place of the enemy's attack. There are few greater threats than a terrorist attack with WMD. To forestall or prevent such hostile acts by our adversaries, the United States will, if necessary, act preemptively in exercising our inherent right of self-defense.[21]

In theory, the unilateral and preemptive use of military power in the face of perceived threats makes sense. However, in practice, these actions have not only resulted in a distancing of traditional allies, but also the establishment of a dangerous precedent within the international community. Ironically, U.S. reliance on preventive war may have doomed its efforts to control the spread of nuclear weapons to rogue states. Iran's efforts to attain nuclear technology and its resistance to international pressure may be the actions of a government operating defensively from what it sees as the perceived threat of invasion. Long-term American efforts to promote regional stability may be more difficult because of the precedent set in 2001 and 2003. An additional second order effect may be the example set for other strong international states.

As the world's only remaining superpower, the United States has the strength and the right to act on its own in support of its vital national interests. However, the policies of preemption and unilateral action have combined to cause great damage to American's global image without enhancing its security. According to Stephen Walt, repudiating this policy is the first step in rebuilding America's reputation within the international community.[22]

The U.S. intervention in Iraq was a war of prevention, fought for regime change, to destroy safe havens for terrorists, and to prohibit the spread of WMD. By acting first and without the support of most major world powers, the United States challenged the contemporary rules governing the use of force. There are defenders and detractors on both sides of the argument, but few will deny that international public opinion has turned against the United States, and American long-term interests and security have been damaged as a result. According to Ivo Daalder and James Lindsey, ". . . No foreign policy decision since America's retreat into isolationism in the 1930s has done more to harm American and global security than the Iraq war."[23] This war ". . . has cost America the trust of its friends and allies around the world — a trust that since 1945 has been instrumental in translating America's economic and military power into global influence and leadership."[24]

Finally, consideration must be given to the costs of 21st century military interventions. According to Richard Betts, both Presidents Bill Clinton and George W. Bush ". . . embraced ambitious goals of reshaping the world according to American values but without considering the full costs and consequences of their grandiose visions . . . [leaving a defense budget] . . . higher than needed for basic national security but far lower than required to eliminate all villainous governments and groups everywhere."[25] A Congressional Budget Office report estimates the cost of funding military operations in Iraq and Afghanistan from September 2001 through the end of FY 2007 as being $604 billion.[26] With few international partners willing or able to help share the costs, the burden for these nation-building efforts falls upon the United States.

LEGITIMACY

The United States has many instruments of national power at its disposal as it seeks to defend its people and vital interests. Whether referring to diplomatic, informational, economic, or military power, Stephen Walt states that "American power is most effective when it is seen as legitimate, and when other societies believe it is being used to serve their interests as well as America's."[27] How one defines legitimacy depends on background and point of view. The word "legitimate" is often used synonymously with the word "legal," but the two have different meanings. Whereas legitimacy is subjective and is based on the dispositions of the interpreter, legality refers to concepts which are ". . . intended to be objective and universal; its meaning is intended to be the same for all actors subjected to it."[28] According to Seyom Brown, ". . . decisions to go to war or to dramatically escalate an on-going war almost always are shaped in part by views, domestic and foreign, as to whether the contemplated actions are legal and moral. Legal is taken to mean consistent with the U.S. Constitution and congressional legislation, but also with treaties to which the United States is a party."[29] Accordingly, a legal military action is one which conforms to the guidelines of the UN charter, as expressed in Article 51.

Decisionmakers must determine whether the United States should be governed by international law or the much more subjective concept of legitimacy. This approach is not without its difficulties, considering that the international community has great trouble coming to a commonly held understanding of what constitutes legitimate action, and cannot agree on the methodology for a test of legitimacy.[30] The only principle most can agree upon is that the concept of legitimacy does matter, to both the American public and also to the international community. According to Ivo Daalder and Robert Kagan,

> To forge a renewed political consensus on the use of force, we first need to recognize that international legitimacy does matter. It matters to Americans, who want to believe they are acting justly and are troubled if others accuse them of selfish, immoral, or otherwise illegitimate behavior. It matters to our democratic friends and allies, whose support may attest to the justness of the cause and whose participation may often be necessary to turn a military victory into a lasting political success.[31]

The struggle to achieve legitimacy is the struggle to win the hearts and minds of the people, and at its core, is a war of ideas. The 9/11 Commission makes it clear that al-Qaeda and other anti-American groups understand the importance of legitimacy, especially in the Islamic world. "If the United States does not act aggressively to define itself in the Islamic World, the extremists will gladly do the job for us."[32] It stands to reason that the United States must do a better job at strategic communication and of explaining ideas, actions, and motives to the international community.

According to Daalder and Kagan, "To sustain broad, bipartisan support for interventions requires that we rebuild a domestic consensus on a fundamental but elusive issue: the question of legitimacy."[33] How best to achieve domestic legitimacy is a challenge for American policymakers. The Constitution outlines a system whereby checks and balances provide the mechanism for ensuring the legality and legitimacy of military force.

The War Powers Act of 1973 was an attempt to assure the proper division of power between the executive and legislative branches of government. As Commander in Chief, the Act allows the President to use force on a temporary basis without congressional approval,[34] but Congress retains the authority to declare war and to raise, fund, and support the armed forces during military intervention.[35] In theory, domestic legitimacy is ensured because no long-term major military intervention can occur without the express approval of the representatives of the American people.

Some question the effectiveness of the War Powers Act since it has not prevented U.S. involvement in long, indecisive wars in the past. The American public remains deeply divided on the question of the war in Iraq, and those divisions continue along party lines in Congress as well. While it is clear that the checks and balances are in place, the United States continues to suffer questions about the legitimacy of its actions. Gaining and maintaining public support for future military interventions will be a challenge for future policymakers. Daniel Byman and Matthew Waxman make the point that linking military action to vital national interests is essential to maintaining U.S. public support. "Support is likely to erode with casualties when vital interests are not at stake, when the public views victory as unlikely, or when the policy elite do not support the policy."[36] The role public opinion played in ending the Vietnam War is of particular relevance in this regard.

To avoid U.S. involvement in long, drawn out, unpopular wars, policymakers have suggested that the United States should consider objective criteria which can be used to govern when, where, and how the United States uses military force in pursuit of its interests. In an attempt to apply specific criteria as litmus tests for employing military force, Colin Powell outlined six basic criteria which should be met before the United States commits forces to combat operations. He contended that military forces should be committed to combat operations only as a last resort and only if vital national interests are threatened; that force should be applied in overwhelming numbers and with the clear intention of winning; that forces should be given clearly defined military and political objectives which are reassessed and adjusted if necessary; and that there must be strong public and congressional support for the campaign.[37]

Some argue that these guidelines are too restrictive and not flexible enough to deal with modern interventions. Branislav Slantchev writes that ". . . the Doctrine is a recipe for inaction and the problem . . . is not that the U.S. gets involved too often but that it gets involved not often enough, and when it does, it is often not with whole-hearted determination because of the perceived need to minimize American casualties."[38]

It is clear, however, that the criteria were intended to help guide domestic discourse and decisionmaking by outlining the kind of issues that need to be considered when determining whether force should be used. Citing a Council on Foreign Relations report, Robert Pauly and Tom Lansford write that the Doctrine is ". . . useful only as a checklist that policy makers can use to ensure that they have carefully thought through a decision for military intervention."[39]

There is a strong link in the minds of the American public between domestic legitimacy and international approval for military action. According to Byman and Waxman,

> The US public will also want to see any military campaign as conforming to international legal norms and its own collective sense of morality, in terms of both the decision to launch military operations and the way operations are conducted. In this regard, international law serves as an imperfect reflection of contemporary morality and an impeachable arbiter of the morality of any action. Actions that appear to violate international law acquire an extra burden to justify themselves in moral terms.[40]

U.S. policymakers have long understood the importance of involving the international community in military interventions. The Truman administration gained legitimacy for the Korean conflict by sending American forces to fight under UN auspices, and the Kennedy administration sought legitimacy by making the case for unilateral action in dealing with the Soviet deployment of missiles to Cuba through the UN. In more recent times, the administration of George H. W. Bush ensured legitimacy by gaining UN support for removing Iraq from Kuwait in 1990. Even though it failed to get UN approval for the use of force in the Balkans, the Clinton administration was able to achieve legitimacy of a sort by working within the NATO-led coalition.

The U.S.-led invasions of Afghanistan and Iraq presented a challenging situation for those proponents of legitimacy. Both conflicts began at the UN and were prosecuted using international coalitions. Both conflicts had supporting resolutions, though some challenge the time gap between the 1991 Gulf War and the U.S.-led invasion of 2003. However, Afghanistan is considered to be legitimate because the link between Taliban support for al-Qaeda and the 9/11 attacks was clear and well-understood by the international community. In spite of the efforts of Colin Powell and Richard Armitage, the George W. Bush administration was never able to establish the link between Saddam Hussein and al-Qaeda , and the U.S. intervention in Iraq has not achieved the same level of legitimacy with the international community. Charles Krauthammer writes that the Afghan war garners more support within the United States because ". . . it's origins are cleaner, the *casus belli* clearer, the moral texture of the enterprise more comfortable. Afghanistan is a war of righteous revenge and restitution, law enforcement on the grandest of scales."[41]

INTERNATIONAL ORGANIZATIONS

Many still consider the UN as the primary institution for defining the legal and legitimate use of force. The UN was originally founded in the aftermath of World War II to ensure international peace and stability and to avoid another global conflict. The UN Charter was drafted with very specific rules governing the use of force and when force can be applied legally by any member of the international community. Article 51 prohibits the threat or the actual use of force with the exceptions of self-defense or Security Council authorization.[42]

Though few will disagree on the theoretical merits of these guidelines, in practice, their implementation raises several problems. First, the Charter was written to address a very different set of challenges than the ones facing today's decisionmakers. The framers of the UN Charter likely did not envision current threats of international terrorism, failing states, and the proliferation of WMD. Michael Glennon writes that the UN envisions a world ". . . governed by objective, universal morality rather than by competition for power and shifting national interests."[43] However, today's reality is that the common good often takes a back seat to the competition for power and the interests of the individual member states. Daalder and Kagan believe that the UN Security Council is divided by conflicting interests, ideology, beliefs about the nature of sovereignty, and the right of the international community to intervene in the internal affairs of nations.[44] The result is a situation where political considerations influence the decisionmaking process to the extent that it leaves an international body which is ineffective and unable to lead. Chris Abbott writes "The problem is that the Security Council's decision to intervene or not intervene in a particular conflict does not reflect internationally agreed objective criteria and legal norms, but the domestic and global imperatives of the Permanent Five."[45]

In addition, recent years have brought the UN a series of internal problems which have caused great damage to its credibility, to include questions of fairness and dedication to the issues surrounding human rights, and charges of corruption in the administration of the oil for food program.[46] No one understood the dilemma facing the UN better than former Secretary General Kofi Annan. In a report to the General Assembly in 2005, he conceded that his organization was formed in a very different period of world history, and that ". . . not all our current practices are adapted to the needs of today." He continued that to survive as a ". . . useful instrument for its Member States and for the world's peoples . . . it must be fully adapted to the needs and circumstances of the 21st century."[47] Natural disasters and humanitarian assistance, the challenges of combating the spread of global jihad and global terrorism, and WMD proliferation, require agile international organizations capable of providing immediate and effective action in defense of peace and stability.

Daalder and Kagan believe that the UN is no longer an effective tool for dealing with today's security challenges. Frustrated by the perceived lack of support from the Security Council for American military action, they argue that the best way to deal with threats to peace and stability is to work through a coalition of democracies.

> A policy of seeking consensus among the world's great democratic nations can form the basis for a new domestic consensus on the use of force. It would not exclude efforts to win (UN) Security Council authorization. Nor would it preclude using force even when some of our democratic friends disagree. But the United States will be on stronger ground to launch and sustain interventions when it makes every effort to seek and win the approval of the democratic world.[48]

Standing organizations or coalitions such as NATO may provide the United States with a viable alternative should UN cooperation fail. NATO was instrumental in bringing the Cold War to a successful conclusion, and to this day boasts the world's only standing, readily useable coalition military capability. According to Ashton Carter and William Perry, NATO provides the security framework for realizing ". . . George Marshall's vision of a Europe united in freedom, peace, and prosperity."[49]

Others argue that this approach would actually perpetuate the problem and create another organization which is even less likely to be effective and more likely to be questioned by the rest of the international community; relying on this approach would actually be counterproductive and might be more harmful than beneficial to American interests. According to Paul Sanders,

> The answer to the problem of the United Nations is not to create something else; it is to use force deliberately, selectively, sparingly and decisively to protect vital U.S. interests and to stop genocide (not civil wars). If America appears to be wise, responsible, and unstoppable in its use of force, we will create our own legitimacy. Democracies and non-democracies alike will respect U.S. actions, even when it is necessary to act outside the U.N. framework.[50]

Whether the answer lies with the UN, NATO, or a coalition of willing democratic nations, it is clear that the United States must work through and include international organizations. Seyom Brown writes, "U.S. foreign policy will always comprise a mix of multilateralism, bilateralism, and unilateralism."[51] The United States may be required to act outside UN guidelines, but it must continue in its attempts to achieve legitimacy through diplomacy. According to Robert Orr, when the United States acts without formal authorization from the UN Security Council, it should continue to work to create alternative strategies to achieve legitimacy.

> Sheer expenditure of effort in this regard helps to generate good will. When the United States follows its own path, it needs to clearly enunciate its interests and the principles at stake that have led it to part ways with other international actors. In all cases, knowing what to expect from the United States—a basic level of predictability—is important to potential future partners in multilateral efforts.[52]

Joseph Nye summarizes the way ahead for U.S. policymakers in the 21st century, stating that "American foreign policy in a global information age should have a general preference for multilateralism, but not all multilateralism. At times we have to go it alone. When we do so in pursuit of public goods, the nature of our ends may substitute for the means in legitimizing our power in the eyes of others."[53]

In the end, there is an undeniable link between legitimacy, multilateralism, and American public support. According to Seyom Brown, "Multilateral direction, authorization, or approval of the use of force by the U.S. abroad confers a degree of legitimacy to military operations, without which it is considerably more difficult to generate the congressional and popular support required to provision and sustain them."[54]

RECOMMENDATIONS

The over whelming lesson of 9/11 is that engagement outside U.S. borders is the only way to ensure peace and security, and that the use of military force is the least preferred method of advancing national interests. While it is clear that there are times when we must use force in support of our interests, policymakers must understand that such interventions are never fast, easy, or cheap. During the Cold War, President Nixon successfully balanced the gap between commitments and resources by trimming military commitments through burden sharing and diplomacy.[55] Robert Orr writes that the United States should pursue multilateralism first, and not as a last resort. "The United States, for all its resources, needs three things that the international community can offer: additional capacity, legitimacy, and burden sharing."[56] When pursuing approval for military action, the United States must seek formal support for its efforts first through the UN. When that body cannot or will not act to support our requests, the United

States should seek informal political consensus with regional organizations or other democracies to form consensus for common action to address a compelling practical necessity. The United States may gain legitimacy even for controversial actions when it works with other multilateral organizations such as NATO, or the European or African Unions as appropriate. Ultimately, the United States must be prepared to act unilaterally and preemptively to ensure the safety and viability of national interests. If this occurs, effective strategic communication will go a long way towards engendering support for our actions and providing the framework for legitimacy. Words without actions can be counterproductive, as Stephen Walt points out,

> . . . defending the legitimacy of American primacy is not primarily a question of "spin" or propaganda, or even cultural exchange. If American foreign policy is insensitive to the interests of others, and if it makes global problems worse rather than better, no amount of public diplomacy is going to convince the rest of the world that the United States is really acting in the best interests of mankind.[57]

If it achieves no other purpose, the U.S. invasion of Iraq has proven that the doctrine of preventive war does not work. Only an imminent threat provides the justification for a preventive strike, and this can only occur if the nation possesses flawless intelligence and unquestioned evidence of a coming strike. In spite of the efforts of Secretary Powell at the UN, the evidence that Iraq possessed WMD and intended to distribute or use them was never strong enough to convince the majority of the international community that war was justified. The absence of any evidence of WMD or significant links between Saddam Hussein and Islamic terrorists made it difficult for the United States to claim legitimacy for its actions in Iraq. Increased levels of violence, even after President Bush declared an end to combat operations, and the scandals of Abu Ghraib and Guantanamo Bay spelled an end to any hopes that the United States had for international help and support.

It is clear that the United States must work harder to engage other nations and attempt to bring them along with us in the pursuit of our vital national interests. The Bush Administration attempted to do this with regards to Iraq, but it had squandered a great deal of its influence when it acted alone and against international opinion in support of its own interests at the expense of the greater good on other issues. The U.S. failure to propose viable alternatives to the Kyoto protocol on global warming and its decision to unilaterally withdraw from the Anti-Ballistic Missile treaty did little to inspire international confidence in U.S. leadership. These events added to international perception that the United States is an arrogant power which cares little for interests outside of its own. To overcome these perceptions and the noncooperation that they engender, the United States must commit itself to resolving issues by peaceful means and to only consider force when diplomatic efforts have failed. By engaging in a strong and effective campaign of public diplomacy, the United States is more likely to find success while defending its interests and maintaining its position as a global leader.

CONCLUSION

The relevance of legitimacy and how it is achieved and maintained is an issue that policymakers will be wrestling with for years to come. The only sure thing is that considerations of legitimacy must be included in any discussion of the exercise of military power. The United States must be willing and able to act unilaterally on vital issues, but part of leadership is working to engage other nations and bring them along with us. As the world's only superpower, it is clear that the United States has the military strength to act unilaterally. However, when the United States acts preemptively, unilaterally, and seemingly without regard to international sentiment, U.S. interests are prone to suffer long-term damage.

Future efforts at military intervention are likely to be complex, demanding, and expensive, and success will be unlikely without U.S. public support and the support of the international community. The way ahead is far from clear, and policymakers must carefully consider when, where, and how we commit our military forces, and seek ways to ensure legitimacy whenever possible. Often times, the right answer is not to intervene. As Jeffrey Record states, "Future enemies undoubtedly will attempt to lure us into fighting the kind of indecisive, protracted, and politically messy wars into which we stumbled in Vietnam and Iraq. But if such wars are, for the United States, wars of choice rather than wars of necessity, we should think more than twice before entering them."[58]

ENDNOTES - CHAPTER 2

1. Ivo H. Daalder, ed., *Beyond Preemption: Force and Legitimacy in a Changing World*, Washington, DC: Brookings Institution Press, 2007, p. vii.

2. *Ibid.*, p. 1.

3. Michael J. Glennon, "Legitimacy and the Use of Force," March 23, 2005, available from *www.un-globalsecurity.org*.

4. Tony Blair, "Speech on the threat of global terrorism," March 5, 2004, linked from 10 Downing Street Homepage at "Speeches on Iraq," available from *www.number-10.gov.uk/ output/Page5461.asp*.

5. Daalder, p. 22.

6. Daniel Thurer, "The 'Failed State' and International Law," *International Review of the Red Cross*, Vol. 836, December 1999, p. 731.

7. Seyom Brown, "Multilateral Constraints on the Use of Force: A Reassessment," *Strategic Studies Quarterly*, March 2006, p. 18.

8. Daalder, p. 23.

9. John M. Handley and Andrew H. Ziegler, "A Conceptual Framework for National Security," January 2004, available from *www.unc.edu/depts/diplomat/archives_roll/2003_10-12/handley_ziegler/handley_ziegler.html*.

10. Rupert Smith, *The Utility of Force*, New York: Alfred A. Knopf, 2007, p. 272.

11. Jeffrey Record, "Back to the Weinberger-Powell Doctrine," *Strategic Studies Quarterly*, Fall 2007, p. 92.

12. Richard K. Betts, "A Disciplined Defense: How to Regain Strategic Solvency," *Foreign Affairs*, Vol. 86, November/December 2007, p. 3.

13. Chris Abbott, "Rights and Responsibilities: Resolving the Dilemma of Humanitarian Intervention," *Journal of Humanitarian Assistance*, October 2005, p. 5.

14. United Kingdom, Parliament, Foreign Affairs Committee, Select Committee on Foreign Affairs, *Fourth Report*, August 14, 2009, available from *www.publications.parliament.uk/pa/cm199900/ cmselect/ cmfaff/28/2813.htm.*

15. Daalder, p. 83.

16. Colin Gray, *The Implications of Preemptive and Preventive War Doctrines: A Reconsideration,* Carlisle, PA: Strategic Studies Institute, U.S. Army War College, July 2007, p. 8.

17. *Ibid.*

18. *Ibid.*, p. 13.

19. *Ibid.*

20. William J. Clinton, *A National Security Strategy for a New Century,* Washington, DC: The White House, October 1998, p. 5.

21. George W. Bush, *The National Security Strategy Of The United States Of America,* Washington, DC: The White House, March 2006, p. 18.

22. Stephen M. Walt, "In the National Interest: A Grand New Strategy for American Foreign Policy," February/March 2005, available from *bostonreview.net/BR30.1/walt.html.*

23. Ivo H. Daalder and James Lindsay, "Restore Trust in America's Leadership," 2007, available from *www.brookings.edu/articles/2007/fall_iraq_daalder.aspx.*

24. *Ibid.*

25. Betts, p. 2.

26. Peter Orszag, *Testimony Before the Committee on the Budget, U.S. House of Representatives*, Washington, DC: Congressional Budget Office, October 2007, p. 3.

27. Walt.

28. Glennon.

29. Brown, pp. 8-9.

30. Glennon.

31. Ivo Daalder and Robert Kagan, "The Next Intervention," *Washington Post*, August 6, 2007, Sec. A, p. 17.

32. National Commission on Terrorist Attacks Upon the United States, *The 9/11 Commission Report,* New York: Norton, 2004, p. 377.

33. Daalder and Kagan, p. 17.

34. Public Law 93-148, *The War Powers Act of 1973*, available from *www.thecre.com/fedlaw/legal22/warpow. htm.*

35. U.S. Constitution, Art. 1, Sec. 8.

36. Daniel Byman and Matthew Waxman, *The Dynamics of Coercion: American Foreign Policy and the Limits of Military Might*, Cambridge, UK: Cambridge University Press, 2002, p. 136.

37. Colin Powell, "U.S. Forces: Challenges Ahead," *Foreign Affairs*, Vol. 3, Winter 1992, p. 5.

38. Branislav Slantchev, "National Security Strategy: A New World Order, 2004," available from *polisci. ucsd.edu/~bslantch/courses/nss/lectures/21-new-world-order.pdf*.

39. Robert Pauly and Tom Lansford, *Strategic Preemption: US Foreign Policy and the Second Iraq War*, Burlington, VT: Ashgate Publishing, 2005, p. 109.

40. Byman and Waxman, p. 133.

41. Charles Krauthammer, "Which Is 'The Real War'?" *Washington Post*, March 30, 2007, sec. A, p. 17.

42. United Nations Charter, Art. 51.

43. Michael J. Glennon, "Idealism at the U.N." *Policy Review*, Vol. 129, February and March 2005, p. 1.

44. Daalder and Kagan, p. 17.

45. Abbott, p. 5.

46. Colum Lynch, "Oil-for-Food Panel Rebukes Annan, Cites Corruption," *Washington Post*, September 8, 2005, sec. A, p. 1.

47. Kofi Annan, *In Larger Freedom: Towards Development, Security and Human Rights for All*, New York: U.N. Secretary General's Office, March 21, 2005, p. 39.

48. Daalder and Kagan, p. 17.

49. Ashton B. Carter and William J. Perry, *Preventive Defense: A New Security Strategy for America*, Washington, DC: Brookings Institution Press, 1999, p. 55.

50. Paul J. Sanders, "Not the Way to Intervene," *Washington Post*, August 13, 2007, sec. A, p. 11.

51. Brown, p. 4.

52. Robert C. Orr, ed. *Winning the Peace: An American Strategy for Post-Conflict Reconstruction*, Washington, DC: Center for Strategic and International Studies Press, 2004, p. 301.

53. Joseph S. Nye Jr., *The Paradox of American Power: Why the Worlds Only Superpower Can't Go It Alone*, New York: Oxford University Press, 2002, p. 163.

54. Brown, p. 9.

55. Betts, p. 2.

56. Orr, p. 299.

57. Walt.

58. Record, p. 94.

CHAPTER 3

AL-QAEDA, THE REVOLUTION IN MILITARY AFFAIRS,
AND THE FUTURE OF WARFARE

Lieutenant Colonel Thomas C. Graves
U.S. Army

INTRODUCTION

With the fall of the Berlin Wall and the demise of the Soviet Union in the 1990s, U.S. policymakers and military planners began an intellectual search for a new national security paradigm. The U.S. military began a program of downsizing its military to capitalize on the peace dividend that resulted from the end of the Cold War. In concert with this reduction in force, military intellectuals, defense analysts, leaders (both civilian and uniformed), and politicians debated the future role of the military in world conflict and how best to organize the remaining forces. This search for a new military paradigm was briefly interrupted when Iraq invaded Kuwait in 1990. This event became the catalyst for President George H. W. Bush to deploy U.S. forces to the Persian Gulf region and eventually launch a war designed to liberate Kuwait. The resulting war, named Operation DESERT STORM, was a classically waged war between a U.S.-led coalition and Iraq; it resulted in an overwhelming victory for the coalition. At the end of the war, the military returned to the United States and continued to downsize.

At the same time it was downsizing its military, the United States was undergoing a tremendous growth in information technology. It was only natural that the debate on the application of military power would include a search for an efficient means to utilize technology in conjunction with a smaller force in order to overwhelm a prospective adversary. The tremendous success of Operation DESERT STORM added to this search for efficiency through technological means. In that conflict, the U.S. military aptly demonstrated the emerging technologies of precision weapons and global positioning systems and gave a glimpse of what some (according to the proponents) would claim was within the realm of the possible for future war.

The search for a revolution in military affairs (RMA) that would allow the U.S. military to dominate all other prospective competitors for years to come centered on the use of cutting edge technology to overwhelm an adversary through the rapid transmission of information. Numerous publications readily grasped the idea of an emerging RMA and provided articles describing how to best identify and take advantage of the changes in technology. The U.S. military implemented plans to transform its forces so as to posture itself to be capable of defeating a future threat with a much reduced force structure and physical footprint. Throughout the 1990s, the debate over RMA continued, and numerous articles, books, and other publications attempted to identify, define, and classify the future of American warfighting. The adherents to RMA theory included noted intellectuals such as Andrew Krepenivich, politicians such as Congressman John Murtha, and military leaders such as Admiral Arthur K. Cebrowski.[1]

An underlying stimulus for the RMA debate of the 1990s was similar to the catalyst for arms races in the past: a concern that failure to adjust to new conditions would lead to a crippling disadvantage relative to one's enemies, irrelevance, and possibly even loss of superpower status.[2] At the time of the events of September 11, 2001 (9/11), the ongoing Department of Defense (DoD) search for the elusive RMA had morphed into a broader concept of transformation—a DoD-wide effort to refashion the entire military in a way that would make maximum use of the RMA. Transformation became the watchword of the military establishment, and every new weapon system, program, or policy was labeled "transformational" to keep pace with current bureaucratic trends and programs. The importance of transformation to the DoD was strongly emphasized with the creation in 2001 of the Office of Force Transformation led by retired Admiral Arthur K. Cebrowski. It was charged with the mission to serve as ". . . the advocate, focal point, and catalyst for transformation within the Department [of Defense]."[3]

Simultaneous to U.S. efforts to achieve an RMA in the 1990s, other state and nonstate actors throughout the world were looking for ways and means that could be used to defeat U.S. military power. At the end of Operation DESERT STORM, it became apparent that most nations would never have the military capacity to defeat the United States on the battlefield and must therefore find alternative means to achieve their strategic objectives. One of these actors, al-Qaeda , developed methods and doctrines that eventually allowed it to stage a devastating attack on the U.S. mainland.

Since that attack, the U.S. military has been focused on the Global War on Terrorism and has conducted major combat operations in Afghanistan and Iraq—in both cases achieving short-term tactical successes on the battlefield but having limited success over the long term at the grand strategic level. In both cases, the U.S. defense establishment heralded the tactical successes of U.S. military power early in the effort.[4] However, over time insurgent forces in Afghanistan and Iraq were able to undermine the short-term tactical success and create a long-term threat that worked against the creation of stable central governments in both nations.

In a 2006 article on defense transformation, Senior Defense Analyst Stephen Biddle cogently described what senior leaders at the Pentagon had sought to achieve. He argued that current U.S. efforts at RMA were aimed at changing "a heavy, slow-moving, Cold War relic into a leaner, faster, higher-technology force that exploits the connectivity of networked information to outmaneuver, outrange, and demoralize enemy forces without requiring their piecemeal destruction in close combat."[5] He added, "Some transformation advocates would even bypass the enemy military in the field altogether, using deep strikes from possibly intercontinental distances to destroy key nodes in a hostile economy or political control system in 'effects based' operations (EBO) that prevail by coercive bombing rather than brute force on the battlefield."[6]

Interestingly, Biddle's summary, applied in a different context, effectively highlights many of the innovations that al-Qaeda embraced in its own effort to find and exploit weaknesses in the U.S. defense posture; indeed if one substitutes the term "al-Qaeda " for the term "American military," it becomes clear that al-Qaeda may have achieved many of the goals articulated for U.S. transformation. In the events of 9/11, al-Qaeda showed that it had bypassed the enemy military in the field altogether, using deep strikes from long distances. It was al-Qaeda that exploited the connectivity of networked information to outmaneuver its enemies. And, it was al-Qaeda that launched a highly demoralizing attack on the U.S. mainland, without requiring the piecemeal destruction of U.S. military forces in close combat.[7]

It is quite possible that in our efforts to effect an RMA, the U.S. military essentially missed the true revolution that was occurring in al-Qaeda. The U.S. military must now refocus its efforts to regain superiority with respect to the true transformation that has fundamentally altered warfare for years to come. This chapter will expand on this concept of al-Qaeda as an RMA. By examining RMA from a conceptual basis, it will establish a functional framework for RMA to include the historical examples of the German Blitzkrieg of World War II and Napoleonic Warfare and the French Revolution, both cited by DoD as examples of revolutionary change in warfare.[8] The framework of RMA will then be applied to al-Qaeda as an organization. Finally, the chapter will examine U.S. Government and military responses to al-Qaeda's RMA, with a focus on developing a more comprehensive solution to warfare under the new RMA paradigm.

RMA AS A CONCEPT

Despite a vast literature on the RMA idea over the last decade, there has never been a clear consensus on the meaning and definition of a true "Revolution in Military Affairs." The number of terms associated with an RMA further complicates the issue. Closely associated terms, such as "Military-Technical Revolution," "Military Revolutions," and "Transformation," all contribute to the confusion. Generally, most authors agree that a true RMA (or military-technical revolution, etc.) is more than simply incremental change in technology, but instead includes changes in technology, organizational concepts, and organizational theory. It is the combination of these factors that separates a true RMA from the normal evolutionary changes in technology. The RMA proponents of the 1990s saw an opportunity for "a drastic shrinking of the military, a casting aside of old forms of organization and creation of new ones, a slashing of current force structure, and the investment of unusually large sums in research and development."[9] Historian Williamson Murray defined RMA as "periods of innovation in which armed forces develop novel concepts involving changes in doctrine, tactics, procedures, and technology."[10] However, Murray also separates the concept of "Military Revolution" from RMA as a "separate and distinct phenomenon."[11] In the past, a military revolution has

> . . . resulted from massive social and political changes that have restructured societies and states, and fundamentally altered the manner in which military organizations prepared for and conducted war. Such revolutions have been unpredictable and to a great extent *uncontrollable*. (emphasis added)[12]

Another viewpoint is expressed by Richard Hundley in his essay, "Characteristics of Revolutions in Military Affairs." In this model, an RMA "involves a paradigm shift in the nature and conduct of military operations which either renders obsolete or irrelevant one or more core competencies of a dominate player; or creates one or more new core competencies, in some new dimension of warfare or both."[13] Under his construct, a competency is defined as "a fundamental ability that provides the foundation for a set of military capabilities."[14] This strengthens the argument that a technology-driven RMA also includes substantial changes in doctrine and organization.[15]

In the 1990s, the wide literature on RMA formed the intellectual foundation, but DoD assumed that it could drive and accelerate the RMA phenomenon to serve its own purposes. Vice Chairman of the Joint Staff Admiral William Owens spoke of a new system-of-systems approach that integrated technology with new military formations and an emphasis on dominant battlefield knowledge—the ability for a military force to understand and respond to its adversary's movements so as to dominate the battlefield. It was "this new system-of-systems capability, combined with joint doctrine designed to take full advantage of these new fighting capabilities, [that was] at the heart of the RMA."[16] It was also this combination of technology, doctrine, and structure that drove the initial publication of *Joint Vision 2010*—"the conceptual template for how we will channel the vitality of our people and leverage technological opportunities to achieve new levels of effectiveness in joint warfighting."[17] In 2002, Defense Secretary Donald Rumsfeld further drew the connection between doctrine, organization, and technology with RMA and the efforts to transform DoD. Speaking to the National Defense University, he stated, "We [DoD] need to change not only the capabilities at our disposal, but also how we think about war. All the high-tech weapons in the world will not transform the U.S. Armed Forces unless we also transform the way we think, the way we train, the way we exercise, and the way we fight."[18]

But none of those in the RMA and transformation debate came to a disciplined, consistent interpretation of the concept. Everyone in the debate used terms that best suited their own ideas and purposes. Thus, attempting to define the different terms becomes an exercise in semantics—interesting but not very useful from a practical standpoint. All of the terms are used interchangeably by different authors and scholars to best fit their own conceptions and purposes. In the final analysis, it is sufficient to acknowledge that rapid (thus potentially revolutionary) change does sometimes occur within societies and military forces, producing a marked advantage for elements that can recognize it and advance it for their own purposes. It is also useful to acknowledge that this type of change is driven by more than one element (such as technology). It is a combination of elements (doctrine, organization, technology, and to a lesser extent other elements such as leadership, logistics systems, etc.) that provides the marked advantage to the organization that embraces it.

THE FRENCH REVOLUTION AND BLITZKRIEG

However RMA is defined, many defense professionals agree that the period of Napoleon and the French Revolution, and the German innovation of Blitzkrieg, achieved substantial success in integrating military capabilities that gave them a marked advantage over their opponents. In both cases, the development of new formations, doctrine, and tactics allowed them to dominate their opponents on the battlefield for a significant period. It took their adversaries years before they could develop a capability that would off-set their enemy's battlefield success and allow for more parity on the field of battle.

The French Revolution and the development of Napoleonic warfare have been viewed by many as a period of profound change. This revolution was marked by the introduction of the *levee en masse* and the development of large citizen armies influenced by patriotism and nationalism.[19] Without the influence of the French Revolution and the huge level of societal change that evolved with it, the *levee en masse* and development of mass armies would have been impossible. However, it would require the military genius of Napoleon to take full advantage of this new capability by developing the command and control structures and organizations that could achieve the marked advantage over its adversaries. Without the development of operational doctrine, corps structures, logistics based on living off the land, and other elements of Napoleonic warfare, the mere existence of a large army would not have ushered in the revolutionary change in warfare.

Likewise, in the development of Blitzkrieg, the Germans used the interwar period between World War I and World War II to greatly advance their military capabilities. This led to the development of a method of integrating air support with tank and infantry formations to dominate the Poles in 1939 and the French (with their British Expeditionary Force coalition partner) in 1940. This development of doctrine and tactics began during World War I and continued following the war with the creation of committees to study the lessons of World War I. Led by Hans Von Seekt, the German military began experimenting with tank formations in 1924, developing techniques that would be further expanded in training exercises at the secret German military school in Kazan, the Union of Soviet Socialist Republics (USSR).[20] The German military combined their new doctrine with technology (such as the development of tactical radios for command and control), allowing them to integrate close air support as a fundamental element of their tactical combat power.[21] After their incredible conquest of France in 1940, many officers on both sides of the war felt that the German Wehrmacht displayed capabilities that were "revolutionary."[22] In many ways, Blitzkrieg drew upon and added to the innovations developed at the end of World War I; but the changes, when brought together and implemented efficiently, had the appearance and effect of a revolution.

It is important to note that much of the DoD emphasis on achieving an RMA in the 1990s was motivated by the success of German advancements in warfare during the period between the World Wars. Many of the early publications from the Office of Force Transformation used Blitzkrieg as an example of transformation, and senior leaders within DoD highlighted the impact of Blitzkrieg on warfare in World War II. During testimony to Congress in April 2002, then Deputy Secretary of Defense Paul Wolfowitz stated, "But by the spring of 1940, with the Germans' lightning strikes across the Meuse and through the Ardennes, it was clear then that blitzkrieg—a term coined by Western journalists to describe this unmistakably new phenomenon—had redefined war and would shape battles for years to come."[23] Likewise, Secretary Rumsfeld specifically mentioned the German Blitzkrieg stating, "what was revolutionary and unprecedented about the blitzkrieg was not the new capabilities the Germans employed, but rather the unprecedented and revolutionary way that they mixed new and existing capabilities."[24] Consequently, the development in the 1920s and 1930s of what would later become known as Blitzkrieg became the DoD de facto benchmark for RMA.

It is also important to note that Blitzkrieg focused on the military's ability to engage in battle at the operational and tactical level. As a parallel, DoD also focused on the operational and tactical levels in their transformational efforts. The outcome of this focus was the development of methods that emphasized precision engagement, use of Special

Operations forces, application of information technologies to urban operations, and other facets. Admiral Arthur Cebrowski, then Director of the Office of Force Transformation in the Office of the Secretary of Defense, summed up the future emphasis on use of force by stating,

> The ultimate attribute of the emerging American Way of War is the superempowerment of the warfighter — whether on the ground, in the air, or at sea. As network-centric warfare empowers individual servicemen and women, and as we increasingly face an international security environment where rogue individuals, be they leaders of "evil states" or "evil networks," pose the toughest challenges, eventually the application of our military power will mirror the dominant threat to a significant degree.[25]

The use of the term, "American Way of War" was not coincidental. In his book of the same name, Russell Weigley identified the American Way of War as historically being focused on annihilation — bringing the full brunt of American industrial and military power to completely destroy an adversary — usually at great cost in both blood and treasure.[26] In Cebrowski's new American Way of War, the cost of war (both in human terms and dollar figures) would be drastically reduced by "super-empowering warfighters" with organizational, doctrinal, and technological developments at the operational and tactical level. It was this focus that drove the pursuit of RMA by the U.S. military throughout the 1990s and would remain the focus of transformation efforts under Secretary of Defense Rumsfeld.

Finally, it is important to note that there remains the view of some theorists that the development of Blitzkrieg was simply an extension of German efforts to solve the tactical problems that plagued the Western Front in World War I. This view of the RMA suggests that it occurred as a natural extension of the desire to manage increasing complexity on the tactical battlefield — an evolutionary approach to development that eventually succeeded in bringing a marked advantage to the German forces in France in 1940.[27] This is significant in that it highlights the tactical and operational nature of the solution set developed by the German Wehrmacht. It must be emphasized that this focus at the operational and tactical levels of war allowed the German Army to dominate the battlefield for a fleetingly short period of time, but did nothing to ultimately achieve the strategic ends of the thousand-year Third Reich. The German Army of World War II never developed a satisfactory approach to warfare at the strategic level and thus found itself doomed to strategic failure despite its tactical and operational prowess.

THE REVOLUTIONARY RISE OF AL-QAEDA

While the U.S. military pursued an RMA along the Blitzkrieg model, another revolution was underway incorporating many of the elements of revolutionary era France. This revolution created by al-Qaeda , the terrorist network responsible for the World Trade Center attacks on 9/11, capitalized on a growing religious and social movement focused on fundamentalist Muslim beliefs. Like the military revolution that had occurred as a result of the radical changes in the French social structure, al-Qaeda would adapt changes in technology and organizational structure to mobilize radical Muslim elements and create an organization that had the capacity to strike globally and achieve strategic results through the minor application of tactical capabilities.

The radical Islamist movement found throughout the Middle East has a variety of roots and causes dating far back into early Muslim history. Throughout this history, radical Islamists have periodically resorted to terror and violence to attain their political or theological goals within their locally limited scope and capacity. However, the modern extremist movement became a powerful global force in the Middle East by capitalizing on several sources of Arab discontent. Despite the fact that radical Muslims come from a variety of religious backgrounds and beliefs (in many cases directly at odds with each other such as Salafist Sunni versus Iranian Shi'a sects), most analysts agree that they are typically motivated by three main factors: the creation of Israel as a nation-state (along with the resulting occupation of Palestinian lands and perceived heavy-handedness by the Israeli authorities);[28] the perception that the United States has imperial designs on the Middle East and unfairly targets believers of Islam;[29] and the desire to create Islamic regimes or, at a minimum, force current Middle Eastern regimes to govern by Islamic principles.[30] These factors are exacerbated by the growing discontent of Middle Eastern youths as a result of social and economic hardship, state totalitarianism, and other considerations.[31]

With the Soviet occupation of Afghanistan in 1979, radical Islamic organizations were motivated by the perceived need to support their fellow Muslims and oust the Soviets from the country. Osama bin Laden was a product of this conflict between fundamentalist Muslim factions and the secular Soviet forces in the nation. As the son of a billionaire construction contractor in Saudi Arabia, bin Laden attended King Aziz University where he earned a degree in civil engineering. Despite not being motivated by religious doctrine as a young man, he relocated to Afghanistan and joined the Afghan Mujahideen (freedom fighters) to fight the Soviet invasion. In Afghanistan he found his calling in life.[32] Once the Soviets were ousted from the country (in 1989), bin Laden turned his energy and organizational skill against a newly identified enemy of Islam — the United States. Using the U.S. "occupation" of Saudi Arabia during the Gulf War as the justification for his cause, he created al-Qaeda (Arabic for "The Base") to expel the United States from Saudi Arabia and protect the Islamic holy sites of Mecca and Medina. In his first religious ruling or *fatwa*, issued in 1996, bin Laden called for all Muslims (specifically Muslim youths) to "push the American enemy out of the holy lands" and begin a war against the "Zionist-Crusader" alliance.[33] His second *fatwa*, issued in 1998, went further, declaring that it was every Muslim's duty to "kill the Americans and their allies — civilians and military . . . in any country which it is possible to do it [kill Americans]."[34]

These religious rulings would have the effect of calling for the modern day equivalent of a transnational *levee en masse* — albeit one that was focused along religious rather than nationalist lines. Osama bin Laden combined this universal motivation of Islamic extremists with new technologies and organizational structures to create a powerful organization with the ability to strike targets throughout the world. Dr. Audrey Cronin has explained that this *levee en masse* (or cyber-mobilization) is still in its infancy, but is irreversible and will have a profound influence on the conduct of future war.[35]

To reach his audience, bin Laden has created a powerful information architecture utilizing the Internet and other information sources to broadcast his message. Developing an Internet and media organization called "Al Sahab" (literally translated in English as "The Clouds"), al-Qaeda produces high quality video and other media accessible by millions through the Internet and other sources. The success of al-Qaeda in this endeavor has increased throughout the last 10 years so that an Internet posting by Osama bin Laden, or one of his lieutenants, now becomes an instant story worthy of heavy international news coverage.[36] This has allowed his *fatwas* and other dictates to be broadcast, not only through al-Qaeda's own Internet pages, but through many other Internet, television, and mass media outlets. By combining this powerful and universal technology with strong religious doctrine and teachings, al-Qaeda has, over the last 6 years, increased its ability to recruit new members and execute terrorist attacks; this has been achieved despite the on-going efforts of the United States and its allies in Afghanistan and elsewhere.

Ironically, the Internet was originally developed by the U.S. military to enhance communications during the Cold War. It was created by the primary DoD laboratory for exploring emerging technology. The Defense Advanced Research Projects Agency (DARPA) designed the Internet (then known as ARPANET) in the 1960s to provide redundant communications in the case of nuclear war. It became a worldwide phenomenon in the 1990s that has been called "the most transforming technological development of our time, rivaling, if not exceeding, the printing press."[37] The ability of al-Qaeda to exploit the Internet (a product designed and created by the U.S. military) in order to wage war *against* the United States is a key element of al-Qaeda's RMA concept.

In addition to integrating Internet technology, bin Laden created a flattened organizational structure to enhance the command and control capabilities of al-Qaeda . Using broad guidance (such as the *fatwa* statement to kill all Americans wherever they are found), he is able to minimize his own importance to the organization and allow subordinates to operate independently to achieve the organizational goals. Some current estimates indicate that even if bin Laden were to die or otherwise be removed from the organization, al-Qaeda would continue unhindered for many years to come.[38] This flattened organizational structure allows the leadership to gain efficiencies in the organizational functions of funding, logistics, manpower, training, and propaganda. Using a network that has associates in at least 75 different countries worldwide, the organization is able to maintain its structure and pursue its goals across a wide range of different cultures and environmental conditions.[39] The July 2007 National Intelligence Estimate, "The Terrorist Threat to the U.S. Homeland," highlighted the growing threat from this networked structure:

> We assess that globalization trends and recent technological advances will continue to enable even small numbers of alienated people to find and connect with one another, justify and intensify their anger, and mobilize resources to attack — all without requiring a centralized terrorist organization, training camp, or leader.[40]

al-Qaeda has been extremely successful in achieving its strategic goals by combining a networked organizational structure with the ability to reach a wide audience and deliver a message that has universal appeal to radical Muslims. Subsequent to the attacks on 9/11, al-Qaeda and associated groups have conducted successful strikes on targets in Algiers, Casablanca, Madrid, London, Istanbul, Riyadh, Jeddah, Karachi, Sharm el-Sheikh, Taba, Mombassa, Kuwait, Mumbai, New Delhi, and Bali.[41] In many instances, these attacks have achieved strategic effects. The most spectacular success was the Madrid train station bombings on March 11, 2004 resulting in 191 civilian deaths. Those attacks directly influenced the outcome of the Spanish elections, scheduled to be held 3 days after the attacks. In those elections, the ruling Popular Party, despite holding a strong lead in the days prior to the attacks, was defeated by the Socialist Party which then promptly withdrew Spanish forces from Iraq, achieving the strategic goal of the al-Qaeda affiliated organization.[42] This success occurred despite the previous 3-year NATO and U.S. campaign against the al-Qaeda leadership in Afghanistan. Other successes have achieved global notoriety, including the train bombings in London and the attack on the nightclub in Bali in October 2002, which killed over 200 civilians (mainly Australians).[43]

What makes al-Qaeda strikingly different from most military organizations is the effort it has put into achieving strategic effects with low cost tactical operations. One analyst characterized al-Qaeda's overarching goals as being "aimed at the overthrow of values, cultures, or societies on a global level through the use of subversion and armed conflict, with the ultimate goal of establishing a new world order."[44] Another way of viewing these goals is that al-Qaeda is prosecuting a global insurgency to achieve major strategic objectives by utilizing small individual organizations with relatively unsophisticated weapon systems. This is most clearly seen by the attacks on 9/11, where a small group of less than 20 operators caused over 3,000 civilian casualties in less than 4 hours.

The end result of this military revolution has been that al-Qaeda continues to prosecute a global war and, despite the efforts of NATO and the United States, has actually increased its capacity to conduct attacks. This effect was achieved without using high technology weapon systems; instead it relied on less sophisticated methods (such as suicide bombers in jet airliners) to attain goals. In achieving their own RMA, al-Qaeda undermined the utility of the U.S. military's core competency of tactical warfighting. Despite a huge effort to physically destroy the al-Qaeda network through the application of tactical force, al-Qaeda has continued to maintain a capability to achieve strategic goals through its own use of selected attacks on specific targets across the world.

THE U.S. RESPONSE TO THE MILITARY REVOLUTION

The U.S. Government has recognized the growing threat from al-Qaeda and has focused on methods of destroying the organization. This increasing acknowledgement of the threat from organizations like al-Qaeda has resulted in the understanding that the U.S. military must be prepared to fight a number of different threats simultaneously. This has helped shape the U.S. defense strategy and subsequently has informed a number of budgeting and programming systems, such as the Quadrennial Defense Review of 2006.[45] It has become clear to the members of the U.S. military establishment that they must develop systems and structures that can respond to a wide range of threats in order to successfully fulfill its mission of defending the nation.

As part of this acknowledgment, the U.S. military is restructuring its forces to be more flexible and responsive to the different threats. Driven by current requirements in Iraq and Afghanistan, the focus has been on changing tactical organizations to meet the battlefield needs of the military in an effort to defeat al-Qaeda and its associated networks by the use of force. The U.S. Army has led the way in this reorganization, changing the basic structure of brigades and battalions to more rapidly deploy and fight at the tactical level. The development of Brigade Combat Teams with enhanced intelligence capability and greater capacity to bring force to bear on the battlefield has been the principle driver behind the reorganization.[46] Likewise, the military has spent a considerable amount of money to counter specific tactics of al-Qaeda -associated groups. This includes the development of vehicles, such as Up-Armored High Mobility Multipurpose Wheeled Vehicles (HMMWVs) and Mine Resistant Ambush Protected (MRAP) vehicles, designed to protect occupants from attacks by improvised explosive devices (IEDs).[47] It also includes development of technologies to defeat improvised explosive devices or otherwise prevent their use by insurgent groups on the battlefield.[48]

However, this reorganization continues to be focused on battle skills and the ability to prosecute the tactical fight. This fits the battle-oriented model for the American Way of War. The United States has a long strategic and cultural tradition of focusing on conventional warfare, while giving less attention to other threats such as terrorism and counterinsurgency. Coupled with this culture is a belief that fighting wars is the purview of DoD—almost to the exclusion of the other entities within the government. Throughout our history, when the nation turned to the use of force to solve a problem, all other elements of the government tended to take a backseat to the efforts of the defense community. As a nation, Americans tend to view military threats only through the lens of military power—the use of weapons and systems to bring about a violent defeat of our enemies. Even the way that Americans discuss the different elements of power (the diplomatic, military, economic, and informational elements of national power), tends to lend itself to a stovepiped conception of distinct categories versus an integrated conception of the various sources of power.[49] This strategic culture is combined with a natural tendency to search for technological solutions to gain efficiencies where possible.

In keeping with U.S. strategic culture, the U.S. military focused its efforts to defeat al-Qaeda in a similar manner to the way it focused its efforts on the search for an RMA—at the operational and tactical levels of war; even as al-Qaeda was focusing operations at the strategic level and spending much less effort at the tactical level, the United States was focusing on capabilities such as precision guided munitions and global positioning systems.

Other efforts to counter al-Qaeda have been made by different agencies within the U.S. Government, but they have been mainly focused on defending the nation against a terrorist attack. The largest of these efforts has been the development of the Department of Homeland Security, consolidating a number of U.S. agencies (the U.S. Coast Guard, Federal Emergency Management Agency, etc.) in an effort to prevent an another 9/11 attack by coordinating the skills and strengths of these myriad organizations. Likewise, the establishment of the Director of National Intelligence to consolidate all national intelligence efforts has also helped prevent further attacks against the United States. However these efforts have not had a substantial effect on the ability to prosecute the war against al-Qaeda 's international network. Audrey Cronin has argued that the U.S. Government's "approach to this growing repulsion [terrorism] is colored by a kind of cultural naïveté, an unwillingness to recognize—let alone appreciate or take responsibility for—the influence of U.S. power except in its military dimension."[50]

RECOMMENDATIONS

The United States must look toward the future of warfare to create the capacity to meet the transnational threat presented by al-Qaeda and its associated network. al-Qaeda has clearly demonstrated that an RMA occurred in the last decade. This revolution, however, was along the lines of the French Revolution vice the development of Blitzkrieg, insofar as it took advantage of significant changes in Islamist social structures and culture to effect its change. Combined with globalization, the rise of information technology (especially the increasing use of the Internet to pass information), and the creation of a decentralized networked organization, al-Qaeda has achieved significant strategic effects without requiring sophisticated weapon systems. They have the ability to effect change globally and to strike when and where it best suits their current strategic needs. Implementing a revolutionary approach, they have succeeded in many respects in reducing the significance of the U.S. military's core competency of battle (in the military sense). As General David Petraeus has affirmed, the U.S. military cannot win the fight in Iraq by itself — it must be won with other sources of power.[51] In this statement he emphasizes the application of military force in *a supporting role complimenting the other elements of national powe*r vice the primary form of warfare.

The answer to this dilemma is that the U.S. military and U.S. Government must look beyond military capability in the pursuit of RMA. As Dr. Cronin has observed, "terrorism is a complex phenomenon; it must be met with short-term military action, *informed by in-depth, long term sophisticated analysis.*"[52] The U.S. Government *in total,* must be viewed as the organization that fights and wins the nation's wars. The United States must go beyond an RMA patterned on developing capabilities that dominate only the kinetic spectrum of military battle — the development of the next version of Blitzkrieg — and instead focus its efforts on defeating organizations and networks across the spectrum of conflict. This is a significant paradigm shift from our current understanding of warfare and government structures. DoD would no longer be the organization solely charged with fighting and winning the nation's wars; instead, the defense establishment would be one component of an entire governmental effort to fight and win the nation's wars, led by an agency or other organization that has the authority to task *all* agencies of the government. Achieving this requires a fundamental shift in thought regarding the functions of a democratic government, and its ability to protect its interests.

The future of warfare resides in the ability to connect *all* elements of power through networking in order to share the information and expertise that resides in each different department. The *2006 Quadrennial Defense Review Report* (QDR) acknowledges that the war on terror,

> . . . is both a battle of arms and a battle of ideas — a fight against terrorist networks and against their murderous ideology. The Department of Defense fully supports efforts to counter the ideology of terrorism, although most of the U.S. Government's capabilities for this activity reside in other U.S. Government agencies and in the private sector.[53]

The QDR report is a great step in the right direction toward building a capability to fight enemies such as al-Qaeda . However, it focuses too much of its effort on defining the structure of the U.S. military for prosecution of the war on terror. It lists specific items that must be developed, purchased, or otherwise employed by the military, but then falls short when describing what must be done to integrate the other elements of national power and apply them to the current fight. Within elements of DoD, the QDR gives specific and pointed guidance, such as "the Department [of Defense] *will . . . transform* Army units and headquarters to modular designs." [emphasis added][54] However, when discussing integration with other elements of the U.S. Government (interagency) the guidance becomes much softer, such as, "the QDR *recommends the creation* of National Security Planning Guidance to direct the development of both military and non-military plans and institutional capabilities." [emphasis added][55] This use of softer language ("will transform" vice "recommends creation") is a subtle acknowledgement that DoD does not have the power or authority to direct other departments or agencies within the U.S. Government.

For the U.S. Government to successfully prosecute war against networked enemies such as al-Qaeda , it must undergo a fundamental shift in the warfighting paradigm. This will require a restructuring of the government and governmental agencies that have previously been overlooked in the pursuit of the operational and tactical RMA. Empowering the Vice President to act as the integrator of the Executive Branch of government would be an example of this paradigm shift. Another example would be the development of a regional combatant command structure where the warfighter or commander would be a senior official from the National Security Council (or a similar organization to be developed in the future). The component commanders for this command would include a flag officer from DoD, an Ambassador from the State Department, a senior official from the U.S. Information Agency, and representatives from other cabinet level organizations deemed necessary for engagement in the region. Vastly increasing the capabilities of agencies other than DoD (such as the Department of State) will be the crucial first step in moving the United States towards a new, more relevant national security paradigm.

This does not preclude the need to continue to develop the kinetic tactical capabilities of the U.S. military. The U.S. military will remain a substantial component (albeit only one of many) in efforts to wage our nation's wars; leveraging technology and other capabilities to dominate the kinetic spectrum of warfare will remain extremely important. Simultaneous to the efforts to reorganize itself, the U.S. Government should pursue technologies that provide network-centric information capabilities throughout the governmental agencies (not just military functions). Information sharing at the highest levels will greatly increase our ability to prosecute warfare at the strategic level. As in any true RMA, the development of capabilities in technology, doctrine, organization, and other elements must be complementary and contribute to a total package of capability as viewed by the entire U.S. Government and not simply DoD. As explained by Antulio Echevarria, the American Way of War should be focused on developing the capabilities to bring strategic success after battle, rather than focused on the effects of battle alone.[56]

There are many other ways to pursue the new RMA, but until we radically rethink how we, as a nation, fight and win our wars, we will continue to fall short in defeating adversaries patterned after al-Qaeda . Whatever capability is developed must take into account the ability to focus all elements of national power to defeat our future adversaries. Many of our future opponents are closely observing our efforts in Afghanistan and Iraq and learning from our mistakes. The future war that we fight will see opponents continue to attempt to marginalize our tactical battlefield capabilities in order to achieve their own strategic goals.

ENDNOTES - CHAPTER 3

1. One website devoted to defense analysis lists 294 separate articles referencing RMA. See "Second Thoughts on the RMA," available from *www.comw.org/rma/fulltext/second.html*. Noted authors include Eliot Cohen, "A Revolution in Warfare"; Michael O'Hanlon, Technological Change and the Future of Warfare"; John Murtha, "A Technological Call to Arms"; Andrew Krepenivich, "Military Experimentation: Time to Get Serious"; Arthur K. Cebrowski, "The American Way of War"; and many others.

2. U.S. Department of Defense, *Conduct of the Persian Gulf War, Final Report to Congress*, Washington, DC: U.S. Government Printing Office, April 1992, p. 27. In his introduction to the DoD formal report on Operation DESERT STORM, then Secretary of Defense Richard Cheney summed up his vision of future war:

> This war [Operation DESERT STORM] demonstrated dramatically the new possibilities of what has been called the "military-technological revolution in warfare." This technological revolution encompasses many areas, including stand-off precision weaponry, sophisticated sensors, stealth for surprise and survivability, night vision capabilities and tactical ballistic missile defenses. In large part this revolution tracks the development of new technologies such as the microprocessing of information that has become familiar in our daily lives. The exploitation of these and still-emerging technologies promises to change the nature of warfare significantly, as did the earlier advent of tanks, airplanes, and aircraft carriers. The war tested an entire generation of new weapons and systems at the forefront of this.

3. *Elements of Defense Transformation*, Washington DC: U.S. Department of Defense, October 2004, p. 11. The publication further explains the role of the Director of Force Transformation, stating, "He monitors and evaluates the implementation of the Department's transformation strategy, advises the Secretary, manages the transformation roadmap process, and helps to ensure that joint concepts are open to challenge by a wide range of innovative alternative concepts and ideas," p. 11.

4. Donald Rumsfeld, "Secretary Rumsfeld Speaks on 21st Century Transformation of U.S. Armed Forces," Speech delivered at the National Defense University on January 31, 2002, available from *www. defenselink.mil/speeches/speech.aspx?speechid=183*.

5. Stephen Biddle, "Iraq, Afghanistan, and American Military Transformation," *Strategy in the Contemporary World: An Introduction to Strategic Studies, 2nd Ed.*, John Baylis, James J. Wirtz, Eliot A. Cohen, and Colin S. Gray, eds., New York: Oxford University Press, 2006, p. 275.

6. *Ibid.*

7. *Ibid.* This play on Biddle's words illustrates al-Qaeda's real accomplishment.

8. *Elements of Defense Transformation*, p. 10.

9. Eliot Cohen, "A Transformation in Warfare," *Foreign Affairs*, Vol. 75, March/April 1997, p. 37.

10. Williamson Murray and MacGregor Knox, "The Future Behind Us," *Theory of War and Strategy, Volume 4*, Carlisle, PA: Department of National Security Strategy, U.S. Army War College, 2007, p. 153.

11. *Ibid.*, p. 156.

12. *Ibid.*, p. 176.

13. Richard O. Hundley, *Past Revolutions Future Transformations*, Santa Monica, CA: RAND, 1999, p. 9.

14. *Ibid.*, p. 9.

15. *Ibid.*, p. 15.

16. Admiral William A. Owens, "Revolutionizing Warfare," *Blueprint Magazine*, January 2000, available from *www.dlc.org*.

17. U.S. Joint Chiefs of Staff, *Joint Vision 2010*, Washington, DC, Office of the Chairman of the Joint Chiefs of Staff, 1996, p. 4. Joint Warfighting is a concept wherein the capabilities of all military services, Army, Navy, Air Force, and Marines, are integrated to achieve synergy and efficiency.

18. Rumsfeld.

19. James S. Corum, *Roots of Blitzkrieg*, Lawrence, KS: University of Kansas Press, 1992, pp. 71-72.

20. *Ibid.*, pp. 132, 193.

21. *Ibid.*, pp. 167-168.

22. Williamson Murray, "Thinking About Revolutions in Military Affairs," *Joint Force Quarterly*, Summer 1997, p. 73.

23. Paul Wolfowitz, "Testimony of Deputy Secretary of Defense Paul Wolfowitz prepared for the Senate Armed Services Committee on Transformation, April 9, 2002," available from *www.globalsecurity. org/military/library/congress/2002_hr/wolfowitz49.pdf*.

24. Rumsfeld.

25. Arthur K. Cebrowski and Thomas P. M. Barrett, "The American Way of War," *Proceedings: The U.S. Naval Institute*, January 2003, p. 42.

26. Russell Wiegley, *The American Way of War: A History of United States Military Strategy and Policy*, Bloomington, IA: Indiana University Press, 1973, p. xxii.

27. Stephen Biddle, "The Past as Prologue: Assessing Theories of Future Warfare," *Security Studies*, Vol. 8, Autumn 1998, pp. 11-12.

28. Anthony H. Cordesman, *The Impact of Terrorism and Extremism on the Regional Balance*, Washington, DC: Center for Strategic and International Studies, March 2004, p. 7.

29. Loren Kelly, *The United States and the Muslim World: Critical Issues and Opportunities for Change*, Stanley Foundation Policy Bulletin, No. 15, January 2005, p. 2. This article served as a report of a conference held in Atlanta, GA.

30. *Ibid.*, This fact was also mentioned by Mr. Cordesman in his CSIS Pamphlet, p. 7.

31. Cordesman, p. 7.

32. Benjamin Orbach, "Usama Bin Ladin and Al Qa'ida: Origins and Doctrine," *Middle East Review of International Affairs*, Vol. 5, No. 4, December 2001.

33. Osama bin Laden, "Declaration of War Against the Americans Occupying the Land of the Two Holy Places," available from *www.pbs.org/newshour/terrorism/international/fatwa_1996.html*.

34. Osama bin Laden, "*Fatwa* to Declare a Holy War Against the West and Israel," available from *www.pbs.org/newshour/terrorism/international/fatwa_1998.html*.

35. Audrey Cronin, "Cyber Mobilization: The New Levee En Masse," *Parameters*, Summer 2006, p. 77.

36. For example, on December 29, 2007, al-Qaeda released a video through their multimedia propaganda agency. This video quickly became a headline story throughout the world, available through multiple Internet sites and other media. This video can be easily accessed through multiple Internet sites by simply conducting a Google search using key words, Osama bin Laden video December 2007.

37. James R. Downey, *Defense Science and Technology Programs, Processes, and Issues: A Strategic Leader's Guide*, Carlisle, PA: Department of Command, Leadership, and Management, U.S. Army War College, April 2007, p. 15.

38. Michael Scheuer, "Can al-Qaeda Endure Beyond bin Laden?" *Terrorism Focus,* Vol. 2, October, 2005, available from *www.jamestown.org/news_details.php?news_id=147*.

39. *Ibid.*

40. National Intelligence Council, *National Intelligence Estimate: The Terrorist Threat to the US Homeland*, Washington, DC: Office of the Director of National Intelligence, July 2007, p. 7.

41. Bruce Riedel, *al-Qaeda : The Return of the Knights*, Washington, DC: The Brookings Institute, July 2007, available from *www.brookings.edu/papers/2007/0725middleeast_riedel.aspx*.

42. Keith B. Richburg, "Madrid Attacks May Have Targeted Elections," *The Washington Post*, October 17, 2004, Sec. A, p. 16.

43. Global Security.org, "Bali Nightclub Bombing," available from *www.globalsecurity.org/security/ops/bali.htm*.

44. Michael F. Morris, "al-Qaeda as Insurgency," *Joint Forces Quarterly*, Vol. 39, Summer 2005, p. 47.

45. *Quadrennial Defense Review Report*, Washington, DC: U.S. Department of Defense, February 6, 2006, p. v. The introduction to the 2006 QDR gives great emphasis to applying lessons learned from operations since 9/11, stating that the report "appl[ies] the important lessons learned from more than four years of war against a global network of violent extremists. . ."

46. Andrew Feickert, *US Army's Modular Redesign: Issues for Congress*, Washington DC: U.S. Library of Congress, Congressional Research Service, May 5, 2006, p. 4.

47. Jim Garamone, "Defense Department Contracts for 2,400 More MRAP Vehicles," *Armed Forces Press Service*, October 19, 2007, available from *www.defenselink.mil/news/newsarticle.aspx?id=47849*.

48. In focusing on the IED problem, DoD established a separate organization headed by a retired four-star general. This organization, The Joint Improvised Explosive Device Defeat Organization, has subordinate organizations located in Iraq (Task Force Troy) and Afghanistan (Task Force Palladin) focused on triage of individual IED attacks. A thorough review of the effect of IEDs and DoD's efforts to combat them can be viewed in a four part series of articles by Rick Atkinson entitled "Left of Boom" published in the *Washington Post* from September 30, 2007, through October 3, 2007.

49. Audrey Kurth Cronin, "Behind the Curve: Globalization and International Terrorism," Michael E. Brown *et al.*, eds., *New Global Dangers*, Cambridge, MA: MIT Press, 2004, p. 449.

50. *Ibid.*, p. 464.

51. "No Military Solution to Iraq," *Cable News Network*, March 9, 2007, available from *www.cnn.com/2007/WORLD/meast/03/08/iraq.petraeus/index.html?iref=newssearch*.

52. Cronin, p. 473.

53. *Quadrennial Defense Review Report*, p. 22.

54. *Ibid.*, p. 43.

55. *Ibid*, p. 85.

56. Antullio J. Echevarria, *Toward an American Way of War*, Carlisle, PA: Strategic Studies Institute, U.S. Army War College, March 2004, pp. v-viii.

CHAPTER 4

AFRICA COMMAND AND THE MILITARIZATION
OF U.S. FOREIGN POLICY

Dennis R. Penn
Department of Defense

INTRODUCTION

The end of the Cold War brought about a new era of remarkable changes in the strategic perspective of the U.S. Government (USG). Within this confluence of changes, two independent threads of thought emerged, evolved, and eventually started to converge. The first thread pertains to the continent of Africa and its rise in strategic value vis-à-vis U.S. national interests. Once relegated to the diplomatic dustbin, Africa surprisingly roared to the top of the foreign policy heap—it was suddenly very strategically important. The March 2006 National Security Strategy states that, "Africa holds growing geo-strategic importance and is a high priority of this Administration . . . our goal is an African continent that knows liberty, peace, stability, and increasing prosperity."[1] The genesis of U.S. renewed commitment to Africa is rooted in large part to its value as an important source of "energy supplies; a possible safe haven for terrorist groups; a transit node of illegal trafficking in drugs, arms, and people; and a growing voice in multilateral institutions."[2] The second thread relates to a momentous shift in U.S. military mission focus. Whereas the military at one time focused almost exclusively on waging war, based largely on the Iraq and Afghanistan experiences, it began a conscious shift in thinking towards preventing war—this is due to the strategic realization that it is more cost effective to prevent war than it is to wage it. The U.S. military adjusted, and continues to adjust, its policy, strategies, and doctrine to include an emphasis on proactive peacetime engagement as a way to achieve national strategy objectives.[3]

The two threads first converged at the U.S. European Command (USEUCOM) Headquarters in Stuttgart, Germany. A geographic combatant command (GCC), USEUCOM's area of responsibility included all of Europe, Russia, Israel, and most of Africa.[4] Through its efforts in the global war on terror (GWOT), USEUCOM pioneered a new approach to theater security cooperation (TSC) and traditional warfighting—a new kind of campaign construct referred to as "Phase Zero."[5] The command operationalized their TSC and capacity-building efforts by collaborating with regional allies and focusing on terrorism's long-term, underlying conditions.[6] With its emphasis on interagency cooperation, coordination, and collaboration, Phase Zero represented a natural evolution in the concept of proactive peacetime engagement. Concurrently, in recognition of the need for a unified response to Africa's growing military, strategic, and economic importance, the Bush administration established a new unified combatant command, U.S. Africa Command (USAFRICOM), on February 6, 2007.[7] USAFRICOM is not like other traditional unified commands in that its focus is first and foremost on war prevention rather than warfighting.[8] Resourced in large part from within USEUCOM itself, the new GCC retains the pioneering TSC and capacity-building focus initiated under the auspices of its parent organization.[9] In addition, USAFRICOM is also pioneering new modes of interagency interaction.[10] The creation of USAFRICOM suggests these threads are inextricably linked, but this is not necessarily true.

Unsurprisingly, not everyone thinks USAFRICOM's approach to proactive peacetime engagement is a good idea. Some in Africa worry that the new command signals a new "western colonialism."[11] Furthermore, Africans are not the only ones expressing apprehension. There are elements within the State Department and the U.S. Agency for International Development (USAID) who voice concern that the military may "overestimate" its capabilities as well as its "diplomatic role" in Africa.[12] The foreign press, never shy about voicing their opinions on U.S. policy, print denouncements such as, "It is therefore disturbing to note that democracy, health, education, economic growth and development are being tied to military interests."[13] Still others contend the GCCs are examples of American proconsuls plying foreign policy.[14] The implication for the new command is that USAFRICOM, as a GCC, represents the next step in the militarization of U.S. foreign policy.

Does USAFRICOM signal a deliberate militarization of U.S. foreign policy? The author posits that this may very well be the case, and the role of USAFRICOM must be managed thoughtfully or it will not engender the intended long-term advantage to the United States. But whether or not the United States is intentionally militarizing its foreign policy may not be the point—what is important is that many perceive it to be the case. Here, perception trumps reality, and in the case of USAFRICOM, perceptions are shaping how the command is accepted within the region and what it can hope to accomplish. If left unchecked, the problem of perception may cause the aforementioned threads to diverge. If this were to occur, the United States would not only waste an opportunity to realize the full potential of what is arguably a genuine revolution in military affairs in regard to prevention of war, but would also fall far short of our stated national objectives in regard to Africa. Over the long term, if they should unravel it would have deleterious effects on U.S.-African relations and spur African states to turn to others, such as the People's Republic of China (PRC), for assistance and strategic partnership.

This chapter argues that the efforts to date represent steps in the right direction, but they are overly reliant on the military for implementation. Consequently, U.S. initiatives only serve to underscore and highlight the appearance of policy militarization. Ultimately this weakens rather than strengthens the link between the two threads. It is therefore ironic that the harder the U.S. military works to implement proactive peacetime engagement, the weaker and more distant the bond becomes between those the military is trying to help and U.S. interests. However, if the proactive peacetime engagement thread were to reflect a nonmilitary lead and include diverse USG participation, the link between threads might actually strengthen. To some degree, the USG is striving to do just this. However, USG efforts to date fall short of the scale of change required, and they do not adequately address the perceptions of militarizing our foreign policy vis-à-vis Africa. This author submits that bold reform is required to ensure the two convergent threads are appropriately interweaved. The policy changes recommended in this chapter could prove to be the level of change required to shift the balance in favor of strengthening the two threads. These changes must be transformational at the strategic level, permanent in nature, and appropriately resourced. To do less will likely mean that the United States, at best, maintains the status quo, and as a direct consequence, it will fall short of meeting its goal of "an African continent that knows liberty, peace, stability, and increasing prosperity."[15] Perhaps more importantly, the failure to pursue these changes would cause the nation to fall short of capturing an essential security paradigm for the emerging 21st century.

AFRICA RISING

Africa is a continent growing in strategic importance. First among the reasons for Africa's rise in strategic value is the continent's underdeveloped natural resources. In some circumstances, Africa will be as important a source for U.S. energy imports as is the Middle East.[16] U.S. interests in Africa also reflect marked concern over transnational issues such as potential terrorist safe havens; transit nodes for illegal trafficking in drugs, arms, and people; Africa's growing stature in multilateral institutions; armed civil conflict; humanitarian crises; the rise of pandemic diseases; and the growing influence of potential competitors.[17] Equally important, as the atrocities in Darfur bear witness, certain elements within Africa continue to "test the resolve of the international community and the United States to prevent mass killings and genocide."[18] Moreover, other nations are also expressing increased interest in Africa; the world's major powers are working aggressively to seek out investments, win contracts, peddle influence, and build political support on the African continent.[19] With respect to access to Africa's oil, natural gas, and other natural resources, the United States is in direct competition with numerous nations to include India, Europe, and the PRC.[20] In many ways, Africa represents the nature and range of security issues confronting the United States in the 21st century. Clearly, Africa demands, and is now getting long wanted and much deserved attention from U.S. policymakers.

U.S. national policy statements in recent years reflect Africa's rise in strategic importance. In July 2003, the Bush administration's African Policy stated that "promise and opportunity sit side by side with disease, war, and desperate poverty" and that this "threatens both a core value of the United States—preserving human dignity—and our strategic priority—combating global terror."[21] In July 2005, President Bush garnered G-8 partner commitment for initiatives that advance U.S. priorities in Africa to include forgiving debt, fighting malaria, addressing urgent humanitarian needs, improving education, boosting development assistance, increasing trade and investment, and broadening support for peace and stability.[22] The March 2006 U.S. National Security Strategy states, "Africa holds growing geo-strategic importance and is a high priority of this Administration," and "the U.S. recognizes that our security depends upon partnering with Africans to strengthen fragile and failing states and bring ungoverned areas under the control of effective democracies."[23] On February 6, 2007, the Bush administration announced its decision to establish a new unified GCC, USAFRICOM.[24]

The formation of USAFRICOM represents a unique internal reorganization of the joint military command structure, creating a new combatant command focused solely on Africa and collaboratively designed with other agencies to help to coordinate USG contributions across the continent.[25] Unlike more traditional unified commands, USAFRICOM concentrates its efforts on war prevention rather than warfighting.[26] The new command supports two primary missions: (1) strengthening security cooperation by creating new opportunities to bolster capabilities; and, (2) enhancing efforts to help bring peace and security by promoting development, health, education, democracy, and economic growth.[27] USAFRICOM works in close partnership with not only other USG elements, but also with African states, regional security organizations, nongovernmental organizations (NGOs), and a variety of other actors.[28] At full operational capability, USAFRICOM's innovative interagency structure will pursue nonkinetic missions across Africa.[29] USAFRICOM will conduct traditional military operations only when directed.[30] As one expert in defense policy and foreign affairs accurately opines, "In many ways, USAFRICOM is a post-Cold War experiment that radically rethinks security in the early 21st century based on peace-building lessons learned since the fall of the Berlin Wall."[31]

To meet its goals and objectives, USAFRICOM must leverage all the elements of U.S. national power — diplomatic, informational, military, and economic (DIME) — through a coordinated interagency effort.[32] Interagency coordination forges the vital link between the military and the other elements of national power, and guides the relationship with NGOs and international organizations.[33] For interagency efforts to be successful, they must be fully integrated and synchronized, achieving unity of effort across the whole of government and beyond.[34] This is no small task, and though the USG has largely come to grips with the critical importance of interagency coordination, it has to date performed poorly in developing and implementing interagency solutions.[35] To avoid repeating previous U.S. interagency missteps, USAFRICOM's architects pioneered a unique approach to interagency coordination within a GCC, placing a senior State Department official as one of two deputy commanders and including an unprecedented number of interagency civilians in key leadership roles throughout the command.[36] The infusion of civilians into the command structure alone will not guarantee success; USAFRICOM must also be able to identify commonly understood objectives and translate those objectives into demonstrable action in a coherent and efficient collective operation.[37] Unity of purpose and effort will flow from interagency integration and other needed changes in policy, strategy, and doctrine.

A REVOLUTION IN POLICY, STRATEGY, AND DOCTRINE

In what constitutes a genuine Revolution in Military Affairs, the U.S. military has fundamentally adjusted its policy, strategies, and doctrine over the past 15 years to emphasize proactive peacetime engagement as a way to achieving national strategy objectives.[38] Proactive peacetime engagement is based on the principle that it is "much more cost effective to prevent conflict than it is to stop one once it has started,"[39] and its efforts are designed to "reassure allies and partners, promote stability and mitigate the conditions that lead to conflict."[40] Evolving to meet the emerging challenges of an uncertain and complex security environment, the concept of proactive peacetime engagement aims to shape the international milieu to meet national interests by creating partnerships and building the capacity of allies and partners.[41] While some may argue that the military has always performed these functions, the military's current focus in conflict prevention did not take root in policy until the fall of the Soviet Empire — the post-Cold War era.[42] This philosophical shift away from a focus on fighting wars to preventing them is at the core of USAFRICOM's mission.[43]

In a critically important step in this evolutionary design, the *Capstone Concept for Joint Operations* (CCJO), published in August 2005, reintroduced the proactive peacetime engagement philosophy via two new joint doctrine concepts designed to minimize the use of armed force and integrate interagency and multinational partners across the full range of military operations.[44] With respect to the first, shaping operations, the ability to maintain peace and prevent conflict or crises is portrayed as equal in importace to the ability to wage major combat operations.[45] The primary focus of peacetime shaping operations, it argues, is to spread democracy by "creating an environment of peace, stability, and goodwill."[46] Concerning the second, stability operations, it states achieving desired political aims by winning war "requires resolving crises, winning conventional combat operations, and ensuring stability in affected areas."[47] This may require the military to help provide a secure environment, initial humanitarian assistance, limited governance, restoration of essential public services, and similar types of assistance.[48] The doctrinal emphasis on shaping and stability operations represents the first step in codifying the military's changing mission focus; that is, do everything you can to prevent war when you can, and then, if you must wage war, do everything you can to end the conflict quickly and reintroduce stability.

Shaping operations fall under the joint doctrine rubric of military engagement, security cooperation, and deterrence.[49] In shaping operations, the military collaborates with numerous domestic and foreign agencies and organizations across a wide range of activities "to protect and enhance national security interests and deter conflict."[50] Combatant commanders complement and reinforce the other instruments of national power and the capabilities of regional allies to shape their areas of responsibility through security cooperation activities.[51] Through its efforts to prosecute the GWOT in Africa, USEUCOM operationalized TSC and capacity-building efforts in a new kind of campaign plan construct called Phase Zero.[52] Also known as the Shape Phase, these operations are continuous and adaptive nonkinetic shaping activities that encompass "everything that can be done to prevent conflicts from developing in the first place."[53]

The ultimate goal of Phase Zero operations is to "promote stability and peace by building capacity in partner nations that enables them to be cooperative, trained, and prepared to help prevent or limit conflicts."[54] In addition, these operations also aim "to enhance international legitimacy and gain multinational cooperation in support of defined military and national strategic objectives."[55] With respect to counterterrorism activities, Phase Zero operations address the underlying conditions that fuel and enable terrorism.[56] Of note, during typical Phase Zero operations, the military will likely play a supporting role rather than a supported role, and the military's programs will be only one part of the much larger overall USG effort.[57] Because these operations are an open-ended, long-term approach to preventing conflict, some consider it "more appropriate to describe Phase Zero as a campaign in and of itself—a new kind of campaign that must be continuously fought by U.S. joint forces in concert with the interagency community and in cooperation with allies and partner nations."[58]

The military's role in stability operations is clarified and codified in Department of Defense (DoD) Directive 3000.05, published in November 2005.[59] The landmark directive defines stability operations as joint military and civilian efforts to establish or maintain order and stability across the full spectrum of a campaign.[60] More notably, DoD Directive 3000.05 establishes stability operations as a core military mission that "shall be given priority comparable to combat operations."[61] In keeping with the ideals outlined in the CCJO, the directive shifts the military's focus from enemy-centric to population-centric effects, emphasizing activities that benefit the indigenous peaceful population over traditional activities that direct action against enemy forces.[62] Successful stability operations require fully integrated and synchronized civil-military efforts.[63] To this end, DoD Directive 3000.05 tasks the military, be it in a leading or supporting role during an operation, to work in close coordination with its interagency and cooperative counterparts to include other U.S. departments and agencies, foreign governments, security forces, global and regional international organizations, foreign and domestic NGOs, and the private sector.[64]

The introduction and inculcation of shaping and stability operations into military policy, strategy, and doctrine since 2005 signals the categorical support of senior leadership for the concept of war prevention. Given the emphasis, it comes as no surprise that the military's take charge, "can do" attitude, coupled with its large resource pool, has literally catapulted the military to the forefront of other government agencies in its ability to implement and support stability operations. As is the case with USAFRICOM, the military is now taking the lead among U.S. agencies in implementing the concept.[65] However, the question remains — should the military be the lead? Both policy and doctrine describe successful shaping and stability operations as closely integrated interagency efforts where the military often plays a supporting vice a supported role.[66] To address the question of who should be the lead, and therefore maximize strategic effect, the Bush administration issued a National Security Presidential Directive (NSPD) in December 2005 assigning a focal point for leading reconstruction and stabilization assistance and related efforts across the USG departments and agencies.[67]

NSPD-44, *Management of Interagency Efforts Concerning Reconstruction and Stabilization*, assigns the Department of State (DoS) the responsibility to "coordinate, lead, and strengthen USG efforts to prepare, plan for, and conduct reconstruction and stabilization missions and to harmonize efforts with U.S. military plans and operations."[68] The directive also establishes a framework to integrate civilian-military coordination and planning activities citing that, when relevant and appropriate, the Secretaries of State and Defense are to integrate stabilization and reconstruction contingency plans with military contingency plans.[69] Furthermore, NSPD-44 charges the DoS with two added functions. First, the DoS is responsible for coordinating stability and reconstruction activities and preventive strategies with foreign countries, international and regional organizations, NGOs, and other private sector entities.[70] Second, the DoS is also responsible for developing strategies to build partnership capacity abroad and for leveraging NGO and international resources for reconstruction and stabilization activities.[71] It is clear in this policy that the Bush administration recognized the criticality of DoS as the central lead in pre-crisis and preventive security cooperation efforts.

PROBLEMS WITH PERCEPTION MANAGEMENT

USAFRICOM's unique approach to proactive peacetime engagement reflects the evolution in policy, strategy, and doctrine described above.[72] In keeping with the precepts of emerging policy and doctrine, USAFRICOM planners are organizing along highly nontraditional lines, designing the command to build both indigenous African security capacities and U.S. interagency collaboration capabilities.[73] To underscore its departure from the norm, USAFRICOM has dropped the traditional "J-code" organizational structure normally associated with combatant command staffs.[74] The formal integration of other department and agency personnel into the organizational structure is another statement of change.[75] USAFRICOM's nontraditional emphasis on development and war-prevention in lieu of warfighting is garnering much widespread praise throughout the USG.[76]

However, the less traditional military focus is also engendering mixed feelings within certain quarters of the government.[77] Some elements within the DoS and USAID express concern that the military may "overestimate its capabilities as well as its diplomatic role in Africa, or pursue activities that are not a core part of its mandate."[78] These concerns are, to a certain extent, justifiable. Though the authority for international engagement belongs to the DoS, the department has no more than 4,000 to 5,000 Foreign Service Officers in the field—far less manpower than what DoD can leverage through its TSC efforts.[79] The DoS also lacks comparable funding and resources required to conduct extensive partner engagement activities such as school and medical projects, coordination visits, training exercises, equipment, and other cooperative activities.[80] The disparity exists in part because Congress made deep cuts in the DoS and other civilian agencies during the 1990s, significantly reducing manpower and foreign aid budget authorizations while retaining significant military capability.[81] In a concerted effort to assuage concerns over its role in the foreign policy arena, DoD press releases are emphatic in pointing out that USAFRICOM is not assuming "a leadership role, rather it will be one in support of efforts of leading countries through our binational and bilateral relationships and the African Union and other multinational organizations."[82]

Yet, despite DoD's statements to the contrary, there are those who believe that USAFRICOM—like the other GCCs—is another example of U.S. military proconsuls plying foreign policy.[83] In ancient Rome, proconsuls were essentially provincial military governors responsible for overseeing military operations, justice, and administration within their provinces.[84] Later, the title referenced colonial governors with similar far-reaching powers.[85] Today, pundits note that U.S. GCCs have "evolved into the modern-day equivalent of the Roman Empire's proconsuls—well-funded, semi-autonomous, unconventional centers of U.S. foreign policy."[86] The GCC's rise in preeminence reflects not only the void left by a weakened DoS, it also reflects a trend in the USG of increasing dependency on the military to carry out foreign affairs in recent decades.[87]

The historic 1986 Goldwater-Nichols Department of Defense Reorganization Act represents a discernable effort to expand GCC powers with the legislation increasing GCC responsibilities and influence as warfighters.[88] As the Goldwater-Nichols Act took root and began to flourish, the Clinton administration further expanded the role of the GCCs by tasking the commands with the mission to shape their regions using multilateral approaches in ways that exceeded the traditional role of the military.[89] The Clinton administration also learned during this period that it could direct DoD to perform more and more duties, to include jobs formerly spread out among the civilian agencies, and that the military would accept them and carry on.[90] Moreover, in addition to executive and legislative efforts to expand the military's mission, the DoD's self-driven shift in emphasis towards proactive peacetime engagement also pushed the military into expanded diplomatic and political roles.[91] By the end of the 1990s, the GCCs were far more than warfighters.[92] The GCCs had grown to "transcend military matters and encroach into all the elements of national power."[93]

The apparent militarization of U.S. foreign policy, though unnoted by most average Americans, is glaringly obvious to foreign audiences acutely aware of shifts in U.S.

policy—particularly in Africa where USAFRICOM is being met with less than euphoria in many states.[94] The Africans, fearing both the reintroduction of Cold War-era arms sales and U.S. support for repressive regimes, are quick to cite hundreds of years of colonial subjugation and "accuse the U.S. of neo-imperialism and resource exploitation."[95] African nations are also concerned that USAFRICOM "will incite, not preclude, terrorist attacks."[96] To exacerbate African fears, poorly conceived references to USAFRICOM as a combatant command "plus" only serve to call greater attention to the command's military mission. Again, concerns such as these are not without foundation. Despite USAFRICOM's focus on a broader soft power mandate designed to build a stable security environment, it is still a military command and, as such, it has "all the roles and responsibilities of a traditional geographic combatant command, including the ability to facilitate or lead military operations."[97]

Regardless of the concerns of Africans and others, USAFRICOM's mission is nonetheless a genuine attempt to establish security through a blend of soft and hard power.[98] To alleviate concerns and offset strategic communication gaffs, both USAFRICOM and the Bush administration continuously emphasized and reiterated the "command's benevolent intentions and nonmilitary character."[99] U.S. strategic communications continue to reassure external audiences, particularly the African nations, that the United States is not pursuing colonial or imperial aspirations on the continent. In an environment where overcoming the challenges Africa faces requires partnership, it is an imperative that the multinational partners do not see the U.S. efforts as predatory or paternalistic.[100]

Yet, despite an aggressive strategic communications campaign, actions continue to speak louder than words and, as a result, there are fundamental questions which have yet to be addressed—questions that serve to undermine both the command's and the USG's credibility in the USAFRICOM initiative. The critical question is why is the military leading an organization whose stated mission is, by definition, largely the responsibility of the DoS? Correspondingly, what message is the USG trying to impart to its foreign partners and those it professes to be helping, when it intentionally places a military commander in a position of authority over his DoS counterpart? Intentional or not, the USG is, via its implementation of USAFRICOM, feeding the perception of a militarization of U.S. foreign policy. Here perception trumps reality and, in the case of USAFRICOM, external perceptions are in turn shaping how the command represents and shapes itself, and limiting U.S. strategic options.

While efforts to date represent steps in the right direction, they are still overly reliant on the military for implementation and, as such, persist in portraying an appearance of policy militarization. This appearance weakens the link between the two threads of an increased strategic focus on Africa and the military recognition of the value of war prevention. Without bold reform to ensure the proper integration of the two convergent threads, they may well unravel to the detriment of U.S. long-term interests. If the threads do diverge, the United States would not only waste an opportunity to realize the full potential of what is arguably a genuine revolution in military affairs; it would also risk falling short of its stated strategic objectives. In the end, Africa may turn elsewhere for aid and assistance—a country like the PRC would like nothing more than to increase its already growing status in Africa. Ironically, as the military increases its proactive peacetime engagement efforts, the weaker the bond grows between the two threads. Yet, the military is a necessary part of any U.S. effort.

On the other hand, if the proactive peacetime engagement thread were to reflect a nonmilitary lead, coupled with a greater diversity in USG participation, the bond between threads may actually strengthen. Today the USG is striving to do just this, but the efforts fall short of the level of change required and do not adequately address the perceptions of militarizing our foreign policy vis-à-vis Africa. The bold steps recommended below, if adopted, might prove to be the degree of change necessary to shift the balance in favor of the proper integration of the two threads and thus ensure success. These steps must be permanent, come with the appropriate resources, provide transformational change starting at the strategic level, and take the next evolutionary leap initiated in the revolution in military affairs noted above — establishing a genuinely integrated and proactive security engagement framework for the 21st century.

MAKING IT RIGHT

What needs to be done is already known. According to a senior USAID official, "It is clearly in the U.S. Government's interest to utilize our toolkit of diplomacy, defense, and development to counter the destabilizing effects that poor governance, corruption, and weak rule of law have on political and economic systems. . . and the threats they pose to vital American interests."[101] Similarly, in a statement regarding the military's role in Africa, the USAFRICOM commander refers to a three-pronged USG approach, with DoD taking the lead on security issues, but "playing a *supporting* role to the Department of State, which conducts diplomacy, and USAID, which implements development programs." [emphasis added][102] Together, these two statements provide a brief glimpse of a solution for prevention of security threats and the demilitarization of U.S. foreign policy — a concept referred to as 3D security engagement. The 3D concept advocates three equal pillars of engagement — diplomacy, development, and defense — all working in unison to address potential security issues such as terrorism, proliferation of weapons of mass destruction, poverty, pandemics, etc.[103] By including development and diplomacy efforts as equal elements of the security strategy equation, the 3D security engagement concept broadens strategic, operational, and tactical options and deemphasizes the militaristic aspect of security engagement. The 3D concept also advances the strategic outlook reflected in policy and doctrine such as the NSPD-44, DoDD 3000.05, and CCJO — that focusing on the root causes of insecurity and preventing conflict leads to stable and sustainable peace.[104]

Within the USG today, the departments and agencies whose mission capabilities most closely represent the 3D security engagement concept are the DoS, DoD, and USAID. These organizations have the responsibilities, authorities, and capabilities needed to reassure allies and partners, promote stability, and mitigate the conditions that lead to conflict.[105] Other elements of the USG, intergovernmental global and regional organizations, NGOs, and even private enterprise and individuals may be integrated into the 3D security engagement process as appropriate. The 3D security engagement concept is not a replacement for the traditional idea of integrated interagency interaction; rather, it is a better way to conceptualize, organize, and implement war prevention activities by circumventing many of the traditional weaknesses of the interagency. Since the "interagency" is not a person, place, or thing, it is not an organizational department or agency of the government. It has no leader and no workforce.[106] The interagency is simply the meeting point where the DoD, DoS, and the other formal agencies of the USG coordinate, cooperate, and collaborate to achieve some objective.[107] It is a process where lines of authority are unclear, and vested interests are often pursued by bureaucratic players.[108] Similarly, the 3Ds do not specifically refer to a particular department or agency, but they do imply lead and hierarchy of common interest. For example, "development" does not refer exclusively to USAID. Instead, it refers more appropriately to the "activity of development" for which USAID plays a leading role and in which DoD or NGOs might be large participants in support of juxtaposed or common interests.

To successfully implement the 3D security engagement concept and mitigate concerns over the militarization of foreign policy, extraordinary political and military leadership at the strategic level and bold reforms in several areas are required. In regard to the latter, the four fundamental impediments outlined below hamper a proper implementation of the 3D security engagement concept. If not resolved, confusion over the militarization of foreign policy will persist, and U.S. strategic objectives will be correspondingly frustrated. The reforms required to overcome these impediments are generally known and easily achievable, even if somewhat contentious. Hence, the recommendations for reform proffered below are not individually novel in and of themselves, but the synergistic effect of their collective implementation could make the 3D security engagement concept a successful security paradigm for a large part of the defense dilemma posed by the 21st century environment. In effect, they address perceptions of foreign policy militarization and complete the revolution in military affairs that started with proactive peacetime engagement.

First, there is no common system for regionally viewing the world within the USG. Departments and agencies define regions differently to facilitate their planning and operational needs. For example, Algeria is considered part of Europe by the DoS and falls under USAFRICOM in DoD. The lack of common regional definitions creates policy seams and overlaps with individual states and in the regions as a whole that often lead to poor coordination and ineffective or conflicting policy decisions and implementation.[109] In addition, the complete absence of consideration of economic and information "regions" further undermines common national strategic direction at the regional level.[110] The simple fix is to require all USG departments and agencies to view the world using the same geographical templates so that regions, seams, and overlaps are commonly understood and addressed.[111]

Second, there is no senior USG functional lead to oversee security engagement efforts in each region. Consequently, efforts lack common purpose, unity of effort, and synergistic effects. Departments and agencies develop individual strategies and compete separately for resources based on ideas that often conflict or are not prioritized and appropriately sequenced. A potential solution is to establish a forward-deployed National Security Council (NSC)-level representative to oversee and lead the 3D efforts in each region. The NSC is the "President's principal forum for considering national security and foreign policy matters with the administration's senior national security advisors and cabinet officials," advising and assisting the President with integrating all aspects of domestic, foreign, military, intelligence, and economic national security policy.[112] Given the high degree of insight into national strategic objectives inherent within the NSC, placing a senior NSC representative to oversee the 3D efforts within each region would ensure that the principal 3D elements—DoD, DoS, and USAID—work toward the same national-level objectives with a common understanding of national-level guidance. It would also lower the perception of a militarized U.S. foreign policy, bringing the use of military power more obviously under civilian control.

Third, currently there are no regional physical constructs—organizations, facilities, or manpower—sufficient to host regional 3D security engagement efforts apart from those of the combatant commands. Establishing 3D centers in each region separate and apart from the existing combatant commands may be costly to implement, but this initiative is essential to develop and implement a successful regional strategy and eliminate all vestiges of a militarized foreign policy. It empowers the senior NSC representative and ensures a balanced and well-reasoned application of U.S. national power. A key consideration for where to place 3D centers should be based on our allies within a region; current and potential partners who may find value and prestige in having such centers located within their nation.

Fourth, DoS and USAID resources are grossly insufficient to implement proactive security engagement activities worldwide. Iraq and Afghanistan have largely overwhelmed current capacity. Forced by circumstance and by policy direction, the U.S. military has taken on many burdens that in the past were the purview of civilian agencies in these theaters and elsewhere; yet, despite its gallant efforts, the military is not suitable as a long-term replacement for civilian involvement and expertise.[113] To provide much needed civilian expertise, free up military forces for other demands, and mitigate the perception and potential for a militarization of foreign policy, the USG should significantly increase civilian capacity and funding for DoS and USAID. Much like the DoS initiative to build a civilian response corps, the USG needs to develop a permanent, sizeable cadre of deployed and immediately deployable civilian experts with disparate skills to supplement or replace existing DoD efforts and meet emerging needs.[114] A robust civilian capability cannot but help to reduce the military footprint in shaping and stability operations.[115] An enhanced civilian capability reduces the temptation to use the military as a first choice and contributes to positive perceptions abroad.

CONCLUSION

Africa is a continent worthy of increased U.S. attention. It is symbolic of security issues confronting the USG in various regions around the world. Founded in the necessity to forge a new security paradigm and an emerging revolution in military affairs in regard to preventing war, the creation of USAFRICOM was a positive but incomplete step forward. The 3D security engagement concept is a further positive step toward a new security paradigm for the United States in the 21st century. The USG must follow these first steps to their logical conclusion. These recommendations offer the additional steps to create a new and viable security paradigm that promises successful implementation of national security objectives throughout the regions of the world. To do less would waste the opportunity to realize the full potential of an ongoing revolution in military affairs and ignore the strategic importance of Africa and other dynamic regions vital to U.S. security interests in the globalized world order of the 21st century.

ENDNOTES - CHAPTER 4

1. George W. Bush, *The National Security Strategy of the United States of America*, Washington, DC: The White House, March 2006, p. 37.

2. Richard L. Armitage and Joseph S. Nye, Jr., Co-Chairs, *CSIS Commission On Smart Power: A Smarter, More Secure America*, Washington, DC: The Center for Strategic and International Studies, The CSIS Press, 2007, p. 22.

3. Gregory J. Dyekman, *Security Cooperation: A Key To The Challenges Of The 21st Century*, Carlisle, PA: Strategic Studies Institute, U.S. Army War College, November 2007, p. 1.

4. Charles F. Wald, "New Thinking at USEUCOM: The Phase Zero Campaign," *Joint Forces Quarterly*, Issue 43, 4th Quarter 2006, p. 72.

5. *Ibid.*

6. *Ibid.*, p. 73.

7. "U.S. To Establish New U.S. Africa Command, AFRICOM," Washington, DC: U.S. Department of State, February 9, 2007, available from *fpc.state.gov/fpc/80454.htm.*

8. William E. Ward, "Questions And Answers About AFRICOM," available from *www.africom.mil/ africomFAQs.asp.*

9. *Ibid.*

10. Sean McFate, "U.S. Africa Command: A New Strategic Paradigm?" *Military Review*, January-February 2008, p. 17.

11. Robert G. Berschinski, *AFRICOM's Dilemma: The "Global War on Terrorism," "Capacity Building," Humanitarianism, and the Future of U.S. Security Policy In Africa*, Carlisle, PA: Strategic Studies Institute, U.S. Army War College, November 2007, p. 8.

12. Lauren Ploch, "Africa Command: U.S. Strategic Interests and the Role of the U.S. Military in Africa," *CRS Report for Congress*, December 7, 2007, p. 6.

13. Michele Ruiters, "Africa: Why U.S.'s AFRICOM Will Hurt Africa," *Business Day*, February 14, 2007, available from *allafrica.com/stories/200702140349.html.*

14. Dana Priest, *The Mission: Waging War and Keeping Peace With America's Military*, New York: Norton, 2004, p. 70.

15. Bush, *The National Security Strategy, p. 37.*

16. Anthony Lake and Christine Todd Whitman, Chairs, "More than Humanitarianism: A Strategic U.S. Approach Toward Africa," *Council On Foreign Relations Independent Task Force Report No. 56*, New York: Council on Foreign Relations, 2006, p. 9.

17. McFate, p. 12.

18. Lake and Whitman, p. 5.

19. *Ibid.*, pp. 9-10.

20. *Ibid.*, p. 9.

21. "An Overview of President Bush's African Policy," Washington, DC: U.S. Department of State, July 11, 2003, available from *www.state.gov/p/af/rls/22364.htm*.

22. "Fact Sheet: U.S. and G8 Renew Strong Commitment to Africa," Washington, DC: U.S. Department of State, July 8, 2005, available from *www.state.gov/p/af/rls/75310.htm*.

23. McFate, p. 15.

24. "U.S. To Establish New U.S. Africa Command, AFRICOM."

25. Ward.

26. *Ibid.*

27. "President Bush Creates a Department of Defense Unified Combatant Command for Africa," Washington, DC: The White House, February 6, 2007, available from *www.whitehouse.gov/newsreleases/2007/02/20070206-3.html*.

28. "Interagency Update," briefing slides with scripted commentary, U.S. Africa Command, December 14, 2007, available from *www.cpms.osd.mil/africom/docs/InteragencyUpdate14Dec2007.pdf*.

29. *Ibid.*

30. *Ibid.*

31. McFate, p. 10.

32. *Joint Publication (JP) 3-08, Interagency, Intergovernmental Organization, and Nongovernmental Organization Coordination During Joint Operations Vol I*, Washington, DC: U.S. Joint Chiefs of Staff, March 17, 2006, p. I-1.

33. *Joint Publication (JP) 3-57, Joint Doctrine for Civil-Military Operations*, Washington, DC: U.S. Joint Chiefs of Staff, February 8, 2001, p. IV-2.

34. *Ibid.*, p. xi.

35. Susanna P. Campbell and Michael Hartnett, "A Framework for Improved Coordination: Lessons Learned from the International Development, Peacekeeping, Peacebuilding, Humanitarian and Conflict Resolution Communities," presented to The Interagency Transformation, Education, and After Action Review Program, Washington, DC, October 31, 2005, p. 4.

36. McFate, p. 17.

37. JP 3-57, p. IV-1.

38. Dyekman, p. 1.

39. James L. Jones, "Statement of General James L. Jones, USMC, Commander, United States European Command before the Senate Armed Services Committee,"March 7, 2006, available from *armed-services.senate.gov/statemnt/2006/March/Jones%2003-07-06.pdf*.

40. *Ibid.*

41. Dyekman, p. 1.

42. McFate, p. 16.

43. *Ibid.*, pp. 16-17.

44. Richard B. Myers, *Capstone Concept for Joint Operations Version 2.0*, Washington, DC: U.S. Department of Defense, 2005, p. 8.

45. *Ibid.*, p. 9.

46. *Ibid.*

47. *Ibid.*

48. *Ibid.*

49. *Joint Publication (JP) 3-0, Joint Operations*, Washington, DC: U.S. Joint Chiefs of Staff, September 17, 2006, p. VII-1.

50. *Ibid.*

51. *Ibid.*

52. Wald, 73.

53. *Ibid.*

54. *Ibid.*

55. JP 3-0, p. IV-27.

56. Wald, p. 73.

57. *Ibid.*

58. *Ibid.*, p. 75.

59. *Department of Defense Directive 3000.05, Military Support for Stability, Security, Transition, and Reconstruction (SSTR) Operations*, Washington, DC: U.S. Department of Defense, November 28, 2005, p. 1-11.

60. *Ibid.*, p. 2.

61. *Ibid.*

62. Secretary of Defense, *Report To Congress On The Implementation Of DoD Directive 3000.05 Military Support For Stability, Security, Transition And Reconstruction, SSTR, Operations*, Washington, DC: U.S. Department of Defense, April 1, 2007, p. 1.

63. *Department of Defense Directive 3000.05*, p. 3.

64. *Ibid.*

65. Ploch, pp. 5-6.

66. JP 3-08, Vol I, p. viii.

67. George W. Bush, National Security Presidential Directive-44, *Management of Interagency Efforts Concerning Reconstruction and Stabilization*, Washington, DC: The White House, December 7, 2005, p. 2.

68. JP 3-08, p. I-6.

69. U.S. Department of State, "President Issues Directive to Improve the United States' Capacity to Manage Reconstruction and Stabilization Efforts," December 14, 2005, available from *www.state.gov/r/pa/prs/ps/2005/58067.htm.*

70. *Joint Operating Concept Version 2.0, Military Support to Stabilization, Security, Transition, and Reconstruction Operations*, Washington, DC: U.S. Department of Defense, December 2006, p. 33.

71. *Ibid.*

72. Berschinski, p. iii.

73. *Ibid.*, p. 6.

74. *Ibid.*

75. McFate, p. 17.

76. Berschinski, p. 7.

77. Ploch, p. 6.

78. *Ibid.*

79. Clarence J. Bouchat, *An Introduction to Theater Strategy and Regional Security*, Carlisle, PA: Strategic Studies Institute, U.S. Army War College, August 2007, p. 6.

80. *Ibid.*

81. Dana Priest, "A Four-Star Foreign Policy?" *The Washington Post*, September 28, 2000, sec A01, available from *listserv.buffalo.edu/cgi-bin/wa?A2=ind0010&L=justwatch-l&D=1&O=D&P=17195.*

82. U.S. Department of State, "U.S. Africa Command, AFRICOM, Update," June 22, 2007, available from *fpc.state.gov/fpc/87094.htm.*

83. Priest, *The Mission: Waging War and Keeping Peace With America's Military*, p. 70.

84. "Proconsul, in Ancient Rome," *The Columbia Encyclopedia, 6th Ed.*, New York: Columbia University Press, 2001-07, available from *www.bartleby.com/65/pr/proconsu.html.*

85. *Ibid.*

86. Priest, "A Four-Star Foreign Policy?"

87. Priest, *The Mission: Waging War and Keeping Peace With America's Military*, p. 14.

88. Tom Clancy, Tony Zinni, and Tom Koltz, *Battle Ready*, New York: Putnam, 2004, p. 319.

89. *Ibid.*

90. Priest, *The Mission: Waging War and Keeping Peace With America's Military*, p. 45.

91. Priest, "A Four-Star Foreign Policy?"

92. Clancy *et al.*, p. 319.

93. Mitchell J. Thompson, "Breaking the Proconsulate: A New Design for National Power," *Parameters*, Winter 2005-06, p. 64.

94. Berschinski, p. 7.

95. *Ibid.*, p. 8.

96. *Ibid.*

97. Ploch, p. 4.

98. Donna Miles, "Gates Assesses 'Soft,' 'Hard' Power Applications in Djibouti," December 3, 2007, available from *www.defenselink.mil/news/newsarticle.aspx?id=48292*.

99. Berschinski, p. 8.

100. Bush, *The National Security Strategy*, p. 37.

101. "Poor Governance a Threat to Democracy in Latin America, U.S. Says: Violence, Corruption, Weak Institutions Can Undermine Progress," Washington, DC: U.S. Department of State, May 25, 2005, available from *usinfo.state.gov/wh/Archive/2005/May/25-60682.html*.

102. Ploch, p. 5.

103. Lisa Schirch and Aaron Kishbaugh, "Leveraging '3-D' Security: From Rhetoric to Reality," *Foreign Policy In Focus, Policy Brief,* Vol. 11, No. 2, November 15, 2006, p. 1.

104. *Ibid.*

105. Jones, p. 12.

106. Michele A. Flournoy and Shawn Brimley, "In Search of Harmony: Orchestrating 'The Interagency' for the Long War," *Armed Forces Journal*, July 2006, pp. 36-39.

107. JP 3-08, Vol I, p. vii.

108. Flournoy and Brimley, pp. 36-39.

109. Clark A. Murdock and Michèle A. Flournoy, "Creating a More Integrated and Effective National Security Apparatus," in Dr. Kent Hughes Butts and Mr. Jeffrey C. Reynolds, eds., *The Struggle Against Extremist Ideology: Addressing the Conditions That Foster Terrorism*, Carlisle, PA: Center for Strategic Leadership, U.S. Army War College, p. 88.

110. Bouchat, p. 6.

111. John E. Pulliam, *Lines On a Map: Regional Orientations and United States Interagency Cooperation*, Strategy Research Project, Carlisle, PA: U.S. Army War College, March 18, 2005, p. 12.

112. JP 3-08, Vol I, p. II-2.

113. Robert M. Gates, "Beyond Guns and Steel: Reviving the Nonmilitary Instruments of American Power," *Military Review*, January-February 2008, p. 6.

114. *Ibid.*, p. 7.

115. *Ibid.*, p. 8.

CHAPTER 5

STRATEGIC BRIDGE TOWARDS COMMUNITY BUILDING:
THE MILITARY'S ROLE

Colonel Lorelei E. W. Coplen
U.S. Army

The phrase "nation-building" — and the U.S. military's role in the concept and its related activities — is an anathema for many in the U.S. military itself, our U.S. Government (USG), elements of civil society at large, and, even among some private commercial enterprises. In general, we prefer terms such as "defense support to civil authorities" or "stabilization, security, transition, and reconstruction (SSTR)" operations to describe the U.S. military's role and responsibilities in regard to civil governance. However, no matter how we frame the concept, it remains that the U.S. military's resources, including its equipment, people, and energy, are now and will continue to be in direct or indirect support of civil governance activities, in both the global and domestic arenas.[1] Although many of the functions of effective governance — especially nation-building — may indeed be the legitimate province of other agencies or entities, the U.S. military is often the first on the scene with the resources to address immediate needs as well as to foster the positive future environment supportive of national interests. Yet, it is equally clear that the contemporary complex world that exists even within our own national borders requires much more than a mere military solution for security, effective governance, and economic prosperity. The U.S. military may initiate the collaboration between agencies and entities of societal sectors, but it may not — and should not — retain a lead role in the process. As indicated in the *Joint Operating Concept, Military Support to Stabilization, Security, Transition, and Reconstruction Operations*:

> Whether responding to a devastating natural disaster or assisting in rebuilding a new domestic order, U.S. military efforts in SSTR operations will be focused on effectively combining the efforts of the . . . militaries with those of USG agencies and multi-national partners to provide direct assistance to stabilize the situation and build self-sufficient host nation capability and capacity. . . .[2]

Given the expectation for the U.S. military to coordinate its efforts with those of other-than-military partners, it behooves the military strategist to do more than simply recognize the complex environment. Instead, the strategist must seek a comprehensive understanding of the other societal actors that may comprise an effective partnership as well as the U.S. military's role in creating or fostering such relationships. In addition, the strategist must review potential organizational models for the collaborative engagement necessary for an environment that is, eventually, independent of U.S. military direct involvement in concert with our own national values. To further that study, this chapter briefly examines the contemporary global environment (which includes our domestic environment) and suggests a collaborative engagement model, the *megacommunity*. It describes the participating entities and proposes the circumstances for building such a community while highlighting the challenges and opportunities in megacommunity collaboration. Finally, it asserts that the USG should continue to expect this type of collaborative engagement by the U.S. military in order to leverage the positive aspects of globalization as "soft power" in a direction that supports our national security interests.

Thomas L. Friedman, in his influential work, *The World is Flat*, proposes that our contemporary global environment is in a newer form of globalization known as Globalization 3.0. Beyond the integrative effects of the Internet and economic programs and policies, Globalization 3.0 empowers the individual to both *compete* and to *collaborate* in the global environment, with related impact on civil society as well as business.[3] Although Friedman does not use the term *civil society* and makes only a few references to multinational corporations (MNCs), he simply and accurately describes the phenomenon of increasing horizontal—that is, flat—partnerships between government, MNCs, and civil society due to overlapping influences, interests, and ideals. This is an environment that includes the increasing influences of private commercial enterprises, often represented by multinational corporations, in partnership with the rising local and global civil society, represented by nongovernmental organizations (NGOs) as well as individual citizens. A scan of headlines and other news stories confirms the complexity and confusion regarding the overlapping roles, responsibilities, and jurisdictions of the various sectors of 21st century society. *The New York Times* recently identified Wal-Mart as "The New Washington," suggesting that "Wal-Mart now aspires to be *like* the government, bursting through political logjams, and offering big-picture solutions to intractable problems."[4] Certainly on the surface, in the immediate aftermath of Hurricane Katrina in 2005, it appeared that private commercial enterprises working together served as a private-sector Federal Emergency Management Agency (FEMA), providing the most basic of services to the disaster-impacted people more effectively and efficiently than the over-burdened, under-resourced, and slow-to-respond government agencies.[5] Yet, does Wal-Mart really want to replace the government? Probably not. However, what should the strategist consider when a MNC such as Wal-Mart publicly avows—backed up by real action in free-enterprise ways not easily matched by the government—to address in its own way some significant domestic and global issues not normally associated with the private sector, such as reducing health care costs for individuals and reducing energy demands on the environment?[6]

In 2008, the acclaimed director, Steven Spielberg, publicly rejected his previous appointment as "artistic consultant" for the Beijing Organizing Committee for the 2008 Olympics. In his statement, Mr. Spielberg specifically protested that "the international community, and particularly China, should be doing more to end the continuing human suffering" in Darfur, where the Sudanese-backed Arab forces have killed and displaced hundreds of thousands of Africans.[7] When Mr. Spielberg speaks, does he represent the USG? No, not likely. Yet, what does it mean to the strategist when a media artist publicly will take on an internationally inflammatory issue that governments appear to tread lightly around?

In this context, Mr. Spielberg serves as a prominent example of "civil society," which is often represented by NGOs and private volunteer organizations (PVOs). Mr. Spielberg is also clearly a *Thought Leader*, an ill-defined term but one that generally describes a person of both innovative ideas and the confidence to promote them.[8] Interestingly, individuals like Mr. Spielberg and other "virtual tribes," with little or no formal affiliation with the traditional NGOs and PVOs, also represent an increasingly global civil society, advocating for their particular social interests separate and distinct from government or private commercial enterprise sectors.[9]

It is not unreasonable to deduce from these examples that private commercial enterprises and business interests, such as MNCs, and civil society, whether an organization or an individual, may perform better than government in advocating, promoting, and potentially resolving selected and complex areas of concern that impact local and global societies — or even that they already perform better than government in particular areas. It is certain that in the near-term, those societal sectors will continue, for their own reasons, to address issues and concerns that may have previously depended upon government endorsement in order to be resolved. Does this mean that the government sector has fallen behind and needs to catch up? Not at all. It does mean that government must recognize the phenomenon and include those actors in planning for functional solutions. When the government sector can collaboratively engage the other sectors of private and civil societies, then together their focused efforts can serve as a component of national soft power, because the very act of collaboration and partnership may reinforce the USG's "ability to attract others by the legitimacy of U.S. policies and the values that underlie them."[10]

In the domestic arena, the USG clearly identifies the requirement for "engaged partnerships at and across all levels" of government and private sectors, as articulated in *The National Strategy for Homeland Security*.[11] Furthermore, it recognizes that our citizens, businesses, and civil society "are our society's wells of creativity, innovation, and resourcefulness" and should therefore be included in addressing comprehensive community revitalization after a domestic disaster.[12] In the global arena, the USG's recognition of the value of partner relationships with the private sector or civil society is not as distinctly stated. However, the USG's continued heavy investment and involvement in many successful international aid programs, such as the African-focused HIV/AIDs assistance, implies an awareness of the positive aspects of collaborative engagement with all other societal sectors. More specifically, the U.S. Department of State's *Advisory Committee on Transformational Diplomacy* suggested in its working group's final report that continued development of the capacity to partner with multilateral organizations as well as "engage nonstate actors," such as private sector and NGOs, is necessary to meet the needs of the State Department of 2025.[13]

Accepting the USG's awareness of the value of combined efforts and resources of the various societal sectors to address solutions for local and global challenges, what might this collaborative engagement look like and how is it achieved? One discernible approach is the *megacommunity* model in which private commercial enterprise, government, and civil society work collaboratively. Megacommunity building and engagement has been described as "a practice ahead of the theory."[14] However, there is existing relevant theory. In 2005, an article in *The Journal of Management* described the collaborative engagement between "the three main societal sectors" — business, government, and civil society — with the unwieldy phrase of "cross-sector partnerships to address social issues (CSSPs [cross-sector social partnerships])."[15] The authors provided a useful model of two primary types of social projects that characterize the CSSPs. The first type is a "transactional" project, which is characterized as short-term, limited in scope, and focused on each partner-entity's self-interest. The second project type is "integrative" or "developmental," characterized as long-term, unconstrained in scope, and more common-interest oriented as regarded by the partner-entities.[16] We fit the megacommunity in the province of this last CSSP type: the integrative, long-term, unconstrained in scope, and more common-interest oriented in the view of the societal sector partners.

Megacommunity model adherents define the term "megacommunity" as "a public sphere in which organizations and people deliberately join together around a compelling issue of mutual importance, following a set of practices and principles that will make it easier for them to achieve results."[17] They suggest five critical elements to the megacommunity model. Two elements are essentially preconditions; these include having "three-sector engagement" (that is, involvement of all three sectors of society) and having "an overlap of vital interests" by the three sectors.[18] The three remaining critical elements are essentially enabling conditions, or those conditions necessary to create a sustainable megacommunity: structure, adaptability, and convergence of effort.[19]

The megacommunity concept indentifies the societal entities of the three-sector engagement as the following: private commercial enterprises, providing resources and capital to fund projects; governments, generally bringing sovereignty as well as the rule of law (and, in most cases, this author suggests that governments bring security to the relationship); and civil society, which provides accountability and "credibility in arenas where business and government fall short."[20] While there are numerous perspectives regarding the strengths and weaknesses each entity or sector brings into the megacommunity, it is generally understood that private commercial enterprises, usually MNCs, can provide collaboration, money, hard infrastructure, technical or knowledgeable people, and local and global economic understanding. On the other hand, MNCs are by nature profit-driven actors, and, as Thomas Friedman indicates: "The cold, hard truth is that management, shareholders, and investors are largely indifferent to where their profits come from or even where the employment is created."[21] Yet, as Max Caldwell of Towers Perrin suggests, companies are increasingly willing "to invest in people and the environment *today*, in order to ensure a viable marketplace in the *future*."[22] This remark begins to explain why corporations are increasingly disposed and perhaps even eager to get involved in local and global societal issues not previously associated with business. One reason may be to counter adverse publicity that depicts MNOs as exploiters of labor and natural resources, concerned only with bottom line profits. A second reason, supportable by the evidence, is that "doing good was, in fact, good for business."[23] Certainly a short review of only a few of the large multinational corporations' annual reports with their related "corporate responsibility reports" or "corporate citizenship reports" reflect this latter paradigm.[24] In summary, the strategist must recognize that the motivations of MNCs and their reputations are sometimes two-edged, perceived as both exploiters as well as developers. Perhaps a more surprising observation, however, is that some individuals or groups, in selected cases, may perceive the MNCs as more legitimate than a particular local government due to requirements for corporate governance transparency lacking in the government sector.

The government sector is more clearly recognized as having social welfare responsibilities. Regardless of form or type, governments are the public face of a legally-defined community or country. Governments can provide legitimacy, oversight, access, and security in ways private commercial enterprises or civil society cannot. However, even where government functionally exists, government members are discovering they "can no longer spend or regulate their way into requisite solutions" and therefore need the resources and talent that is available through the private sector or the support of civil society.[25] At the same time, in some functional or geographical arenas, governments no longer retain their legitimacy — or never had it. As H. Lee Scott Jr., Wal-Mart's Chief

Executive Officer (CEO), observed recently to his employees, "We live in a time when people are losing confidence in the ability of government to solve problems."[26] This observation is especially true, obviously, in the situations where the government sector is weak, corrupt, incompetent, or simply does not exist.

As described above, private and government sectors are easily recognized in most cases by even a lay observer. Civil society, however, seems more amorphous. The World Bank provides a definition of civil society that, while not succinct, is certainly comprehensive. According to the World Bank, *civil society* is represented by:

> . . . the wide array of non-governmental and not-for-profit organizations that have a presence in public life, expressing the interests and values of their members or others, based on ethical, cultural, political, scientific, religious or philanthropic considerations.[27]

Certainly the NGOs and PVOs bring to the megacommunity passionate people, talent, potential for local or functional information and intelligence, long-term outlook, and often a legitimacy that neither government nor the private sectors can always attain. On the other hand, NGOs and PVOs also suffer from a dual-edged reputation in certain areas, often depicted as idealistic and naïve in their parochial approaches. Yet, even the NGOs and PVOs have discovered that although globalization, especially through the effect of the Internet and other global media, has given them a greater voice than ever before, there is also a corresponding increase in demand for their own expertise and energy. They too are competing for funding and donations, moving towards private commercial enterprises and the government sector to better pursue their own interests and concerns on behalf of their constituents and causes.[28]

The requirement to leverage the strengths, and compensate for the weaknesses, of each of the societal sectors leads to the special collaboration advocated in the first precondition of the megacommunity model, three-sector engagement. The second precondition to megacommunity formation is obvious. For the three sectors to engage, they need to have an overlap of interests, sometimes described as shared issues or mutual concerns, as well as a shared sense of moral concern, local impact, and overall responsibility. In many cases, but not all, such interests will reflect a geographic or demographic focus, such as regional water rights or women's education. Further, megacommunity adherents propose that where there is an interest or concern shared by the three societal sectors, a latent megacommunity already exists.[29] However, the conditions needed for a megacommunity to exist—latent or overt—are not enough to sustain the relationship. Therefore, the megacommunity model also proposes three additional elements for long-term community sustainment—structure, adaptability, and convergence.

These critical elements serve as enabling conditions and are important to note in order to obtain the full benefits of this collaborative engagement, especially for the military strategist considering this approach. *Structure* suggests that the megacommunity must have an explicit formative stage with clearly defined properties, terminology, protocols, objectives, and understanding of each other's social networks, thereby facilitating the common effort. In other words, although the collaboration may be latent, or appear naturally occurring, at some point each actor must concur with a given overarching purpose and means to communicate in order to sustain the megacommunity. *Adaptability* ensures that the megacommunities remain open to new ideas, members, and activities;

no closed organization can remain healthy and, therefore, sustainable in the long-term.[30] The *convergence* of commitment toward mutual action, which may occur spontaneously, such as during a natural disaster, or deliberately, focuses on the specific overlapping interest. However, the model suggests that rarely will the various sectors come together as a sustainable megacommunity on their own, "they must be consciously made to converge."[31] One actor or subgroup must initiate the convergence, *serving as a strategic bridge that connects the separate societal sectors to form the collaborative engagement of a megacommunity*.

Therefore, the role of a strategic bridge is critical to megacommunity formation and for leveraging the benefits of the subsequent collaborative engagement. Strategic bridging organizations function to connect diverse entities to work on social or developmental issues. Strategic bridging is vital when other parties cannot work directly with each other for physical or logistical reasons; or choose not to collaborate initially due to human dynamic concerns such as lack of trust or cultural tradition. However, strategic bridges are more than mediators or mere facilitators; they have their own agendas as well. According to Sanjay Sharma *et al.,* "unlike mediators, bridges enter collaborative negotiations to further their own ends as well as to serve as links among domain stakeholders" and have motivational factors that are egoistic (voluntary or self-serving), altruistic (mandated or problem focused), or a mix of the two factors.[32] A collaborative engagement proposal that is transnational, or trans-sector, in geography or function will likely require a strategic bridge to create the opportunity for commitment convergence among the diverse societal sectors.

A strategic bridge organization serves to synthesize "the problem domain for the island organizations in terms of the bridge's own interests."[33] The bridging organization seeks to control the actions and influence the results of a collaborative engagement in a manner that best suits the bridge, egoistically, altruistically, or both, even as the bridge recognizes and appreciates the shared interests and agendas with other organizations. Consequently, the strategic bridge often will be the initiator of the megacommunity convergence as well, in order to define the environment and the range of potential solutions in a manner that favors or ensures the achievement of its own aims and interests.

The United Nations (UN) offered itself as a strategic bridge in its report, "Strengthening of the United Nations System," which states that "the convening power and moral authority of the United Nations enable it to bring often conflicting parties together to tackle global problems" which includes nonstate actors such as members of private and civil societies.[34] The report highlights UN efforts to initiate megacommunity approaches to a wide-range of global issues and shared concerns, but there are other examples of strategic bridge organizations in recent years as well. For example, the U.S. military often serves as a strategic bridge in both domestic and global arenas, initiating the collaborative engagement that forms the megacommunity. Why the military? One reason may be that the U.S. military is perceived as readily available, such as in regional combatant commands, or can be made available, such as our National Guard. Often the U.S. military is already in place and very aware of the overlapping vital interests necessary to form a megacommunity collaboration that addresses a complex issue. Another reason the U.S. military becomes a strategic bridge is its capability to provide the security that is an essential prerequisite for collaborative engagement to flourish, particularly in areas with dysfunctional governments or immature civil societies. However, a final reason is that at this time the U.S. military remains better resourced than any other agency within the USG. As Conrad Crane states:

> . . . the harsh historical reality is that the world's greatest nation building institution, when properly resourced and motivated, is the U.S. military. . . the United States has rarely accomplished long-term policy goals after any conflict without an extended American military presence to ensure proper results from the peace.[35]

How does a strategic bridge, U.S. military or otherwise, "begin a responsiveness-oriented megacommunity"?[36] The megacommunity model proposes the following six "guideposts":

1. *Identify and empower the stakeholders* — know who should be in your "full panorama of allies" but also how to provide space for their own participation style;

2. *Be an initiator* — do not hesitate to seek players who can assist in resolution, and engage them "as full partners";

3. *Embrace interdependence* — "plan, train, and rehearse the methods by which these separate but interrelated organizations will function together";

4. *Allow for ambiguity* — accept the confusion that may exist when organizations may perceive themselves as having overlapping responsibility, and continue communication;

5. *Reward collaboration* — do not punish cooperative behavior, but "create incentives that encourage it"; and,

6. Strengthen your social networks — develop your contact list![37]

The model suggests that these guideposts free leaders of societal sectors "from the notion that they must control outcomes and events unilaterally" when it is obvious that the complexity of the issue or situation makes single-point authority impossible, and ensures a work environment that permits the entire megacommunity to continue developing "an ever-expanding circle of resources, capabilities, and talents."[38]

It is important to note the challenges that are inherent in megacommunity collaborative engagement. Resistance to collaborative engagement is generally based on two dominant concerns: the structure and the ideology. The structural concern is founded on the belief that "there is no institution with the capability and responsibility to design a coherent . . . approach . . . and to connect it to the essential players."[39] Certainly the megacommunity model, as described earlier, also identifies the need for deliberate structure as an enabling condition for megacommunity sustainment. However, this concern can be resolved by the development of a common partnership culture. A partnership culture will likely have many components to ensure its viability, but the most important may be a common vocabulary or terminology.[40] Larry Cooley suggests that common terminology might start with a definition of *partnership*, which he believes "is generally understood to entail a voluntary pairing of two or more entities working together to achieve a result beneficial to each party . . . a sharing of risks and rewards."[41] He also identifies topic areas that must be addressed for any partner-organization relationship to be successful, many of which apply to the megacommunity concept as well:

- Alignment of the participating organizations' expectations.
- Development of codified "best practices."
- Recognition of work required that is either within or outside of the participating partners' "core interests."
- Recognition of resources that may be "tied" by regulation or tradition.
- Addressing problems of scale.
- Determining the role of trust and relationships between partners.
- Acknowledge the emerging problems of intellectual property and competition.[42]

Despite the difficulties inherent in some of these topic areas, Cooley asserts there is a "growing recognition that success is most likely when partnerships have strong and evident links to partners' core interests, when partners invest significant time and effort in understanding one another's motives and methods, and when partners retain a clear exit option."[43] Given the scope of the challenges of developing agreed-upon structure, the role of a strategic bridge organization is even more apparent. Without the initiating actor, the diverse societal sectors may not overcome their differences to find enough similarity in interests and approach to address the complex issue at hand.

The other main area of resistance to collaborative engagement is ideological. For example, even advocates for the increasing influence of civil society express concern that "the notion of global civil society only partially overcomes the limitations civil society at the national level faces with regard to ensuring development and democracy."[44] Ironically, cooperation and collaboration with either government or private sectors may challenge NGO and PVO legitimacy as well as regulate traditional civil society "to a marginal, merely nominal role in the greater scheme of things."[45] Other observers express concern that the involvement of MNCs in corporate social responsibility (CSR) projects in weak states, such as those in Africa, may actually undermine local and national governments by providing those services that "governments ought to be doing."[46] Megacommunity adherents, however, argue that ideological mistrust and miscommunication among sectors can be resolved with education and experience, and the benefits of collaborative engagement vastly outweigh the risks to the separate societal entities.

Given the advantages of the three societal sectors of collaborative engagement, what are the circumstances for the military strategist that lend themselves to megacommunity formation? One framework for analysis is embedded in *The National Security Strategy*, which addresses three levels of engagement: conflict prevention and resolution; conflict intervention; and post-conflict stabilization and reconstruction.[47] Using these three levels, it is possible to address megacommunity formation, substituting the term *crisis* in place of *conflict*. The term *conflict* is not encompassing enough to address the impact of natural or manmade disasters such as storms, floods, or drought situations. Therefore, *crisis* is a more inclusive term.

In a U.S. military-initiated megacommunity, we are invariably preventing or resolving crises. As the historical cliché of the Treaty of Versailles reminds us, in practice, the post-crisis period is often simultaneously a pre-crisis period. The *Joint Operation Planning Guide* defines the activities of the pre-crisis (conflict) prevention and resolution level of engagement as *shaping*, designed:

... to dissuade or deter potential adversaries and to assure or solidify relationships with friends and allies. . . executed continuously with the intent to enhance international legitimacy and gain multinational cooperation in support of defined national strategic and strategic military objectives.[48]

In another U.S. military reference, *shaping operations* "describe the long-term, integrated joint force actions taken *before or during crisis* to build partnership capacity, influence nonpartners and potential adversaries, and mitigate the underlying causes of conflict and extremism."[49] These military sources refer to the myriad of programs a megacommunity collaborative engagement can address in selected regions to prevent crisis. Many, if not most, of the geographic combatant commands' Theater Security Cooperation programs may be examples of the U.S. military serving as a strategic bridge to a latent megacommunity collaborative engagement in a pre-crisis period. For further illustration, Thomas P. M. Barnett describes the security concerns of the Non-Integrating Gap—the countries and regions where the positive influences of globalization have yet to reach. As he explains, Gap regions are prone to crisis and conflict; therefore, getting Gap countries "above the line" (which he defines as an annual per capita Gross Domestic Product [GDP] above $3000) may increase the probability for a stable and secure environment that reduces the penchant for crisis and conflict. However, that level of financial commitment requires significant foreign direct investment (FDI); it cannot be done with the constrained resources of either government or civil sector programs.[50] It requires a megacommunity.

The military strategist can refer to the well-documented Hewlett-Packard (HP) Company investment in engineering education and infrastructure in Africa as an example of building a megacommunity to address under-resourced Gap regions. After an earlier success in Latin America in addressing engineering education in a multistakeholder collaboration, in 2006 the concept was turned to Africa. According to Barbara Waugh, the director of University Relations at HP Company, knowledge may be the only factor of production available for small and land-locked countries with negligible natural resources, and therefore knowledge production is a natural fit for the developing economies of many Non-Integrating Gap countries and regions, such as those found in Africa.[51] As previously observed in Latin America, all societal sectors in Africa benefited from the HP-initiated megacommunity. HP, as a MNC, was able to partner with the World Federation of Engineering Organizations (WFEO), representing over 90 countries as a civil society organization. Because the partnership was not HP-led, simply HP-initiated, the collaboration eventually included other MNCs, some small companies, and engineering academics that normally avoided corporate partnerships, "to join an effort in a manner that also had subsequent reciprocal benefits outside of the African-focused megacommunity."[52] Civil society, represented by the engineering society and academics, benefited from the regional access the HP-initiative provided to them. Finally, the local governments that participated in the programs achieved greater indigenous knowledge capacity, thereby increasing potential for improved economic status. This case study illustrates for the military strategist how the three societal sectors working together in a megacommunity at both regional and functional levels (Africa and technology development), impacted the developing African nations and may have assisted those countries to get above the $3,000 per capita GDP mark that Barnett references, thereby reducing the factors that create an environment ripe for crisis.

Another level of engagement is crisis intervention and its immediate aftermath. Sometimes referred to as the consequence management or response period, the *National Strategy for Homeland Security* definition of *incident management* is "a broader concept that refers to how we manage incidents and mitigate consequences across all . . . activities, including prevention, protection, and response and recovery."[53] This statement describes the classic environment for megacommunity collaborative engagement, and the events surrounding Hurricane Katrina in 2005 provide a prime case study of a megacommunity formed in response to crisis. Arriving as a Category V hurricane to the Gulf Coast on August 29, 2005, Katrina ultimately displaced over one million people, with a death toll of more than 1,700, and still untotaled damage to three states in the billions of dollars.[54] Megacommunity model advocates remind us that although FEMA and various local and state authorities are criticized for lack of preparation and an inadequate response to the situation, it was not these governments that failed. It was the megacommunity that failed because it failed to preexist or to converge appropriately.[55]

According to some sources, there were attempts in the pre-landfall hours and in the immediate aftermath to establish a megacommunity approach to the emerging crisis. Perhaps due to the unavailability of local government or civil society sectors, themselves devastated by the storm, the private sector commercial enterprises emerged as the strategic bridge, initiating a megacommunity response. Leveraging existing relationships among selected corporations and their leaders, the private sector eventually contributed over $1.2 billion dollars and hundreds of thousands of employee volunteer hours to recovery efforts.[56] Although many corporations can rightly claim hero-status for their individual and collective efforts to assist in the immediate aftermath and subsequent recovery in the region, two companies have emerged as icons in the Katrina pantheon: Wal-Mart and Home Depot. Serving in a limited way as the strategic bridge organization, the private sector, represented in part by these corporations, utilized their vast databases, transportation, and storage facilities to anticipate the requirements of and respond to a regional community readying for survival and recovery. These organizations openly shared their information to government sectors at the local and federal level and civil society as represented by the traditional NGOs and PVOs in an attempt to facilitate collaboration and to leverage individual efforts.

Although, by many accounts, the megacommunity approach above state level may have been problematic during the Katrina crisis, it appears that the ad hoc megacommunity enjoyed great success at local levels. The private sector provided resources to the civil sector for disbursement while the government—represented in this case by the U.S. military—provided increasing security for the immediate survival and recovery periods. The Katrina case study further demonstrates how interdependent the societal sectors are in regard to each other while achieving the most effective solutions. Without the contribution of civil society and the security provided by a government, the vast capacities and resources of the private sector can literally sit idle in parking lots or warehouses, untapped and unused.

The reconstruction period of the Hurricane Katrina megacommunity case study is still in progress. Such a period reflects the last level of engagement, post-crisis, which paradoxically may be simultaneously the pre-crisis period for a follow-on crisis event or series of events. Home Depot, as a continuing example, remains engaged in a classic megacommunity—working recovery and revitalization efforts at all levels, from individual home owner discounts to local school playgrounds to reforestation efforts of state parks throughout the Gulf Coast region—remaining in close coordination with government and local civil society to determine the appropriate methods to employ combined resources.

One of the challenges for megacommunity formation is that in the crisis period, any one of the three societal sectors may not be immediately responsive to establish a collaborative relationship. For example, many failed or failing states may have a dysfunctional government that inhibits or prohibits the provisions of services to the people, including security.[57] Some states may have a significant lack of private commercial enterprises, because, as Barnett reminds us, FDI "does not flow into war zones, because it is essentially a coward."[58] That is, companies may be eager to take advantage of available labor and resources, but not at risk to their assets and personnel.[59] Finally, a state may have an immature or nonexistent civil society, complicating the three-sector engagement expected of megacommunity collaboration. Yet, the absence at the local or regional level of any particular societal sector does not have to prohibit the formation of a megacommunity. It may only mean that the strategic bridge organization needs to look to another level of that societal element to bring into the megacommunity the requisite expertise and energy.

The recent Kenyan post-election crisis and its apparent resolution provide insights into post-crisis megacommunity formation, to include the multilevel approach to the three-sector engagement. In January 2008, President Mwai Kibaki and the opposition leader Raila Odinga became the de facto rival leaders of warring tribes masquerading as political factions. The tensions began shortly after the disputed late December 2007 elections when it appeared the votes may have been rigged in favor of Kibaki, although both sides claimed vote fraud. Street protests became violent as the police tried to assert control. Ultimately, more than 850 people were killed and 250,000 displaced in less than 30 days.[60] Sixty days later, Kenya was again quiet due in significant part to a megacommunity approach to the crisis resolution: the strong Kenyan civil society, the influence of the private sector, and, in this case, international governmental pressure and political intervention in the place of a functional state government. To illustrate, Ambassador Michael Ranneberger, U.S. Ambassador to Kenya, credited the crisis resolution to Kenya's strengths: "a dynamic civil society . . . the enormous democratic space . . . an increasingly modern and booming private sector. . . ."[61] He reiterated that four factors brought the warring parties to the current peace: the people's voices, "heard through civil society"; the international economic and diplomatic pressures; the pragmatism of the opposing parties' leaders; and "the skilful and forceful direction of Kofi Annan," representing the international government sector as a strategic bridge organization.[62] The value of the megacommunity collaborative engagement does not end at this point, however. Ambassador Ranneberger is among other Kenya-based voices that clamor for Kenya to utilize the new opportunities provided by peace to develop long-term solutions to continuing Kenyan challenges "through the Government, the corporate sector, civil society organizations and Kenya's international partners."[63] While it is too early to determine if the megacommunity model will be sustained and result in long-term stability and continued modern economic and democratic development in Kenya, it certainly seems to be the most appreciated approach at this juncture.

Although it is important to study the megacommunity successes, it is as important to consider the conditions that are not conducive to this collaborative approach. A megacommunity approach, which by nature requires an inherent sense of the greater good by all actors and an ability to consider and appreciate the agendas of other entities, is at greatest risk of failure when the sector actors are unreasonable or uncompromising, perhaps represented by rigid or self-interested leaders, or with irreconcilable interests or unbridgeable culture gaps. An example of a culture gap was presented in a study in *The Journal of Corporate Citizenship* of oil company collaboration while addressing CSR issues in Azerbaijan and Kazakhstan. The authors began their study by asking if international oil companies (IOCs) should be expected — by themselves or with any other societal sector — to be involved in nation-building activities or concerns. They concluded that the IOCs were inherently engaged in the micro-CSR activities such as local labor use, provision of local services, and in some cases, cultural institution or research sponsorship. However, in almost all cases, they noted the IOCs remained clear of any indication of interference in host-nation government policy formation. The authors refer to macro-CSR activities as those that would appear to directly involve IOCs in sensitive host-nation policies, such as social equality, good governance, and transparency regarding oil production revenue. The paradox of participation, according to the study authors, is that international civil society, often represented by NGOs, expects more direct involvement in these sensitive government policies by the MNCs. Yet, as the study indicates, any public advocation by the IOCs of those same issues can result in MNC loss of operating freedom, and potentially, their corporate assets in the host-nation.[64] Therefore, in this study the limited IOC CSR-initiatives established in these emerging petro-states failed to survive. The MNCs found it difficult to overcome the cultural barriers of operating in countries with no tradition of nongovernment sector inclusion in governmental affairs. The companies were also unprepared to accept the risk inherent with offending the uncompromising host-nation government regarding CSR-initiatives. Still, the authors suggest that IOCs' ultimate sustainability for the future in those petro-states resides in their ability to address macro-CSR issues either unilaterally or in alliance with NGOs, other multilateral development organizations, and government, where the MNCs, the NGOs, and others use each other's strengths to offset their own organizational short-comings.[65]

The ongoing drama that characterizes the President Hugo Chavez-led Venezuelan government may be an example of uncompromising public sector leadership that could frustrate the value of megacommunity approach. Among his various posturing, he recently entwined his state oil company in a legal dispute with Exxon Mobil, a U.S.-based corporation that shares the same two Louisiana refineries with the Venezuelan company.[66] He has tried — and succeeded in varying degrees — to limit the interaction of civil society in his country by ensuring that all their funding flows through his governmental agencies for disbursement.[67] On all fronts, Chavez seems to defy the pragmatic logic implied in megacommunity formation and sustainability. Therefore, while Chavez leads Venezuela, the megacommunity concept may not work in addressing the economic well-being of the people or the regional security and stability. However, any strategic approach to Venezuela — as well as with similar geographical or functional challenges — must include all the sectors of the collaborative engagement model. A unilateral approach, while appealing for its near-term appearance of efficiency, is unlikely to be effective in our globally-linked world and less likely to be in our long-term national interest.

Should the private sector or civil society advocacy replace the governmental sector? No, it is unreasonable to expect that a MNC, or a Hollywood director as a representative of civil society, alone can resolve the Darfur crisis or similar concerns, no matter how well-connected or resourced. Yet, in combination with other megacommunity entities, such as the government sector, their actions may enhance the use of the USG's soft power and lead to solutions that are appropriate for our long-term interests. Does the government sector have to be able to function like a private commercial enterprise? No, for as *The Wall Street Journal* indicated in 2005, "FEMA is never going to operate with the agility of a FedEx . . . that's the nature of competition."[68] Even Scott reported that Wal-Mart "can't do more than our own part, we are not the federal government, there is a portion we can do, and we can do it darn well."[69] However, the government must promote efforts to move beyond mere recognition of "unleashing the power of the private sector," and build megacommunities that forge partnerships with private and civil societal sectors to address our domestic and global interests and goals.[70]

As part of this promotion, the U.S. military must be prepared to be the initiators, or strategic bridges, for megacommunity formation. In the past, especially in the realms of failed states or in the absence of fully functioning government, the U.S. military acting as a strategic bridge initiator often had the secondary role of arbitrator between the civil society and private commercial enterprises. Now, with the burgeoning positive relationships between civil society and private sectors, the military must not become the outsider in a megacommunity. Therefore, it is imperative that the military strategist have a more comprehensive understanding of the megacommunity concepts and the other societal actors in order to understand their own agendas and to leverage their capabilities towards collaborative solutions. The U.S. military continues to be the critical strategic bridge organization, often as the only member of the megacommunity with the capacity and knowledge to "understand how to intervene and influence others in a larger system that [we] do not control."[71] At the same time, the U.S. military must not only be prepared to relinquish the initiating leadership role as the megacommunity convenes, but should actively seek to create the conditions for other entities to lead and monitor the continued three-sector engagement.[72] After all, "good strategy flows from understanding the nature of the environment and *creating a symmetry and synergy of objectives, concepts, and resources* that offer the best probability of achieving the policy aims," and the military remains at the center of U.S. national security, at home and abroad.[73]

ENDNOTES - CHAPTER 5

1. The author leaves to others the argument of whether nation-building or its ilk is a traditional, but forgotten, aspect of the U.S. military's *raison d'etre*, or whether it is a novel concept to address. For the purposes of this chapter, she accepts that the U.S. military is now and will be engaged in the activities that are often associated with nation-building. For a summary of the discussion, see David B. Haight, *Preparing Military Leaders for Security, Stability, Transition, and Reconstruction Operations*, Strategy Research Project, Carlisle, PA: U.S. Army War College, March 12, 2007.

2. *Military Support to Stabilization, Security, Transition, and Reconstruction Operations*, Joint Operating Concept, V. 2, Washington, DC: The Joint Staff, December 2006, p. iii.

3. Thomas L. Friedman, *The World Is Flat: A Brief History of the Twenty-First Century*, 2d Ed., New York: Farrar, Straus, and Giroux, 2006, p. 11.

4. Michael Barbaro, "Wal-Mart: The New Washington," *The New York Times*, February 3, 2008, Sunday Opinion section, p. 3.

5. "Private FEMA," *The Wall Street Journal*, September 10, 2005, available from *www.opinionjournal.com/forms/printThis.html?id=110007238*.

6. Barbaro.

7. Frederik Balfour, "China: Spielberg's Olympic-Sized Snub," *Business Week*, February 13, 2008, available from *www.businessweek.com/print/globalbiz/content/ feb2008/gb20080213_989993.htm*.

8. *Thought Leader*, available from *en.wikipedia.org/wiki/Thought_Leader*. Although various other definitions of the phrase "Thought Leader" exist, the Wikipedia entry most characterizes the influence of Mr. Steven Spielberg on his professional community and perhaps civil society writ large. Lieutenant Colonel Richard C. Coplen, U.S. Army, Retired, used the term during discussion with the author on February 16, 2008, regarding Mr. Spielberg's protest announcement about Darfur.

9. This example also illustrates another growing phenomenon of the civil society sector. The increasing influence of contributing members that advocate and share their opinions in ways that are individual-based, personalized, and inventive, usually through global technological and media means.

10. Joseph S. Nye, Jr., "The Decline of America's Soft Power," *Foreign Affairs*, May/June 2004, available from *www.foreignaffairs.org/20040501facomment83303/joseph-s-nye-jr/the-decline-of-americas-soft-power.htm*.

11. George W. Bush, *National Strategy for Homeland Security*, Washington, DC: Homeland Security Council, October 2007, p. 33.

12. *Ibid.*, p. 38.

13. U.S. Department of State, Advisory Committee on Transformational Diplomacy, *Final Report of the State Department in 2025 Working Group*, available from *www.state.gov/secretary/diplomacy/99774.htm*.

14. Lieutenant Colonel Richard C. Coplen, U.S. Army, Retired, in private conversation with author, February 7, 2008. Coplen is a current employee of Booz-Allen-Hamilton, BAH, and participated as an audience member in a BAH presentation regarding Megacommunities, same date.

15. John W. Selsky and Barbara Parker, "Cross-Sector Partnership to Address Social Issues: Challenges to Theory and Practice," *Journal of Management*, Vol. 31, December 2005, p. 849.

16. *Ibid.*, p. 850.

17. Mark Gerencser, Fernando Napolitano, and Reginald Van Lee, "The Megacommunity Manifesto," August 16, 2006, available from *www.strategy-business.com/resilience/ rr00035.*

18. Chris Kelly, Mark Gerencser, Fernando Napolitano, and Reginald Van Lee, "The Defining Features of a Megacommunity," June 12, 2007, available from *www.strategy-business.com/li/leadingideas/li00029.*

19. *Ibid.*

20. *Ibid.*

21. Friedman, p. 245.

22. Max Caldwell, "Uncovering the Hidden Value in Corporate Social Responsibility," *The Journal of the EDS Agility Alliance*, Vol. 3, February 11, 2008, available from *www.eds.com/services/whitepapers/.*

23. Barbaro.

24. Several examples are readily available for public reading at any library or on line. For this chapter, the author most closely read Chevron, Exxon Mobil, and Home Depot reports. See Chevron at *www.chevron. com/globalissues/corporateresponsibility/2006/;* Exxon Mobil at *www.exxonmobil.com/Corporate/community_ccr. aspx;* and Home Depot at *www. homedepotfoundation.org/.* An illustration of selected MNCs' embrace of societal issue involvement can be found in Rex W. Tillerson's statement in his company's 2006 Corporate Citizenship Report. Mr. Tillerson is the Chairman and Chief Executive Officer of Exxon Mobil, and he begins his remarks with the following: "Exxon Mobil's primary responsibility is to produce the energy the world needs in an economically, environmentally, and socially responsible manner . . . global in scale. Our approach . . . is pragmatic, with a long-term perspective . . . that will help ensure reliable, affordable energy for people around the world." In another example, Home Depot's corporate responsibility is exercised through the Home Depot Foundation, and its report reads less global in focus but yet very attuned to domestic issues of housing and urban renewal in keeping with their product and service.

25. Gerencser, Napolitano, and Van Lee.

26. Barbaro.

27. The World Bank, "Approach to the World Bank's Engagement with Civil Society," available from *go.worldbank.org/3L5WS8C510.*

28. Gerencser, Napolitano, and Van Lee.

29. *Ibid.*

30. Kelly *et al.*

31. *Ibid.*

32. Sanjay Sharma, Harrie Vrendenburg, and Frances Westley, "Strategic Bridging: A Role for the Multinational Corporation in Third World Development," *Journal of Applied Behavioral Science*, Vol. 30, December 1994, p. 461.

33. *Ibid.*, p. 470.

34. The United Nations General Assembly, *Strengthening of the United Nations System*, 58th session, June 11, 2004, p. 9.

35. Conrad C. Crane, "Phase IV Operations: Where Wars are Really Won," *Military Review*, May-June 2005, p. 28.

36. Douglas Himberger, David Sulek, and Stephen Krill, Jr., "When There is No Cavalry," *Strategy + Business*, Autumn 2007, available from *www.strategy-business.com/press/article/07309?pg=all&tid=230*.

37. *Ibid.*

38. *Ibid.*

39. George C. Lodge and Craig Wilson, "Multinational Corporations: A Key to Global Poverty Reduction — Part II," *YaleGlobal Online*, January 5, 2005, available from *yaleglobal.yale.edu/article.print?id=6672*.

40. An example of the discrepancies with terminology is the use of the word *governance*. In the world of private or civil sectors, governance refers to management, policies, and transparent procedures. However, in government study, governance refers to the method of managing the institutional services and the political processes.

41. Larry Cooley, "2+2=5: A Pragmatic View of Partnerships between Official Donors and Multinational Corporations," Lael Brainard, ed., *Transforming the Development Landscape: The Role of the Private Sector*, Washington, DC: Brookings Institution Press, 2006, p. 109.

42. *Ibid.*

43. *Ibid.*, pp. 118-123.

44. Glenn Brigaldino, "Stepping Beyond Civil Society: Prospects for the Multitudes of Resistance," *Global Policy Forum*, April 5, 2007, available from *www.globalpolicy.org/ngos/intro/general/ 2007/0405stepbeyond.htm*.

45. *Ibid.*

46. Witney W. Schneidman, "Multinational Corporations and Economic Development in Africa," *CSIS*, July 25, 2007, available from *forums.csis.org/africa/?p=44*.

47. George W. Bush, *The National Security Strategy of the United States of America*, Washington, DC: The White House, March 2006, p. 15.

48. *Joint Publication (JP) 5-0, Operation Planning*, Washington, DC: The Joint Staff, December 26, 2006, p. IV-35.

49. U.S. Department of Defense, *Irregular Warfare,(IW), Joint Operating Concept, JOC*, Washington, DC: U.S. Department of Defense, September 11, 2007, p. 16.

50. Thomas P. M. Barnett, *The Pentagon's New Map: War and Peace in the Twenty-first Century*, New York: The Berkley Publishing Group, 2004, p. 4. Barnett coined the phrase, "Non-Integrating Gap," to describe "the regions of the world that . . . constitute globalization's 'ozone hole' . . . where connectivity remains thin or absent." The connectivity he refers to includes "the flows of people, energy, money, and security," p. 205.

51. Barbara Waugh, "HP Engineers a Megacommunity," November 6, 2007, available from *www.straegy-business.com/li/leadingideas/li00050?pg=all&tid=230*. She also highlights in her article that China, India, and several Middle East nations are already heavily invested in capacity building in the region.

52. *Ibid.*

53. Bush, *National Strategy for Homeland Security,* p. 31.

54. Business Roundtable, "Recent Disasters: The Partnership Response;" available from *www. respondtodisaster.com/mambo.*

55. Himberger, Sulek, and Krill.

56. Business Roundtable.

57. Daniel Thurer, "The 'Failed State' and International Law," December 31, 1999, available from *www. icrc.org/Web/Eng/siteeng0.nsf/html/57JQ6U.* While there are many definitions of a failed state, I prefer the one offered by Dr. Daniel Thurer of the University of Zurich and the International Committee of the Red Cross: "The 'failed State' is one which, though retaining legal capacity, has for all practical purposes lost the ability to exercise it."

58. Barnett, pp. 239-240.

59. *Ibid.*

60. Brian Hull, "FACTBOX-Facts about Kenya's Post-Election Crisis," *Reuters,* January 29, 2008, available from *www.reuters.com/articlePrint?articleId= USL294301368.*

61. Michael Ranneberger, "Turning Political Crisis into Opportunity," *Daily Nation Online,* March 9, 2008 , available from *www.nationmedia.com/dailynation/ printpage.asp?newsid=118584.*

62. *Ibid.*

63. Sam Makinda, "Deal Should Go Beyond Power Sharing," *allAfrica.com,* March 6, 2008, available from *allAfrica.com/stories/printable/200803061050.html.*

64. Lars H. Gulbrandsen and Arild Moe, "Oil Company CSR Collaboration in 'New' Petro-States," *The Journal of Corporate Citizenship,* Winter 2005, p. 20, available from *ProQuest.*

65. *Ibid.*

66. "Venezuela's Chavez Says Could Sue Exxon Mobil," *Reuters,* February 17, 2008 , available from *www.reuters.com/articlePrint?articleId-USN1764515220080217*; and "Exxon's Wrathful Tiger Takes on Hugo Chavez," *Economist.com,* February 14, 2008, available from *www.economist.com/world/la/ PrinterFreindly. cfm?story_id=10696005.*

67. Stephen Johnson, "Venezuela's New Chokehold on Civil Society," *The Heritage* Foundation, July 7, 2006, available from *www.heritage.org/Research/LatinAmerica/em1005.cfm*; and "Keep Venezuelan Civil Society Free," *Transparency International,* July 26, 2006, available from *www.transparency.org/layout/set/print/ news_room/latest_news/press_releases/2006.*

68. "Private FEMA."

69. Michael Barbaro and Justin Gillis, "Wal-Mart at Forefront of Hurricane Relief," *Washington Post*, September 6, 2005, available from *www.washingtonpost.com/wp-dyn/content/article/2005/09/05/AR2005090501598.html*.

70. Bush, *National Strategy for Homeland Security*, p. 32.

71. Gerencser, Napolitano, and Van Lee.

72. Kelly, *et al.*

73. Harry R. Yarger, *Strategic Theory for the 21st Century: The Little Book on Big Strategy*, Carlisle, PA: Strategic Studies Institute, U.S. Army War College, p. 31.

CHAPTER 6

DEFINING CRITERIA FOR HANDOVER
TO CIVILIAN OFFICIALS IN RELIEF OPERATIONS

Colonel John Bessler
U.S. Army

On April 18, 1906, an earthquake of 8.3 Richter magnitude struck along the San Andreas Fault near the city of San Francisco. The fire that resulted from the tremors was devastating. In a city of 400,000 people, the combination of the earthquake and fire left 550 dead, but the true magnitude was manifested in the 220,000 homeless and the total loss of the city's commercial industrial center. Federal relief efforts included mobilization of National Guard assets, but despite the magnitude of this disaster, after 6 weeks the Guardsmen were demobilized and sent home, having accomplished all missions required to the satisfaction of the state and local officials. The key milestones associated with this withdrawal included, but were not limited to, the restoration of utilities outside the burned area, the closure of the missing persons' bureau, debris removal completed from the downtown area, resumption of retail trade, and stabilization of food lines.[1] During this period, as in all disasters, normal social and economic activities ceased or were dramatically degraded. How long an emergency period lasts is generally a factor of the society's capacity to react and cope with a disaster. In the case of the San Francisco earthquake, the end of the emergency phase was characterized by achievement of four milestones: a generalized cessation of search and rescue, a restoration of law and order and a feeling of security by the locals, a drastic reduction in emergency mass feeding and housing, and clearance of debris from principal arteries.[2]

In the 21st century as populations and global temperatures continue to rise, there will be increased competition for resources and a strong potential for friction between and among nations. This increased competition will often end in conflict. Additionally, global climate change will likely cause an increasing number of natural disasters such as cyclones, hurricanes, and similar events; all with accompanying human suffering. Often in these situations, U.S. military forces will be utilized because they are the most readily available, well-resourced, capable, and large organized entities which can alleviate immediate suffering and provide needed aid. Fortunately, as the California earthquake vignette illustrates, the U.S. military has a long history of intervention in disaster and humanitarian assistance as well as assisting with post-conflict stability operations. This long history has similarly led to an accompanying plethora of doctrine to assist both the commander and planner. But what is missing in the doctrine is guidance on how to create an exit strategy from these sorts of missions—a way of defining the metrics needed to transition these relief efforts from one of primarily military control back to civilian control.

In the past, no aspect of these kinds of operations has been more problematic for American military forces then the transition back to civilian control. While it is widely agreed that civilian and international organizations must as soon as possible take on those missions that were initially carried out by the military,[3] the difficulty is in defining the handover criteria which varies from crisis to crisis. Particularly in disaster relief operations, the U.S. military is often asked to stay longer than is prudent because the host nation or the people they are assisting feel that the military provides the only sure sense of security, dependability, and safety in a very traumatic situation—a sense of assurance that civil organizations are unable to provide at that particular moment. This is especially challenging when the crisis is of such a magnitude that the civil police force is absent and normal law and order begins to break down. In these situations, the military may have to wean the civilians from the military presence in order to enable the host government or civil authorities to reassert themselves as fully empowered and capable to deal with the circumstances.[4]

The four milestones that were achieved in the aftermath of the San Francisco earthquake correlated with the National Guard's relief from responsibility and transfer to civilian authorities and could well serve as guidelines for disengagement criteria that might be useful today. Building on these, this chapter proffers three models by which commanders can define their exit metrics and illustrates each in three distinct relief operations. First, U.S. joint and service doctrine, U.S. policy, and other agency positions associated with such operations at home and abroad is reviewed, and three examples of exit metrics are introduced. Second, three cases studies involving U.S. military disaster assistance are used to examine the issues of domestic and permissive overseas environment exit criteria: Hurricane Andrew, Hurricane Katrina, and the U.S. intervention to assist the victims of the 2005 Indonesian tsunami. While these are relief operations, the issues are remarkably similar in post-conflict operations. Lastly, this chapter will attempt to draw some conclusions and recommendations for the future, as disaster relief and post-conflict operations, most assuredly and most unfortunately, will only continue to be a growth industry.

CURRENT DOCTRINE

The civilian spectrum with whom the military must interface is varied and challenging. Not only do commanders have to interface with the locally distressed civilians, but also with informal neighborhood leaders and elected or paid officials from all levels—local, regional, state, and national. The military also often interacts with personnel representing governmental and nongovernmental relief organizations who may have been in the region for years prior to the military's arrival, or whose lead elements often deploy nearly as rapidly as the military does, such as U.S. Agency for International Development's (USAID) Disaster Assistance Response Teams (DARTs) and the Red Cross.[5] The civilian view of the disaster, what needs to be done, what the civilians expect the military to provide, and even how the crisis and emerging tasks will be defined, may be different from the military's view, and this difference must be resolved in the earliest days of the response. Coordinating and cooperating with these different groups may prove to be one of the military's greatest challenges, and yet they may well prove to be among the greatest enablers, depending on the nature of the crisis and how the military engages them. Because it is the civilians to whom the military will eventually leave the recovery and reconstruction tasks for completion, it is imperative they are contacted at the earliest opportunity.

Current joint doctrine describes operational termination as so critical to success that it is the first thing to be determined when designing any military operation. Knowing the conditions that must exist before military operations can terminate and how to preserve gained advantages is crucial to achieving the national strategic end state.[6] *Joint Publication (JP) 3-07.6, Joint Tactics, Techniques, and Procedures for Foreign Humanitarian Assistance,* states that two of the three most critical functions that a Joint Force Commander (JFC) must accomplish early in the planning process are to ascertain and articulate a clearly identifiable end state, and to determine transition or termination criteria for the operation — the conditions that must exist before either should occur.[7] Determining these conditions for stability operations and support operations is particularly difficult. The Joint Warfighting Center's *JTF Commander's Handbook for Peace Operations* emphasizes the ambiguity and difficulty in identifying these conditions by quoting *Field Manual (FM) 100-23, Peace Operations*: "Transitions may involve the transfer of certain responsibilities to nonmilitary civil agencies. . . . Transitions in peace operations may have no clear division between combat and peacetime activities, they may lack definable timetables for transferring responsibilities, and be conducted in a fluid, increasingly political environment."[8]

JP 3-07.6 provides specific planning doctrine and describes criteria for termination or transition as being based on events, measures of effectiveness, availability of resources, or other various metrics. A successful harvest or critical facilities' restoration in the crisis area are examples of the types of events that might trigger mission termination. An acceptable drop in mortality rates, a certain percentage of dislocated civilians returned to their homes, or a marked decrease in requests for support are potential statistical criteria that may prompt the end of the involvement of U.S. forces. Essentially, when non-Department of Defense (DoD) organizations such as the Office of Foreign Disaster Assistance (OFDA), the United Nations (UN), the Red Cross, local authorities, or others, have marshaled the necessary capabilities to assume the mission, U.S. forces execute a transition plan.[9] Because these organizations are normally civilian agencies with less ability to rapidly mobilize, U.S. military doctrine advocates that forces remain in place until these organizations have sufficient capacity to relieve the military of these duties. *Joint Publication (JP) 3-08, Interagency, Intergovernmental Organization and Nongovernmental Organization Coordination during Joint Operations,* provides an excellent checklist for planners to use when the need to coordinate with local, regional, national, and international nongovernmental organizations (NGOs) arises. While it is not a complete list of tasks, it is a good resource to guide commanders and planners in developing a list appropriate to the relief effort to which they are deployed.[10]

The U.S. Army conducts full spectrum operations to accomplish its missions in both war and in operations other than war. Full spectrum operations include offensive, defensive, stability, and support operations. The 2003 version of *Field Manual (FM) 3-07, Stability Operations and Support Operations,* defines "support operations" as those generally conducted in response to emergencies and natural or manmade disasters, and to relieve or reduce suffering. Support operations meet the immediate needs of civil authorities or designated groups for a limited time until they are able to accomplish those tasks without military assistance. This version goes on to describe two categories of support operations: domestic support operations (DSO), and those which support foreign humanitarian assistance (FHA). Disaster relief operations are further described as having three stages: response (roughly corresponding to the emergency phase described above), recovery, and restoration. Both DSO and FHA are limited in scope and duration. The military's role is often most intense in the response stage, diminishing steadily as the operation moves into the recovery and restoration stages. Response operations normally focus on those life-sustaining functions required by the population in the disaster area. Recovery operations begin the process of returning the community infrastructure and services to a status that satisfies the needs of the population. Military forces normally redeploy as operations transition from the response to the recovery stage.[11]

In any support operation, the military's role is normally associated with maintaining or restoring essential services and activities to mitigate damage, loss, hardship, or suffering. In DSO, long-term relief is primarily a local and state responsibility with appropriate federal support; for FHA, U.S. responsibility is at the national level. FM 3-07 acknowledges that there is no specific menu of tasks a commander can complete to achieve success, and the FM focuses on characteristics and concepts, "aiming more at broad understanding than at details of operations;" leaving the latter to the commander on the ground.[12] In response to an emergency, however, FM 3-07 does focus relief tasks on lifesaving measures to alleviate the immediate needs of a population in crisis, including security and the provision of medical support, food, water, medicines, clothing, blankets, and shelter. In some cases, it involves transportation support to move affected people from a disaster area to areas with more infrastructure or security. Relief operations also involve the restoration of minimal infrastructure and create the conditions needed for longer-term recovery, and include establishing and maintaining the minimum safe working conditions needed to protect relief workers and the affected population. These operations may also involve repairing or demolishing damaged structures; restoring or building bridges, roads, and airfields; and removing debris from critical supply routes and relief sites. However, unless repairing major structures is essential to lifesaving activities (like a destroyed bridge to reconnect a population center with medical facilities), major repair and restoration tasks normally are relegated to the reconstruction phase.[13] In the absence of more concrete doctrinal guidance, this list could well serve as the baseline for transition tasks, but the commander must still tailor it to the facts on the ground. The military's ultimate aim remains to transition relief functions to civilian organizations as rapidly and efficiently as possible.

A major challenge facing military commanders is the relationship between their forces and civilians. There are three groups of civilians in any relief effort: (1) the populace being assisted; (2) NGOs and other private organizations; and (3) the local, regional, and international governmental officials involved, as well as responsible U.S. Government officials. Technical and cultural differences aside, civilian visions of the desired end state, the conditions that constitute the end state, and the nature and sequencing of the tasks required to create those conditions may be vastly different than that of the military. Understanding the expectations and capabilities of all parties is a critical element and, in fact, affects all three transition models discussed in this chapter. Civilians will be engaged long after the military has departed. It is also essential to understand the differences in interpretation between the military and the civilian end states to get agreement on transition criteria.[14]

A critical dynamic to bear in mind is: "The deployment of ground forces [for whatever reason] into any region [at home or abroad] and the approach they take to the [local] population will immediately affect the population's daily life, perceptions, and politics—for better or worse, depending on the viewpoint of the inhabitants."[15] Ignoring this dynamic may have negative effects, not the least of which might be a loss of the legitimacy—however temporary—of the local government in the eyes of the local populace. If U.S. military forces are viewed as able to provide more and better services, including the establishment of an environment relatively free from looting, vandalism, or crime, then one of the unintended consequences of the military's presence might very well be a growing reluctance on the part of the targeted population to accept local civil authority during the recovery phase.

In Army and joint doctrine, security is identified as an activity common to both types of relief operations.[16] Both domestically and overseas, providing a safe and secure environment for the local population as well as the relief workers is critical to success. Security is an essential element that must be established prior to the military transitioning out of the area of operations. In the case of DSO, DoD Directive 3025.12 contains specific guidance concerning the use of military assets during civil disturbances. Federal military forces can be authorized to assist civil authorities to restore law and order when the magnitude of the disturbance exceeds the capabilities of local and state law enforcement agencies, including the capabilities of the National Guard.[17]

In FHA, security is also a significant consideration. The type of environment— permissive, uncertain, or hostile—will dictate the level of required security forces. In a permissive environment, this may be nothing more than enough forces to prevent desperate populations from overrunning distribution points. The fact remains that there is a security aspect to both types of support operations, if only to allow civilian agencies to operate safely and uninhibited from either the population being helped on the one hand, or hostile forces on the other.[18]

Exacerbating both support and security issues is the dynamic that different sectors of a neighborhood, county, province, or country recover or transition at different rates. This means that the military cannot simply up and pull out of everything and everywhere on a single day, but must gradually contract its footprint and phase itself out; this too must be a consideration in the initial planning. Departure does not have to be a long process, but it can often be extended over quite a prolonged period. An excellent illustration of the latter can be found in New Orleans where, years after Katrina, National Guard troops continued to bolster New Orleans' hurricane-depleted police force, while the city and its police force worked to bounce back from Hurricane Katrina and clamp down on violent crime.[19] Without security for both relief workers and citizens, the transition from emergency to recovery cannot successfully move forward.

POLICY AND CIVIL SECTOR PROGRESS

Recognizing an increasing likelihood of troop deployments for humanitarian assistance following the end of the Cold War, beginning in 1997, the *National Security Strategies* (NSS) and *Quadrennial Defense Reviews* (QDRs) described military intervention for humanitarian assistance operations as both necessary and expected.[20] In these documents, it is clearly the national vision that relief operations should be of limited duration and designed to give the local authorities the breathing room and the opportunity to restore order and services before withdrawing troops. In spite of a brief flirtation with unilateralism, the George W. Bush administration adopted a similar logic.[21]

The primary U.S. Government organization most engaged with foreign relief today is the United States Agency for International Development's (USAID) Office of Foreign Disaster Assistance (OFDA). OFDA provides humanitarian assistance to save lives, alleviate human suffering, and reduce the social and economic impact of humanitarian emergencies around the world.[22] OFDA only responds to a foreign crisis when the U.S. Ambassador or Chief of Mission in an affected country declares an emergency. In addition to providing U.S. relief resources when responding to natural disasters or civil conflict, OFDA often fields special response teams to assess, report, coordinate, and enable relief efforts by international aid organizations and the host nation.[23] The OFDA Field Operations Guide (FOG) is issued to team leaders deploying to disaster areas. It provides information on OFDA responsibilities, reference materials, checklists, lists of available commodities, and general information on disaster activities, to include working with U.S. military forces responding to the crisis. The FOG has even been cross-referenced with Sphere guidelines as described below, but the FOG fails to provide any guidance for an exit strategy.[24]

In 2004, President Bush directed the formation of the Department of State's new Office of the Coordinator for Reconstruction and Stabilization (S/CRS). This purpose of this office is to address long-standing concerns over what is seen as inadequate planning mechanisms for overseas stabilization and reconstruction operations, a failure of interagency coordination in carrying out such tasks, and a lack of capabilities among the nonmilitary departments and agencies.[25] Developed primarily for post-conflict operations, S/CRS nevertheless provides a robust source of information and capabilities that can be applied to relief operations, as many of the same tasks in post-conflict scenarios are concomitant with relief operations. This office has developed a menu of literally hundreds of essential tasks that can be used by commanders for planning and defining exit metrics. When fully staffed, S/CRS will provide a ready resource for either stability or support operations.

The NGO community's Sphere Project was launched in 1997 by a group of humanitarian NGOs, including the Red Cross and Red Crescent, to better codify relief requirements and standards. Collating input from over 220 relief organizations, the Project published a handbook to assist the relief community in determining the metrics of success during intervention—the Sphere standards.[26] The Sphere standards generally address water supply, hygiene, sanitation, food, shelter, and health issues as minimum standards. However, there are conflicting opinions as to the applicability of the Sphere Project standards' use in disaster relief operations. Among the criticisms are: the standards are focused on relief camps, not the devastated area as a whole; politicians can use the standards to obscure the underlying causes of the misery (if other than a natural act); and the standards are inappropriate in cases where the normal living conditions were below the Sphere standards before the disaster.[27] Moreover, the overwhelming list of tasks, while a good reference for relief leaders to use in asking the right questions about quality of life standards, is so exhaustive and detailed that contemporary use by the military in developing measures of effectiveness is problematic.[28]

Much good work has been done recently in compiling lists of tasks for relief workers to accomplish and the standards towards which to strive. However, the reality is that each relief effort is unique in its scope and challenges. Commanders and planners have at their disposal the doctrine and guidelines, described above, as well as the tools and resources of S/CRS and international relief organizations to consider while planning and conducting relief operations. But none of these provide specific metrics or tools to determine when or under what conditions to transition tactical and operational control to civil authorities during relief operations.

PROPOSED METRICS MODELS

DoD must become better prepared to execute support missions, for it is clear that relief operations are here to stay. Current doctrine provides a good conceptual basis for planning but fails to adequately address criteria for transferring control from the military to civilian government and NGOs. Likewise, the S/CRS and Sphere Project initiatives make important contributions to the understanding and conduct of relief operations but do not address military-civilian transition—i.e., an appropriate exit strategy for the military. Such transition guidance is sorely needed, but given the uniqueness of each situation a standard set of criteria may not apply. To that end, this chapter proffers three conceptual models by which commanders can define their own exit metrics. These three models are referred to as negotiated conditions, objective conditions, and requests for assistance/tracking capacity.

The negotiated conditions model can be described as the efforts of a military staff, very early in a crisis, to closely interact with civil officials, as well as with civilian humanitarian effort representatives, to determine a coordinated response to the crisis, and to jointly determine the exit timeline and milestones. This may be the most recurrent model for anticipated disasters—such as hurricane or typhoon landfalls. Enough lead time or prior planning must exist to ensure a rapid linkup between civilian officials with access to policy decisionmakers, such as the Federal Emergency Management Agency (FEMA), USAID, and the supporting military.

When the amount of destruction is unanticipated, very rapid, or the damage is of such a scope as to overwhelm the ability of civilian officials to cope, an objective conditions model may be a better option. Objective conditions are a known set of parameters by which a military staff tracks progress in a relief scenario where the disaster's true magnitude and requirements are unknown or ambiguous. During relief planning, military staffs use predetermined metrics to monitor progress, shift effort, and gauge the relief effort's progress. These predetermined criteria normally are modified to fit the particular situation and can change throughout the operation itself. Usually in situations where objective conditions are used, the military takes the lead until civilian authorities are better able to contribute meaningfully to the process.

A request for assistance (RFA)/tracking capacity model is a third approach. It refers to a two-fold staff tracking mechanism. An RFA is a request for support or assistance. Requests can be for either a commodity, such as water or medical supplies, or for a service, such as transportation or medical evacuation. RFAs are normally made to the military relief operation's representatives by a local official or relief organization. In this model, military planners and civilian representatives (such as from USAID or the Red Cross) jointly monitor how many RFAs are received, prioritized, and addressed across the various regions within a given area over time. As RFAs diminish in various areas, the military staff develops some applicable threshold metric that when exceeded allows the military effort to be shifted elsewhere or terminated. Tracking capacity is a metric tool which enables the on-site military commander to monitor the growing support capacity of other agencies that are providing assistance in the area of operations, such as NGOs, international governmental organizations (IGOs), as well as reconstituted local, state, and national agencies.

These models allow a commander to address the uniqueness of his own mission situation and to develop meaningful, tailored criteria. They make use of what is known about relief operations without proposing arbitrary and inappropriate exit metrics. The following three disaster relief operations, two at home and one abroad, illustrate how these models were used to determine the conditions and criteria for transitioning from military to civilian control.

Hurricane Andrew.

Until Katrina, Hurricane Andrew was the most economically devastating natural disaster to hit the United States, making landfall on August 24, 1992, south of Miami, FL, and again on August 26 near Morgan City, LA. The President declared a major disaster in both areas, authorizing federal relief effort. The 2nd U.S. Army established Joint Task Force (JTF) Andrew on August 27, which ultimately involved over 24,000 service members. The JTF's mission was to provide humanitarian support, reflected in the key tasks expressed in the commander's intent:

> "immediately begin to operate feeding and water facilities; provide assistance to other (local, state, and federal) agencies in the receipt, storage, and distribution of relief supplies, with an end state to get life support systems in place and relieve initial hardships until non-DoD, State, and local agencies can reestablish normal operations throughout the area of operations." [29]

The commander's intent nicely captured what are termed immediate response guidelines.[30]

Immediate response authority allows on-scene commanders and those ordered to support relief efforts to assist in the rescue, evacuation, and emergency medical treatment of casualties; the maintenance or restoration of emergency medical capabilities; and the safeguarding of public health. Immediate response may also include firefighting, water, communications, transportation, power, and fuel related tasks, as well as the authority to provided immediate assistance in clearance of debris, rubble, and explosive ordnance from public facilities to permit rescue or movement of people and restoration of essential services.[31] While broad in its scope, it is not a blanket authority for any specific level of support and the focus is on expediting transition of relief support to civilians.

Among JTF Andrew's primary operational objectives was creating the conditions to help the communities themselves to be an integral part of the recovery process; in other words, enabling them to facilitate the return to normalcy. Responding to the commander's intent and key tasks, the initial response of the JTF focused on six critical areas of emergency services: providing food, water, shelter, sanitation, medical supplies and services, and transportation, with the objective of easing the suffering. The JTF was deployed to ensure that local residents had access to life-saving measures and means. As such, it provided much-needed relief in these areas and was generally hailed as a success by local and state authorities and the media.[32]

The early establishment of a strong working relationship between the military and the lead federal agency, FEMA, was initiated by the 2nd U.S. Army when it appointed a Defense Coordinating Officer (DCO) to serve as liaison between DoD and FEMA. This officer established contact with FEMA on August 23 — before Andrew made landfall — and by the time the JTF was operational, many of the requirements were identified, relationships were built, and much of the coordinating structure was in place. This early cooperation persisted throughout the mission and proved to be a force multiplier for the JTF.[33]

Despite the lack of previous transition criteria, the excellent interface between the JTF staff and FEMA bridged the gap. Their close relationship enabled both the military and the civilian authorities to agree on the need for measuring the success of operations and to arrive at a consensus on an end state; namely, the capacity of state and local governments to shoulder the burden of providing essential public services, specifically sanitation, water, power, and emergency rescue and medical support.[34] Early and cooperative JTF interface with local, regional, and federal officials led to a list of key milestones on which all parties could agree — negotiated criteria. This enabled the JTF to work towards a civil-authority endorsed list of tasks which, when accomplished, signaled that the military mission was complete. Using these criteria as metrics, the JTF was able to withdraw after approximately 20 days, when the key milestone of "schools reopened" was met. The use of negotiated conditions to determine transition milestones, when hammered out collaboratively with the civil authorities, is a useful technique when the just-alerted commander may only have a writ to provide immediate response, and little else to go on.

Hurricane Katrina.

The damage wrought by Hurricane Katrina in 2005 was unprecedented in scope in the United States: over a million people displaced; 1,300 storm related fatalities; over five million people without power, some for weeks; and economic damage estimated at nearly 200 billion dollars. The federal disaster declarations covered an area of the United States roughly the size of the United Kingdom.[35] The federal response was equally massive in immediate and long-term aid and military support. The DoD contributed substantial support to state and local authorities, including search and rescue, evacuation assistance, provision of supplies, damage assessments assets, and public safety. Ultimately nearly 25,000 active and 50,000 National Guard personnel, 200 aircraft, and 20 ships were committed to the affected states of Louisiana, Mississippi, and Texas.[36]

For example, subordinate to JTF Katrina, the 82nd Airborne and portions of the 24th Marine Expeditionary Unit (MEU) spent 3 weeks working with local, state, and federal disaster-response agencies helping victims of Hurricane Katrina and then Hurricane Rita.[37] The JTF Katrina commander and his staff used the military primarily for rescue operations, security operations, medical support, clearing debris, and opening transportation arteries to enable local, state, and federal officials and volunteer organizations to deliver critical supplies. The National Guard was used in law enforcement operations when necessary, under their Title 32 status. The latter was particularly crucial when over two-thirds of New Orleans' police force failed to show up for work, either because their own homes were devastated, traffic arteries were closed or flooded, or it was in their judgment simply too dangerous a place to work in the storm's immediate aftermath.[38] In fact, National Guardsmen were still patrolling some parts of New Orleans years after the fact.[39]

According to the U.S. Army Center for Lessons Learned (CALL) database regarding DoD's Hurricane Katrina response, the overarching purpose stated by the President and pursued by JTF commanders at all levels was to empower local or county governments to rebuild their communities—not to do it all for them. Hence, for the JTF, the critical issue was restoring capacity (such as emergency medical services, availability of clean water, and open transportation routes) so the local, state, and volunteer civil agencies could deliver supplies and services and begin to rebuild. To do this, the JTF commander and staff adopted six objective conditions to pursue, expressed as tasks. Progress toward these conditions, in their judgment, would empower civil authorities and provide a measure for evaluating success in the ambiguous circumstances they found themselves in. First among these tasks was influencing the local government and public service agencies to accept a leading role in the support and rebuilding efforts. The second task was influencing the federal government (through FEMA) to target resources towards those parishes or localities most in need. Connecting local leaders with the available resources and assisting them to establish relationships with the proper agencies was their third measure. Influencing media to highlight the plight and rebuilding efforts of these parishes served as a fourth measure. The fifth key task was to directly assist the local populace with short-term, high-impact civil-military engineering projects. And finally, they measured their degree of success in assisting local officials to develop transition plans which would allow for continuing long-term solutions.[40] The JTF Katrina experience provides a second model for establishing metrics for transition—an objective conditions model.

Progress in regard to these operational level tasks varied initially based on the participants' level of understanding and the differing magnitudes of damage sustained by the various communities. For the most part, the tactical execution of tasks centered around those normally associated with disaster relief: rescue, water and food distribution, sanitation, emergency shelter, and debris removal. Once these primary tasks were adequately addressed, military and civilian officials were able to look ahead to longer-term recovery.[41]

Conditions improved at different rates across the disaster area and resulted in some unanticipated results and confusion. As conditions improved in some areas of operation, a new dynamic emerged wherein the populace and civilian officials became dependent on military support. In several areas, the transition to civilian responsibility met with extreme reluctance on the part of local officials and citizens who, after the trauma and aftermath of this catastrophe, did not feel secure with the military's departure. In these cases, military units had to wean the local population, government, and economy from the relief effort's resources.[42] Moreover, in some cases, small unit leaders became so identified with their supported communities that they felt significant pressure during the drawdown to continue support, notwithstanding the fact that the need was greater in other areas.[43] In short, the citizenry in several parishes and neighborhoods lost faith in their local and regional elected officials, and, until that was restored, the announcement of the military's impending departure was not happily received. Perhaps a more visible presence by local leaders and officials at the neighborhood, city, and county levels earlier in the relief operation, coupled with progress reports by the military highlighting milestones and progress by the civil-military team might have alleviated some of the populace's angst.

To be sure, the turnover to civilian relief agencies and authorities is anticipated and collaboratively determined so that it is an integral part of planning, and the public is appropriately informed. Ideally, all planning is accomplished in collaboration with supporting relief agencies and local and state leaders. Such a collaborative relationship among the military, civilian relief organizations, and local and national officials ensures better prioritization of efforts and more effective use of resources. A collaborative relationship should be established at the earliest opportunity, but in the absence of an immediate proactive civil-military relationship, a model like the objective conditions model serves well. In the wake of a crisis so devastating, and a civilian response slow to realize its enormity, the objective conditions model enabled JTF Katrina to work proactively toward transition until such time as the local, state, and federal authorities were capable of assuming a more robust role.

Tsunami Relief.

On December 26, 2004, at 7:38 a.m. local time, a 9.15-magnitude earthquake struck off the west coast of the Indonesian island of Sumatra. It was rapidly followed by 15 smaller earthquakes across the region. Altogether these seismic events lasted for 10 minutes and produced a number of tsunamis — large destructive ocean waves. The height of the individual tsunamis differed radically from area to area, depending on the direction the shoreline faced and the depths of the surrounding waters. Along the coastlines of Thailand and Sumatra, some waves reached over 30 feet in height, though most were half that height. Many people who survived a first wave assumed that the worst had passed, only to be swept away by a second, often larger, wave that arrived a few minutes later. By the end of the disaster, over 225,000 people were declared dead or missing, entire towns and villages had totally vanished, and the shorelines of northwestern Indonesia and other affected countries were permanently altered.[44]

Within 72 hours of the tsunami strikes, the U.S. Navy had established JTF 536 at Utapao, Thailand.[45] It also established three Combined Support Forces (CSFs), one in support of each of the three hardest-hit countries: Sri Lanka, Thailand, and Indonesia. Named Operation UNIFIED ASSISTANCE, this relief operation was essentially a naval force from the 7th Fleet augmented by teams from USAID. The U.S. effort was soon joined by Australia, Japan, and Singapore. Focusing on assisting the overwhelmed governments of the hardest-hit countries, the multinational force conducted search and rescue, delivered supplies, and provided medical support. With the arrival of international relief agencies, additional support and supplies began pouring in. As a result of their internal politics, the Indonesian Government reluctantly accepted U.S. support, but with the major caveats that U.S. forces maintain a minimal footprint ashore and that all U.S. personnel be withdrawn before March 1.[46] In adhering to this request, the U.S. commitment was for just under 2 months.

JTF 536's humanitarian mission ultimately revolved around a number of tasks including providing search and rescue, water, food, and medicines to the survivors. In addition, JTF personnel conducted damage surveys, cleared debris from key locations, and assisted in organizing relief packages from the arriving bulk supplies. All U.S. military personnel were withdrawn by February 23, 2005.[47] Throughout the mission, U.S. naval commanders were constrained not only by the Indonesian government's caveats of accepting assistance only with a hard end date and limited footprint, but also by U.S. imposed force-protection measures which required all U.S. personnel to be offshore by sundown each day.[48]

In one sense the hard end date set by the Indonesian government made it easy for the military planners to develop a transition mindset. It forced them to consider transition tasks beginning on January 2 before support vessels had fully closed on the area of operation.[49] Despite this mindset, the sheer scope and totality of the devastation made it initially difficult to determine what assistance was needed, in what capacity, and when that assistance would no longer be needed. *Joint Publication (JP) 3-57, Doctrine for Joint Civil Affairs,* states that transitions should occur when the mission has been accomplished or when the President and Secretary of Defense so direct.[50] But in this case, defining "mission accomplished" would be a tough nut to crack,[51] if for no other reason than the totality of the devastation. And neither doctrine nor the directive codifying the end date answered the questions of how to measure progress and effectively transition out of the support mission.

Advance representatives of USAID flowed into the area along with the Navy and quickly formed civil-military teams with the JTF and the CSFs.[52] Nongovernmental relief organizations, some already in country before the tsunami, greeted the JTF as it arrived. In discussing the end state for operations in the region, more than one recommended that Navy planners use the Sphere standards as the desired outcomes for each country. However, the civil-military teams comprised of USAID representatives and Navy planners decided that these standards were not feasible. In many cases in the affected regions, the standards of living did not meet Sphere standards before the disaster, consequently achieving the standards was impractical. For this reason, as well as the exhaustive nature of the Sphere list, planners and USAID team members rejected the Sphere standards in their search for appropriate transition metrics and looked internally for an appropriate mechanism.[53]

In managing the relief operation, the JTF-USAID team developed a system whereby they tracked RFAs for the various areas. These RFAs were used throughout the operation to validate, coordinate, and prioritize requests for assistance from international relief agents and local officials ashore.[54] Using RFAs, USAID's military liaison officers afloat with the Navy helped track the volume, type, destination, and closure of RFAs. Hence, RFAs greatly enhanced the coordination in the civil-military effort. Since a declining number of RFAs indicated less need for military assistance, Lieutenant General Robert Blackmon, the CSF Commander, settled on tracking the number of RFAs as one metric to determine his transition termination progress.[55] When a minimum threshold of requests was crossed in an area, local efforts could be relinquished to others and military operations could be shifted or ended.

Throughout the 6 weeks of the Navy's involvement, relief organization participation, international support, and host country abilities continued to grow as the world mobilized to assist the hard hit victims. In his guidance for transition, the Commander directed the military footprint to slowly shrink when RFAs for military assistance decreased or were passed to aid agencies.[56] To further help visualize progress towards their own eventual withdrawal, the JTF staff tracked the capacity of non-CSF organizations as those organizations expanded their footprint in country. In doing this, they used four capabilities-based categories as further metrics: (1) coordination (essentially command and control — how capable the organizations were in coordinating continued relief); (2) health services (how capable the organizations were in providing disease control measures); (3) engineering (capacity of the organizations to provide basic sanitation, water, and engineering support); and (4) transportation (capacity of the organizations for water and supplies distribution in-country as well as intercountry delivery).[57] This easy to understand, capabilities-based system, coupled with the RFA tracking system, provided simple, clear metrics for measuring progress and managing transition.

The technique of tracking RFAs and evaluating civil capacity provides another successful approach for determining when to transition relief operations to civil control. Defining transition in terms of a minimum threshold in requests for assistance worked exceptionally well in this case. Measuring the growing capacity of incoming relief organizations and others was equally effective. Coupled with an early transition mindset and a determined effort to develop effective relationships among the military, USAID, NGOs, and local officials, an RFAs/tracking capacity model is another proven methodology for managing transition to civilian control.

THE MODELS CONSIDERED

The three cases researched for this chapter reinforce current doctrine which identifies three essential activities as decisive in successful relief operations: (1) ensuring security; (2) restoration of essential services (herein defined as immediate life saving, access to potable water and food, basic sanitation, and access to medical facilities); and (3) early interaction between the on-site military commander and civilian officials. These three activities are critical to success and are present in each relief effort case.

Security must be achieved before services can be reliably restored — indeed, establishing security is first among essential services. Essential services in relief operations are defined as those elements of basic life support required to protect human life and safeguard public health: emergency rescue and emergency medical treatment, clean water, food, shelter, access to medical services, and clearance of debris from major arteries in order to provide access. Yet, both security and essential services are enhanced by a collaborative and cooperative effort to merge military and civilian planning and execution. For the military commander, such coordination is essential in order to accomplish the military relief mission and to determine when and how to transition responsibility to the civil sector.

Transition is a crucial aspect of relief operations. The end of military operations does not mean the end of relief operations. The relief organizations and local, state, and national authorities are on the ground before the military shows up and will remain long after the military departs. When and how the transition occurs are key decisions in the military planning process. While in the decisive activities, the commander must either choose or develop a mission and situation specific model by which he can measure success and determine a glide path to disengagement. The case studies reveal three distinct models by which a relief effort commander and his staff can attack the problem of identifying metrics for transition.

Negotiated conditions appear to work well in situations where local government and relief officials are willing to interact early and collaboratively with military staffs deployed to assist. Establishing a positive civil-military relationship as soon as possible and developing a true interagency approach at all levels clearly enhances the potential for success of the relief effort. However, this model will be difficult to use if the staff is unfamiliar with or unwilling to deal with civilians; if it adopts a we-they attitude; or if it fails to organize effectively to deal with the myriad of civilian agencies (local, state, federal, and NGO) which will likely flood the area and headquarters. The commander must eventually effectively organize his staff to receive and interact with the civilians in any event, regardless of the model chosen, but proactively seeking collaboration on the end state and effective metrics significantly enhances success.

The objective conditions model may be a better alternative when the scope of the devasta-tion is overwhelming, the ability to judge the magnitude of the disaster is wanting, or civilian agencies are incapable of productively assisting. Establishing critical and objective conditions to provide broad guidance to subordinates is an effective technique by which to visualize what is required for transition. However, these broad conditions must be carefully translated into discrete productive tasks or the actual military forces interfacing with the populace may waste effort or performing activities that are not aligned with the intent of higher headquarters. Nesting intent to the lowest level is paramount with this model. In addition, ensuring that a strong strategic communications plan exists as soon as possible to empower the civilian agencies and officials, and aggressively building an effective civil-military relationship also facilitate the application of this model.

The RFAs/tracking capacity model used in the tsunami case study can also be used to measure success. RFAs are quantifiable and are easily tracked by a headquarters. They provide a fairly simple way to illustrate to officials and commanders the progress being made in various areas. However, the Sphere standards debate offers an important lesson learned in regard to transition criteria: military staffs should avoid building overly-detailed or ambitious lists for humanitarian relief. A simple, quantifiable list of measures, developed in conjunction with NGOs and government officials at all levels, and vetted through relief experts such as USAID liaison personnel provides a more realistic and attainable transition framework, regardless of the actual tasks. Tracking capacity validates the RFA indicators and quantifies how capable arriving enablers are, but these must also be specific. If too general, they will not convey an accurate picture to the commander and they will complicate transition planning. Again, in this model, it is incumbent on all involved to ensure the civil-military linkage is strong. It is imperative that a collaborative effort be made to identify the disengagement plan because civilian officials and NGOs have differing perspectives from the military, and among themselves, as to when they are capable of assuming responsibility for relief operations.

Few operations are as complex as a major relief effort and that is why other organizations involved typically look to the military as the lead at the outset. The men and women in uniform who are on the spear's point have never failed the nation at home or abroad; they are masters at mobilizing resources and coordinating large operations. As we look at a future of greater demands, commanders and staffs confronting potential relief operations must remain mindful of the ambiguities and complexities that will confront them in planning and executing these operations. They must also be mindful that other military requirements exist, or may arise, and that any relief operation should have an appropriate military ending point. Whether choosing to use objective criteria, negotiated criteria, or RFAs/tracking capacity to define mission success, commanders and staffs owe it to all those involved to think through to the ending point, to know when it has been reached, and to neither rush nor extend it.

ENDNOTES - CHAPTER 6

1. J. Eugene Hass, Robert W. Kates, and Martyn J, Bowden, eds., *Reconstruction Following Disaster*, Cambridge, MA: The MIT Press,1977, p. 5.

2. *Ibid.*, p. 3.

3. Conrad C. Crane and W. Andrew Terrill, *Reconstructing Iraq: Insights, Challenges, and Missions for Military Forces in a Post-Conflict Scenario*, Carlisle, PA: Strategic Studies Institute, U.S. Army War College, February 2003, p. 43.

4. U.S. Army Center for Army Lessons Learned, "Disaster Response, Hurricanes Katrina and Rita, Initial Impressions Report, # 06-11," Ft Leavenworth, KS: U.S. Army Center for Army Lessons Learned, CALL, February 2006, p. 89.

5. USAID Speeches: "Briefing on Humanitarian Assistance To Iraqis in the Event of War," February 25, 2003, available from *www.usaid.gov/press/speeches/2003/sp030225.html*.

6. *Joint Publication (JP) 5-0, Joint Operational Planning*, Washington, DC: The Joint Staff, December 26, 2006, p. IV-5.

7. *Joint Publication (JP) 3-07.6, Joint Tactics, Techniques, and Procedures for Foreign Humanitarian Assistance*, Washington, DC: The Joint Staff, August 15, 2001, p. I-9.

8. *JTF Commander's Handbook for Peace Operations*, Ft. Monroe, VA: The Joint Warfighting Center, June 16, 1997, p. V-1.

9. JP 3-07-6, p. IV-22.

10. *Joint Publication (JP) 3-08, Interagency, Intergovernmental Organization and Nongovernmental Organization Coordination During Joint Operations*, Vol. I, Chap. III, Washington, DC: The Joint Staff, March 17, 2006.

11. *Field Manual (FM) 3-07, Stability Operations and Support Operations*, Washington, DC: U.S. Department of the Army, February 2003, pp. 1-1, 1-6, 6-12. An October 2008 revision of this FM integrates stability and support operations in light of the Iraq and Afghanistan wars. While the concepts articulated are similar, the 2003 version vocabulary is more useful in conceptualizing transition metrics as developed herein.

12. FM 3-07, p. iv.

13. *Ibid.*, pp. 6-11.

14. JP 3-08, Vol I, p. IX.

15. *Field Manual (FM) 1, The Army,* Washington, DC: U.S. Department of the Army, June 14, 2005, pp. 3-9.

16. FM 3-07, pp. 1-14, 1-22, 2-16. See also JP 3-07.3, pp. IV-15 thru IV-16.

17. *Ibid.*, p. 6-21. DoD Directive 3025.12, "Military Assistance for Civil Disturbances, MACDIS," Washington, D.C.: U.S. Department of Defense, February 4, 1994, available from *www.dtic.mil/whs/directives/corres/pdf/302512p.pdf.*

18. *Field Manual (FM) 3-05.40, Civil Affairs Operations,* Washington, DC: U.S. Department of the Army, September 29, 2006, pp. 3-7.

19. "Louisiana: Extension of Guard Watch in New Orleans," *New York Times,* Associated Press, January 10, 2008.

20. William S. Cohen, *Report of the Quadrennial Defense Review,* Washington DC: U.S. Government Printing Office, May 1997, p. 8.

21. William J. Clinton, *A National Security Strategy for a New Century,* Washington, DC: The White House, May 1997, p. 9; George W. Bush, *The National Security Strategy of the United States of America,* Washington, DC: The White House, March 2006, pp. 47-48, and introductory presidential letter.

22. "USAID from the American People," USAID website, Humanitarian Assistance, available from *www.usaid.gov/our_work/humanitarian_assistance/disaster_assistance.,*

23. *USAID Field Operations Guide for Disaster Assessment and Response, 4.0,* Washington, DC: U.S. Government Printing Office, February 2005, p. xix.

24. *Ibid.*

25. Nina M. Serafino and Martin A Weiss, *Peacekeeping and Post-Conflict Capabilities: The State Department's Office for Reconstruction and Stabilization Report for Congress,* Washington, DC: Congressional Research Service, The Library of Congress, Order Code RS22031, April 2005, p. 1.

26. Andre Griekspoor and Steve Collins, *Raising Standards in Emergency Relief: How Useful are Sphere Standards for Minimum Humanitarian Assistance?* September 29, 2001, available from *www.pubmedcentral.nih.gov/articlerender.fcgi?artid=1121289#id2730650.*

27. *Ibid.*

28. James Daniels, "Operation Unified Assistance, Tsunami Transitions," *Military Review,* January-February 2006, p. 51.

29. "CINCFOR Hurricane Andrew After Action Report, Vol I," Fort McPherson, GA: United States Forces Command Headquarters, November 20, 1992, p. 4.

30. FM 3-07, pp. 6-11.

31. *Ibid.*, pp. 6-11.

32. "CINCFOR Hurricane Andrew After Action Report, Vol. I," p. 4.

33. Jerold E. Brown, *"Humanitarian Operations in an Urban Environment: Hurricane Andrew, August-October 1992,"* Fort Leavenworth, KS: U.S. Army Command and General Staff College, School of Advanced Military Studies, p. 425, available from *www-gsc.army.mil/ carl/download/csipubs/Block/chp12_Block%20by%20 Block.pdf.*

34. "CINCFOR Hurricane Andrew After Action Report Vol. I,"p. 15.

35. Mark R. Arn, "Department of Defense's Role in Disaster Relief," Civilian Research Project, p. 2, available from *www.dtic.mil/cgi-bin/GetTRDoc?AD=ADA461435&Location=U2&doc=GetTRDoc.pdf.*

36. "Preliminary Observations on Hurricane Response," Washington, DC: U.S. General Accounting Office, February 2006, p. 4.

37. "Port of Wilmington Welcomes USNS Peleliu with 82nd Airborne, 24th Marine Expeditionary Unit Cargo Back From Hurricane Relief," October 7, 2005, available from *www.ncports.com/web/ncports.nsf/ pages/051007+Hurricane+Relief.*

38. Donna Miles, "Military Leaders Describe Recovery Mission," September 3, 2005, available from *www.defenselink.mil/news/Sep2005/20050903_2609.html.*

39. "Louisiana: Extension of Guard Watch in New Orleans."

40. U.S. Army Center for Army Lessons Learned, p. 90.

41. *Ibid.*, p. 89.

42. *Ibid.*

43. "After Action Review MSJTF Wright, HQ 265th EN Bn, Marietta to CP Shelby to Lyman and Return, DATES: 2 SEP 05-23 SEP 05," Fort Leavenworth, KS: U.S. Army Center for Army Lessons Learned, p. 1.

44. Bruce A. Elleman, ed., *Waves of Hope: The U.S. Navy's Response to the Tsunami in Northern Indonesia,* Newport Papers No. 28, Newport, RI: Center for Naval Warfare Studies, U.S. Naval War College, February 2007, pp. 6-7.

45. *Ibid.*, Appendix I.

46. *Ibid.*, p. 111.

47. *Ibid.*, Appendix I.

48. Elleman, p. 89.

49. PACOM AAR, "CSG Indonesia-Transition," Revision 4, March 31, 2005, Powerpoint Briefing, available from *team.apan-info.net/QuickPlace/tsunami,* provided by Mr. Jim Long, PACOM Lessons Learned Specialist, slide 1.

50. *Joint Publication (JP) 3-57, Civil-Military Operations,* Washington, DC: U.S. Joint Chiefs of Staff, July 8, 2008, p. B-4.

51. Daniels, p. 51.

52. PACOM AAR, slide 1.

53. Elleman, p. 88.

54. "CSF-CSG RFA Form," Operation Unifed Assistance Tsunami Relief Information Exchange Portal, p. 1, available from *team.apan-info.net/QuickPlace/tsunami/PageLibrary0A256F7F000E4863.nsf/h_Toc/332D39 D97656389F0A256F8900172461/?OpenDocument*.

55. Daniels, p. 51.

56. Elleman, p. 93.

57. PACOM AAR, slides 4-5.

CHAPTER 7

ECONOMIC AND RECONSTRUCTION CONSIDERATIONS
IN A FAILED STATE

Colonel Roger H. Westermeyer
U.S. Air Force

As the United States enters the 7th year of the Global War on Terrorism and continues its herculean efforts to rebuild the nations of Afghanistan and Iraq, it is evident that nation-building in failed states is of U.S. strategic importance for the foreseeable future. In December 2005, the President issued National Security Policy Directive (NSPD)-44 establishing the Department of State (DoS) as the lead agency for Stability, Security, Transition, and Reconstruction (SSTR) activities, and directed the Department of Defense (DoD) to integrate its SSTR contingency plans and operations with the DoS.[1] DoD subsequently published DoD Directive (DoDD) 3000.05, *Military Support for Stability, Security, Transition, and Reconstruction Operations,* which established stability operations as a core U.S. military mission comparable to combat operations. Further, it directed that U.S. military forces "shall be prepared to perform all tasks necessary" to establish order when civilians cannot do so.[2] The directive broadly states that stability operations include: help to rebuild institutions such as security forces, correctional facilities and judicial systems; revive/build the private sector, economic activity, and construction of necessary infrastructure; and, develop representative governmental institutions.[3] This chapter provides recommendations and prioritization of the many steps required to restore economic activity and rebuild related infrastructures and institutions.

First, nation-building and economic restoration require a coordinated international, U.S. interagency, and DoD joint approach. Formation of the Department of State's new Office of the Coordinator for Reconstruction and Stabilization (S/CRS) and issuance of DoDD 3000.05 were good initial steps that hopefully will feed into larger international/ United Nations (UN) efforts. The whole of the U.S. Government needs to jointly plan and exercise economic nation-building strategies and tasks in order to be prepared to execute them when called upon, and they need to capture lessons learned from previous nation-building efforts to improve future operations.

One lesson that continues to be relearned is the need for economic development at the early stages of nation-building. Often, once security has been reestablished, the priority has been to hold free elections as soon as possible. Unfortunately, rebuilding the economy is often delayed because it is considered a lower priority long-term issue. Although rebuilding an economy does take considerable time, it is a misguided approach to wait until later in the nation-building effort to begin rebuilding the economy because a stable economy and low unemployment are essential for security and stability, as evidenced in Iraq. In 2004, when Task Force Baghdad analyzed attacks in its area of operation, they found "a direct correlation existed among the level of local infrastructure, unemployment figures, and attacks on U.S. soldiers."[4] Similarly, in the British counterinsurgency campaign in Malaysia (1948-60), the British counterinsurgency expert, Sir Robert Thompson, stated that three forces influenced the Malaysian population: nationalism; religion and culture;

and economic well-being. Of the three, he gave primacy to economic well-being, stating that "however powerful nationalist or religious forces may be, that of material well-being is as strong if not stronger."[5] It appears that this lesson has been finally institutionalized in U.S. Army *Field Manual (FM) 3-24, Counterinsurgency*, where it states that ." . . lasting victory comes from a vibrant economy, political participation, and restored hope."[6]

With this lesson hopefully firmly entrenched in the American psyche, the next question is how to go about rebuilding the economy of a failed state and in what priority tasks should be executed. There is no precise template that will work in every situation, but there are some universal principles that can be applied. The best way to approach this overwhelming challenge is to consider the tasks from a short-term and mid/long-term perspective. In the short term, it is necessary to first reestablish security and provide humanitarian assistance. No economy can rebuild if the people are starving and there is no security. Lack of security in Iraq and Afghanistan continues to hamper economic revitalization of both these countries. Second, essential services, such as safe drinking water, health care, sanitation, garbage removal, and electricity, need to be provided as quickly as possible. Though directed at meeting the immediate needs of the populace and winning the hearts and minds in a counterinsurgency operation, these essential services are also critical to rebuilding the economy. Some of these services can be provided quickly and cheaply, (i.e., trash removal), while others such as electricity may require both immediate and long-term reconstruction solutions.

Closely linked to providing essential services and building on security is finding employment for the populace. After civil war or conflict, unemployment rates are usually very high, and as stated previously, high unemployment leads to instability as unemployed young males are quite susceptible to recruitment by an insurgency or are otherwise forced to turn to illegal and violent activities to provide for themselves and their families. In Iraq the workforce experienced great economic hardship, with the unemployment rate exceeding 50 percent after the war.[7] There is no doubt that these harsh conditions directly contributed to insurgent support and greater instability, which in turn slowed economic progress. There are three tools available to support short-term employment and restoration of essential services: the Commander's Emergency Response Program (CERP), Provincial Reconstruction Teams (PRTs), and the formal contracting apparatus. CERP provides commanders in the field with a tool to rapidly execute small projects, which expedites local small scale humanitarian efforts and supports stabilization, builds rapport with the local populace, helps earn trust and confidence, and enhances the legitimacy of U.S. and coalition forces and the host nation.[8] Similarly, the widely publicized PRTs provide integrated teams of professionals to execute short- to mid-term projects to restore services, rebuild infrastructure, and employ the local populace. The idea is to create small teams comprised of military and civilian agencies that can provide security while conducting quick-impact projects that win the hearts and minds of the local people.[9] Finally, awarding government reconstruction and services contracts to local firms is also an effective way to employ locals and stimulate the economy. In Iraq, the Joint Contracting Command-Iraq/Afghanistan (JCC-I/A) established the "Iraq First" program which mandates that DoD contracts go to Iraqi businesses whenever possible.[10] In one 18-month period, some 3,900 Iraqi businesses received U.S. contracts at a *monthly* value of over $100 million. These contracts ranged from construction, to material goods production, to professional services across a variety of sectors. More importantly, this direct economic stimulus generated more than 100,000 Iraqi jobs.[11] Other methods to increase employment include cash-for-work programs, transitional assistance to farmers and micro-entrepreneurs, and vocational training programs.

Next in the economic rebuilding process are long-term initiatives such as establishing the rule of law, implementing a sound financial system, stimulating public and private investment, energizing industrial operations, rebuilding infrastructure, promoting entrepreneurs, developing human capital, rebuilding social institutions, and instituting sound trade and tax policies. But the phrase "long-term" is a bit of a misnomer because most of these initiatives need to begin as soon as possible and in small ways are initiated in the near- and mid-term. They are drivers or enablers of economic activity, and without them the economy will not flourish. Paul Collier, an Oxford University economist and leading expert on African economies, argues that external peacekeepers and economic growth have proven to be more critical than political reform in preventing a return to conflict.[12] Of these initiatives, establishing sound rule of law is probably the most critical and the most challenging. Moreover, the rule of law is not only essential to reviving an economy it is essential to reestablishing the legitimacy of the government and providing for the stability and security of the state. Therefore, reestablishing the rule of law should begin immediately in any nation-building effort.

The rule of law includes criminal law with an inherent criminal justice system, public law with accountability and transparency, and economic law to include property, contracts, and torts. Law must be supported by a competent police force with investigative and enforcement capability, an independent judicial system to adjudicate disputes and criminal and civil cases, and a penitentiary system. In regards to economic law, conditions are not likely to improve unless the legal building blocks for private economic activity are in place.[13] One important lesson in establishing the rule of law is to balance the existing law and customs/culture with a more modern and global legal framework. It requires good judgment and knowledge of various legal systems along with the local culture in order to select what to retain and what to discard in reestablishing a viable legal system that is locally accepted and provides for international economic integration.

Concurrent with reestablishing the rule of law is the imperative to establish a viable public and private financial banking sector. Viable financial services support not only private development but daily life and economic activity. One common approach to establishing financial services is the establishment or revitalization of a central bank. In Iraq, the Coalition Provisional Authority revived the insolvent Central Bank of Iraq and gave it authority similar to the U.S. Federal Reserve.[14] Steps should also be taken to establish and encourage private banking. For example, the expansion and growth of "electronic funds transfer (EFT)-capable private financial institutions are critical to stimulating sustained economic growth and moving from a cash-based society to a modern economy."[15] In concert with establishing financial and banking systems, it is important to have a stable currency and a low rate of inflation. Many failing states make the mistake of printing money to finance war or fund peacetime reconstruction efforts, and the subsequent out of control inflation leads to the collapse of the economy and chaos. To stabilize the currency and curtail inflation requires the will to exercise fiscal control and sound monetary policy.

Related to financial services is the need for robust private and public investment to grow a struggling economy. Most failed states have limited resources for public investment, but those few that do should make funding available to private firms and individuals. One commonly-used approach is micro-loans. Micro-loans are just that, small dollar loans to individuals and small enterprises to encourage economic activity and business growth. This tool can build an economy from the ground up. In addition to public funding, steps to encourage private investment are also very beneficial. Of course, security and the rule of law are key to private investment and business growth, but post-conflict countries also need to focus on pragmatic, short-term actions to reduce obstacles to competition. These include reducing the costs and time required to register a business, removing or simplifying licensing requirements, removing export or import restrictions to allow more players in the market, and reducing the burden of regulations wherever possible.

Another important step for the revitalization of the economy and for encouraging entrepre-neurial activity is to privatize public enterprises. Much caution should be given to privatization early in the nation-buiding process; otherwise the rich and corrupt may benefit to the detriment of the poor. In Iraq, the Ministry of Industry and Minerals issued a public solicitation to privatize 13 large state-owned factories, and on January 10, 2008, the Government of Iraq announced the first award of joint ventures to three Iraqi-European financial consortiums.[16] It is anticipated that 15,000 jobs will be created under the terms of these transactions. In addition to privatization and investment, it is also critical to restore idled industrial capacity in formerly industrialized states. Industrial activity feeds upon itself and restarting idle factories and industrial centers can jumpstart an economy and employ hundreds of thousands. Doing so requires an infusion of public and private funds and an environment conducive to trade. Grants are a useful tool in giving idle factories and centers the financial resources to restart operations.

One of the most expensive and time-consuming challenges to restoring an economy is building and repairing critical infrastructure. This includes but is not limited to roads, bridges, electrical capacity (both production and distribution), sanitation, water, and irrigation systems, communication networks, ports, airports, hospitals, clinics, schools, and everything else in between. The difficulty lies in funding and prioritizing the many infrastructure needs of failed states—in balancing overwhelming short-term demands with sensible long-term development. One approach is to look at which elements are the key enablers that will open economic growth and foster state stability to meet short-term needs while building for the future. In Iraq, for instance, due to poor communication infrastructure, it was decided to build a fiber optic communication backbone and network. This network was not only instrumental in meeting the need for immediate public communication, but it also aided the fledgling financial and banking institutions as well as other private sector business development.[17] Of course, the status and needs of infrastructure are different in each state, and each requires independent and careful analysis. Building or repairing roads is often the critically important construction priority in states that depend on the transportation of agricultural products for economic viability, but they can be built with an eye to future economic expansion. In a similar manner, electrical capacity is essential to both the well-being of the populace and economic activity in modernizing states and can be developed with both in mind. Trade-offs and tough prioritization decisions are inevitable, but comprehensive analysis can create innovative synergies.

Sound economic and trade policies and institutions are important for long-term economic growth and must be encouraged. These include laws that favor industry, appropriate tariff and tax regulations, and honest as well as strong border control to regulate trade. In addition, states benefit enormously from fiscal discipline and sound monetary policy. In Iraq, since 2003, all tariffs on inbound goods have been suspended, essentially making Iraq a completely free open market for all international goods so as to encourage trade.[18]

Another difficult to grasp but essential element for economic prosperity is social capital. Social capital includes trust, public spirit, community participation and volunteerism, a sense of well-being, and optimism. Such elements serve as the grease in the machine of economic activity as well as the lubricant of a smoothly functional society. Ways to build social capital include establishing security and the rule of law, satisfactory delivery of basic public services, transparency in governance, and use of voluntary organizations.[19]

Last, but not least in rebuilding a nation and its economy, is improving human capital. This includes rebuilding educational and health care systems. Human capital is the most vital aspect of building long-term economic growth, and a vibrant educational system is the cornerstone of building human capital. Educational needs run the gamut from primary education and literacy, to trade and farming skills, to higher level and professional education. Education and health care lead to a quality workforce, a competitive economy, and a viable society in a globalized world order.

In the 21st century, nation-building is an essential strategic competency for the U.S. Government. The DoD is an instrumental player because of its role in security and its inherent capabilities. Revitalizing the economy is probably the most important element in rebuilding a failed state. The cornerstones of economic viability, as well as state stability, are security and the rule of law. Short-term priorities for rebuilding an economy include providing security and humanitarian relief, restoring essential services, and providing employment. In the mid- and long term, priorities include establishing the rule of law, implementing a sound financial system, stimulating public and private investment, energizing industrial operations, rebuilding infrastructure, promoting entrepreneurs, developing human capital, rebuilding social institutions and social capital, and implementing sound economic policies. Of course, every nation-buiding effort is different, and there is no template that can be universally applied. Each situation requires comprehensive analysis and sound judgment that focuses on the basics, establishes priorities, and makes informed trade-offs between short- and long-term objectives. The U.S. military must be prepared to participate in the essential economic and reconstruction activities on the ground and in the planning and strategy processes.

ENDNOTES - CHAPTER 7

1. George W. Bush, "NSPD-44 Management of Interagency Efforts Concerning Reconstruction and Stabilization," Washington, DC: Office of the President, December 2005, available from *www.fas.org/irp/ offdocs/nspd/nspd-44.html*.

2. DoDD 3000.05, *Military Support for Stability, Security, Transition, and Reconstruction Operations,* Washington, DC: Department of Defense, November 28, 2005, available from *www.dtic.mil/whs/directives/ corres/pdf/300005p.pdf.*

3. *Ibid.,* p. 1.

4. Peter W. Chiarelli and Patrick R. Michaelis, "Winning the Peace: The Requirement for Full-Spectrum Operations," *MilitaryReview,* Vol. 85, No. 4, July-August 2005, pp. 6, 10.

5. Robert Thompson, *Defeating the Communist Insurgency: The Lessons of Malaya and Vietnam,* New York: Frederic A. Praeger, Inc., 1966, p. 63.

6. *Field Manual (FM) 3-24, Counterinsurgency,* Washington DC: U.S. Department of the Army, December 15, 2006, pp. 1-27.

7. U.S. Agency for International Development, USAID, "Employment Participation and Unemployment in Iraq," Washington, DC: U.S. Government Printing Office, May 2007.

8 ."Iraq Reconstruction: Lessons in Program and Project Management," July 2006, Washington DC: Special Inspector General for Iraq Reconstruction, p. 94, available from *www.sigir.mil/reports/pdf/Lessons_ Learned_March21.pdf.*

9. Stewart Patrick and Kaysie Brown, "The Pentagon and Global Development: Making Sense of the DoD's Expanding Role," Working Paper 131, Washington DC: Center for Global Development, November 2007, p. 6.

10. Paul A. Brinkley, "Restoring Hope: Economic Revitalization In Iraq Moves Forward," *Military Review,* March-April 2008, p. 11.

11. *Ibid.*

12. "USAID: A Guide to Economic Growth in Post-Conflict Countries," Washington, DC: USAID, Economic Growth Office Bureau for Economic Growth, Agriculture and Trade, October 4, 2007, available from *https://www.businessgrowthinitiative.org/SiteCollectionDocuments/EG%20Guide_Final.pdf.*

13. Robert Rotberg, *When States Fail,* Princeton, NJ: Princeton University Press, 2005, p. 189.

14. Laura Landes, "Follow the Money: The Army Financial Corps and Iraqi Financial Independence," *Military Review,* March-April 2008, p. 86.

15. Brinkley, p. 11.

16. *Ibid.,* p. 14.

17. *Ibid.,* p. 10.

18. *Ibid.,* p. 16.

19. Rotberg, p. 225.

CHAPTER 8

THE ORGANIZATION FOR SECURITY AND COOPERATION IN EUROPE:
A CASE STUDY FOR A RETURN TO MULTILATERALISM

Lieutenant Colonel Gary Espinas
U.S. Army

International partnerships continue to underpin unified efforts to address 21st century challenges. Shared principles, a common view of threats, and commitment to cooperation provide far greater security than the United States could achieve independently. These partnerships must be nurtured and developed to ensure their relevance even as new challenges emerge. The ability of the United States and its allies to work together to influence the global environment is fundamental to defeating 21st century threats. Wherever possible, the United States works with or through other nations, enabling allied and partner capabilities to build capacity and develop mechanisms to share the risks and responsibility of today's complex challenges.

Joint Publication (JP) 1[1]

States pursue foreign policy interests through a variety of means including multilateralism, an approach in which several states work in concert with one another to achieve their common interests.[2] Multilateralism generally occurs within the framework of an international organization, such as the North Atlantic Treaty Organization (NATO), European Union (EU), or Organization of American States (OAS). The principal advantages of international organizations are their capacity to make services and expertise available to members, to give voice to consensus, to provide a convenient means of contact between states that are otherwise estranged, to allow verbal argument to substitute for more violent forms of confrontation, to serve as repositories for problems that are not ripe for resolution, and to handle issues while tempering and constraining national rivalries.[3]

The Organization for Security and Cooperation in Europe (OSCE) is one such international organization. Within this forum, headquartered in Vienna, Austria, 56 member countries collectively pursue comprehensive security in Europe through dialogue and transparency measures that bind members together in a cooperative framework. The OSCE proved to be an important security forum during the Cold War when mutual distrust over military capabilities gave rise to tensions between the NATO and Warsaw Pact alliances. A fear that the Red Army could overrun Western Europe in a surprise attack had existed since the earliest days of the Cold War. In the immediate aftermath of World War II, the Soviet Union had 175 army divisions—five times as many as the United States, Britain, and France combined.[4] This concern was reflected in National Security Council (NSC)-68, the U.S. Cold War-era containment strategy that was developed in late 1949-early 1950. NSC-68 stated that "the inability of either side to place any trust in the other puts a premium on a surprise attack against us."[5] However, it was not until the mid-1970s that both sides took concrete steps toward reducing this tension.

These initial steps included a series of measures first agreed to in the Helsinki Accords of 1975. Signed by the United States, the Soviet Union, Canada, and 32 European countries under the auspices of the then-named Conference on Security and Cooperation in Europe (the CSCE became the OSCE in 1994), the Helsinki Accords broke new ground by creating the first confidence and security-building measures in Europe. These politically-binding measures included the prior notification of major military maneuvers for exercises exceeding 25,000 troops and an invitation for observers to witness the maneuvers. As stated in the Helsinki Accords, the purpose of these measures was "to promote contacts and mutual understanding."[6] Following these first measures, a number of subsequent measures have been negotiated and are contained in the *Vienna Document of the Negotiations on Confidence and Security-Building Measures*. Known simply as the Vienna Document, this set of politically-binding measures was agreed upon in 1990 and later updated in 1992 and 1999.

Confidence and Security-Building Measures (CSBMs) underpinned the belief that if information regarding the numbers of military forces, equipment, and personnel stationed in Europe were provided to all other parties, the tensions that gave rise to two world wars in Europe could be abated. These measures continue to be implemented today and include *inter alia* an annual exchange of information on military forces and major weapon and equipment systems, visits to military installations, demonstrations of new types of major weapon and equipment systems, evaluations, and inspections.[7]

The value of CSBMs in enhancing security can be described by the concept of "mutual restraint," the activity by which adversaries mutually wish to restrict the means and places in which they act out their antagonism so as to add stability and predictability to their relationship.[8] Agreed reciprocal measures can reduce the possibility of a surprise attack, limit deployments, reduce armaments, and decrease the size and limit the structure of armed forces to temper the likelihood that differences between states will lead to war.[9] The fact that CSBMs continue to be implemented to the present day attests to their on-going value in contributing to European security.

Another key contribution associated with the OSCE is the Treaty on Conventional Armed Forces in Europe (CFE), which member states often refer to as the cornerstone of European security. All signatory parties to the CFE Treaty are member states of the OSCE. The treaty's implementation and negotiating body is also colocated with the OSCE in Vienna. Signed on November 19, 1990, by the 22 countries which comprised NATO and the Warsaw Pact,[10] the CFE Treaty established parity, transparency, and stability in the balance of conventional military forces and equipment in an area of Europe stretching from the Atlantic Ocean to the Ural Mountains. The treaty established equal lower levels for five categories of offensive conventional armaments, including battle tanks, armored combat vehicles, artillery, combat aircraft, and attack helicopters.[11] Prior to the CFE Treaty and the Vienna Document, the withdrawal by the Soviet Union of large amounts of equipment beyond the Urals had caused concern in the West.[12]

Reflecting on the value of the OSCE's contributions to European security, U.S. Under Secretary of State Nicholas Burns recently stated, "There's no question that over the years the OSCE has gained international prominence for the pioneering work it has done on the concept of cooperation and cooperative security. This concept links security among nations with respect for human rights within nations. That has been the secret of the OSCE and that is what made it unique."[13]

THE OSCE: EUROPE'S PREEMINENT SECURITY ORGANIZATION

Our European allies and partners continue to view the OSCE as an important forum for enhancing peace and security in Europe. In addition to implementation of the Vienna Document, the OSCE provides an important forum for political negotiations and dialogue in the areas of early warning, conflict prevention, crisis management, and post-conflict rehabilitation.[14] Recently, the OSCE has taken on new activities in the management and disposal of excess small arms and light weapons and stockpiles of conventional ammunition. The international community has recognized the OSCE for its expertise in these activities. The *OSCE Handbook of Best Practices on Small Arms and Light Weapons*, published in 2003, was highlighted by the UN during a 2006 conference dedicated to the eradication of these dangerous stockpiles.[15]

Given the value our European allies and partners place in the OSCE and the opportunities for dialogue it provides, the United States should take full advantage of the organization to advance its own politico-military agenda in Europe. This was demonstrated in 2006 when the U.S. European Command (USEUCOM) provided OSCE with two briefings that described its Theater Security Cooperation Plan activities in the OSCE region. The briefings, entitled *External Factors Affecting the OSCE Security Environment* and *Addressing Common 21st Century Threats*, were warmly welcomed by the OSCE as important contributions to its security dialogue. The briefings also provided USEUCOM an opportunity to promote its security initiatives before an audience in which 53 of the 56 member countries are located within USEUCOM's area of responsibility or area of interest.

With the recent exception of the U.S. 3-month chairmanship of the OSCE Forum for Security Cooperation in the fall of 2003,[16] the United States has not played an active role in OSCE politico-military activities since the late 1990s, when the United States was a key player in negotiations for the 1999 revision of the Vienna Document. During the Cold War, the CSCE provided a unique forum in which the United States was able to engage the Soviet Union in constructive dialogue. The parties worked together in implementing the CSBM regime and in conducting CFE treaty inspections. In the immediate aftermath of the Cold War, the CSCE/OSCE helped to shape the post-Cold War security environment. In 1992 the United States was instrumental in establishing the Forum for Security Cooperation (FSC), the autonomous decisionmaking body which is responsible for politico-military activities in the OSCE. The United States also played an important role during the 1990s in negotiating the CFE Treaty, the Vienna Document, and the Treaty on Open Skies,[17] all of which are significant pillars of the European security architecture, with ties to the OSCE. In recent years, however, the United States has largely underutilized the OSCE, and the factors underlying this shift in strategy are examined below.

RECENT TRENDS IN U.S. FOREIGN POLICY: A SHIFT AWAY FROM THE OSCE

Three trends in U.S. policy toward European security and arms control help explain the shift of the U.S. approach to the OSCE. First, the United States has displayed a tendency to focus on NATO to advance its politico-military and security interests in Europe. In his remarks during the 1997 signing of the NATO-Russia Founding Act, President Bill

Clinton stated that:

> we are building a new NATO. It will remain the strongest alliance in history . . . it will work closely with other nations that share our hopes and values and interests . . . it will be an alliance directed no longer against a hostile bloc of nations but instead designed to advance the security of every democracy in Europe, NATO's old members, new members, and nonmembers alike."[18]

Since the demise of the Soviet Union, U.S. support for NATO enlargement has been an impor-tant goal, as demonstrated by the growth of the Alliance from 16 to 26 nations. In 1999, Hungary, Poland, and the Czech Republic joined NATO; in 2004, Estonia, Latvia, Lithuania, Slovenia, Slovakia, Bulgaria, and Romania became Alliance members. A number of other countries have also expressed their interest in joining NATO, including Albania, Croatia, the Former Yugoslav Republic of Macedonia, Georgia, Montenegro, and the Ukraine, so further enlargement should be anticipated. Support for a transformed NATO is shared by the U.S. Congress. Indiana Senator Richard Lugar, the top Republican on the Senate Foreign Relations Committee, said in 2007 that "If NATO is to continue to be the preeminent security alliance and serve the defense interests of its membership, it must continue to evolve and that evolution must include enlargement."[19]

NATO has also established a forum to provide a separate dialogue with Russia. The signing of the NATO-Russia Founding Act in 1997[20] created a cooperative framework and established a new security partnership between Russia and the Alliance. President Clinton highlighted that under the Act, NATO and Russia would "consult and coordinate and work together."[21] This new partnership includes a forum known as the NATO-Russia Council (NRC), which provides the parties with opportunities for consultation, joint decision, and joint action on a wide range of issues,[22] although this forum has not had great success.

Another perceived advantage of NATO is a strong sense of cohesion and a set of values closely shared by the Alliance members. Unlike NATO, there is no collective defense arrangement within the OSCE. The OSCE, whose membership includes Russia, countries of the former Soviet Union, and several neutral states, presents a group that is more diverse than NATO. However, while NATO has 26 members, the OSCE provides a broader audience of 56 countries and 11 partner countries.[23] There are many potential opportunities to be gained by tapping into this audience, which comprises the largest regional security organization in the world. On this point, member countries fondly quip that the OSCE region spans from Vancouver to Vladivostok.

A second trend demonstrated by the United States has been a reluctance to adopt new arms control agreements and measures, with the major exceptions of the Moscow Treaty on Strategic Offensive Reductions (2002) and the Convention on Conventional Weapons Agreement on the Explosive Remnants of War (2003). While current CSBMs proved their worth during the Cold War—and their on-going implementation reflect a continuing value—the United States has shown a recent preference not to negotiate new CSBMs, which are a core competency of the OSCE. In 2006, Russia introduced two CSBM proposals that required additional reporting requirements for the deployment of military forces within the OSCE region. The proposals, which addressed large-scale military transits and the deployment of foreign troops on the territory of other countries, were viewed by many as an attempt to primarily target U.S. military forces, since the United States deploys most of the troops that would be subject to the reporting requirement. The basis for the Russian proposals was summed up by Russian Chief Arms Control Delegate Mikhail Ulyanov, who explained that "less relevant issues from the point of view of European security frequently take priority while the problems that should be at the heart of the Forum's mandate are relegated to second place. As a result, the 'political-military tools' of the OSCE devised in the 1990s are becoming increasingly outdated, and the Forum's current work has lost much of its direction."[24]

While Russia's proposals were not agreed to, the United States also objected to other, more benign, measures. A 2006 proposal coauthored by Belgium and France for a CSBM to establish reporting requirements that would combat the illicit transportation by air of small arms and light weapons was similarly rejected by the United States. A third trend has been U.S. concern that new activities undertaken by the OSCE could duplicate efforts underway in other international bodies. This concern is, in part, driven by limited resources. U.S. Government officials have argued that discussions of most politico-military activities should take place in the appropriate international body where the relevant expertise resides. Discussions within other forums are seen to be duplicative or interruptive, and thus costly. Activities related to export controls over Man-Portable Air Defense Systems (MANPADS), for example, are discussed under the Wassenaar Arrangement on Export Controls for Conventional Arms and Dual-Use Goods and Technologies Activities, a convention with 40 participants whose secretariat is headquartered in Vienna. Likewise, nonproliferation activities under the Nuclear Non-Proliferation Treaty are discussed by the International Atomic Energy Agency (IAEA), also headquartered in Vienna; and activities under the Chemical Weapons Convention are discussed in the Organization for the Prohibition of Chemical Weapons (OPCW), headquartered in The Hague, the Netherlands.

This view, however, can be shortsighted. Several members of the OSCE-FSC believe that many politico-military issues are crosscutting in nature, so a complementary discussion should take place within the FSC as well. For example, the FSC adopted a decision in 1996 that required all members to ensure the timely ratification of the Chemical Weapons Convention (CWC). Member states were also required to provide each other with written information regarding the status of their ratification processes. The FSC performed a useful contribution with this effort since all OSCE member states are signatory participants to the CWC. In November 2005, the FSC successfully reported 100 percent ratification of the CWC.

Another example is an FSC decision taken in 2004 entitled *OSCE Principles for Export Control of Man-Portable Air Defense Systems (MANPADS)*. This decision complemented the Wassenaar Arrangement's efforts to prevent the spread of MANPADS into the illicit market. Under the decision, the FSC adopted the Wassenaar Arrangement's principles governing export controls over MANPADS and made them binding on OSCE member states as well. As these examples demonstrate, the OSCE can provide an important contribution to regional security by raising awareness of activities taking place in other international bodies and by providing reinforcing mechanisms through the adoption of binding decisions. The illicit proliferation of chemical weapons and MANPADS poses serious threats to all nation-states, so raising these issues in an FSC forum should be seen as a value-added contribution and not a distraction.

A NEW APPROACH FOR ADDRESSING POLITICO-MILITARY ISSUES IN THE OSCE

The United States can promote its security interests by using the OSCE security dialogue. Closer cooperation with the organization should be made an important element of the U.S. strategic relationship with Europe. The principal advantage of the OSCE, dating back to its origin under the Helsinki Accords, has been its ability to bring member countries to the table where they can discuss common security concerns. This offers an opportunity for the United States to enhance this dialogue by addressing the new threats of the 21st century. To do so will require taking concrete steps that the United States could help lead. The United States should seek not only to elevate its own participation, but to improve the forum's activities as well. The United States should pursue three objectives in the OSCE: (1) shift responsibilities within the OSCE to better address security issues, (2) update the FSC agenda to better address 21st century threats and challenges, and (3) reexamine previously-agreed measures for their continuing utility. Each of these objectives is discussed below.

Objective 1: Shift Responsibilities within the OSCE to Better Address Security Issues.

The OSCE divides its activities into three areas of responsibility, or "baskets." They are: (1) politico-military, (2) economic and environmental, and (3) the human dimension. Within the current OSCE organizational structure, activities fall under the authority of one of two bodies, each of which has separate decisionmaking authority: the Permanent Council and the FSC. The Permanent Council is responsible for economic and environmental issues, the human dimension, and the nonmilitary aspects of security. The Permanent Council meets weekly for political consultations and decisionmaking on these activities. Normally, each member country's Permanent Representative to its diplomatic mission to the OSCE is its representative in the Permanent Council.

The other OSCE decisionmaking body is the FSC, which is responsible for politico-military security issues. The FSC is a separate, consultative and decisionmaking body for arms control and CSBMs that meets weekly in Vienna. The head of each member country's arms control delegation to the OSCE, normally a senior diplomat, is its representative in the FSC. Closely associated with the FSC are the international implementation bodies associated with the two major arms control treaties in Europe: the Treaty on Conventional Armed Forces in Europe and the Treaty on Open Skies. The forums normally meet on a monthly basis in Vienna and are named the Joint Consultative Group and Open Skies Consultative Commission, respectively.

Under this organizational arrangement, security issues are divided between the Permanent Council and the FSC. As earlier noted, the Permanent Council is responsible for the nonmilitary aspects of security. Also known as *soft* security issues, nonmilitary security activities include *inter alia* border security, container security, and passport and document security. In contrast, the FSC has responsibility for *hard* security issues. These include arms control and CSBMs, as well as recently undertaken activities relating to the management or disposal of small arms and light weapons and excess stockpiles of conventional ammunition. While the Permanent Council is responsible for soft security issues, it normally does not consult on this subject during its weekly plenary meeting. Instead, the Permanent Council assigns these discussions to a sub-Permanent Council Working Group on the Non-Military Aspects of Security. Almost without exception, the representative to this working group discussion is the FSC representative, not the Permanent Representative. This participation reflects a view held by most member states that there is in fact little distinction between military and nonmilitary aspects of security. The OSCE, however, divides the discussion between two separate and autonomous bodies.

To provide better unity of effort, one decisionmaking body should be made responsible for all security issues. This responsibility would best be assigned to the FSC since the preponderance of security issues discussed in the OSCE pertain to the hard security issues under the purview of the Forum. The Permanent Council Working Group on the Non-Military Aspects of Security could be disbanded so that the Permanent Council can focus exclusively on human dimension and economic/environmental issues. Under this arrangement, the nebulous distinction between hard and soft security issues that currently exists would be eliminated. The Permanent Council and the FSC would continue to enjoy separate decisionmaking authority, since neither body has this overall responsibility within the OSCE.

Objective 2: Update the FSC Agenda to Better Address 21st Century Threats.

The current agenda of the FSC is based on two decisions adopted by the FSC in 1996. The first decision, *A Framework for Arms Control*, provides the intellectual basis for the FSC's current work. The decision establishes arms control measures, including disarmament and confidence and security-building, as the foundation for comprehensive and cooperative security in Europe.[25] The second decision, the *Development of the Agenda of the Forum for Security Cooperation*, provides specific issues that the FSC should address; in effect, its mandate. These issues consist of implementing agreed upon arms control measures and seeking ways of strengthening existing arms control agreements and CSBM regimes. An annex to the decision provides a comprehensive list of suggested activities that could be considered so as to strengthen existing agreements and regimes. However, in reviewing the list of suggested topics, one quickly concludes that the suggested activities have little relevance to the reality of 21st century threats. Suggestions include the extension of CSBMs to naval activities; an exchange of information on internal security forces; cooperation in defense conversion; regular seminars on military doctrine; a unilateral declaration of weapons ceilings; transparency with regard to structural, qualitative and operational aspects of armed forces; voluntary participation, on a national basis, in a verification and information exchange of regional regimes; and studying the possibility of creating nuclear-free zones in Europe.[26]

The FSC agenda should be updated to better reflect current security challenges and to facilitate their broader discussion within the forum. The current FSC agenda offers little flexibility for a discussion of topics outside its current mandate of arms control and the CSBM regime. Where the forum has succeeded in taking on additional topics, agreement has often been reached by exception, and has required the overcoming of bureaucratic obstacles and resistance. Yet to its credit, the FSC has periodically succeeded in taking on new activities; for example, discussions of chemical and nuclear nonproliferation and obligations concerning the illicit proliferation of small arms, light weapons, and MANPADS. The FSC should continue to focus on pertinent issues and enable their discussion through a broadened and more relevant agenda. This broadened agenda should be captured in a revised decision that outlines a new FSC mandate. Relevant topics that ought to be addressed include counterterrorism, narcotics trafficking, proliferation of weapons of mass destruction (WMD) and effects, border security, energy infrastructure security, and pandemic disease, to identify a few. These threats reflect the true challenges of the 21st century, in contrast to the previous Cold War threat of the Warsaw Pact. Today's threats are transnational in character and require the collective efforts of a multilateral body such as the OSCE to effectively address them.

An example of how the United States has engaged the FSC to better address a major challenge of the 21st century was a recent U.S. initiative regarding the implementation of UN Security Council Resolution (SCR) 1540. The resolution, adopted in 2004, obligates all 192 UN member states to take certain measures to prevent the proliferation of WMD, related materials, and their means of delivery. Since combating WMD is a vital U.S. national security interest, the White House launched an initiative to encourage implementation of UNSCR 1540 following its adoption by the Security Council. Recognizing the value of the broad OSCE audience, in 2006, the United States proposed that the FSC host an international conference devoted to the implementation of UNSCR 1540. The conference led to similar U.S.-initiated meetings in other regions of the world. Of particular note, the FSC conference produced a binding FSC decision in which all OSCE member states pledged to implement UNSCR 1540 on a national basis. The decision was subsequently endorsed by every OSCE Foreign Minister at the 2006 meeting of the OSCE Ministerial Council in Brussels, Belgium.

It is important to note that the goal of broadening the FSC agenda would be to provide additional opportunities for dialogue, which is the forum's greatest benefit, and not to take responsibility from other international bodies for their activities. First, the FSC, with a limited secretariat staff, lacks the capability to do so, and second, the true strength of the OSCE resides in the contributions of individual member states, not the organization. Also noteworthy is language in the 1996 decision on the *Development of the Agenda of the Forum for Security Cooperation* that recognizes the importance of avoiding duplication. Citing two examples, the decision states that "the participating states will consider . . . measures for complementing (but not duplicating) the international community's efforts in relation to an effective solution regarding anti-personnel landmines and in relation to the fight against terrorism."[27]

An enhanced security dialogue could help raise awareness of common concerns, complement discussions taking place elsewhere, and find useful and unique ways by which the FSC could make value-added contributions. An improved dialogue could greatly complement the advancement of U.S. efforts elsewhere.

Objective 3: Reexamine Previously-Agreed Measures.

Concurrent with the effort to update the FSC agenda, the OSCE should examine the utility of previously-agreed measures. Do these measures continue to be as relevant today as when they were agreed? A reexamination of existing arms control and CSBM activities might reveal that some activities are out-of-date and require revision. To illustrate, Vienna Document reporting thresholds requiring notification of certain major military exercises have long ago become obsolete since military exercises taking place in Europe today are on a much smaller scale than in previous years. This provision has therefore gone unexercised for quite some time. Additionally, Vienna Document activities such as inspections, evaluations, visits to military installations, and demonstrations of new types of major weapons and equipment systems, while proven useful during the Cold War when used to counter the Soviet threat, appear less significant today. Taken at face value, these activities appear to have dubious utility in fighting current threats such as terrorism and the proliferation of WMD. However, where certain existing measures require updating, other measures will likely continue to be useful. Several Vienna Document activities, including those just named, have been important mechanisms for continued engagement with Russia and for the promotion of democratic ideals with regard to former republics of the Soviet Union that are now OSCE member states. Therefore, a review of current measures would not automatically call for their elimination, but would likely point to ways to better meet today's threats and challenges.

Under this objective, the CFE and Open Skies Treaties would not be made part of a review. While both treaties are implemented in Vienna, their association with the OSCE is only tangential, owing to the fact that a number of OSCE members are also signatories to the two treaties. A discussion of either treaty, such as the current impasse over ratification of the Adapted CFE Treaty, would therefore not belong to an FSC discussion, but in the relevant body such as the Joint Consultative Group, for example.

CONCLUSION

The threats and challenges of the 21st century security environment are too daunting and complex for the United States to address without the participation of other countries, particularly our European allies and partners with whom we successfully navigated the Cold War. The importance of working with multinational partners was underscored by then Secretary of State Condoleezza Rice in a speech delivered in 2005. Speaking before an international audience in Paris, France, Rice said,

> America stands ready to work with Europe on our common agenda, and Europe must stand ready to work with America. After all, history will surely judge us not by our old disagreements but by our new achievements. The key to our future success lies in getting beyond a partnership based on common threats, and building an even stronger partnership based on common opportunities, even those beyond the transatlantic community.[28]

Rice added that the United States and Europe had to

> adapt to new circumstances—and we are doing that. NATO has enlarged not only its membership, but its vision. The Organization for Security and Cooperation in Europe now operates not only on a continent whole, free, and at peace, but beyond Europe as well. The agenda of U.S.-EU cooperation is wider than ever, and still growing, along with the European Union itself.[29]

The importance of working with multinational partners is similarly captured in the 2007 version of U.S. joint warfighting doctrine. *Joint Publication (JP) 1, Doctrine for the Armed Forces of the United States*, provides the intellectual and foundational underpinnings for the employment of the U.S. armed forces in the current security environment. In support of this chapter's main argument, the manual states,

> international partnerships continue to underpin unified efforts to address 21st century challenges. Shared principles, a common view of threats, and commitment to cooperation provide far greater security than the United States could achieve independently. These partnerships must be nurtured and developed to ensure their relevance even as new challenges emerge. The ability of the United States and it allies to work together to influence the global environment is fundamental to meeting 21st century threats.[30]

The OSCE is specifically singled out in JP 1 as a multilateral structure under which multinational operations can take place.[31] The cooperative framework and set of interlocking agreements established by the Helsinki Accords that gave rise to the OSCE should form a founda-tion for how we can collectively address current challenges today. The greatest contribution the OSCE offers is as a forum for mutual dialogue in which member countries can exchange ideas, keep each other informed, and reach consensus on collective ways to address common threats in the OSCE region. The United States should engage the OSCE to its full advantage in the advancement of U.S. security interests in Europe. To date, much of this potential remains largely untapped.

ENDNOTES - CHAPTER 8

1. *Joint Publication (JP) 1, Doctrine for the Armed Forces of the United States*, Washington, DC: U.S. Joint Chiefs of Staff, May 14, 2007, p. VI-1.

2. "Multilateralism," available from *en.wikipedia.org/wiki/multilateralism*.

3. Charles W. Freeman, Jr., *Arts of Power: Statecraft and Diplomacy*, Washington, DC: U.S. Institute of Peace Press, 1997, p. 38.

4. Ernest R. May, ed., *American Cold War Strategy: Interpreting NSC 68*, Boston, MA: Books of St. Martin's Press, 1993, p. 3.

5. The Executive Secretary, "NSC-68: A Report to the National Security Council," *Naval War College Review*, Vol. 27, May-June 1975, p. 85.

6. "Document on Confidence-Building Measures and Certain Aspects of Security and Disarmament," *The Final Act of the Conference on Security and Cooperation in Europe*, August 1, 1975, available from *www1.umn.edu/humanrts/osce/basics/finact75.htm*.

7. Organization for Security and Cooperation in Europe (OSCE), *Vienna Document 1999 of the Negotiations on CSBMs*, November 16, 1999, available from *www.osce.org/documents/fsc/1999/11/4265/_en.pdf*.

8. Freeman, Jr., p. 83.

9. *Ibid.*

10. The 16 NATO members at the time were Belgium, Canada, Denmark, France, Germany, Greece, Iceland, Italy, Luxembourg, the Netherlands, Norway, Portugal, Spain, Turkey, United Kingdom, and the United States. The six Warsaw Pact members were: Bulgaria, Czechoslovakia, Hungary, Poland, Romania, and the Soviet Union.

11. *Treaty on Conventional Armed Forces in Europe (CFE)*, available from *www.globalsecurity.org/military/world/russia/cfe-treaty.htm*.

12. *Ibid.*

13. Nicholas Burns, Under Secretary of State for Political Affairs, "Intervention to the 15th OSCE Ministerial Council," statement, OSCE Ministerial Council, Madrid, Spain, November 29, 2007, available from *osce.usmission.gov/archive/2007/11/Burns_MC_11_29_07.pdf*.

14. *The Organization for Security and Cooperation in Europe Home Page*, available from *www.osce.org/about*.

15. The "United Nations Conference to Review Progress Made in the Implementation of the Program of Action to Prevent, Combat, and Eradicate the Illicit Trade in Small Arms and Light Weapons in All its Aspects" took place in New York, June 26-July 07, 2006.

16. The Forum for Security Cooperation (FSC) is the decisionmaking body in the OSCE responsible for politico-military issues. Since 2002, the FSC Chairmanship has rotated every 4 months, according to the French alphabetical order.

17. The Treaty on Open Skies establishes a program of unarmed aerial surveillance flights over the entire territory of the participating states. The treaty was designed to enhance mutual understanding and confidence by giving all participants the ability to gather information about military forces and activities that might be of concern to them. The treaty has 34 signatories and entered into force on January 1, 2002. "Treaty on Open Skies," is available from *en.wikipedia.org/wiki/Treaty_on_Open_Skies*.

18. President Bill Clinton, "Remarks at a Signing Ceremony for the NATO-Russia Founding Act," statement, Paris, France, June 02, 1997, available from *findarticles.com/p/articles/mi_m2889/is_n22_v33/ai_19664903*.

19. David McKeeby, "U.S. Endorses Future NATO Expansion," April 10, 2007, available from *www.america.gov/st/washfile-english/2007/April/20070410165101idybeekcm4.331607e-02.html*.

20. *The Founding Act on Mutual Relations, Cooperation and Security between NATO and the Russian Federation* was signed in Paris on May 27, 1997, by the Heads of States and Governments of the North Atlantic Alliance, the Secretary General of NATO, and the President of the Russian Federation.

21. Clinton.

22. "Fact Sheet: NATO-Russia Council," Washington, DC: The White House, May 28, 2002, available from *www.whitehouse.gov/news/releases/2002/05/20020528-3.htm*.

23. The OSCE has five Asian Partners for Cooperation (Afghanistan, Japan, the Republic of Korea, Mongolia, and Thailand) and six Mediterranean Partners for Cooperation (Algeria, Egypt, Israel, Jordan, Morocco, and Tunisia).

24. Mikhail Ulyanov, "Statement by Mr. Mikhail Ulyanov, Head of the Delegation of the Russian Federation to the Vienna Talks on Military Security and Arms Control at the Meeting of the Forum for Security Cooperation," statement, OSCE Forum for Security Cooperation (FSC), Vienna, Austria, September 13, 2006, available from a limited access website of which the author is a member.

25. OSCE-FSC, "A Framework for Arms Control," Vienna, Austria: Organization for Security and Cooperation in Europe, December 1, 1996, FSC Decision Number 8/96, available from a limited access website of which the author is a member.

26. OSCE-FSC, "Development of the Agenda of the Forum for Security Cooperation," Vienna, Austria: Organization for Security and Cooperation in Europe, December 1, 1996, FSC Decision Number 9/96, available from a limited access website of which the author is a member.

27. OSCE, *Lisbon Document 1996*, p. 25, available from *www.osce.org/item/4049.html*.

28. Condoleezza Rice, U.S. Secretary of State, "Remarks at the Institut d'Etudes Politiques de Paris—Sciences Po," Paris, France, February 8, 2005, available from *www.state.gov/secretary/rm/2005/41973.htm*.

29. *Ibid.*

30. JP 1, p. VI-1

31. *Ibid.*

CHAPTER 9

REDEFINING SECURITY COOPERATION:
NEW LIMITS ON PHASE ZERO AND "SHAPING"

Colonel Thomas M. Rhatican
U.S. Army Reserve

The first, the supreme, the most far-reaching act of judgment that the statesman and commander have to make is to establish. . . . the kind of war on which they are embarking; neither mistaking it for, nor trying to turn it into, something that is foreign to its nature.

—Carl von Clausewitz
On War[1]

In February 2008, the U.S. Army introduced a new operational doctrine to capture and apply recent changes to national security policies and multiservice, joint military doctrine. In U.S. Army *Field Manual (FM) 3-0, Operations*, senior Army leaders reaffirmed that the Army has analytically looked into the future and determined that our nation will continue to be "engaged in an era of persistent conflict—a period of protracted confrontation among states, non-state, and individual actors increasingly willing to use violence to achieve their political and ideological ends."[2] The new field manual is a self-described revolutionary departure from past doctrine, and it anticipates a complex and multidimensional environment "increasingly fought among the people."[3]

The new FM provides what it calls the intellectual underpinnings of how the Army will train, equip, and fight in this new environment, and boldly notes that "victory in this changed environment of persistent conflict"[4] will only come if met by military operations that are closely coordinated with "diplomatic, informational, and economic efforts."[5]

If we are truly facing an era of complex and persistent conflict, an era that will require the "protracted application"[6] of the military, as well as civilian agencies and organizations, are civilian and military leaders heeding the warning of Carl von Clausewitz? If chaos, chance, and friction dominate pre- and post-conflict operations as much today as in the time of Clausewitz,[7] are today's leaders providing the policy guidance and doctrinal clarity necessary for the military to prepare for and conduct a "perpetual war?"[8]

In the 5 years since the end of the ground war in Iraq, the debate continues about the future use and role of the military against state and nonstate actors, and the complexities of military involvement in both pre- and post-conflict operations. Francis Fukayama warns that pre- or post-conflict nation-building requires that an early distinction be made between a country that requires development, or the complete transformation of the society and its institutions, or a country that requires only reconstruction.[9] Reconstruction is possible when the "underlying political and social infrastructure has survived the conflict or crisis,"[10] and the society can be returned to its pre-conflict state. He warns that "failed states are not modern states minus the resources,"[11] and that as evidence from Iraq and Afghanistan suggests, special skills and precautions are required to effectively intervene and then manage such a complex, volatile, and costly undertaking.

In the capstone publication of joint military doctrine, *Joint Publication (JP) 1, Doctrine for the Armed Forces of the United States*, geographic combatant commanders (GCCs) are called to be actively engaged in shaping such failed or failing states by "employing all instruments of national power—diplomatic, informational, military, and economic."[12] The question must then be asked: Do military commanders and their staffs understand the complexities and subtleties of nation assistance or nation-building? Are they prepared for their new core role in post-conflict reconstruction and stabilization? More important, in a pre-conflict environment do they understand the complexities and dangers of trying to intervene and possibly stave off the collapse of a failing state?[13]

It is likely that the Global War on Terrorism (GWOT) will continue to generate an interest on the part of GCCs to operationalize pre-conflict Theater Security Cooperation activities.[14] But without the benefit of a unifying strategy and a method of interagency control, combatant commanders should be wary of such incremental efforts.[15] In fact, if not carefully coordinated, even well-intended pre-conflict shaping activities designed to improve the training and capabilities of the host military or provide urgent humanitarian relief may actually complicate our foreign policy objectives, or worse yet, undermine our overall national security interests.

This chapter therefore examines the benefits of limiting Phase Zero (shaping) activities to full spectrum military operations,[16] and distinguishing it from pre-conflict security cooperation activities designed to build the economic and security capabilities of our partners and allies. Also examined are the benefits of better linking our security cooperation strategy to the direction and control of the National Security Council (NSC) to ensure that our security cooperation activities are integrated and synchronized with a an overarching security cooperation strategy.

SHAPING EVOLVES WITHOUT A CLEAR PURPOSE

General Anthony Zinni (U.S. Marine Corps, Ret.), never one to shy away from international humanitarian assistance missions or nation-building exercises as commander of U.S. Central Command in the late 1990s, expressed concern about the increased pressure to use military forces to counter asymmetric threats caused by failing states, terrorists, international drug trafficking, and the general threat of the proliferation of weapons of mass destruction (WMD). As early as September 2003, only months after the conclusion of the ground war in Iraq, General Zinni fortuitously shared concerns about the growing complexity of the U.S. military's mission in Iraq and Afghanistan in light of the current trend of peacetime and wartime missions. He observed that simply defeating the enemy in the field was clearly no longer enough to win wars, but also acknowledged that U.S. forces are not properly configured for operations beyond the breaking and killing phase of war, and that "American officers lack the strong mix of non-combat skills needed in order to engage arrays of cultures and organizations at the edge of the empire."[17]

Drawing on his experiences in Vietnam, General Colin Powell also expressed his general wariness to use troops for anything but decisive military engagements for fear of endless entanglements, a position often interpreted to mean his general opposition to the use of troops for peacekeeping or nation-building.[18] Other officers also share concerns about the possible erosion of core military competencies as the number of new missions and new necessary skills squeeze out training time and resources that could have been used for traditional warfighting. Still others cite the possible loss of legitimacy and trust as a profession if the military assumes too many nontraditional roles and is perceived as stepping outside of its expertise and "jurisdiction."[19]

While current military doctrine is replete with references calling first for the application of nonmilitary resources to resolve potential conflicts,[20] should we be concerned about the emerging role of GCCs in displacing or overshadowing broader U.S. foreign policy objectives? Do GCCs exercise an inordinate amount of influence over the U.S. Department of State and other U.S. Government (USG) agencies operating within the combatant commander's area of responsibility even during periods of relative stability and peace? Some fear that the commanders may take advantage of vague doctrine governing interagency coordination and grant themselves the authority to be first among equals, and perhaps otherwise apply military solutions to regional challenges best resolved through diplomatic and economic measures.[21] Critics believe that with bountiful resources and an open-ended mandate, GCCs are sometimes engaging with "countries that seem far outside the U.S. sphere of influence or concern,"[22] or acting in many ways like Roman proconsuls.[23]

In fairness to the GCCs, overall U.S. security depends in part on the USG's ability to develop viable, long-term security cooperation strategies throughout the world. In an effort to comply with national security strategies, the Department of Defense (DoD) requires the GCCs to develop contingency plans and crisis action plans to respond to security threats, and to likewise develop separate but related Theater Security Cooperation (TSC) plans to integrate diplomatic, information, and economic sources of national power to prevent crises that may later warrant military intervention. Integrating diplomatic and economic activities is no easy task, so the question needs to be asked: Are the GCCs and their staffs well-suited to take the lead in developing our nation's security cooperation plans?

BRIEF OVERVIEW OF SECURITY COOPERATION PLANNING AND FUNDING

Initiated by President Clinton and Secretary of Defense William Cohen in 1997, Security Cooperation Planning evolved during a period of strategic ambiguity immediately following the end of the Cold War. It was a time for the United States to take a advantage of a strategic opportunity to best promote U.S. national interests.[24] At the time called Theater Engagement Planning, the Chairman of the Joint Chiefs of Staff introduced a new planning methodology for a new type of nonkinetic engagement process. But many leaders within the DoD had reservations about the relevance of the so-called engagement plan. Hadn't they already been engaging with the political and military leaders of the countries within their respective areas of operation (AORs)?[25]

From the time of its inception as an engagement strategy, most of the activities were referred to as shaping activities. In fact, the word *shaping* was used interchangeably to mean almost any activity taken to prepare for a future contingency. The overuse of the word shaping led to real and perceived overlaps with our broader diplomatic and development assistance efforts at the Department of State and at the U.S. Agency for International Development (USAID). Adding to the confusion, TSC development in the early years had been purposefully stovepiped and not shared outside of the DoD until reviewed by the Chairman of the Joint Chiefs of Staff and approved by the Secretary of Defense.[26]

Today, overall U.S. Security Cooperation Strategy is derived from the President's National Security Strategy and a number of other defense related strategies, directives, and plans.[27] But the intent of shaping remains much the same as it did in the late 1990s. It includes taking actions to enhance bonds between possible future coalition partners, using the military to prevent or deter crises from developing, and, if a crisis does occur, taking action to secure the use of facilities to best provide access for follow on troops and equipment.[28]

Today, combatant commanders and service chiefs are tasked by the Secretary of Defense to work with DoD staff to promulgate regional and country specific plans and to align resources and activities.[29] These resources and activities are most easily broken down into two categories: (1) Title 10, U.S. Code, or funds and programs managed and funded within the Army's resource planning system (PPBES); and (2) Title 22 U.S. Code, or funds and programs controlled by the State Department but administered within the DoD by the Defense Security Cooperation Agency. Title 22 activities include peacekeeping operations, International Military Education and Training (IMET), foreign military financing, and foreign military sales (the largest security assistance program).[30] The very popular Foreign Internal Defense (FID) program is also included within Security Assistance.[31]

In recent years, two new programs and nontraditional funding mechanisms have come under scrutiny by several leading members of Congress (and have caused some controversy at the Department of State [DoS]). First, the 2006 National Defense Authorization Act (Section 1206) granted the DoD the authority and funding to train and equip foreign militaries and police forces at the direction of the President, but without approval by the DoS.[32] Section 1206 funding was increased from $200M in 2006 to $300M in 2007 for use in up to 14 countries, and due to recent changes, may now be used at the sole discretion of the DoD.[33] Authorization for this type of activity would normally require the coordination and approval of the DoS as part of the Title 22 Security Assistance activities.

Second, DoD recently received approval to create a Combatant Commander Initiative Fund (CCIF) to allow combatant commanders to conduct joint military exercises; military education and training; humanitarian assistance and civic projects to include medical and veterinary care; and the construction of schools, wells, transportation systems, and sanitation systems.[34] The most evident example of the new CCIF is the operation in the Horn of Africa (HOA) operating out of Camp Lemonier, Djibouti.

Congressional criticism and concern appears to be leveled at both the method and the cost of the programs. Without clear strategic doctrine and without a planning process that integrates experts at the DoS and USAID who perform many of these tasks as part of their profession, some fear that well-meaning commanders may not be taking all of the necessary diplomatic precautions. Local populations rarely see our role as benign or disinterested, and external interventions of any kind invariably provoke resentment or even a nationalist reaction by a determined few.[35] So what is it that we gain by deploying small groups of soldiers on reconstruction, development, or humanitarian assistance missions? As an example, do we lose credibility and acceptance from the Muslim populations in Africa when we overtly link our military with developmental initiatives?[36] And if it is true that "praise for good results is accorded stingily; and blame for problems, freely,"[37] shouldn't we at least assign responsibility for complex stabilization efforts to an agency or organization in the best position to weigh all of the long-term benefits and risks?

RECONCILING NSPD-44 AND DoDD 3000.05

In late 2005, the President issued National Security Presidential Directive (NSPD)-44 to empower the Secretary of State to take action to better coordinate reconstruction and stabilization efforts in countries that are "at risk of, in, or in transition from conflict or civil strife."[38] NSPD-44 clearly states the primacy of the DoS over all agencies, to include the DoD, for the purpose of coordinating and carrying out all laws and policies related to foreign policy, to include the harmonization of such policies with U.S. military plans and operations. NSPD-44 also contemplates both pre- and post-conflict operations focused on reconstruction and stabilization.

Within weeks of the President's announcing NSPD-44, the DoD issued Directive 3000.05, describing the DoD's plan to support the DoS's new reconstruction and stabilization effort. DoDD 3000.05 directs that the subordinate military services elevate stability operations as a core mission on par with combat operations, and directs all services to be prepared to perform a complete array of civilian tasks as part of stability operations "when civilians cannot do so."[39]

Some would suggest that the DoD's combatant commanders are not organizationally or culturally equipped to conduct a wide array of predominantly civilian-type tasks,[40] and that the military may never be able to adequately adapt to duties that are not part of its culture.[41] Echoing similar concerns, it is argued that civilianizing the core mission of the military may actually break down the jurisdiction of the profession or the very heart of where the military's expert knowledge is applied.[42] As such, the boundaries of the profession become increasingly unclear to leaders outside the profession as well as to the members of the military profession itself, perhaps weakening their professional identity and commitment, but also making it increasingly harder for the military to say no to almost any task.[43]

In the end, did DoD Directive 3000.05 finally resolve any possible disputes over the military's proper jurisdiction and role in nation-building? By directive of the Secretary of Defense, stability operations are now at an equal level of importance as combat operations. As such, it is argued the tasking to develop new required skills, capabilities, and traditions should end "the military's long-standing cultural aversion to the use of the U.S. military power for nation-building,"[44] and that we should refocus our energy and resources on improving the capabilities of the military, and not worry so much about integrating the DoS and the rest of the interagency.[45]

Since the issuance of NSPD-44 and DoDD 3000.05, it is evident that the DoS has struggled to develop and fund the creation of the civilian response teams needed for civilian led reconstruction and stabilization efforts. Locked in a perceived zero-sum game with Congress, many in the State Department believe that increased spending on

Iraq, Afghanistan, and the GWOT seriously hinders the reconstruction and stabilization operations at State.

In contrast, over the same period and as a result of the operations in Iraq and Afghanistan, the Defense budget mushroomed and enabled the DoD to shift resources to humanitarian and development aid at a time when State and USAID had their funding limited by the Congress and the White House.[46] To his credit, the disparity in funding and the limits on operations at the DoS had not gone unnoticed by Secretary of Defense Robert M. Gates. He has repeatedly spoken in favor of increased funding and support of the DoS and even testified before Congress in support of the DoS request for 1100 new employees in the FY 09 budget.

In November 2007, Secretary Gates also gave a speech calling for the revival of our nonmilitary instruments of national power, and for increased funding of foreign affairs programs that "remain disproportionately small relative to what we spend on the military and to the importance of such capabilities."[47] He noted that the total foreign affairs budget for the DoS was less than what the DoD spends on health care coverage alone, and that the entire number of foreign officers equals the crew size of one aircraft carrier. "What is clear to me," he said, "is that there is a need for a dramatic increase in spending on the civilian instruments of national security—diplomacy, strategic communication, foreign assistance, civic action, and reconstruction and development."[48]

Hampered by his role in an administration that left office in January 2009, Secretary Gates called on national military leaders to change the way in which the military approaches security cooperation and stabilization operations. "If forced by circumstances," he said, "service members must be prepared to step up and perform civilian-related tasks,"[49] but he also warned that the preferred method is to always have civilians doing the things that they do best.

In a very practical way, Secretary Gates was also trying to protect and preserve the military's resources and its profession. "After all, civilian participation is both necessary to making military operations successful and to relieving stress" on our armed services.[50] He then noted that more robust civilian capabilities would make it less likely that military forces would need to be used in the first place—where "local problems might be dealt with before they become a crisis."[51]

In 2008, Secretary of State Condoleezza Rice noted that if the DoS and USAID did not improve their expeditionary capabilities to deploy civilians with the necessary skill sets, that the military would continue to step in to perform many civilian functions and create a situation that she warned would erode the core functions of both the DoD and the DoS—a point in which she noted that she and Secretary of Gates were in complete agreement.[52] So until the DoS is adequately funded, and in light of increased pressure to counter nonstate actors and terrorists associated with the GWOT, the key question is: Should the DoD continue to take the lead in creating security cooperation activities and otherwise helping to shape or operationalize our foreign policy?

THEATER SECURITY COOPERATION—WHO IS IN CHARGE?

In December 2006, the GOP-led Senate Committee on Foreign Relations released a bi-partisan report critical of the DoD and its policies and practices with regard to TSC and shaping. In a report titled, "Embassies as Command Posts in the War on Terror," the Committee noted that the demands on U.S. embassies have risen exponentially, and that their vital role in coordinating and supporting a broad, interagency effort to fight terrorism lacks people, equipment, and funding.[53] The report included four major points:

First, it noted that the number of DoD personnel in noncombatant countries has risen dramatically, and has caused blurred lines of authority between the DoD and the DoS that hamper interagency decisionmaking at the embassy level.

Second, inadequate funding of DoS staff and functions have decreased their relative strength to pursue long-term, noncoercive efforts in diplomacy, strategic information program-ming, and economic assistance. Perceived gaps caused by lack of funding have been filled by a well-funded DoD, thus creating a shift to the DoD in setting U.S. foreign policy. For example, the report notes that "just as Defense has ramped up its involvement in humanitarian aid and development aid, State and USAID have had to scale back some operations due to the 'Iraq tax' and budget limitations."[54] The report also noted that budget cuts at USAID affected both personnel and programs, and are repeatedly cited as a deficiency in the U.S. campaign against extremism in susceptible regions of the world.[55]

Third, the Committee noted that increased funding to the DoD for its self-assigned missions is creating an overlap of missions and increased friction with non-DoD agencies. As the role of the military continues to expand, DoS and embassy officials are concerned that the DoD will chafe even more at the methods of operation already coordinated and directed by the embassy leadership.

Fourth, the Senate Report cites evidence that host countries are questioning the increased role of the U.S. military in problems seen as not lending themselves to military solutions. While host nation militaries may welcome U.S. military presence, some elements of their governments and society are suspicious of U.S. coercion—and if the trend continues, it could undermine DoS broad bilateral relationships and efforts is support of the GWOT. For example, in Uganda and then in Ethiopia, military civil affairs teams and humanitarian action teams helping local communities build wells, erect schools, and other small development projects, came under suspicion by local authorities for taking sides. In Ethiopia, they were ordered out of the region to prevent sparking further cross-border hostilities.[56]

During congressional hearings on the creation of U.S. Africa Command (AFRICOM) in the summer of 2007, testimony echoed many of the concerns identified in the Senate Committee report. The United States was having difficulty convincing the Africans of a shared concern for international terrorism and for the need for an AFRICOM headquarters on the continent. Most African countries continued to broadly define terrorism in terms of local unrest and violence—not as an issue to be dealt with militarily as against a foreign threat. Some African leaders reported that the United States habitually underestimates the significance of local violence to their security, and that the United States believes that the violence is not enough of a significant international threat (by U.S. standards) to warrant notice or action.[57] If true, perhaps the U.S. position is simply a reflection of our military-centric view of the overall security concerns of our allies and partners.

During the Vietnam War, Ambassador Robert W. Komer noted that civilian and military leaders in Washington miscalculated and misunderstood the complexities of the political socio-economic factors at play in the earliest stages of the conflict, and too quickly committed to a military solution that later significantly "unbalanced our response."[58]

Today, Ambassador Robert B. Oakley echoes Ambassador Komer's concerns and argues that the ambassador and embassy country teams are the "critical intersection where plans, policies, programs, and personalities come together,"[59] and that interagency country teams are in the best position to measure an appropriate response. In an effort to avoid unintended violence, Oakley recommends that a combatant commander's authority should be limited to the actions of deployed forces only engaged in active hostilities. All other military elements working on missions in-country should be under the authority of the ambassador, to include intelligence personnel and special operations forces — with a memorandum of agreement between the ambassador and the geographic combatant commander making clear the ambassador's authority relative to the increased number of special operations forces and SOF missions.[60] As a small but important practical matter, and as a way to circumscribe the peacetime shaping activities in-country, he recommends that assigned DoD personnel fall within the supervisory rating and evaluation scheme of the ambassador, mirroring the rating scheme of other non-military personnel assigned to the embassy.[61]

Some of Ambassador Oakley's contemporaries within the DoS question whether the DoD has become more robust not only in terms of numbers and resources, but also "in the ways they think they can operate under this still not terribly well-defined authority of the chief of mission."[62] Other foreign service officers argue that the war on terrorism may create a steady-state battlefield, and they worry that if the battlefield is everywhere, then even greater guidance will be needed to deconflict the traditional roles and responsibilities of foreign officers and the military.[63] One senior State Department official asks: Has the military relegated foreign service officers to the usefulness of "third rate soldiers as opposed to first-rate diplomats?"[64]

At a National Press Club event in September, 2007, General David Petraeus hailed Ambassador Ryan Crocker as "my great diplomatic wingman."[65] If war zones are military turf, and diplomats are logically the wingman in that type of operational environment, the question must be asked: When, if ever, under the current doctrine of full spectrum operations, does the general become the wingman to the ambassador? If the conflict is persistent, and requires the protracted application of the military, what are the logical checks on diligent military planners and commanders who feel they need to operationalize Phase Zero to fulfill their role in a new core mission.[66]

LIMITING PHASE ZERO (SHAPING) TO FULL SPECTRUM OPERATIONS

Within 8 months of the issuance of DoDD 3000.05 and the elevation of stabilization to a core mission (and core competency), the Chairman of the Joint Chiefs of Staff published *Joint Publication (JP) 3-0, Operations*, and *Joint Publication (JP) 5-0, Operations Planning*. In JP 5-0, security cooperation planning is distinct and separate from joint operations planning.

Joint operations planning includes contingency and crisis action planning for full spectrum military operations, to include stabilization operations; and stabilization operations include Phase Zero (shaping). Unlike joint operations planning, security cooperation plans are promulgated by combatant commanders and service chiefs in accordance with the DoD's Security Cooperation Guidance and in consultation with U.S. agencies that represent other instruments of power to include the U.S. chiefs of mission (ambassadors) in the commander's area of responsibility.[67] Therefore, and consistent with joint doctrine, Phase Zero (shaping) activities and security cooperation activities are the products of two separate plans.

But while joint doctrine defines separate *planning* processes for Phase Zero (shaping) and security cooperation, it defines the respective *activities* as much the same: enhancing bonds and increasing capabilities of partners, preventing conflicts and crises, and maintaining operational access for follow on forces.[68] So how does the DoD distinguish the two?

Historically, much of the control and funding for security cooperation activities has fallen under the purview of the State Department, and security cooperation activities have been applied throughout the world in areas in which the United States wants to shape our national security. In fact, in an effort to differentiate the respective roles of the DoS and the DoD with respect to security cooperation planning, JP 3-0 still acknowledges that the DoS is always a principal agency (and often the lead agency) responsible for U.S. efforts to "protect and enhance national security interests and deter conflict."[69] DoS controls the funding for many critical Title 22 programs, to include foreign military sales and foreign military financing. DoD therefore encourages combatant commanders and other joint force commanders to maintain working relationships with the chiefs of U.S. missions and the State Department, and describes the Theater Security Cooperation (TSC) plan as the framework in which joint force commanders will "continually employ military forces to *complement and reinforce* other instruments of national power."(emphasis by author.)[70]

But in recent years, and as noted in the Senate Foreign Relations Committee Report, the DoD has willingly assumed a larger role in humanitarian aid, development, and other areas once managed almost exclusively by the State Department and USAID. As a result, the DoD is blurring the line between the historical application of security cooperation activities and the new Phase Zero (shaping) activities.

To maximize the full effect of security cooperation and Phase Zero (shaping), and to add some clarity to their doctrinal application, it would be better to limit the application of Phase Zero (shaping) to the following two methods: First, Phase Zero should only be applied in a linear, progressive manner once a military campaign commences. In this case, Phase Zero operations would immediately follow security cooperation activities. For example, if a GCC had already been gathering information and creating tentative plans for access to a country's airfields and ports as part of its contribution to the TSC plan, shaping activities may include the logical follow on tasks. These tasks may include the completion of necessary contracting services for logistics and support, conducting rehearsals, or completing the final coordination with host nation or multinational military and security forces. Consistent with the joint publications, Phase Zero operations will continue to include actions that prevent conflict but at the same time best facilitate the possible arrival and onward integration of military forces.

Second, Phase Zero activities should only be applied as part of an on-going military campaign with forces engaged in full spectrum operations (or a mix of defensive, offensive, and stability operations). The GCC would be engaged in full spectrum operations where, by definition, Phase Zero operations are conducted in areas of relative peace, and the GCC would try to safeguard the peace while simultaneously taking action to ensure that military forces would have access to the area as needed.

Limiting Phase Zero (shaping) activities to an operational construct, and not letting it freely overlap with security cooperation activities, is consistent with the balance of operations chart in JP 3-0 that depicts and defines shaping operations not in isolation, but as part of the continuous application, a three-part mix of offensive, defensive, and stability operations.[71] Phase Zero (shaping) activities should therefore remain operationally focused, and in concert with host nation and multinational partners to preserve peace or prevent conflict but with a heavy emphasis on safeguarding military access. Security cooperation, reflecting at times the more complicated nature of a targeted fragile state, focuses on more complex, and long-term interagency solutions to promote stability and peace and requires a different conceptual framework.

A NEW FRAMEWORK FOR INTERAGENCY SECURITY COOPERATION

In a study produced by the Atlantic Council of the United States, Colonel Albert Zaccor provides a helpful analytical framework in support of the creation of a new interagency security cooperation plan that supports all foreign policy objectives while maintaining our "focus on forward defense."[72] Zaccor shares the concerns of other critics of the current system, and agrees that if defined too broadly, security cooperation has the potential to be a "surrogate for foreign policy."[73]

His analysis includes a review of three important areas in support of an interagency security cooperation plan: (1) the creation of broad security cooperation goals (to include political will),[74] (2) the need for more integrated planning, and (3) the removal of likely obstacles to the creation of a fiscally sound, integrated, and effective security cooperation plan.

First, security cooperation goals focus on the creation of sound, long-term relationships with civilian and military leaders to secure information (or gain access to the host nation's sources and data), and to secure access to airports, ports, and possible troop facilities. Relationships are based on trust, mutual interest, and a common understanding of the threat,[75] but most importantly, security cooperation relies on the creation of adequate capabilities and the political will to use them.

The United States must leverage the capabilities of our allies and partners to fill the gaps in our own security shortfalls in a region.[76] One of the true tests for measuring the possible effectiveness of military capabilities does not rest with the military, but rather with the careful assessment of the host nation's shared security interests, its political interests, and its record of cooperating with the United States in other areas of mutual interest.[77] For example, do the current leaders of the country have a history of cooperation with the USG in all matters of mutual interest with regard to trade, commerce, alliances, and treaties? In broader terms, do the country's leaders believe that they share a common fate with us, or even a shared interdependence in the international community? If so, they are more likely to see cooperation as beneficial.[78] Or does the country have a pressing political situation that might make cooperation with the United States only temporarily undesirable, as with Germany and Turkey when U.S. diplomats asked for military assistance in Iraq?[79]

To this end, this type of assessment and recommendation necessarily relies on the input of many experts, to include the military. But a final decision on security cooperation investments and programs will require an interagency decision linked to the broader interests of both the partner country and the United States.

In recent years, the United States met with some success in developing capabilities in partner countries and then securing the cooperation of their leaders to apply their new security capabilities against shared threats. The Georgia Train and Equip Program is widely viewed as a success story because it reflected our ability to create partner capabilities that were later exercised by the Georgian leadership to remedy both Georgia's internal security concerns as well as our international security concerns in that region.[80] The United States pooled $65M from a combination of security cooperation sources to train 2,600 Georgian soldiers who later rooted out terrorists in the Panski Gorge region — the original objective of the program. Bordering on Turkey and Russia, Georgia seeks entry into the European Union (EU) and NATO, and has been a willing partner in U.S.-led coalition operations, to include sending 600 troops for operations in Iraq.[81]

The Trans-Sahel Counterterrorism Initiative (TSCTI) is another example of a successful (but expensive) security cooperation effort in northwestern Africa. Requiring $508M in FY 2008, TSCTI now includes 10 states and a successful program to protect borders, deny safe havens, track movement of terrorists, and improve general cooperation in the region against international terrorism.[82] TSCTI also reflects our ability to improve the military and security capability of select partner countries, as well as generate the political willingness to exercise that capability for mutual gain.

Second, Zaccor identifies the peculiar need for better integrated planning in the current operating environment that includes not only terrorism, drug trafficking, and the proliferation of WMD,[83] but also AIDS epidemics, international organized crime, climate change and population migrations, and the emerging threat of countries like China seeking to secure energy reserves in Africa. As such, the temptation is for the United States to be more fully engaged throughout the world. So the challenge will be one of economizing on our costs in the current counterterrorism campaign, costs that are already high and "almost certainly not sustainable."[84]

To be effective, a new security cooperation strategy must reflect a new institutional culture. The strategy must build broad capabilities in much the same way that the Army has adopted Doctrine, Organization, Training, Leadership, Materiel, Soldier Systems/ Personnel, and Finances (DOTLMS-PF) to "capture all of the factors that go into the creation of a truly capable" force.[85] Likewise, and despite our multiplicity of government programs and good intentions, our foreign partners and allies rightfully expect us to speak with one voice.

Finally, Zaccor identified a number of obstacles to achieving a fiscally sound, integrated, and authoritative security cooperation effort. The current system of security cooperation lacks a common conceptual understanding, or doctrine, and the funding system remains "underfunded, fragmented, and inflexible."[86] For example, the Foreign Assistance Act prohibits using Foreign Military Assistance funds to support law enforcement organizations in foreign countries, with exceptions only for counternarcotics and customs.[87] This type of stovepiped funding hinders a broader USG effort to improve host nation law enforcement or gendarmerie, and reflects a lack of organizational structure and lines of authority necessary to best apply our resources.[88] In his conclusion,

Zaccor recommends the elimination of our "hierarchical and program driven approach . . . controlled by policy 'fiefdoms',"[89] and instead, the adoption of an interagency program patterned after the current DoD Security Cooperation model but with national Security Council playing an integral role.[90]

NATIONAL SECURITY COUNCIL: PROVIDING CLARITY AND BALANCE

In 1947, only 2 years after the conclusion of World War II, national leaders had quickly identified the need for greater interagency coordination. The National Security Act of 1947 was a seminal decision that created the National Security Council and the Central Intelligence Agency, and set the stage for the creation of the DoD 2 years later. Most important, it was an acknowledgement by national leaders that while the war had certainly been successful, there were still significant weaknesses or gaps between foreign and military policy, as well as gaps between the military and civilian agencies.[91] Testimony and reports provided to the Senate Armed Services Committee at the time called for the deliberate integration of domestic, foreign, and military policies to keep foreign and military policies mutually supporting and in balance.[92] In the end, the 1947 Act captured the consensus of the wartime policymakers on the need for better interagency coordination in both policy development and execution.[93]

Today, reorganizing and redirecting an even larger national security apparatus will be no easy task. But the continued pursuit of uncoordinated strategies in the current security environment may bear serious long-term consequences. The lessons learned from our immediate post-conflict stabilization and reconstruction efforts in Iraq are well known, but the response has been slow and inadequate. Instead of clarifying and explaining the strategic role of security cooperation, shaping operations, and stability operations, the USG permits all three to move incrementally forward in fits and starts.

In July 2004, the DoS initiated and created a new Office of the Coordinator for Reconstruc-tion and Stabilization (S/CRS) with a broad tasking to lead and coordinate interagency efforts to prevent or prepare for post-conflict situations. With little funding, and little support outside the DoS, S/CRS had minimal impact until December 2005, when President Bush issued NSPD-44 designating the DoS as the lead agency for all stabilization and reconstruction efforts. Patterned after a number of similar programs in other countries, S/CRS began to fill three pools of civilian experts to assist in civilian-centric stabilization tasks, and to coordinate and deconflict interagency efforts in selected hot spots around the world.

However, S/CRS lacks the political support and bureaucratic clout necessary to garner the funding needed to fully organize and perform its mission.[94] Its current FY 2009 budget request for $248.6M is for on-going start up costs only. Deployment costs would require additional funding estimated to range in the hundreds of millions of dollars,[95] making it a target for yet more Congressional scrutiny and likely cutbacks.[96] As such, it reflects the same general lack of authority, funding, and capabilities of NSPD-44,[97] limiting it for now as a program with only long-term potential.

Is it possible to create an interagency structure that can close the gaps and effectively handle day-to-day operations while simultaneously preparing for future challenges and opportunities? Can we fashion a proactive, long-term, and sustainable national security strategy that will help the United States maintain a strategic security advantage? While some call for legislation mirroring the scope and significance of the Goldwater-Nichols Act of 1986, others recommend that we first revisit the thought process embraced by President Dwight Eisenhower as he struggled to reconcile the seemingly unsustainable policies contained in National Security Memorandum 68.[98] As a military officer, he knew that long-term planning was difficult to sustain when daily operations kept the commander and the staff preoccupied,[99] and he was determined to fix it.

In an effort to capture all of the many divergent theories of how to counter the growing Soviet threat, President Eisenhower gathered a team of experts from outside the mainstream and outside the controlled chaos of day-to-day operations and planning. He called it "Project Solarium" after the afternoon debate he had with his Secretary of State, John Foster Dulles, in the solarium of the White House; a conversation that the President felt mirrored the great disparity of thought on the subject of the country's long-term national security. The results of the project captured the wide range of opinions and options on how to best deal with the long-term strategic threat presented by the Soviet Union. In the end, the President and the NSC were able to thoughtfully weigh the benefits and risks of each strategy, and to select the strategies that ultimately formed the core of the security policy directive.[100]

With only minor exceptions, the NSC has produced little to no long-term strategic thinking and security guidance since Project Solarium.[101] For over 50 years, the NSC staff system has been marked by an overall trend of "declining ability or willingness . . . to perform strategic threat assessment and planning."[102] As such, calling on the NSC in its present form to take the lead in creating and then managing a long-term, interagency security effort would be unwise. The NSC requires a new mandate, and a new structure capable of providing sound, well-informed, and long-term security guidance, as well as a bureaucracy capable of managing and leading the policy within the interagency.

Michele Flournoy and Shawn W. Brimley propose the creation of a holistic, interagency Quadrennial National Security Review (QNSR) that would identify an overarching strategy and incorporate all instruments of national power. The QNSR would also produce an authoritative classified planning document directing the National Security Advisor and the Cabinet Secretaries to develop particular courses of action.[103] Nested within the NSC, Flournoy and Brimley propose to create a staff of strategic planners "insulated from day-to-day demands and crisis management."[104] Others recommend the creation of long-term planning cells, perhaps with an executive director reporting to the National Security Advisor, and at all times thoroughly insulated from the existing agencies to avoid creating an organization of detailees, serving at the whim of, and still loyal to, their home departments.[105]

It is within this framework that a new security cooperation effort could flourish. As directed in National Security Presidential Directive-1, it is already the duty of the NSC and the NSC System to "coordinate executive departments and agencies in the effective development and implementation" of "domestic, foreign, and military policies relating to national security."[106] The current DoD theater security cooperation framework offers a suitable starting point from which the NSC could better direct and control the efforts of agencies already engaged in various degrees of security cooperation planning.

CONCLUSION

The DoD deserves credit for its attempts to integrate interagency contributions into Theater Security Cooperation plans. In an age of persistent conflict, the DoD is creating new doctrine and planning models that attempt to integrate all USG security interests. But the pressure of the current operating environment is causing the DoD to reevaluate the limits of its core military functions, and to consider the addition of many new civilian competencies within Phase Zero (shaping) operations as TSC activities. In an effort to avoid the inadvertent creation of a surrogate foreign policy, and to avoid creating the impression that the USG does not speak with one voice, the DoD is more mindful of the strategic hazards created by operationalizing Phase Zero and blurring the lines between the roles and duties of the military and civilian agencies (e.g., the DoS and USAID). Therefore, and in an effort to preserve clarity and understanding, Phase Zero (shaping) activities should be limited to full spectrum military operations. Security cooperation activities, while currently the product of DoD-led planning, should instead be developed and implemented as part of a new NSC organization. If given the authority and organizational structure, the NSC system is in the best position to manage the complexities of engaging our allies and partners, and will provide the strategic guidance, authority, and resources necessary to develop and protect our short- and long-term national security interests.

ENDNOTES - CHAPTER 9

1. Carl Von Clauswitz, *On War*, Michael Howard and Peter Paret, eds. and trans., Princeton, NJ: Princeton University Press, 1984, p. 88.

2. *Field Manual (FM) 3-0, Operations*, Washington, DC: U.S. Department of the Army, February 27, 2008, foreword.

3. *Ibid.*

4. *Ibid*, p. viii.

5. *Ibid.*

6. *Ibid.*, p. vii.

7. *Ibid.*, p. viii.

8. Thomas P. M. Barnett, *The Pentagon's New Map*, New York: Berkley Books, 2004, p. 159.

9. Francis Fukuyama, *Nation-building: Beyond Afghanistan and Iraq*, Baltimore, MD: Johns Hopkins University Press, 2006, pp. 4-5.

10. *Ibid.*

11. *Ibid.*

12. *Joint Publication (JP) 1, Doctrine for the Armed Forces of the United States,* Washington, DC: U.S. Joint Chiefs of Staff, May 14, 2007, p. I-1.

13. *Department of Defense Directive 3000.05,* Washington, DC: U.S. Department of Defense, November 28, 2005, p. 2, available from *www.dtic.mil/whs/directives/corres/html/300005.htm.* DoD provides guidance to all services to be prepared to conduct stability operations "across the spectrum of peace to conflict . . . and to perform all tasks necessary . . . when civilians cannot do so."

14. General Charles F. Wald, "New Thinking at EUCOM: The Phase Zero Campaign," *Joint Forces Quarterly,* 4th quarter 2006, p. 73.

15. Thomas S. Szayna *et al., U.S. Army Security Cooperation: Toward Improved Planning and Management,* Santa Monica, CA: Rand Corporation, 2004, p. xv.

16. For specific information on joint strategic planning, see *Joint Publication (JP) 5-0, Joint Operation Planning,* Washington, DC: U.S. Joint Chiefs of Staff, 13 April 1995.

17. General (Ret.) Anthony Zinni, speaking at the Marine Corps and U.S. Naval Institute Forum 2003, September 4, 2003, Arlington, VA, quoted in Laurent Guy, "Competing Visions for the U.S. Military," *Orbis,* Fall 2004, pp. 705-706.

18. Colin Powell's overall concerns about the use of military forces, and his specific concerns about the need for an exit strategy to avoid endless entanglement, are often taken together and interpreted to mean that the United States should avoid peacekeeping and nation-building exercises. See also *www.foreignaffairs. org/19921201faessay5851/colin-l-powell/u-s-forces-challenges-ahead.html.*

19. James Burk, "Expertise, Jurisdiction, and Legitimacy of the Military Profession," Lloyd J. Matthews, ed., and Project Director Don M. Snider, *The Future of the Army Profession,* 2nd Ed., Boston, MA: Custom Publishing, 2005, p. 54.

20. JP 1, p. VII-1. JP 1 is the capstone of the joint military doctrine. While it often makes reference to interagency coordination, cooperation, and communication, it does not describe the manner or process in which it will be accomplished. "Military operations must be coordinated, integrated, or deconflicted with the activities of other agencies of the USG, IGOs, NGOs, regional organizations, the operations of foreign forces, and activities of various HN agencies. . . ."

21. Mitchell J. Thompson, "Breaking the Proconsulate: A New Design for National Power," *Parameters,* Winter 2005-06, p. 65.

22. Dana Priest, *The Mission,* New York: W. W. Norton & Company, 2003, p. 74. In Australia, "extensive military-to-military contacts during the 1990s came under review in 2000. According to Australian defense planners, the review found that, in time, engagement activities were being carried out rather promiscuously, often times under questionable rationales, with ill-defined objectives and without identifiable payoffs to Australian interests."

23. *Ibid.,* pp. 61-77.

24. Thomas M. Jordan, Douglas C. Lovelace, and Thomas-Durrell Young, *Shaping the World Through Engagement: Assessing the Department of Defense's Theater Engagement Planning Process,* Carlisle, PA: Strategic Studies Institute, U.S. Army War College, April 2000, p. 2.

25. *Ibid.,* p. iii.

26. Zinni, pp. 135-136. Today, GCCs are much more inclusive of nonmilitary input in the creation of TSCs and may rely on their Joint Interagency Coordination Groups (JIACG), Political Advisor (POLAD), and input from each respective Chief of Mission from each country in the GCC's area of responsibility.

27. Jefferson P. Marquis, Richard E. Darilek, Jasen J. Castillo, Cathryn Quantic Thurston, Anny Wong, Cynthia Huger, Andrea Mejia, Jennifer D. P. Moroney, Brian Nichiporuk, and Brett Steele, *Assessing the Value of U.S. Army International Activities*, Pittsburgh, PA: RAND Arroyo Center, 2006, p. 5. In addition to the NSS, other documents from the DoD include the *National Military Strategy, Quadrennial Defense Review, Strategic Planning Guidance, and the Security Cooperation Guidance.*

28. *Joint Publication (JP) 3-0, Joint Operations,* Washington, DC: U.S. Joint Chiefs of Staff, September 17, 2006, p. V-3.

29. Marquis *et al.,* p. 5. An excellent summary of security cooperation planning, with charts is provided on pages 5-10.

30. Szayna, p. 49. It is important to distinguish Title 22 activities controlled by DoS from the Title 10 programs administered by the Army. The Army insists that it does not simply divide its security cooperation resources among the combatant commands, "but rather maintains a global capability and makes allocations to best support the overall strategy." See *U.S. Army Regulation (AR) 11-31, Army International Security Cooperation Policy,* October 24, 2007, p. 3. In addition, JP 5-0 lumps all of the security cooperation activities, Title 10 and 22, into six categories described on p. I-3.

31. *Joint Publication (JP) 3-07.1, Joint Tactics, Techniques and Procedures for Foreign Internal Defense (FID),* Washington, DC: U.S. Joint Chiefs of Staff, April 30, 2004, p. V-8.

32. U.S. Congress, Senate Foreign Relations Committee Report, "Embassies as Command Posts in the Anti-Terror Campaign," 109th Cong., 2nd Sess., December 15, 2006, available from *www.fas.org/irp/congress/2006_rpt/embassies.html.*

33. *Ibid.,* pp. 7-8.

34. *Ibid.,* p. 9.

35. Richard K. Betts, "A Disciplined Defense: How to Regain Strategic Solvency," *Foreign Affairs,* November/December 2007, p. 74.

36. Kurt Shillinger, "A New U.S. Command Paradigm and the Challenges of Engagement in Africa in the 21st Century," written testimony submitted to the House Committee on Foreign Affairs, Subcommittee on Africa and Global Health in the hearing on "Africa Command," August 2, 2007, available from *foreignaffairs.house.gov/110shi080207.htm.*

37. Betts, p. 74.

38. George W. Bush, National Security Presidential Directive (NSPD)-44, Washington DC: The White House, December 7, 2005.

39. *Department of Defense Directive 3000.05,* p. 2.

40. Thompson, p. 66.

41. James Q. Wilson, *Bureaucracy: What Government Agencies Do and Why They Don't Do It,* New York: Basic Books, Inc., 2000, p. 95, quoted in Michael B. Siegel, "Clarity and Culture in Stability Operations," *Military Review,* November/December 2007, p. 102.

42. Burk, p. 49.

43. Don M. Snider, "The U.S. Army as Profession," in Lloyd J. Matthews, ed., and Project Director, Don M. Snider, *The Future of the Army Profession*, 2nd Ed., Boston, MA: Custom Publishing, 2005, pp. 26-27.

44. John F. Troxell, "Presidential Decision Directive-56: A Glass Half Full," Joseph R. Cerami and Jay W. Boggs, eds., *The Interagency and Counterinsurgency Warfare: Stability, Security, Transition, and Reconstruction Roles*, Carlisle, PA: Strategic Studies Institute, U.S. Army War College, 2007, p. 44.

45. *Ibid.*, p. 26.

46. Shawn Zeller, "Who's in Charge Here?" *Foreign Service Journal*, December 2007, p. 25.

47. Robert M. Gates, "Beyond Guns and Steel: Reviving the Nonmilitary Instruments of American Power," *Military Review*, January-February 2008, p. 8.

48. *Ibid.*

49. *Ibid.*

50. *Ibid.*

51. *Ibid.*

52. Condoleezza Rice, "On Transformational Diplomacy," speech at Georgetown University, Washington, DC, February 12, 2008, available from *www.state.gov/secretary/rm/2008/02/100703.htm.*

53. U.S. Congress, Senate Foreign Relations Committee Report, p. 3.

54. Zeller, p. 25.

55. *Ibid.*

56. *Ibid.*, p. 24.

57. J. Peter Phram, Ph.D., "Africa Command: A Historic Opportunity for Enhanced Engagement— If Done Right," testimony before the U.S. House of Representatives, Committee on Foreign Affairs, Subcommittee on Africa and Global Health, August 2, 2007, available from *foreignaffairs.house.gov/110/pha080207.htm.*

58. Robert W. Komer, *Bureaucracy at War: U.S. Performance in the Vietnam Conflict*, Boulder, CO: Westview Press, 1986, p. 5.

59. Robert B. Oakley and Michael Casey, "The Country Team: Restructuring America's First Line of Engagement," *Joint Force Quarterly*, 4th quarter 2007, p. 146.

60. *Ibid.*, pp. 152-153.

61. *Ibid.*, p. 152.

62. Zeller, p. 20.

63. *Ibid.*, p. 28.

64. *Ibid.*

65. General David Petraeus, quoted in Gerald Loftus, "Speaking Out: Expeditionary Sidekicks? The Military Diplomatic Dynamic," *Foreign Service Journal,* December 2007, pp. 16-17.

66. Loftus, p. 16.

67. JP 5-0, p. I-4. Additional planning guidelines and procedures are described in the *Chairman of the Joint Chiefs of Staff Manual (CJCSM) 3113.01A, Responsibilities for the Management of Security Cooperation,* as well as in *Joint Publication (JP) 3-08, Interagency, Intergovernmental Organization, and Nongovernmental Organization Coordination during Joint Operations,* Washington, DC: U.S. Joint Chiefs of Staff, 17 March 2006 Vol. 1.

68. See JP 3-0, p. V-3, and JP 5-0, p. I-3, for a comparison of Phase Zero (shaping) and security cooperation, respectively.

69. JP 3-0, p. VII-1.

70. *Ibid.*

71. JP 3-0, pp. V-1 - V-2.

72. Albert Zaccor, "Security Cooperation and Non-State Threats: A Call for an Integrated Strategy," The Atlantic Council of the United States, Occasional Paper, August 2005, p. 8, available from *www.acus. org/docs/0508-Security_Cooperation_Nonstate_Threats_ Zaccor_Albert.pdf.*

73. *Ibid.,* p. 7, footnote 38.

74. *Ibid.,* p. 6. Zaccor briefly describes the difference between Security Assistance activities such as Foreign Military Sales (FMS), Foreign Military Financing (FMF), the International Military Training and Education Program (IMET), and other programs governed under the Foreign Assistance Act, with policy direction provided by the DoS; and compares it to Security Cooperation, a much broader term that, in addition to Security Assistance, includes categories of activities to include combined exercises, military-to-military contacts, combined education, and humanitarian assistance.

75. *Ibid.,* pp. 8-10.

76. Jenifer D. P. Moroney *et al., Building Partner Capabilities for Coalition Operations,* Santa Monica, CA: Rand, 2007, p. xi.

77. Jennifer D. P. Moroney, Adam Grissom, and Jefferson P. Marquis, *A Capabilities-Based Strategy for Army Security Cooperation,* Santa Monica, CA: Rand, 2007, p. xiv.

78. Marquis *et al.,* p. 42.

79. *Ibid.,* p. 41.

80. Maroney *et al., "Building Partner Capabilities for Coalition Operations,"* pp. 55-61.

81. *Ibid.,* p. 59.

82. *Ibid.,* pp. 72-73.

83. Zaccor, p. 22.

84. *Ibid.*, p. 24.

85. *Ibid.*, p. 25.

86. The Phase III Report of the U.S. Commission on National Security/21st Century, The "Hart-Rudman Report," Draft Final Report, January 31, 2001, p. 53, available from *www.rense.com/general10/roadmap.htm*.

87. Zaccor, p. 38.

88. *Ibid.*, p. 33.

89. Kurt M. Campbell and Michele A. Flournoy, *To Prevail: An American Strategy for the Campaign Against Terrorism*, Washington., DC: The CSIS Pres, 2001, p. 158, quoted in Zaccor, p. 44.

90. Zaccor, p. 41.

91. Charles A Stevenson, "Underlying Assumptions of the National Security Act of 1947," *Joint Forces Quarterly*, 1st quarter 2008, p. 130.

92. *Ibid.*, p. 131.

93. *Ibid.*

94. Nora Bensahel and Anne M. Moisan, "Repairing the Interagency Process," *Joint Forces Quarterly*, 1st quarter 2007, p. 107.

95. John E. Herbst, "Briefing on Civilian Stabilization Initiative," On-The-Record Briefing, Washington, DC, February 14, 2008, available from *www.state.gov/s/crs/rls/rm/100913.htm*.

96. Bensahel and Moisan, p. 107.

97. *Ibid.*

98. Michele A. Flournoy and Shawn W. Brimley, "Strategic Planning for National Security: A New Project Solarium," *Joint Forces Quarterly*, 2nd quarter 2006, p. 82.

99. *Ibid.*

100. *Ibid.* The project was named "Project Solarium" after the late-afternoon debate President Eisenhower had with John Foster Dulles on May 8, 1953, in the White House solarium. They discussed and argued about the true nature of the Soviet threat and the necessary long-term security strategy to counter it.

101. *Ibid.*, p. 84.

102. *Ibid.*

103. *Ibid.*, pp. 85-86.

104. *Ibid.*, p. 86.

105. Bensahel and Moisan, p. 107. They propose creating a cell of permanent employees (not detailed from other agencies) within the NSC that would focus separately on three areas: strategic planning, crisis management and coalition building, and liaison and strategic communication. For more information on a project intending to replace the National Security Act of 1947, see the Project on National Security Reform

(PSNR) described by Robert B. Polk, "Interagency Reform: An Idea Whose Time Has Come," Joseph R. Cerami and Jay W. Boggs, eds., *The Interagency and Counterinsurgency Warfare: Stability, Security, Transition, and Reconstruction Roles*, Carlisle, PA: Strategic Studies Institute, U.S. Army War College, 2007, p. 321.

106. National Security Presidential Directive (NSPD)-1, *Organization of the National Security Council System*, Washington, DC: The White House, February 13, 2001.

CHAPTER 10

KNOW BEFORE YOU GO:
IMPROVING ARMY OFFICER SOCIO-CULTURAL KNOWLEDGE

Lieutenant Colonel James C. Laughrey
U.S. Army

> On one hand, you have to shoot and kill somebody; On the other hand, you have to feed
> somebody. On the other hand, you have to build an economy, restructure the infrastructure,
> build the political system. And there's some poor Lieutenant Colonel, Colonel, Brigadier
> General down there, stuck in some province with all that saddled onto him, with NGOs
> [nongovernmental organizations] and political wannabes running around, with factions
> and a culture he doesn't understand. These are now [the] culture wars that we're involved
> in. We don't understand that culture.
>
> —General (Ret.) Anthony Zinni[1]

Language capabilities and cultural knowledge have emerged as closely related but separately identified critical capabilities during Operations IRAQI FREEDOM and ENDURING FREEDOM. The United States found itself with significant forces deployed to conduct counterinsurgency and stability operations where the support of the indigenous population and daily contact with that same population combined with the support to indigenous government agencies and security forces were critical to success. Unfortunately, the U.S. Army found itself in this same situation about 40 years ago. In Vietnam, the Army lacked the language skills and the cultural knowledge necessary to interact positively with indigenous populations and allied armed forces. Consequently, it attempted to correct these deficiencies with temporary solutions. To address the current dearth of culture-related capabilities, the U.S. Government, the Department of Defense (DoD), and the Army have belatedly started initiatives to overcome these shortfalls. Some programs are focused on the civil education arena, while others seek to enhance military education and training.

This chapter examines these Army programs to determine if they are sufficient to meet the current and future challenges associated with developing the *socio-cultural* knowledge needed to operate effectively in another country. For the purpose of this chapter, "socio-cultural knowledge" includes, but is not limited to society, social structure, culture, language, power and authority structures, and interests.[2] In conducting this examination, this chapter will first define the character of war that is expected to challenge the United States in an era of persistent conflict. As the character of the war will be more focused on irregular warfare (IW) and stability, essential components of these types of warfare, and support and transition to reconstruction operations (SSTRO), are described.

Since history informs decisionmakers, this paper illustrates several lessons learned from our decades-long experience in Vietnam. Then our experiences in Iraq and Afghanistan, as related to socio-cultural skills, are examined to frame the subsequent discussion of the DoD and Army policies, programs, and initiatives to provide these needed skills.

Since this research identifies deficiencies, it concludes by providing observations and recommendations for pre- and post-commissioning education that improves the language proficiency of the officer corps and provides incentives for officers to improve their educational background in other areas of socio-cultural knowledge.

AN ERA OF CONSTANT CONFLICT

Secretary of Defense Robert Gates was unambiguous when he told senior Army leaders and others that "unconventional wars—[are] the ones most likely to be fought in the years ahead, . . . [that these wars are] . . . fundamentally political in nature, . . . [and] . . . success will be less a matter of imposing one's will and more a function of shaping behavior—of friends, adversaries, and most importantly, the people in between."[3]

General George Casey, the Chief of Staff of the Army, has agreed publicly with the Secretary that we are in "a period of protracted confrontation among state, non-state and individual actors, . . . [and that] . . . we're seeing the precursors of that now in Iraq and Afghanistan."[4] A key strategic issue is to understand the nature and character of these wars in order to meet their diverse challenges.

The character of war is what differentiates types of war from one another. For example, conventional conflict, counterinsurgency, and strategic nuclear war are three distinctly different types of war. Furthermore, individual wars within a type can be different from each other as illustrated by the insurgencies in Malaya, Algeria, Vietnam, Iraq, Afghanistan, and Northern Ireland. The character of war informs us as to the specific causes of the conflict, how the war is prosecuted, and the objectives of the belligerents. It is the character of war that determines the requirement for socio-cultural knowledge.

Multiple guest speakers at the U.S. Army War College during the 2007-08 academic year commented that "the nature of war has changed"[5] or "the nature of war changed on 9/11."[6] However, noted strategic thinker Colin S. Gray is correct when he cites and interprets recognized theorist Clausewitz, noting that "the use of warfare to pursue political goals . . . is eternal in nature yet ever-changing in character . . . war is violence threatened or waged for political purpose."[7] This distinction is more than academic. It provides the general objective and *raison d'être*, if not the precise *casus belli* of a war. Characterizing the types of conflicts that the United States is likely to face helps us to develop capabilities and concepts to achieve our strategic and operational objectives.

Secretary Gates and General Casey, as cited above, have spoken of unconventional war with Iraq and Afghanistan as the precursors of the type of conflicts that we are likely to find ourselves facing in the future. Academics, former senior military officers from other countries, and civilian defense analysts agree and have provided additional detail and analysis. Rupert Smith, a retired British General that commanded forces in Ireland, United Nations (UN) forces in Bosnia, and was the Deputy Commander of the North Atlantic Treaty Organization (NATO) forces during Operation ALLIED FORCE believes that the "new . . . paradigm of war [is] war amongst the people . . . in which the people . . . all the people . . . are the targets, objectives to be won, as much as an opposing force."[8] Civilian analyst Colin Gray noted that "irregular warfare may be the dominant form of belligerency for some years to come," while Ralph Peters agrees that we will fight unconventional opponents in failed or failing states.[9]

132

The message is clear as senior Defense officials, senior Army leaders, and leading defense analysts all believe that counterinsurgency and stability operations like those in Iraq, Afghanistan, Somalia, Bosnia, and Kosovo are not atypical conflicts that the Army or the nation can ignore once they are over as occurred following the Vietnam war. We find ourselves most likely to engage in conflicts that demand irregular warfare (IW); major combat operations (MCO); and stability, support, and transition to reconstruction (SSTRO) operations as illustrated in Figure 1. SSTROs and counterinsurgency (COIN), a main subset of irregular warfare, are likely to be the most commonly encountered mission sets.

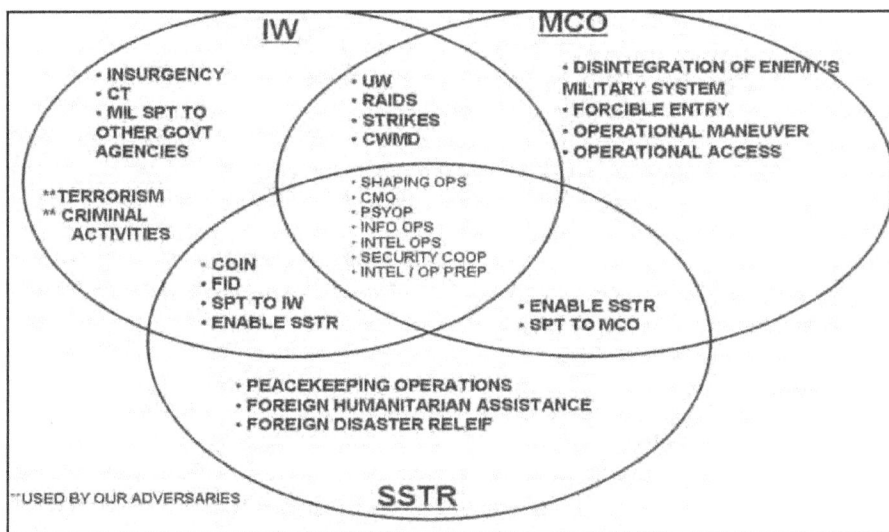

Figure 1. Irregular Warfare, Major Combat Operations, and Stability, Support, and Transition to Reconstruction Operations Interrelationship.[10]

THE CHARACTER OF IRREGULAR WARFARE AND STABILITY OPERATIONS

The character of IW, particularly the COIN subset, and stability operations is different than the character of conventional conflict associated with MCO. Conventional conflicts associated with MCO typically involve two warring nation states, and combat is characterized by kinetic force-on-force operations until one side surrenders or can no longer continue to fight. The focus of MCO is on the opposing government and the opposing military. The objective of these conventional operations and conflicts can range from limited tactical operations to regime change.

Insurgencies are civil wars, and they occur because a government has sufficiently alienated a portion of the populace to the extent where that faction has taken up arms against the government. SSTROs occur because an event caused the collapse of legitimate governance and essential services. The focus of COIN and stability operations shifts from the opposing government and military forces to the population and the government, as illustrated in Figure 2, and typically we are working with a host-nation government.

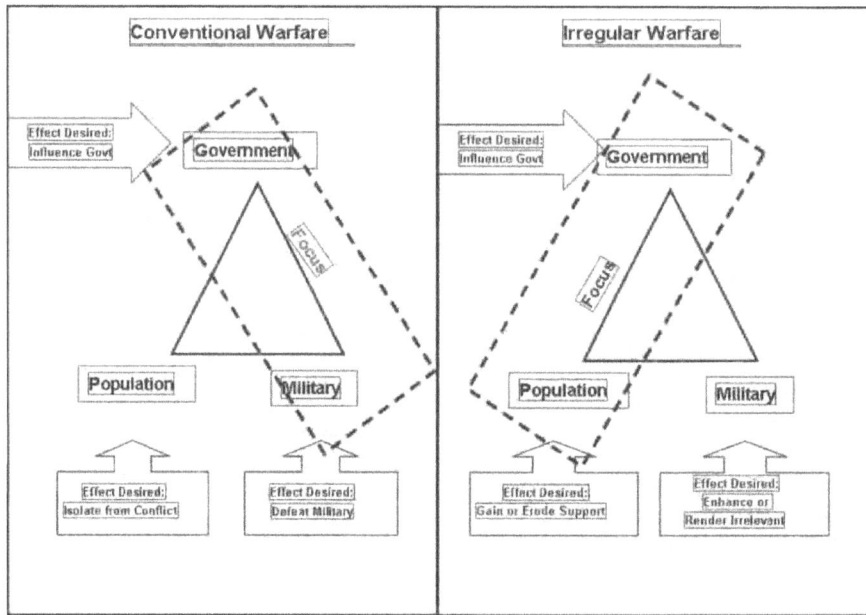

Figure 2. Focus of Operations: Conventional versus Irregular.[11]

Our strategic objective in COIN and SSTRO is to create or strengthen legitimate government institutions that meet the economic and social needs of the populace. Our intermediate objective, as retired General Rupert Smith observes, is to:

> . . . establish a condition in which the political objective can be achieved by other [nonmilitary] means and in other [nonkinetic] ways. We seek to create a conceptual space for diplomacy, economic incentives, political pressure and other measures to create a desired political outcome of stability, and if possible democracy.[12]

Achieving these conditions and objectives means that the majority of the populace must consent to be governed, and that armed insurrection becomes socially unacceptable.

The population in a nation beset by insurgency generally falls into three categories. There is a portion of the population that supports the government, a portion that supports the insurgency, and a portion that is unallied. The population generally is the center of gravity for both the insurgents and the COIN force, with the unallied portion of the populace a critical vulnerability and capability for both sides. For the COIN or SSTRO force to win over the populace, it must "be able to offer the populations of countries effected by war the hope that life will be better for them and their children because of our presence, not in spite of it."[13]

Figure 3 shows lines of activity and strategic objectives for COIN and SSTRO that are designed to win over the populace and establish a legitimate government capable of providing for the population's social and economic needs. Security and civil-military operations that place our troops in a close and regular relationship, if not a partnership, with the populace are necessary to support each line of operation. Obviously, the institutions and services provided must achieve political "buy-in" and acceptance from the population, or they will not receive popular support. This means that junior leaders must have socio-cultural knowledge, not just awareness. COIN expert David Kilcullen was blunt when he wrote in an article targeting company commanders, "neglect this knowledge, and it will kill you."[14]

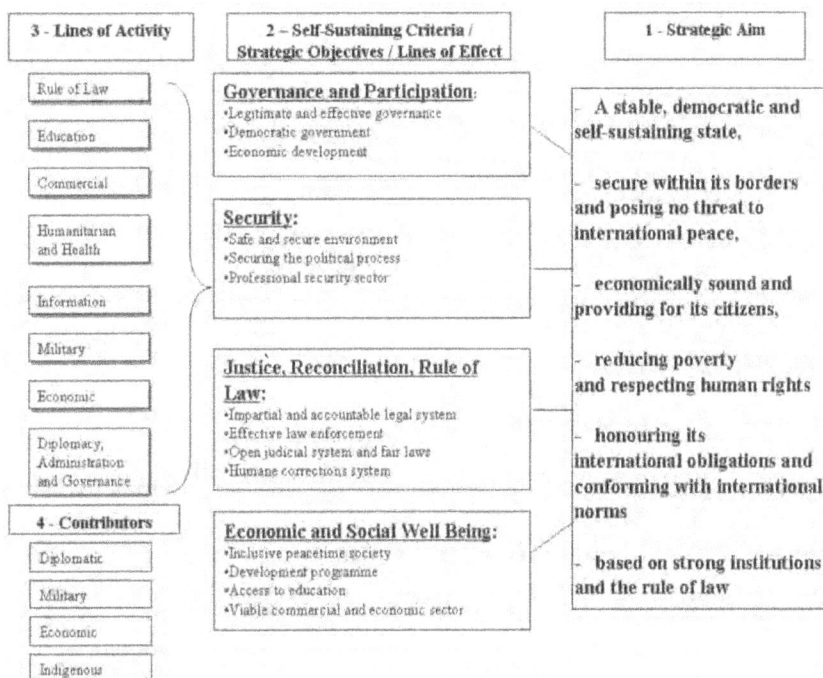

Figure 3. Lines of Activity to Strategic Aim Linkage.[15]

Theory and doctrine tell us that the focus of COIN and SSTRO is on the population and the host-nation government. The campaign in both cases is designed to gain the consent of the population for the establishment of a capable government, and to remove their support for the insurgents in the case of COIN. To do this, U.S. and allied forces must establish relationships with the population that range from the acquiescence of the populace to the presence of our forces, to outright partnership. Socio-cultural knowledge is critical to establishing those relationships according to accepted theory.

The United States has engaged in COIN operations before and is currently engaged in two major COIN operations. Two key questions that this chapter will now answer are: (1) Has the historical record borne out the necessity for socio-cultural skills? (2) How has the Army fared in ensuring that deploying Soldiers had the socio-cultural knowledge to effectively operate? One historical case study of Vietnam and two modern ongoing case studies of Iraq and Afghanistan provide insights to help answer these questions. These case studies are used because they required the large-scale use of U.S. conventional units and personnel as COIN forces in advisory roles and in the civil operations and reconstruction role. The scope of missions in these countries exceeded, or exceeds, the capacity of Special Forces units specifically organized and trained for the COIN and SSTRO mission set, and this was not the case in other late 20th century and early 21st century operations.

THE ARMY AND SOCIO-CULTURAL KNOWLEDGE IN VIETNAM

The United States began its active involvement with COIN operations in the Republic of Vietnam (RVN) by sending advisors to the country in 1955. The advisory effort peaked in 1970, with 14,332 personnel in the country. Beginning in 1965, U.S. combat units deployed to the country, with troop strength peaking at 550,000 in 1968-69. U.S. Soldiers found themselves on a battlefield that placed them among the South Vietnamese people on a daily basis—a culture completely different from their own in terms of religion, social mores, language, and environment. Advisors were faced with the additional task of trying to train and influence Vietnamese counterparts. In order to prepare combat troops and advisors for their mission, the Army developed a variety of training courses during the course of the conflict.[16]

Officer Education and Training.

From 1962-65, generic COIN doctrine, theory, and techniques were taught in classes at West Point and Reserve Officers' Training Corps (ROTC) departments. These classes emphasized counterguerilla operations, the requirement to win the support of the populace, and the need to improve conditions within the assisted country. Classes continued at branch level courses, the U.S. Army Command and General Staff College, and at the U.S. Army War College. Vietnam-specific education and training was limited to tactical scenarios in kinetic operations, although a guest lecture component of training courses utilizing Vietnam veterans might have included some socio-cultural topics.[17]

In 1966, psychological operations (PSYOP) was added as a mandatory topic for Cadets and within branch schools. The objective of the courses was to educate officers to evaluate all of their actions in a COIN campaign "with an eye toward its possible psychological and political effects," and former Chief of Staff of the Army General Harold K. Johnson provided additional guidance in 1967 with the intent that all military personnel would have a greater understanding of the elements of the socio-cultural aspects of counterinsurgency.[18] The overall impact was that COIN topics received an even greater emphasis, and increased course time devoted to generic socio-cultural topics in the officer education system from 1966-72. After 1972, the "no more Vietnams" mindset, combined with the focus on conventional operations in Europe, resulted in a steady reduction of COIN and SSTRO topics in the Officer Education System.[19]

Conventional troops, including officers, received training on the general principles of COIN operations such as patrolling and ambushes, and troops arriving in Vietnam received a lecture emphasizing humane and legal conduct towards the populace. Vietnam-bound infantrymen received a 16-hour orientation before leaving the United States.[20] In spite of this training, "racism, ethnocentrism, haughtiness, and callousness" were exhibited by U.S. Soldiers who "had difficulty relating to the Vietnamese, whose non-western culture, alien language, and comparatively primitive standard of living made them appear inferior in the minds of some Soldiers."[21] This type of conduct exhibited by even a relatively limited number of Soldiers, with the My Lai Massacre the most extreme example, can easily have a strategic impact on a COIN campaign in terms of domestic and international opinion, as well as sowing mistrust among the populace in the area of operations.

Advisor Education and Training.

Personnel assigned to advisory duty in Vietnam received additional specialized training beyond that given to officers and enlisted men in U.S. combat units. The U.S. advisory effort in the RVN started in 1955 with just 342 personnel and culminated with over 14,000 advisors deployed in 1970. The U.S. advisor role was originally limited to support for the Army of the RVN (ARVN) units as they trained and conducted operations. These advisors found themselves with "three roles: a US Army officer following orders and supervising US subordinates, a member of an [ARVN] unit sharing its experiences and bonding with his [ARVN] counterpart, and a mediator interpreting and communicating between his [ARVN] counterpart and US superiors."[22] Thousands of officers found themselves fulfilling these three functions. Socio-cultural knowledge would have assisted in the bonding process and in translating perspectives and actions between U.S. and ARVN units and personnel. As we shall see later, the Army was not particularly successful in equipping advisors to meet these challenges.

As the conflict and U.S. involvement evolved, advisory teams were added at the Province and District level, which involved approximately 88 locations. The number of personnel assigned to these teams expanded with the creation of the Civil-Operations and Revolutionary Development System (CORDS) and the mission of providing economic, governance, and security assistance at the local level.[23] CORDS was charged with the pacification of the populace by improving governance, security, and the economy at the local level. This meant that officers assigned to CORDS advisory positions found themselves involved with social, political, and economic issues at the lowest levels of Vietnamese society, which required an even greater degree of socio-cultural knowledge than needed by the advisors in ARVN units. Training and education underwent substantial changes to prepare advisors to meet these increased requirements.

The initial advisor course, attended by officers destined for assignment with ARVN units, was 4 weeks long. After a small number of iterations, the course was expanded to 6 weeks, which included just 46 hours of Vietnamese language training and 25 hours of area studies.[24] Language training eventually constituted 50 percent of the course content and included native speakers as the instructors. By contrast, a 1970 U.S. Marine Corps (USMC) advisor course included 6 weeks of immersion language training. Personnel designated for advisory assignments at the battalion, province, and district level eventually received 8-12 weeks of language training at the Defense Language Institute. [25]

In the later stages of the war, the senior advisers assigned to the province and district levels as part of CORDS attended a total of 48 weeks of training prior to deployment. These advisors received over 195 hours of area studies and country orientations/ updates, roughly equivalent to four or five three-credit courses at a university; and 1,139 hours of language training, roughly equivalent to 16 five-credit language courses. [26] The heavy investment made in language training and the most extensive area studies training offered to U.S. personnel belies the complexity and challenge of meaningful socio-cultural education. The Army found, despite early attempts to provide socio-cultural education on the cheap in terms of time, that there was no quick fix for providing advisors with the required education that would allow them to accomplish their missions.

Despite the increases in educational content, the advisors and their Vietnamese counterparts provided feedback that indicated that the advisors still lacked the necessary socio-cultural knowledge. Advisors noted that language was the most important capability that they lacked since "Interpreters, although useful, have many drawbacks . . . they introduce inevitable inaccuracies into conversations [and] discourage frank exchange of views . . . permitted by private talk between a counterpart and his advisor."[27] One immediate effect described by an advisor was that the advisors became "victims of the language barrier . . . not fully aware of what was going on around them . . . This . . . was a crippling weakness, since few interpreters could or would render faithfully what they heard."[28] Another advisor summarized the impact of the lack of socio-cultural knowledge, thus:

> We did not understand what was going on in Vietnam. We were in a foreign land among people of a different culture and mindset. . . . The information sent across the cultural divide was not the information received. There was a disconnect. One thing was said and another thing was heard. One thing was meant and another thing was understood. . . . Meaning, intent, and truth were lost in translation.[29]

We can conclude that the Army tried to conduct the advisory mission in Vietnam on the cheap in terms of the time devoted to educating the advisors. When the short training courses were identified as inadequate, the Army did adapt and provide increased time for educating advisors, focusing on the key area of language and other socio-cultural knowledge topics. What the Army determined, though, was that a dedicated corps of officers devoted to the nation-building skill set was needed.

Vietnam: Genesis of the Foreign Area Officer Program.

In 1966 the Army created a board, led by Lieutenant General Ralph E. Haines, Jr., tasked with evaluating officer education. The board recommended the expansion of the Foreign Area Specialist Program, an intelligence focused specialty, and the merger of Civil Affairs and Psychological Operations into a specialty designated the Military Assistance Officer Program (MAOP). The vision for the MAOP program was to create a cadre of

6,000 officers to fill G-5, S-5, advisor, and other positions requiring nation-building and politico-military expertise.[30]

The MAOP officers were to receive "language training and civilian graduate schooling in anthropology, economics, foreign affairs, government, international relations, political science, psychology, public administration, or sociology."[31] However, the program was cut in the post-war period when the Army refocused itself on conventional operations. The MAOP program and the Foreign Area Specialist Program were merged to form the Foreign Area Officer (FAO) Program, which is still with us today. In contrast to the 6,000 MAOP officers envisioned by the Haines Board, there are only 1,083 FAOs in the Army as of 2006 and 1,414 FAOs in all of the services.[32]

Final Thoughts on Vietnam and Socio-Cultural Awareness.

The Army devoted significant resources and time to education and training on the broad principles of COIN. It was clearly aware of the importance of the criticality of the nonmilitary lines of operations required for victory in a COIN, and in the case of the officer corps, it implemented pre- and post-commissioning education and training programs. Despite this effort, the United States generally, and the Army specifically, had a difficult time winning over the Vietnamese populace. There are numerous reasons for this failure that go well beyond the scope of this chapter—tour lengths, the quality of the draftee Army, and the constant movement of units to different areas are just three factors that arguably contributed to U.S. failure.

In the area of socio-cultural education and training, the Army's efforts were largely unsuccessful. Conventional units received minimal training, and the troops were unable to bridge the socio-cultural divide to win over the Vietnamese people. Advisors to ARVN units fared somewhat better since they received increased levels of language and cultural education and were given the opportunity to establish a rapport with a limited group of South Vietnamese. The CORDS Program had the greatest success. Its personnel, particularly the senior advisors, received up to a year of education in socio-cultural knowledge areas, worked in one area of the country, and were in a position to establish a rapport with Vietnamese counterparts.

There are five broad conclusions that emerge from the Vietnam socio-cultural training and education effort. First, counterinsurgency education and training needs to include COIN theory, socio-cultural education and training specific to the area of operations, and training in tactics, techniques, and procedures (TTPs). Second, language training is the most important knowledge area since fluency is key to situational awareness and, in the case of advisors, allows for accurate private conversations with counterparts. Third, socio-cultural knowledge areas are only slightly less important than language as societal thought processes, norms, and historical factors shape the worldview of allies and the target population. Socio-cultural knowledge provides the required background for mutual understanding, and for the development of programs that do not alienate the indigenous population. Fourth, effective socio-cultural education requires a significant investment in resources and there is no quick fix or shake-and-bake solution. Finally, finding the time and resources to provide comprehensive socio-cultural education, and education regarding the nonmilitary components of a COIN campaign, was virtually impossible outside the most extensive advisor courses.

When the Army finished its involvement in Vietnam, it shifted its focus back toward conventional operations designed to defend NATO against the threat from the Warsaw Pact. The COIN and nation-building emphasis of the 1960s fell largely by the wayside and became the domain of the Special Operations Forces (including Civil Affairs and PSYOP). By the time U.S. forces entered Afghanistan and Iraq the Army did not "have any doctrine, nor was it educated and trained, to deal with an insurgency. . . . After the Vietnam War, we purged ourselves of everything to do with irregular warfare or insurgency because it had to do with how we lost that war."[33]

AFGHANISTAN AND IRAQ

How the United States, and the Army in particular, entered Afghanistan in October 2001, and Iraq in March 2003, is well-documented. In both countries, the Army found itself engaged in long-term COIN and nation-building operations on a scale not seen since Vietnam and for which it was unprepared, as noted above. There is no metric that this author has found that measures the level of cultural awareness. There are several indicators that, with caution, are usable. These indicators, which are based on vignettes from both countries as well as comments of Iraqis and American soldiers, point to a shortfall in socio-cultural skills.

Indicators.

The anecdotal evidence from Afghanistan and Iraq provide compelling testimony to the Army's lack of socio-cultural preparedness. In Afghanistan, the Special Forces units, which belonged to the Special Forces Group tasked with linguistic and cultural specialization in the U.S. Central Command (CENTCOM) Area of Responsibility (AOR), were reduced to showing tribal and village elders a narrated digital video disc (DVD) on a laptop computer due to a lack of language capacity. The DVD explained why the U.S. units were in Afghanistan. All fine and well, but how were the Soldiers supposed to follow-up the DVD so as to establish a rapport and gain the support of the local Afghan leaders? The situation did not improve by 2006, when only six of the more than 55,000 officers in the U.S. Army had a documented ability to speak Pashto, the dominate language of the area along the Pakistani border and southern Afghanistan, where the security situation is the least stable.[34]

In Iraq our strategic assessment of culture was flawed on two counts. First, we interpreted membership in the Ba'ath Party as being pro-Saddam instead of realizing that some individuals were party members for employment purposes. We also interpreted anti-Saddam attitudes as pro-American, and we misjudged the resentment that the long-term presence of foreign forces in the country would create.[35] At the operational level, U.S. Commanders engaged local tribal sheikhs in the aftermath of the fall of Baghdad in the belief that they could control the insurgency and other types of violence without understanding tribal structures or the credibility of the sheikhs.[36] These missteps clearly indicate a lack of knowledge in several of the areas that constitute socio-cultural knowledge.

Ample anecdotal evidence is available regarding a lack of socio-cultural knowledge at the tactical level in Iraq. A lack of language capability, independent of any other socio-cultural knowledge, negatively impacted the ability of U.S. forces to recognize individuals wanted for detention. For example, immediately after the fall of Baghdad, U.S. units received lists of license plate numbers for key leaders of the Saddam regime that were still at large. The concept was for U.S. vehicle checkpoints to compare license plates with the list. Unfortunately, the list was printed using English letters and Arabic numbers while Iraqi license plates use Arabic letters and numbers.

Two National Public Radio reports, one in 2007 and the other in February 2008, highlighted continuing language issues. A lack of language capability among U.S. units resulted in a dependence on indigenous translators and negatively impacted the ability of our troops to determine the reliability of Iraqi security forces, identify problems affecting the local population, or to win the trust of the populace. In the 2007 report, U.S. troops operating with Iraqi forces in Baghdad conducted a raid on a suspected Shi'a militia weapons cache site. Nothing was found. The Iraqi translator later translated what one Iraqi soldier said to his comrades in the presence of the U.S. Soldiers, none of whom spoke Arabic. The Iraqi soldier told his comrades that the weapons the search was intended to find were, in fact, at the house of his mullah a short distance away.

In the 2008 story, U.S. forces were conducting a patrol in a Sunni Arab neighborhood of Mosul, a city where the Sunni Arab and Kurdish tensions are high, with the Arabs viewed as outsiders and whom the Kurds wished to push out of the city. The U.S. platoon leader asked a resident, through his Iraqi Army interpreter (a Kurd), what problems, if any, the resident was having. The translated response was that there was trouble with insurgents in the area. The translator with the NPR team later told the U.S. news personnel that the resident had actually complained about searches, theft, and harassment by Iraqi Army units composed of Kurdish personnel. The U.S. Army unit left ignorant of the real complaint and, in fact, allied with the unit that the residents view as oppressors and thieves.

Statements by both American and Iraqi personnel also point to deficiencies in the other areas of socio-cultural knowledge and their negative impact on operations. Multiple junior officers indicated that they were not prepared to overcome the cultural issues, which were described by one officer as "overwhelming."[37] Iraqi officers agree with the assessment of the junior officers.

This author met with Iraqi officers on multiple occasions from 2003-06 to include a meeting in 2006 with Iraqi officers ranging in rank from major to colonel who came from all of the major ethnic and sectarian groups in the country. When asked if U.S. troops were any better at relating to the Iraqi populace in 2006 versus 2003, the answer was a resounding "no" from all Iraqis. As the discussion went on, they acknowledged that there were incremental improvements, but cited racial epithets that the Iraqi populace now understands, a lack of language capability, and multiple examples of Arab and Islamic custom that still caused problems with the populace. The Iraqi officers also pointed out that the assignment of advisors junior in rank created real discipline issues within Iraqi units. Additionally, a lack of socio-cultural skills and linguist support crippled the initial advisor effort.

The initial U.S. advisor teams fielded in 2003-04, were largely pulled from units already deployed in Iraq. A Center for Army Lessons Learned report found that there was no standardized training for advisors. These advisors had no language capability and no specialized socio-cultural education to prepare them to work with Iraqi units. Advisors complained of support from native linguists who were not conversant in English or a lack of any interpreter support at all.[38] The Army also established a training base for advisors at Fort Riley, KS, in mid-2006 with a program of instruction that is reminiscent of its Vietnam predecessors. The 8-week long course consists of 24 hours of culture immersion training, 10 hours of simulated meetings with indigenous officials, and 42 hours of language training (30 hours of classroom instruction and 12 hours of language lab). Note that these class hours almost exactly mirror the 25 cultural and 46 language training hours given in the 6-week long Vietnam Advisors Course, which provided inadequate socio-cultural knowledge and skills for bridging the socio-cultural gap.[39]

Successes.

This is not to say that the entire picture is bleak, and that there are not significant examples of socio-cultural knowledge among leaders and Soldiers. General David Petraeus during each of his three tours in Iraq, Lieutenant General Peter Chiarelli, and Colonel H. R. McMaster all conducted operations based on socio-cultural knowledge, and their units enjoyed significantly greater success than those units that did not bridge the cultural gap.[40]

In Tal Afar, the 3d Armored Cavalry Regiment under the command of Colonel McMaster underwent a relatively thorough socio-cultural awareness training and education program prior to deployment. Colonel McMaster produced a 7-page reading list on COIN, Islam, Arab customs, and Iraqi history and politics. The officers of the Regiment held discussion groups on the readings, and any trooper could expect Colonel McMaster to ask pointed questions. The regiment also sent two troopers per platoon to basic Arabic language courses at a local college for 5 weeks prior to deployment. This gave some platoons one Soldier out of every eight that possessed a basic knowledge of Arabic, which Middle East Foreign Area Officer Mike Eisenstadt noted "pays huge dividends, for it demonstrates the kind of respect for the local population and their traditions that helps establish rapport and build relationships."[41]

This training and education enabled the regiment to establish a rapport with the local populace, who in turn provided intelligence. One cavalryman related the story of how residents in one neighborhood insisted on fixing a Bradley Fighting Vehicle that had thrown a track, providing chai (tea) for the Soldiers while the residents did all of the work.[42] Such was the rapport with the local Iraqis that the mayor of the city appealed directly to General Casey (the MNF-I commander at the time), Secretary of Defense Donald Rumsfeld, and President George Bush to have the unit remain beyond its scheduled return to the United States. McMaster's local training and education effort had produced a unit that could successfully wage a COIN campaign in a very alien cultural environment. His was not the only success, but it stands out as one of the best publicized.

It is apparent that U.S. forces have enjoyed local successes, failures, and many challenges in the socio-cultural arena. Success in the early years of both conflicts appears to have depended heavily on unit leaders and less on the training and education provided by the institutional Army. The next key issue that deserves examination is to determine what the Army and the DoD have done to educate and train forces for the current and future operating environment, and what impact this training has had.

CURRENT POLICIES, PROGRAMS, AND CAPABILITIES

Awareness of our shortfall in socio-cultural knowledge started soon after the September 11, 2001 (9/11) attacks. The rediscovery of COIN theory and doctrine as the long-term nature of the U.S. commitments in both Iraq and Afghanistan became apparent and brought the socio-cultural knowledge topic to the forefront of capabilities discussions in concert with other topics. Between 2004 and the end of 2006, *Military Review* published 19 articles on COIN and SSTRO related topics, a trend that was matched in *Parameters*. Socio-cultural knowledge, referred to by some authors as cultural awareness, cultural savvy, and cultural understanding, along with language skills, were commonly mentioned as required knowledge areas in these professional journal articles.

More official studies echoed the opinions presented in the professional journals. *The Defense Science Board 2004 Summer Study on Transition To and From Hostilities* found that the DoD lacked adequate capacity for language and knowledge of other cultures. *The Defense Language Transformation Roadmap* notes that, "Post 9/11 military operations reinforce the reality that the Department of Defense needs a significantly improved organic capability in languages . . . and regional area skills."[43] Army officer language qualifications and degree backgrounds supported this assessment.

As of October 2006, 5 years after the invasion of Afghanistan, the U.S. Army had just six officers, four in Special Forces, with an official Pashto language rating. Table 1 displays the number of officers that had ratings in a selection of languages that might serve well in the crisis spots of the post-Cold War and post-Colonial world. Language capacity for the Arab world is particularly limited to just 910, or just 1.6 percent of the Army officer corps at the time the data was compiled.[44]

Language	Total
Egyptian Arabic	80
Standard Arabic	693
Mandarin Chinese	230
French	1358
Hindi	36
Kurdish	1
Pashtu	6
Farsi	99
Russian	861
Spanish	3370
Urdu	31
Total	6765

Table 1. Army Officer Selected Language Capacity.

As Table 2 shows, officers with degrees directly relevant to socio-cultural knowledge or that might have a socio-cultural knowledge application (e.g., general history, political science, public policy, and administration) were held by 16.5 percent of the officer corps. Eliminating degrees in economics, history, political science, and public policy and administration reduces the number of relevant degree holders to just 2.6 percent of the officer population. Area or regional studies degree holders comprise just 1.28 percent of Army officers.[45] These numbers are almost certain to climb in the coming years as the DoD and the Army respond to the recognized shortfall in socio-cultural knowledge as major DoD policies, and the supporting service programs, take effect.

	BA	MA	PhD	Total
African Studies	0	26	0	26
Anthropology	0	0	0	0
Arabic and Arab Studies	0	20	0	20
Area Studies	76	36	0	112
Asian Studies	20	160	0	180
Economics	527	33	1	560+
History	3438	274	46	3758
International Studies	22	16	3	41
International Relations	682	362	13	1057
Latin American Studies	5	142	0	147
Middle East Studies	6	57	0	63
Political Science	3103	139	19	3261
Public Policy and Public Admin	0	47	2	49
Russian and Soviet Area Studies	11	148	0	159
Sociology	0	0	0	0
Strategic Intelligence	N/A	233	N/A	233
			Total	9107
			Area or regional studies	707

Table 2. Army Officer Degrees Relevant to Socio-Cultural Knowledge.

National and DoD Socio-Cultural Policy Initiatives.

Two federal programs open to the civil populace are designed to increase the number of citizens with socio-cultural knowledge. The National Security Education Program provides opportunities for undergraduate students to study abroad in countries other than those in Western Europe. Students that accept the grants or fellowships must then serve in the federal government, preferably in a national security position. Another component of this program provides assistance to citizens with fluency in a foreign language to learn English. A third component seeks to create a civilian reserve language corps by funding college education and volunteers who will serve the nation in times of crisis.[46]

The purpose of the National Security Language Initiative is to increase K-16 language education in strategic languages such as Mandarin Chinese and Standard Arabic. Funds are provided to public school systems and universities to increase and improve their language education capacity. The stated goal of the program is to educate "2,000 advanced speakers of Arabic, Chinese, Russian, Persian, Hindi, and Central Asian languages by 2009."[47]

The DoD has produced separate instructions for the management of FAOs and the management of DoD language and regional proficiency capabilities. An annual FAO program assessment and a Defense Language Roadmap are supporting documents. The FAO policy directed the agencies, services, and combatant commands to identify their FAO requirements in a relatively unconstrained manner. The instruction also directed the services to ensure that FAOs have a career path that includes general officer or flag rank opportunities.[48] In response to this instruction, the Services will increase the number of FAOs from 1,164 in 2005 to 2,159 by 2012, with the Army having the greatest increase from 739 in 2005 to 1,021 by 2012.[49]

The DoD language management instruction and its roadmap details the departmental oversight of language and regional proficiencies; establishes goals for improving the number of active, reserve, and civilian personnel that can speak a foreign language; and tracks the careers of language specialists and FAOs. Some of the tasks detailed include the requirement for junior officers to have language training, improve study abroad opportunities, and incorporate regional studies topics into "professional military education and predeployment training."[50] The instruction also details regional proficiency levels in order to standardize the assessment of an "individuals awareness and understanding of the historical, political, cultural (including linguistic and religious), sociological (including demographic), economic, and geographic factors of a foreign country."[51]

Socio-Cultural Education and Training for Army Officers.

In response to the demands of the current and future operating environment, the requirements of the DoD instructions regarding language, regional proficiency, and FAO management, the Army instituted changes in education at the U.S. Army Military Academy at West Point, NY, and in ROTC programs. West Point Cadets are required to take two semesters of a foreign language, and starting with the class of 2009, the nontechnical majors must take four semesters of a foreign language. The Academy also increased the number of Cadets that are participating in Foreign Academic Individual Advanced Development Program with its semester abroad programs and shorter 7-10 day programs. In academic year 2007-08, approximately 140 Cadets participated in semester abroad programs, while a further 390 attended the shorter overseas programs.[52]

ROTC Cadets are encouraged to take language courses when it is feasible, in the words of one defense official speaking on a nonattribution basis. Additionally, Cadets in their senior year receive instruction on cultural awareness from their ROTC instructors, and as part of the National Security Education Program, DoD provided $24 million to four universities to provide enhanced language education and overseas studies opportunities.[53] Finally, ROTC Cadets can compete for Olmstead Scholarships, which fund study opportunities, or overseas opportunities offered through their universities.

Socio-cultural education for commissioned officers has changed little. The socio-cultural education requirements of the Infantry Officer Basic Course are an excellent example. Socio-cultural knowledge training consists of self-taught modules on the country specific culture for either Iraq or Afghanistan. The Iraq requirement consists of just 89 pages of material on Iraqi culture, history, customs, and geography. A foreign language requirement utilizing the self-paced Rosetta Stone software takes approximately 12 hours to complete. Online testing is the method for tracking student completion of these course requirements. Classroom time with a live instructor consists of just 1 hour on cultural awareness, although more than an additional 39 hours are dedicated to Stability Operations and course field training is COIN focused.[54] While the author was unable to find any socio-cultural training requirements for the Captain's Career Course, the TRADOC Cultural Center at Fort Huachuca, AZ, has prepared training support packages for these courses.

Officers attending Intermediate Level Education receive 201 hours of COIN related education, of which just 6 hours are on general socio-cultural topics. Students are also required to take a regional studies course and can pick from four electives that are focused on the Middle East, Iraq, Afghanistan, China, or Korea. Students with orders sending them to Iraq or Afghanistan receive 24 hours of classroom language instruction and are required to complete an additional 32 hours of computer-based education using the Rosetta Stone software. As Figure 4 shows, the Rosetta Stone Software does not bring the student anywhere near achieving a minimal official language rating.[55]

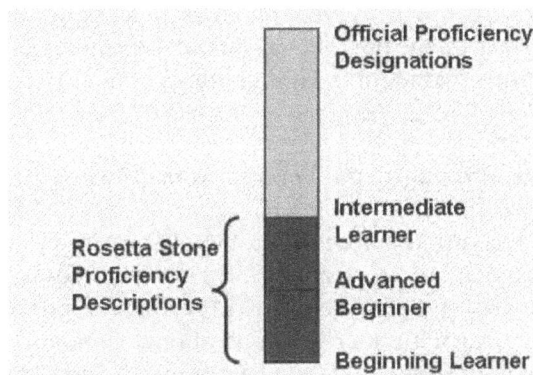

Source: U.S. Army Command and General Staff College.
Figure 4. Language Proficiency Upon Completion of Rosetta Stone Training.

Senior Service College (SSC) students are required to take a regional studies elective course that consists of 30 hours of class time in the case of the U.S. Army War College. Other blocks of instruction in the curriculum provide single class periods covering COIN and stability operations theory, and some practical discussion of the strategic and operational level factors for COIN and SSTRO. Guest speakers, depending on the topic, contribute to the socio-cultural portion of SSC education. There is no language education requirement, but language classes and the Rosetta Stone software are available.

The Army has clearly tried to adapt precommissioning education and professional military education to provide officers with some socio-cultural knowledge, with the focus obviously upon operations in Iraq and Afghanistan. While some knowledge is better than no knowledge, the Army should be realistic about the level of regional expertise or language fluency that officers will achieve. The regional studies hours are, at best, comparable with the regional studies education provided in the 6-week Vietnam advisors course. Officers today receive fewer hours of language training than the Vietnam era advisors, and a large percentage of today's training is not with an interactive human instructor.

Just as the Vietnam advisors found themselves inadequately trained to bridge the language and cultural barriers, our officers today are almost certain to find themselves in the same situation. Our training and education system finds itself in the same situation that instructors noted in the early stages of the Vietnam War as they lamented the lack of time and other resources needed to properly train their students as illustrated by the following comment:

> We cannot give a complete course in geography, political science, applied psychology, comparative religions, ethnology, aesthetics, economics, and the tactics and techniques of counter guerrilla operations—it just cannot be done. Yet knowledge in all of these areas is vital to success in counterinsurgency operations. . . . [56]

At best, today's socio-cultural knowledge education for officers can provide them with survival level capabilities that will prevent them from making egregious errors and demonstrate an effort to learn on the part of U.S. military personnel. With this examination completed, five observations that identify shortcomings in the DoD and Army programs are now identified.

Observations on Policies, Programs, and Foreign Area Officers.

This chapter's first observation is that the National Security Education Program, the National Security Language Initiative, and the DoD instruction for language and regional proficiency management are too language-centric. The clear emphasis of these programs is on increasing language capacity, a critical operational capability. Brigadier General Michael Vane and Lieutenant Colonel Daniel Fagundes observed that "a Soldier might speak a language, but unless he has solid political, military, and strategic knowledge, he is useless as an adviser . . . the reverse is not necessarily true, however."[57] Nonlanguage education in socio-cultural topics can produce officers that can plan and lead effective operations in a foreign culture.

Second, the goal of creating a language corps of 2,000 civilian linguists by 2009, particularly linguists that will deploy when and where needed seems optimistic. Compare this goal to the fact that, as noted earlier, the Army officer corps had just six Pashto speakers by 2006, 5 years after invading Afghanistan. Language courses are typically long, often taking a year or more to achieve minimal fluency. Effective courses also require a low instructor to student ratio, making student throughput a real constraint on producing trained personnel. We should also remain aware that many foreign officers are extremely rank conscious when dealing with advisors, which means that we should provide officers with the requisite language ability to fill these assignments.

Third, while the increase in the number of FAOs is a good personnel decision since they provide the best combination of service experience, language capability, and regional expertise, they are not a panacea for the current shortfall in language or regional expertise among the officer corps. It seems unlikely that the Army will substantially increase the number of FAOs in the force beyond what is currently planned, although this would make an excellent use of some of the authorized increase in total Army end strength. FAOs are expensive to produce, costing the Army an average of $143k, and it takes 4 to 5 years to produce a qualified FAO.[58]

Furthermore, increasing the number of FAOs to match the force of 5,000-6,000 Military Assistance Officers that was recommended during the Vietnam conflict would cost at least $570m and would take an unknown number of years, given the limited capacity of our graduate area studies and language programs. Finally, there are nine regional FAO specialties.[59] This means that the anticipated force of 1,021 Army FAOs will provide an average of 113 of these socio-cultural experts per region—a number that is clearly insufficient to meet the requirements of the tactical force in operations of the same scope as Iraq or Afghanistan, and also to fill the higher level (and often Joint Duty Assignments List [JDAL]) assignments the FAO corps is intended to fill. Additionally, FAOs are not suited to fill some tactical level assignments, since their tactical skills will have certainly eroded during the years spent in the educational pipeline.

Fourth, the current effort to provide some socio-cultural knowledge in the Officer Basic, Captain's Career, and Intermediate Level Education (ILE) courses appears boiler plated. Sheila Miyoshi Jager differentiated between "the kinds of cultural knowledge that are required at the tactical level . . . is quite separate from the cultural knowledge that are required to formulate grand strategy and policy."[60] This implies that the socio-cultural portion of the ILE curriculum, already noted as too short, does not provide the socio-cultural knowledge needed for majors that will go to joint duty assignments in the J-2, J-3, and J-5 directorates at the combatant commands, or joint and Department of the Army assignments in Washington, where they are involved in the operational and strategic levels of war.

Finally, not all senior Army leaders appear to agree with the need for U.S. Soldiers to bridge the language and culture gap. Brigadier General Daniel Bolger, in a article on how to be an advisor in Iraq, writes of enabling the Iraqis to reach across the culture and language barriers.[61] This appears to miss the point that attempts by U.S. personnel to reach across the language and culture divides makes a favorable impression on the Iraqis, and the ability to do so allows the U.S. advisors to have situational awareness, as opposed to their predecessors in Vietnam.

In summary, current programs and policies appear to either focus too heavily on language skills as a panacea, vice an enabler, for socio-cultural awareness. Current education programs are focused on tactical level skills, and the task of providing socio-cultural education that provides real language and regional expertise, like the 48-week training program for senior CORDS advisors in Vietnam, exceeds time and other resource requirements the Army can, or will, provide. With these observations, this chapter identifies options that could increase the socio-cultural education level of the officer corps.

THE WAY AHEAD

Improving the socio-cultural knowledge of our officer corps would improve the Army's strategic, operational, and tactical capabilities across the spectrum of conflict. Colin S. Gray noted that while cultural expertise is not a panacea for the difficulties that we have encountered in Afghanistan and Iraq, "there is no mode of warfare, conducted in any environment, wherein the enemy's strategic culture is of no importance."[62] Gray adds that this is particularly true in irregular wars which "are won or lost in the minds of the local people . . . If we do not understand what is in those minds, what they value and how much they value it, success secured . . . will most likely only be temporary."[63]

The FAOs are our socio-cultural experts. Their training program includes 2 years at a university studying the history, sociology, economics, geography, and politics of their target region or country. This is followed by attendance at language school and then 1 year of in-country training. The key point is that the FAOs are educated at universities and not at military schools for the nonlanguage portion of their education. The Army needs to leverage the universities in the precommissioning phase of an officer's career beyond the current level of effort.

Precommissioning Initiatives.

First, the United States Military Academy (USMA) is overdue for a comprehensive reassessment of its curriculum, particularly for Cadets majoring in the humanities or social sciences. The academy, in keeping with its roots as the nation's first engineering school, has a curriculum that requires Cadets majoring in these subject areas to take four semesters of advanced mathematics, four semesters of science, and three semesters of engineering. Math majors are also required to take the three semester engineering sequence. As former Army officer Andrew Exum observes, these academic requirements are unmatched in any similar curriculum at a civilian university and are questionable as to whether they truly prepare officers to meet the needs of the nation in the contemporary operating environment.[64]

Simply cutting the math and science requirements in half and dropping the superfluous engineering courses would allow the addition of seven more semesters relevant to socio-cultural knowledge or the relevant major for the individual. This would allow an addition of two more semesters of language education, which brings the total semesters of language to six for humanities and social science majors and four for math majors. Language training for the humanities and social sciences majors would continue through the senior year instead of terminating at the end of the junior year, which currently gives the Cadet 1 year for the language skills to perish. Additionally, there would still be room after the addition of more language courses to add courses that contribute to socio-cultural knowledge. The result would come closer to producing the pentathlete officer the Army seeks for its ranks upon commissioning, and this adjustment appears, on the surface, to be a no-cost or low-cost initiative.

The second main precommissioning initiative involves the Reserve Officers' Training Corps (ROTC). ROTC is the true center of gravity for the Army officer corps because 55.2

percent of Army officers were commissioned out of the ROTC programs in 2000, and ROTC accounted for two-thirds of new Army officers in 2006.[65] ROTC Cadets should also face more stringent language requirements, and the Army should create programs that encourage Cadets to major in fields that are more directly related to socio-cultural expertise. ROTC programs currently lack even the minimal two semesters of language required by West Point, ROTC Cadets are simply encouraged to take foreign language courses. Nearly 100 percent of ROTC Cadets have French or Spanish language classes available to them, 60 percent have access to Russian classes, and over 30 percent have standard Arabic and Mandarin Chinese instruction available.[66] Nonscholarship ROTC Cadets should have a two-semester language requirement, while Cadets on scholarship should have a four-semester requirement, similar to Cadets at USMA. This is a no-cost initiative. A low-cost initiative might provide an additional stipend for successful completion of coursework in the more difficult languages or pay for the language courses of the nonscholarship Cadets if they take the more difficult languages.

The Army should also consider prioritizing scholarship awards to applicants or currently enrolled Cadets that choose to major in a field directly relevant to socio-cultural knowledge such as area studies, regional or country history, politics, and anthropology. Again, this is a no-cost initiative. Other alternatives could provide additional stipend funds or scholarships for Cadets majoring in these relevant fields. Finally, the Army should reopen or expand ROTC programs in the large cities, particularly those in the northeast where there are large immigrant populations.[67]

Officer Professional Military Education Initiatives.

Post-commissioning education initiatives will tend to be more expensive in terms of money and manpower than precommissioning initiatives. Military or U.S. Government run programs have costs that include training base overhead (personnel and facilities) and a loss of personnel time when officers attend the education or training opportunity. Attendance at civilian institutions or those run by other government agencies still incurs a period where the officer is drawing pay but is not in a normal duty assignment, and there are tuition costs as well.

The Army currently sends approximately 250 officers per year to advanced civil schooling. These officers are given 12-18 months to complete all degree requirements before returning to a regular assignment. For many officers this is perceived as a relatively poor deal; since school attendance usually follows assignments in units that deployed to Iraq or Afghanistan; requires the officer to compress 2 years of course work into a shorter time frame; and the officer probably returns to a deploying unit. The Army should study the cost effectiveness of the following three initiatives, which are relatively high-cost compared to other proposals in this chapter. First, the Army should grant these officers an additional 6 months for degree completion if they are working towards a socio-cultural knowledge related degree. Second, the Army should create a secondary specialty code that designates officers completing an advanced degree that focuses on a critical region as a provisional FAO, with eligibility to serve in nonlanguage coded FAO positions on COCOM staffs or in Washington. These officers could serve in language coded positions if they have a documented capability. Third, the Army should guarantee a follow-on assignment of up to 12 months for some form of in-country study or 24 months in an interagency duty position (e.g., USAID or the State Department) following graduate school if the degree is in an SSTRO or socio-cultural knowledge related field.

The Army should propose a review of the Joint and Combined Warfighting School curriculum. Currently officers attending the course take one regional elective that meets once per week. If there is empty space in the curriculum, it might allow more additional time for regional studies courses or other socio-cultural knowledge course work. This would allow more time for students to transition from the tactical level socio-cultural knowledge they developed as junior officers to operational and strategic level socio-cultural knowledge. It would also better prepare them for follow-on assignments at the regional combatant commands.

Two other initiatives, one no cost and the other relatively high, conclude this chapter's recommendations. The no cost initiative is the implementation of regionally-focused management for the 34A Strategic Intelligence career field. All 34A officers attend graduate school at the National Defense Intelligence College (NDIC). The majority of their subsequent assignments are at the COCOM level or higher, typically working regional or country-desk intelligence accounts. Currently FA34 officers are assigned worldwide wherever an opening at the right grade is available. For example, this means that an officer who focused his or her graduate studies on the Middle East and then spends 3 years at U.S. Central Command becoming a regional or subregional expert, may never work the region again following that initial assignment. Consequently, Human Resources Command should work to assign FA34 officers in billets that build deep socio-cultural expertise in a region, as opposed to moderate or shallow expertise in several regions. A Middle East focused officer might, for example, attend the NDIC and regionally focus on the Middle East, then serve at U.S. CENTCOM, move to the Middle East Division of DIA, and then move to Army-Central Command or its supporting intelligence brigade. At the end of that last theoretical tour, the officer would have 8-10 years experience working Middle Eastern issues. Our current assignment process almost guarantees that this hypothetical officer would follow the CENTCOM tour with an assignment to USPACOM or Korea, and then move to a CONUS assignment that focused on neither the Middle East nor the Pacific.

Finally, for long-term advisor commitments like Iraq and Afghanistan that exceed the capacity of Special Forces to carry out the mission, the Army should develop lengthy advisor training courses similar to those for CORDS personnel in Vietnam. To recoup the training time and expense, advisors would need to serve tours of more than 1 year in duration or serve repeatedly in advisor duty positions. The Army developed special incentive programs during Vietnam to attract officers to the CORDS program and could easily do so again. This is a high-cost option compared to the 6-week advisor training we currently have.

CONCLUSION

Socio-cultural knowledge matters at all levels of warfare. Socio-cultural expertise is required for developing national level policy, theater engagement plans, operational plans at all levels of war, and for the conduct of tactical operations. Individuals with socio-cultural expertise, or at least deep socio-cultural awareness, matter. Well-known senior leaders like General David Petraeus and Lieutenant General Peter Chiarelli in Iraq, General John Abizaid in Central Command, and Lieutenant General David Barno in Afghanistan were all recognized as successful commanders. They all possessed educational backgrounds that provided them with, at the least, an appreciation for the importance of socio-cultural factors in a COIN environment.

Social cultural awareness also matters at the operational or tactical levels. Colonel H. R. McMaster, the commander of the highly effective clear, hold, and build operations in Tal Afar later helped develop the surge strategy and continues to advise General Petraeus, holds a Doctorate in Military History with an emphasis on Vietnam and COIN. Lieutenant Colonel John Nagl also has an advanced degree and was a key member of the team that wrote the new COIN manual. Major Greg Ryckman, a South Asia Foreign Area Officer, had focused his thesis research on a forgotten country called Afghanistan while living in Pakistan, and was the only officer in the CENTCOM headquarters in the fall of 2001 and winter of 2002 with relevant socio-cultural knowledge of that country.

The point is this, it does not take thousands of officers with relevant knowledge or academic backgrounds to have a significant and positive impact on current and future operations, or on the Army as an institution. Even relatively modest increases in the number of officers with advanced socio-cultural knowledge or academic fields relevant to irregular warfare and SSTRO will significantly increase the effectiveness of our armed forces as they continue to protect U.S. interests in an era of persistent conflict.

ENDNOTES - CHAPTER 10

1. General (Ret.) Anthony Zinni, Address to the Marine Corps Association, Quantico, VA, September 23, 2003.

2. *Field Manual, (FM) 3-24, Counterinsurgency,* Chicago: University of Chicago Press, 2007, p. 84.

3. Robert M. Gates, "Remarks as Delivered by Secretary of Defense Robert M. Gates, Washington, DC, Wednesday, October 10, 2007, to the Association of the United States Army," available from *www. defenselink.mil/speeches/speech.aspx?speechid=1181.*

4. General George Casey, "Remarks at the National Press Club, August 15, 2007," available from *www. army.mil/-speeches/2007/08/15/4436-army-chief-of-staffs-remarks-at-the-national-press-club/*; and "The Brookings Institution Maintaining Quality in the Force: A Briefing By General George W. Casey, Jr., Tuesday, December 4, 2007," available from *www.army.mil/-speeches/2007/12/04/7139-army-chief-of-staff-remarks-at-brookings-institution-dec-4th-2007/index.html.*

5. While a student at the U.S. Army War College during the 2007-2008 academic year, the author heard multiple guest speakers make this comment.

6. *Ibid.*

7. Colin S. Gray, *Another Bloody Century,* London: Weidenfeld and Nicolson, 2007, p. 380.

8. General Sir Rupert Smith, *The Utility of Force,* New York: Random House, 2007, p. 6.

9. Gray, p. 382; and Ralph Peters, *Fighting for the Future,* Mechanicsburg, PA: Stackpole, 1999, p. 133.

10. SOKF-J9 Futures Directorate, "Irregular Warfare JOC," MacDill AFB, FL: U.S. Special Operations Command, available from *www.dtic.mil/futurejointwarfare/strategic/cdeday1 _iwjoc.ppt.*

11. *Ibid.*

12. Smith, p. 272.

13. Lieutenant General Peter W. Chiarelli and Major Stephen M. Smith, "Learning From Our Modern Wars: The Imperatives of Preparing for a Dangerous Future," *Military Review,* September-October 2007, available from *usacac.army.mil/CAC/milreview/English/ SepOct07/indexengsepoct07.asp.*

14. David Kilcullen, "Twenty-Eight Articles: Fundamentals of Company-level Counterinsurgency," *Military Review,* May-June 2006, available from *usacac.army.mil/CAC/milreview/English/MayJun06/webpdf/ BoB_Insights_Reviews_Letters_MJ06.pdf.*

15. U.K. Ministry of Defense, UK D Strat Plans/JDCC, "Generic Strategic Campaign Planning Briefing to JFCOM CCF Seminar," briefing slides with commentary, MacDill Air Force Base, U.S. Central Command, March 2005.

16. Robert D. Ramsay, *Advising Indigenous Forces: American Advisors in Korea, Vietnam, and El Salvador,* Fort Leavenworth, KS: Combat Studies Institute Press, 2006, pp. 27-29.

17. Andrew J. Birtle, *U.S. Army Counterinsurgency and Contingency Operations Doctrine 1942-1976,* Washington, DC: Center for Military History, 2006, pp. 261-266.

18. *Ibid.,* p. 456.

19. *Ibid.,* pp. 455-461. See also pp. 477-484.

20. *Ibid.,* p. 463.

21. *Ibid.,* pp. 402-404.

22. Ramsay, pp. 27-35.

23. *Ibid.,* pp. 35-37.

24. *Ibid.,* pp. 39-43.

25. *Ibid.* The Province Senior Advisers and District Senior Advisers received 60 hours of country orientation and background during a 6-week basic course and an additional 135 hours of area orientation and mission specific knowledge areas (e.g., rural development, advisor techniques, situation updates).

26. *Ibid.,* pp. 39-43.

27. *Ibid.* p. 46.

28. *Ibid.*

29. *Ibid.*

30. *Ibid.,* pp. 62-63; and Birtle, pp. 442-443.

31. *Ibid.*, pp. 62-64.

32. *FY 2006 DOD Foreign Area Officer Annual Review and Report*, Washington, DC: U.S. Department of Defense, 2006, p. 5, available from *https://www.g357extranet.army.pentagon.mil/DCSExtranet/damossf/Documents/FY06%20Annual%20DoD%20FAO%20Report%20070510.pdf*.

33. General Jack Keane, as quoted in FM 3-24, p. xiv.

34. Data compiled from the Army Human Resources Command data base, October 11, 2006.

35. Andrew Stewart, *Friction in U.S. Foreign Policy: Cultural Difficulties with the World*, Carlisle, PA: Strategic Studies Institute, U.S. Army War College, 2006, p. 9.

36. Lieutenant Colonel Michael Eisenstadt, "Iraq Tribal Engagement Lessons Learned," *Military Review*, September-October 2007, p. 23, available from *usacac.army.mil/CAC/milreview/English/SepOct07/indexengsepoct07.asp*.

37. Leonard Wong, *Developing Adaptive Leaders: The Crucible Experience of Operation Iraqi Freedom*, Carlisle, PA: Strategic Studies Institute, U.S. Army War College, July 2004.

38. Thomas E. Ricks, "Flaws Cited in Effort To Train Iraqi Forces," *The Washington Post Online*, November 21, 2006, available from *www.washingtonpost.com/wp-dyn/content/article/2006/11/21/AR2006112100171_pf.html*.

39. "The Fort Riley Training Mission (FRTM) Standard (60-Day) Training Model Notes, Fort Riley, KS: 1st Brigade Transition Training Team, November 29, 2007, available from *www.riley.army.mil/units/trainingteam.aspx*.

40. See also Major General David Petraeus, "Learning Counterinsurgency: Observations from Soldiering in Iraq," *Military Review*, January-February 2006, available from *usacac.leavenworth.army.mil/CAC/milreview/English/JanFeb06/Petraeus1.pdf*; and Major General Peter Chiarelli, "The Requirement for Full-Spectrum Operations, *Military Review*, July-August 2005, available from *usacac.leavenworth.army.mil/CAC/milreview/download/English/JulAug05/chiarelli.pdf*.

41. David R. McCone, Wilbur J. Scott, and George R. Mastroianni, *The 3rd ACR In Tal'afar: Challenges And Adaptations*, Carlisle, PA: Strategic Studies Institute, U.S. Army War College, 2008, available from *www.strategicstudiesinstitute.army.mil/pdffiles/of-interest-9.pdf*; and Eisenstadt, p. 25.

42. McCone *et al.*, p. 18.

43. "Defense Language Transformation Roadmap 2005," Washington, DC: Department of Defense, available from *www.defenselink.mil/news/Mar2005/d20050330roadmap.pdf*.

44. Data compiled from the Army Human Resources Command internal data base on October 11, 2006.

45. *Ibid.* The author acknowledges that eliminating economics, history, political science, public policy, and administration degrees in determining the number of officers with socio-cultural relevant degrees, as some of those degrees are almost certainly in non-U.S. history, foreign political topics, or other relevant subfields of the major degree. Unfortunately, the Human Resources Command database does not offer this level of fidelity in an officer's educational background.

46. "National Security Education Program," *Institute of International Education Home Page*, available from "Programs Portal," *www.iie.org/programs/nsep/default.htm*; and *The National Security Education Program Home Page*, available from *www.ndu.edu/nsep/*.

47. "National Security Language Initiative," January 5, 2006, *The United States State Department Home Page*, available from "Undersecretary for Public Diplomacy and Public Affairs," *www.state.gov/r/pa/prs/ps/2006/58733.htm*.

48. *Management of the Department of Defense (DoD) Foreign Area Officer (FAO) Programs Department of Defense Instruction 1315.20*, Washington, DC: U.S. Department of Defense, September 2007.

49. *U.S. Department of Defense 2006 Annual Foreign Area Officer (FAO) Report*, Washington, DC: U.S. Department of Defense, 2007, p. 5, available from *https://www.g357extranet.army.pentagon.mil/DCSExtranet/damossf/Documents/FY06%20Annual%20DoD%20FAO%20Report%20070510.pdf*.

50. *U.S. Defense Language Transformation Roadmap*, Washington, DC: U.S. Department of Defense, 2005, p. 7, available from *https://www.g357extranet.army.pentagon.mil/DCSExtranet/damossf/Documents/Defense%20Language%20Roadmap.pdf*.

51. *Department of Defense Instruction 5160.70 Management of DoD Language and Regional Proficiency Capabilities*, Washington, DC: U.S. Department of Defense, 2007, p. 18, available from *https://www.g357extranet.army.pentagon.mil/DCSExtranet/damossf/Documents/Official%20Signed%20DoDI%205160%2070.pdf*.

52. Donna Miles, "Language, Cultural Studies Gain More Focus at Service Academies," American Forces Press Service, May 25, 2007, available from *www.defenselink.mil/news/newsarticle.aspx?id=46142*.

53. "Department of Defense Announces the ROTC Language and Culture Project," Washington, DC: Department of Defense, May 08, 2007, available from *www.defenselink.mil/releases/release.aspx?releaseid=10844*.

54. Lieutenant Colonel Lance Davis, "2-11th Infantry Battalion (Infantry Basic Officer Leaders Course [IBOLC] Command Briefing)," briefing slides, available from *https://www.benning.army.mil/ibolc/welcome/2-11th_Command_Brief_ _13mar08.ppt*; and Defense Language Institute, "Iraq in Perspective" and "Iraq Familiarization," available from *fieldsupport.lingnet.org/index.aspx*.

55. Ralph O. Doughty, "Irregular Warfare & Stability Operations at USACGSC," June 26, 2007, briefing slides, available from *www.oft.osd.mil/initiatives/ncw/docs/SSTR%20and%20PME%20Presentations/Doughty.ppt*.

56. Quote from Infantry School Report, Report of the Infantry Instructors' Conference, July 15-19, 1963, pp. 105-106, 108-109, as quoted in Birtle, p. 262.

57. Brigadier General Michael A. Vane and Lieutenant Colonel Daniel Fagundes, "Redefining the Foreign Area Officer's Role," *Military Review*, May-June 2004, available from *usacac.leavenworth.army.mil/cac/milreview/download/English/MayJun04/vane.pdf*.

58. *U.S. Department of Defense 2006 Annual Foreign Area Officer (FAO) Report*, p. 5.

59. *Ibid.*

60. Sheila Miyoshi Jager, *On The Uses Of Cultural Knowledge*, Carlisle, PA: Strategic Studies Institute, U.S. Army War College, 2007, p. 4.

61. Brigadier General Daniel Bolger, "So You Want To Be An Adviser," *Military Review*, March-April 2006, available from *usacac.leavenworth.army.mil/CAC/milreview/English/MarApr06/Bolger.pdf*.

62. Colin S. Gray, *Irregular Enemies And The Essence Of Strategy: Can The American Way Of War Adapt?* Carlisle, PA: Strategic Studies Institute, U.S. Army War College, 2006, p. 34, available from *www.strategicstudiesinstitute.army.mil/pubs/display.cfm?PubID=650*.

63. *Ibid.*, p. 25.

64. Andrew Exum, "Are U.S. Military Academies Preparing Graduates for Today's Wars?" January 29, 2007, available from *www.washingtoninstitute.org/print.php?template= C05&CID=2559*; and "Curriculum Overview," briefing slides, available from *www.dean.usma.edu/Curriculum/CurriculumBriefing.pps*.

65. "Population Representation in the Military Services," Washington, DC: Office of the Assistant Secretary of Defense, Force Management Policy, November, 2001, available from *www.defenselink.mil/prhome/poprep2000/html/chapter4/chapter4_3.htm*; and Greg Jaffe, "Urban Withdrawal: A Retreat from Big Cities Hurts ROTC Recruiting," *The Wall Street Journal*, February 22, 2007, available from *www.classroomedition.com/archive/07apr/ 07apr_additional_urbanwithdrawal.pdf*.

66. Gail H. McGinn, "Statement of Mrs. Gail H. McGinn, Deputy Under Secretary of Defense for Plans and the Department of Defense Senior Language Authority before the Senate Armed Services Committee Subcommittee on Emerging Threats and Capabilities," April 25, 2007, available from *www.dod.mil/dodgc/olc/docs/testMcGinn070425.pdf*.

67. Jaffe's article highlights St. Johns University, one of two remaining ROTC programs in New York City, where 40 of the 120 Cadets speak a second language. Jaffe also points out that there is no ROTC program in the greater Detroit area with its large Arab-American population, and that New York City (population 8.2m) currently produces fewer officers for the Army (34) than Alabama (pop. 4.5m, 174 officers).

CHAPTER 11

EL SALVADOR, IRAQ, AND STRATEGIC CONSIDERATIONS FOR COUNTERINSURGENCY

Lieutenant Colonel James F. Glynn
United States Marine Corps

Insurgency: The organized use of subversion and violence by a group or movement that seeks to overthrow or force change of a governing authority.

—Joint Publication 1-02[1]

INTRODUCTION

Insurgency as a form of war is not new. Colonial freedom fighters in this country utilized it. Napoleon's adversaries employed it. The Zionist movement used it. It was evident in Algeria in the 1950s, Vietnam in the 1960s, Afghanistan in the 1980s, and countless other examples. In the 20th century alone, Vietnam was the 48th small war fought somewhere in the world. Since the end of the Cold War, insurgencies have proliferated—not the least of which is Iraq.[2] Why has insurgency endured for centuries? What makes it so popular in this age? With so much experience to draw from, why does it remain difficult for governments to counter, or even prevent, an insurgency? One possible explanation of the persistence of insurgency is its ability to undermine an existing government. For democratic forms of government, this is particularly challenging because the power of the government is derived from the very same civil population that an insurgent cause seeks to influence.

The U.S. Government, and particularly the U.S. military, faced its largest insurgent challenge in Vietnam, where over the course of a decade a number of lessons emerged at the strategic, operational, and tactical levels. Arguably, the most important lesson of the Vietnam War for the U.S. military was you can win the majority of the battles but still lose the war. In other words, and with due deference to the military theorist Carl von Clausewitz, without an enduring, definitive link between the political objectives and the military effort, victory is not certain.[3] That lesson seemed destined to be relearned in Iraq with the emergence of an insurgency following the U.S.-led invasion that dethroned Saddam Hussein in 2003. A great question loomed: Do democracies have the ability to defeat insurgencies?

Historically, examples of the defeat of insurgencies exist, such as the British in Malaya. Extensive research has been invested in examining the political and military policies, strategies, tactics, and techniques applied by the antagonists in both successful and unsuccessful insurgencies. No single case, however, can be utilized without first understanding its full context—political, social, and military. For example, Bernard Fall offered that using Malaya as an example for future counterinsurgent efforts was unworkable. In his opinion, credit is infrequently given to the opposition for its mistakes, and when the communist insurgents in Malaya decided to confront the British in a straight forward military operation they, predictably, failed.[4] However, a greater insight is that the adaptive nature of insurgency has made its defeat illusive and difficult to codify. The adaptability of insurgencies is perhaps the most important reason democracies have not been properly prepared to fight them, and why this method of warfare has grown in popularity in the emerging global world order.

In the spring of 2005, it was rumored that the U.S. administration was considering pursuing a strategy for Iraq called the Salvadoran option, referring to U.S. involvement in Central America in the 1980s.[5] When then Secretary of Defense Donald H. Rumsfeld was asked at a news conference about the utility of using El Salvador as a model for countering the insurgency in Iraq, he stopped short of categorically denying it and declined any further comment.[6] While El Salvador is perhaps one of the least studied insurgencies, its study offers a unique and valuable perspective for successfully countering insurgency. It is considered a successful modern counterinsurgency effort by many, and it offers a number of strategic insights for the policymaker and the military strategist. Both the U.S. and Salvadorian experiences with counterinsurgency and regime change in El Salvador during the 1980s is prescient of the 21st century challenges confronting democracies around the world. However, understanding the specific context for El Salvador is critically important before its insights can be generalized and applied in another counterinsurgent effort.

This chapter examines the strategic environments that confronted El Salvador and the United States and the role that U.S. interests played in El Salvador's war. The seven dimensions of the Manwaring paradigm, or Small Wars Operations Research Directorate (SWORD) model, are introduced and used as the backdrop for analysis of the U.S. involvement in El Salvador from a strategic perspective.[7] In the course of doing so, legitimacy, unity of effort, and time emerge as the most critical dimensions of modern insurgency. In turn, these critical dimensions specifically suggest conclusions about the relevance of the El Salvador counterinsurgency to that of Iraq, and to counterinsurgency in general.

EL SALVADOR BACKGROUND

El Salvador declared its independence from Spain in 1821, as did most of Central America. Despite participation in a short-lived federation of Central American states, El Salvador endured a number of wars with its Central American neighbors and several revolutions of its own. For the first 70 years of the 20th century, military dictatorships governed El Salvador and a ruling elite of right wing military officers and landed oligarchy emerged. Beginning in the 1970s, however, international trade and the creation of a regional market spurred significant economic growth in El Salvador. Ultimately the oligarchy pursued their own economic interests at the expense of the majority who were peasant farmers, as international demand for El Salvadoran goods, particularly coffee, grew.[8] Discontent among the El Salvadoran population increased as societal inequality and economic disparity widened. For example, landless peasants increased from 12 percent in 1960 to 40 percent in 1975.[9] The growing inequities and unrest created tensions among and within the oligarchy, military, and Church.

Beginning in 1960s, a civil war ensued between the government, run by the right-wing National Conciliation Party (PCN), and a number of left-wing anti-government guerrilla factions, represented most notably by the Farabundo Marti National Liberation Front (FMLN). The FMLN and others conducted attacks on bridges, electricity supplies, and irrigation systems, and even temporarily occupied towns.[10] By the late 1970s, consistent political, economic, and social problems created enough unrest in El Salvador that in 1979 a military coup ousted the country's ruler, General Carlos Humberto Romero, and then the more moderate and centralist Jose Napoleon Duarte soon assumed a provisional presidency. The decade following the coup was volatile as the El Salvadoran government and military, with U.S. economic and military assistance, countered a growing insurgency. The El Salvadoran government, the insurgents, and the United States were ill-prepared for the disorder that arose from 50 years of authoritarian rule.[11]

President Duarte was immediately challenged by the need to bring to justice right-wing death squads that were responsible for the murder of Archbishop Oscar Romero in March 1980 and three American nuns later that year.[12] Even with U.S. support of the El Salvadoran government, an estimated 30,000 people were killed by right-wing death squads backed by the military. President Duarte suffered the political consequences of failing to gain control over the death-squads and was defeated in an election in March 1982. Two years later, in an election that turned out 80 percent of the El Salvadoran voting population, he was elected as President, and initiated negotiations with the FMLN that led to a peace agreement 8 years later. By that time, however, an estimated 75,000 people had been killed in El Salvador as a result of violence between the government and insurgents.[13]

From 1980-92, the U.S. Government funded extensive political and social reforms in El Salvador to help undermine the revolutionary insurgency. The left-leaning orientation of the FMLN, supported by Cuba and combined with tacit Soviet Union support of guerrilla forces in neighboring Nicaragua, led the United States to also provide extensive military aid and training to counter communist influence in the conflict. These U.S. efforts had effects at many levels within El Salvador. Most importantly, at the strategic level they had a significantly positive effect on the ability of the El Salvadoran government to pursue long-term stability and security. Eventually, El Salvador established an enduring democratic government and inclusive economic growth, which has led some to conclude that the U.S. strategy to counter the insurgency in El Salvador should be a model for other efforts, particularly in Iraq.

U.S. INTERESTS IN EL SALVADOR

President James Monroe's proclamation of 1823 disparaging European intervention and colonialism in the Western Hemisphere, subsequently known as the Monroe Doctrine, was the long-standing measure for evaluating U.S. national interests in Central America. The known presence of Soviet missiles in the hemisphere created the Cuban Missile Crisis in 1962, and no Soviet missiles in Cuba became a vital national interest. The notion of another communist incursion into America's backyard was unpalatable to U.S. policymakers, and the ongoing violence in El Salvador and the Nicaraguan revolution seemed to indicate outside intervention. With the Cold War looming large in the minds of many within the administration of President Jimmy Carter, the outcome of the 1979 El Salvadoran coup was interpreted as an opportunity to support a moderate, centrist government.[14] The vital interest of American continents free of Soviet influence would be well served.

The inauguration of President Ronald Reagan in January 1981 brought even greater emphasis on defeating the Soviet Union, and in particular the spread of communism around the world. In Central America, U.S. aid to El Salvador increased throughout President Reagan's two terms in office. For example, monetary aid went from $264.2 million in fiscal year 1982 to $557.8 million in fiscal year 1987.[15] The United States also provided military support teams to assist in training and advising the El Salvadoran armed forces, but the lack of U.S. domestic support at the time precluded the introduction of U.S. combat troops on any large scale.[16] Ultimately a democratically governed El Salvador prevailed but at great human cost. United Nations (UN) involvement in negotiating an enduring agreement between the government and the FMLN played a significant role in helping end the armed struggle, but the dissolution of the Soviet Union played an even larger part in minimizing the international influence of communism, eliminating outside support, and assuaging U.S concerns over Soviet influence.

THE SWORD MODEL

In 1984, then Vice Chief of Staff of the Army General Maxwell Thurman, a veteran of the Vietnam War, recognized the challenge of ongoing U.S. involvement in the insurgency in El Salvador and sought to avoid repeating the quandary that Vietnam had presented the military.[17] General Thurman commissioned the Strategic Studies Institute of the U.S. Army War College to study the strategic and doctrinal issues associated with U.S. involvement in insurgencies. In response, Dr. Max G. Manwaring developed two studies that analyzed 69 small wars, virtually all which had occurred since World War II.[18] The studies identified 72 variables that were ultimately whittled down to seven dimensions of insurgency. Dr. Manwaring moved to the SWORD of U.S. Southern Command, and the results of his studies were published as the SWORD model, or Manwaring paradigm, in 1992.[19]

The model identified legitimacy, unity of effort, information/intelligence, isolation, actions of intervening power, indigenous military capabilities, and external military support as the dimensions common to, and influential in, every insurgent conflict. These seven dimensions are strategic-level variables that predicted the outcome of the studied insurgent conflicts with a 90 percent accuracy rate.[20] This research suggests that despite the unique context of every insurgent conflict or irregular war, specific consideration, evaluation, and management of these variables in the development and implementation of the ends-ways-means of strategy are most likely to resolve conflict in a politically effective manner.

The lasting value of Dr. Manwaring's research is evident in the U.S. Army and Marine Corps *Field Manual (FM) 3-4 (MCWP 3-33.5), Counterinsurgency*. It reinforces Dr. Manwaring's assessment of the myriad factors in insurgent warfare that make it so complex. The preeminence of legitimacy and unity of effort in countering insurgency is demonstrated by dedicating much of the first two chapters to discussing them. Of equal importance is the element of time. FM 3-24 acknowledges the relative and contextual nature of time in operational planning, but it is equally applicable to policy and strategy.[21] The advantage one side can generate against another in insurgency is often relative. In other words, it is a matter of comparison at a given moment in time in a given context. The moment of advantage may be short-lived, or it may persist. In either case, awareness of the temporal dimension of insurgency must be considered at every level of the conflict.

Dr. Manwaring argues that every element of the SWORD model plays an important part in the analysis of an insurgency.[22] He is entirely correct in his conclusion, however, for the policymaker and military strategist consideration of *legitimacy* and *unity of effort* over the course of *time* is most prescient. The strategic primacy of legitimacy, unity of effort, and time is evident in El Salvador's struggle to defeat its insurgency in the 1980s, and the Savadoran struggle makes obvious the significance of these three variables for the counterinsurgency efforts in Iraq.

THE MODEL APPLIED

Legitimacy.

> In [Peace Operations] PO, legitimacy is perceived by interested audiences as the legality, morality, or fairness of a set of actions. Such audiences may include the U.S. public, foreign nations, civil populations in the operational area, and the participating forces. If a PO is perceived as legitimate by both the citizens of the nations contributing the forces and the citizens of the country being entered, the PO will have a better chance of long-term success. . . . The perception of legitimacy by the U.S. public is strengthened if there are obvious national or humanitarian interests at stake. Another aspect of this principle is the legitimacy bestowed upon a local government through the perception of the populace that it governs.[23]

The single most important dimension in the development of counterinsurgency strategy is legitimacy. In fact, U.S. joint military doctrine for military operations other than war (MOOTW) published in 1995 declared, "legitimacy is frequently a decisive element." [24] Within the SWORD model, legitimacy is defined as the moral right to govern.[25] It is, in essence, an unwritten contract between the governing establishment and those it governs based on confidence that the governing body will engage in activities that are in the best interests of the governed. At a minimum, these activities include security, economic, and key social aspects of legitimacy. Ultimately those subject to the actions of a governing body must believe that governing actions are taken in their collective best interest in order for the government to maintain legitimacy. If the interests and needs of the governed are not met or there is a perception that they cannot be sustained, then legitimacy begins to erode and political vulnerabilities are exposed.

Political power is the central issue in insurgencies and counterinsurgencies, as each side strives to get the people to accept its authority to govern as legitimate. Nation-states whose governments have achieved legitimacy are relatively invulnerable to destabilizing actions whether internal or external.[26] For example, the constitutional monarchy of the United Kingdom (UK) has reigned for centuries and endured many challenges to its authority from domestic challengers and international enemies. Because of its legitimacy in the eyes of the governed, the times that have tested the monarchy the most have often been those that have unified it the best as was evident in World War II. Hence, quite often the strategic center of gravity in insurgency warfare is legitimacy, which is perception-based and typically expressed through public opinion. El Salvador is an example of the preeminence of legitimacy as a dimension against subversion in any war.

A slow start on the part of the government and armed forces of El Salvador in implementing social and economic reforms following the 1979 coup created opportunities for opposition groups.[27] The FMLN, in concert with other left-wing elements, countered with popular promises to build the working class and redistribute wealth.[28] El Salvador's President Jose Napoleon Duarte intuitively recognized the political significance of the emerging discontent and implemented the changes necessary to surpass the promises of the FMLN and deliver results in a more timely manner.[29]

The promulgation of relatively effective reforms such as holding elections, developing a bureaucratic capability to promote economic growth, particularly in the agriculture industry, and demonstrating the ability to widely distribute commercial and financial resources to the society as a whole went a long way toward reinforcing the legitimacy of the Duarte government. The reforms were not perfect or all-encompassing, but they were tangible and more effective than anything the opposition could produce, which resulted in a perception among the people that the government was making concerted efforts to enact changes for the collective good.

Unity of Effort.

> Unity of effort emphasizes the need for ensuring that all means are directed to a common purpose. In [Peace Operations] PO, achieving unity of effort is often complicated by a variety of international, foreign, and domestic military and nonmilitary participants, the lack of definitive command arrangements, and varying views of the objective.[30]

Unity of effort is advocated throughout U.S. joint military doctrine and has made its way into the U.S. Government's interagency discussions and publications. For example, the October 2007 U.S. Department of State's *Counterinsurgency for U.S. Government Policy Makers: A Work in Progress* emphasizes the "complementarity of purpose and unity of effort required for interagency and international counterinsurgency operations."[31] The importance of unity of effort in counterinsurgency is monolithic because of the myriad of government and interest groups that vie for both influence and legitimacy. David J. Kilcullen coined the term "conflict ecosystem" in reference to the many participants in an insurgency and the resultant counterinsurgency efforts.[32] As illustrated in Figure 1, the conflict ecosystem is a complex system of legitimate and recognized government and nongovernmental organizations (NGOs), as well as the insurgents and a number of less obvious and often illegal actors. The following graphic depicts the complexity of gaining and maintaining unity of effort in this environment.

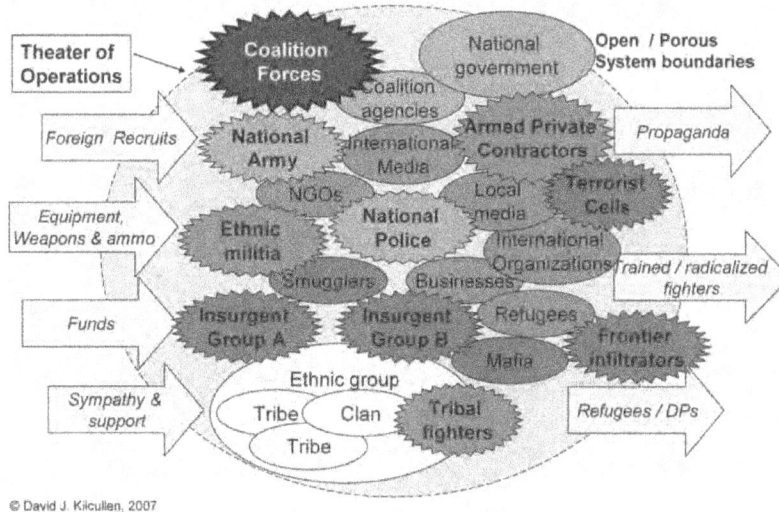

The Conflict Ecosystem

Figure 1. Kilcullen's Conflict Ecosystem.[33]

The SWORD model defines unity of effort as "the necessary organization to coordinate and implement an effective unity of political-diplomatic, socio-economic, psychological-moral, and security-stability effort against those who would destroy the government."[34] It is the act of centering all efforts on the ultimate political objective of survival, with particular emphasis on legitimacy. To achieve effectiveness against an enemy whose objective is to undermine the legitimacy and authority of the government, the efforts of all elements of power, at every level, must be unified in order to survive. In other words, strategic clarity is mandatory for unity of effort.[35] In particular, links between political and diplomatic efforts, sociological and economic factors, and security and stability efforts must be formalized to the maximum extent possible and reinforced regularly. Historical examples abound of the plight of nations unable to establish unity throughout their effort, from Hannibal's defeat of the Romans in the Battle of Cannae in 216 BC, to the British defeat in the American Revolutionary War. Unity of effort is simple in theory but difficult in practice.

Whatever relationship is established between the myriad elements involved in a counterinsurgent effort, all aspects of establishing unity of effort must be managed both vertically and horizontally. Vertical unity refers to establishment of unity of effort among the government's and insurgents' own organizational structures. Horizontal unity refers to the unity of effort established among the government or insurgents with external actors. The complexity of establishing and maintaining vertical and horizontal unity of effort is daunting for any government given the many additional NGOs and intergovernmental organizations (IGOs) that participate in a mature conflict ecosystem.

Building unity of effort in El Salvador was a continuous work in progress, and even when the UN brokered a peace agreement, unity of effort was a relative term. The government of El Salvador had merely done a better job of achieving unity than had the FMLN. Both sides organized to the extent necessary for survival, and perhaps even moderate success, but not to the degree required to win.[36] Thomas Pickering, U.S. Ambassador to El Salvador from 1983 to 1985, said:

> We had neither the doctrine nor the support, nor the coordination in the United States government that would really be required to deal effectively with that kind of operation. I don't think we ever developed it; we still are kind of ad hoc in our way of viewing the problems. That is really quite a critical comment.[37]

The El Salvadoran government, like the insurgents, was debilitated by discord among their subordinate political and military organizations. In the early 1980s, the vertical unity of the El Salvadoran government was inhibited by strife between the extreme-right and more centrist politicians.[38] The rift led to contradictory policies and insubordinate actions and was substantial enough that it resulted in the murder of politicians on both sides.[39] This lack of unity, and its resultant violence, undermined governmental legitimacy benefiting the insurgent position. The insurgents, however, had misgivings within their own effort about their objectives, let alone the best ways for achieving them. The former El Salvadoran insurgent Marco Antonio Grande lamented, "The Salvadoran problem was seen by the left as a problem of class struggle and a seizure of power, not as a problem of how to democratize the system."[40] As a result of such varying views on the ends for the insurgent effort, the FMLN was ultimately unable to consolidate the necessary effort to sufficiently exploit the El Salvadoran government's weaknesses and, as a result, slowly lost its own legitimacy.

A second example highlights the horizontal aspect of unity of effort. The United States, through its military support teams, encouraged the Salvadoran armed forces to grow into an image of their U.S. counterparts.[41] The result was a formidable military force most comfortable in conventional, battalion-size operations ill-suited for the sustained counterinsurgency operations required. Such a mirror imaging approach to developing the Salvadoran armed forces inhibited their effectiveness and confidence. Not only did it demonstrate the absence of a clear understanding of the dynamics of the insurgency at the time by the U.S. military, it was also a manifestation of lagging horizontal unity of effort between the United States and El Salvador. As a result, the success of the El Salvadoran Army in countering the insurgency was largely an extension of President Duarte's other strategic initiatives and assistance.[42]

Time.

> Of all the many dimensions of strategy, time is the most intractable. Compensation for deficiencies elsewhere and correction of errors are usually possible. But time lost is irrecoverable. The Western theory of war pays too little attention to war's temporal dimension.[43]

166

The dimension of time is perhaps the least analyzed of the elements of strategy formulation, yet its impact is wide and profound. Mistakes are made and corrections are applied in any conflict, but the time expended in the course of so doing affords the opposition the opportunity to utilize time with greater effect. In the absence of more tangible assets at their disposal, time is a weapon that insurgencies covet and use calculatingly.

Mao Tse-Tung recognized time as a strategic consideration as exemplified in his advocacy for protracted struggle. For example, he acknowledged the effect time had on the logistics and morale of the Japanese force that occupied China and mandated, "energies must be directed toward the goal of protracted war so that should the Japanese occupy much of our territory or even most of it, we shall still gain final victory."[44] History has demonstrated that an insurgent cause can prevail if it is able to outwait its opponent while making progress in the legitimacy dimension. The insurgencies in Algeria and Vietnam are two 20th century examples of the value of strategic patience. They also demonstrate the inherently slow pace of counterinsurgency operations, a fact that has bedeviled democratic governments and Western culture.

El Salvador's struggle against insurgency, like so many others, illustrates the strategic importance of time. Even in the most restrictive of timelines, the organized insurgent effort in El Salvador lasted from 1980-92, and it concluded only after years of the government and the FMLN negotiating through a variety of intermediaries and venues. During those 12 years, a strategic-level competition for domestic and international legitimacy existed. For example, in the United States the national interest, strategy, and success in El Salvador were the subject of considerable debate. Additionally, the demise of the communist government of the Soviet Union played a pivotal role in focusing Soviet national interests domestically, which terminated their continued support of the FMLN, both directly and through Cuba.[45]

Colin Gray observed that the mindset needed to combat an irregular enemy is not one that comes easily to Western militaries or strategic culture.[46] An examination of nearly every war since 1700 by the Australian historian Geoffrey Blainey offers an explanation. Blainey's book, *The Causes of War*, noted, "Nations confident of victory in a forthcoming war were equally as confident that war would conclude quickly."[47] Because of this optimism, patience is a virtue that many nations, particularly Western nations, do not possess. Furthermore, democracies depend on the leadership of elected representatives who serve a finite and relatively short period in office, a fact for which their adversaries have developed a deep appreciation. Consequently, the insurgent approach has frequently utilized time to overcome their material disadvantages.

CORRELATIONS TO IRAQ

There is a natural desire to rely on historical experience to acquire an understanding of the dynamics of a current predicament, but fundamental to any such comparison is the understanding of the context surrounding both cases. From the preceding analysis, there are aspects of Salvadoran and U.S. strategy in El Salvador that are valuable to examining the situation in Iraq today. The following discussion, utilizing the analytical elements of legitimacy, unity of effort, and time, provides a comparison of the El Salvador and Iraq insurgencies.

Legitimacy—Correlating El Salvador and Iraq.

The conflict in El Salvador was viewed internationally, even in the 1980s, as a situation where insurgency fomented predominantly through the tacit support of outsiders. As a result, it acquired an international standing as another in a growing list of proxy wars between the East and West. Internal to El Salvador, however, it was a protracted struggle for political power, and at the same time a matter of daily survival for the people of El Salvador. The core of the struggle was establishing an enduring government that would run the country based on political, social, and economic values that were recognized by the people as legitimate. If that could be accomplished by the government, to a level that negated the FMLN's promises and abilities, the government's battle for legitimacy would be won.

The U.S. contribution to El Salvador was viewed by most in El Salvador as legitimate. Certainly from the perspective of the El Salvadoran government, U.S. economic and military aid was the linchpin that facilitated the realization of many government political, economic, and social reforms that positively influenced the population. Furthermore, U.S. military assistance, and the U.S. insistence on improving the human rights record of the El Salvadoran armed forces, improved the military's capabilities and standing throughout the country.

Though assistance to El Salvador was largely viewed among U.S. elected representatives as a necessary investment in both the Cold War and Latin America, U.S. involvment also faced considerable opposition because of the El Salvadoran military's alleged human rights abuses; a perceived lack of political, economic, and social progress in El Salvador; the emergence of the Iran-Contra affair; and partisan U.S. domestic politics. If it were not for President Reagan's personal commitment to defeating communism in Latin America and his election to a second term, waning American public support of U.S. national interests in El Salvador may have collapsed before communist support for the opposition failed.

Seen as a proxy war internationally, there was no organized opposition or consensus to U.S. support of the government of El Salvador. Though Mexico and France recognized the FMLN as a "representative political force" in 1981, they later influenced the insurgents to reassess their strategy in 1988 and pursue a negotiated settlement.[48] By 1992, the UN had officiated an extended process of negotiation that resulted in a peace agreement for El Salvador. The international legitimacy of the outcome in El Salvador was substantiated by the UN's role as both observer and verifier of the agreement, and by donor countries in their capacity to fund reforms.[49]

In contrast, the legitimacy of the Government of Iraq, as late as 2008, was cause for considerable concern. In a March 2007 BBC/ABC poll, 53 percent of the Iraqis polled expressed dissatisfaction with the way the Iraqi government was performing, compared with 33 percent in 2005.[50] The same poll showed that much of the pessimism stemmed from a perception that life had not noticeably improved. The Iraqi government of Prime Minister Nouri Al-Maliki was installed in 2006 to serve until 2010. To the degree the serving government is unable to secure the confidence of the people of Iraq, the government's legitimacy will be eroded.

The U.S. National Strategy for Victory in Iraq, published in November 2005, clearly establishes the objective of "a new Iraq with a constitutional, representative government that respects civil rights and has security forces sufficient to maintain domestic order and keep Iraq from becoming a safe haven for terrorists."[51] If, however, the Iraqi government is ultimately unable to gain and maintain the confidence of the people through measurable improvements in social and economic conditions, their ability to achieve a near-term political reconciliation within a very fractured society may well pass. This is not to say that the end state is not achievable—certainly the first, nor the second, elected leader of El Salvador achieved the national objective of peace and unity—but more time will be necessary to attain it.

Iraqi perceptions of the legitimacy of U.S. actions within Iraq depend considerably on the audience solicited. For much of the Sunni population, who surrendered power and prestige with the demise of the Ba'ath party, the U.S. invasion was an illegal occupation, while most of the Kurdish populace of Iraq viewed the same actions as liberating. The Shiite community was arguably of the liberated mindset early on, but some factions, such as Muqtada Al Sadr's Mahdi Army and Sadr Bureau, evolved over time toward a position desiring an end to the occupation now.

In late 2007, a convergence of Iraqi opinion about continued U.S. military presence in their country materialized. In November 2007, focus groups conducted by the U.S. military, comprised of Iraqis of all sectarian and ethnic groups, believed the U.S. military invasion was the root of the violent differences among them and viewed the departure of occupying forces as the key to national reconciliation.[52] The absence of the perception by Iraqis of any denomination viewing the continued U.S. presence in their country as legitimate undermines the effectiveness of U.S. efforts and has deleterious effects on an Iraqi national government already plagued with skepticism about its legitimacy from those it is intended to serve.

Within the U.S. population, the unexpected ongoing conflict in Iraq has proven to be a divisive political issue, much more so than the U.S. involvement in El Salvador was in its time. Much of the divisive fervor is easily attributable to the continued deployment of large American military forces to Iraq, which was not the case in El Salvador. Other reasons include a failure to make the case for vital U.S interests, and partisan politics. Strong signals of a mandate for change to the U.S. strategy in Iraq were sent by the American people in the 2006 mid-term elections, and were confirmed in the 2008 Presidential election. All of these represent challenges to legitimacy.

The insurgency in El Salvador spanned three U.S. presidential election cycles and was somewhat divisive in its time, but the pace and proliferation of media coverage dramatically increased at the turn of the century. These changes pose new problems in attaining and sustaining legitimacy. The fast-paced media cycle and the availability of information and opinions regarding issues such as Iraq provides a continuing realtime venue for the repeated and minute scrutiny and challenging of the national interest and objectives, and critiques of progress toward achieving those national objectives. While this is the purpose of a free and open media in a democracy, the process subjects issues and decisions to constant exposure to, and often distortion of, the Western, and particularly

American, prism of impatience. In the minds of many Americans, if the United States has not achieved its objectives within 5 years of committing to involvement, then they are either inappropriate, or they are not going to be attained in a timely manner to make the continued expenditure of national treasure, particularly American sons and daughters, worthwhile.[53]

The U.S.-led multinational coalition operates in Iraq at the request of the Iraq government and with UN Security Council approval, which theoretically provided the coalition with international legitimacy. Yet, the lack of growth in the international political and military coalition that supports Iraq raises questions. A robust political, economic, or military commitment on the part of a regional ally such as Saudi Arabia or Jordan, or even a European ally such as Germany or France, would bolster the international commitment to the reconstruction of Iraq. Absent such a commitment, the true international perception of legitimacy must be reevaluated to determine why there is a lack of international resolve. Is it because of a concern about the Iraqi government, or the unwillingness to become involved so long as there is a robust American presence in Iraq, or a combination of such factors? Considerable opportunity for improvement in international legitimacy will grow when other nations, and the UN, recognize Iraq as a sovereign state and become involved in the long-term stability and growth of the country.

Unity of Effort—Correlating El Salvador and Iraq.

It was previously identified out that unity of effort, as it pertained to the protagonists in El Salvador, was evaluated on a relative scale. None of the elected governments during the period of 1980-92 was particularly unified in their action by Western standards, but compared to the FMLN they were able to maintain unity at a higher level for a longer period of time. El Salvador's government consistently pursued improvement of political, economic, and social conditions, as well as military reforms, and the effort produced tangible results that the FMLN was unable to overcome. Furthermore, despite debate among U.S. lawmakers, economic and military aid to El Salvador remained reliable.[54] In contrast, support to the FMLN, whether it came directly from the Soviet Union or through Cuba or Nicaragua, withered as the Communist empire collapsed.

Unity of effort within the Iraq government remains a pivotal issue in determining the future of the nation. The ability of the elected Shiite, Sunni, and Kurdish representatives to establish a political system that facilitates compromise and resolution of issues is the cornerstone of legitimacy for the government and is the foundation of defeating the insurgency. A December 2007 Pentagon report indicated that despite a reduction in violence in Iraq in the 3 months leading up to the report, the Iraqi government had made little progress in improving the delivery of electricity, health care, and other essential services.[55] The report also noted, "The government of Iraq's improvements in budget execution have translated into minimal advances in the delivery of essential services to the people of Iraq, mainly due to the sectarian bias in targeting and execution of remedial programs."[56] While the Iraqi infrastructure upon which essential services rely was in poor condition prior to the demise of the Saddam Hussein regime, it is the inability of the current government to create sufficient unity of effort that prevents it from meeting the people's expectations. One of the great truths of modernity is that when the people perceive that their government cannot improve their condition, that the government will not be long tolerated.

Conversely, neither al-Qaeda in Iraq, nor any other insurgent subsidiary, has delivered tangible improvements of any scale in these areas either, so a window of opportunity still exists if the El Salvadoran example of *unity of effort is relative* holds true. How long that temporal window remains open is perhaps the ultimate question.

Time — Correlating El Salvador and Iraq.

Twelve years of protracted political and military conflict transpired before political reconciliation occurred in El Salvador. During that time, the number of military forces and advisers ebbed and flowed as the momentum vacillated between the government and the insurgents. The shock of the collapse of the Soviet Union in 1991 significantly contributed to the willingness of the FMLN to compromise, but the ability of the government to use the dimension of time to achieve unity of effort and enhance its domestic and international legitimacy placed it in a stronger position to negotiate a compromise with the FMLN that resulted in a favorable peace.

As of this writing, Iraq has had nearly 5 years of a growing insurgency vying for legitimacy. The insurgency's failure to achieve unity and provide a cohesive and credible vision for the future has allowed the Iraqi government the same rare privilege of time afforded the El Salvadoran government. Time is required to sever the unity of the insurgents and discredit their legitimacy as in Al Anbar province, and other parts of Iraq.[57] Such a use of time and the achievement of momentum must, however, correlate with positive improvements in the unity and legitimacy of the Iraqi national government if stability is to become a continuing reality. The government must be viewed as acceptable, fair, and legitimate by the majority of the people of Iraq regardless of their sectarian or ethnic affiliation. Furthermore, the government must provide sufficient internal security and support to allow economic and social evolution to occur on a scale acceptable to the Iraqi people. Only when the people realize tangible improvements, embrace progress, and build a new national identity will success be realized. History has demonstrated that failure to create success will provoke some governing alternative to emerge and present its bid for legitimacy. In El Salvador, it took several national governments to achieve results acceptable to the people, so it is reasonable to expect that it could take more than one government in Iraq as well.

CONCLUSION

The strategic template provided by history rarely directly applies from one situation to the next. The myriad elements and influences that combine at one point in time to produce armed conflict, in these cases insurgencies, are not entirely the same notwithstanding the many similarities they might share. El Salvador in the 1980s and Iraq circa 2008 are alike in the absence of national unity and identity, the involvement of interest groups external to the country, and a significant investment on the part of the United States to cultivate a central government and military forces that will support stability within the region. As a result of these similarities, it has been suggested that the success of the past U.S.

171

model for involvement in El Salvador should be used to formulate a strategy for Iraq today. While there is value in this endeavor, any such process must be tempered with an appreciation of the unique circumstances of the two nations and the two periods in time. For example, there was no belief among El Salvadorans that the United States created the strife that initiated the insurgency that plagued El Salvador for over a decade. On the other hand, in Iraq, many perceive the United States did foment the conditions that led to an insurgency. Nonetheless, examination of the success of the El Salvadoran government in overcoming its insurgent challenge highlights several dimensions of Dr. Manwaring's model that, if successfully adhered to, can lead to success in Iraq.

First, the public-at-large must be persuaded of the legitimacy of the government and its actions. The people of a country ravaged by an insurgency must view their government as the legitimate national authority; one that is acting on their behalf to provide security and to improve their economic and social conditions. Equally important, if the United States, as an outside power, is supporting the threatened government, then the United States must achieve and sustain acceptable legitimacy within the threatened country, among the international community, and at home. Lack of legitimacy by the United States in the host nation, or abroad, greatly complicates the acquisition of international support, and of operations of any sort on the ground. Both El Salvador and Iraq demonstrate that the need to convince the American public, and to maintain their conviction, are two different, yet equally important aspects of domestic legitimacy that policymakers cannot ignore. In the spectrum of conflict where insurgency falls, American public support is very often the strategic center of gravity and must be assessed and addressed as such.

Unity of effort is a common theme within counterinsurgency theory and doctrine, yet creating it tends to be elusive. At its essence, insurgency is diametrically opposed to the targeted government—survival is at stake for both antagonists. Thus, insurgents seek to sever the influence and discredit the government with the population at every opportunity.[58] Clausewitz proposed that "war is merely the continuation of policy by other means."[59] "Other means" is a revolutionary concept of war that Vladimir Lenin and Mao Tse-Tung embraced in proposing their theories of insurgency.[60] Mao's little red book codified the idea that physical confrontation is but one of several necessary ways to achieving political objectives in an insurgency.[61] Consequently, the whole of the threatened government must work together to achieve an "effective unity of political-diplomatic, socio-economic, psychological-moral, and security-stability effort against those who would destroy the government."[62] Likewise, the U.S. national security professional must appreciate that no enemy today would logically seek to engage in a solely military confrontation with the United States. As such, the United States and her allies must anticipate insurgency and build unity of effort through a coherent marriage of their own national interests with shared strategic objectives in the counterinsurgent effort. This enables international and domestic resolve to be established on a foundation that will most likely endure the many assaults it will face in countering an insurgency while bolstering the legitimacy of the threatened government.

Time is a critical dimension to consider in any endeavor against an insurgency. The French and U.S. experiences in Indo-China as well as the El Salvadoran civil war confirm that time has strategic significance to all parties in conflict. For the insurgent, time can be used as a substitute for a lack of material goods in attaining their political objectives. For the government, legitimacy and unity of effort possess a temporal element. For example, leaders in democratic governments must consider the impact of time on policy decisions that span subsequent election cycles. Both legitimacy and unity of effort tend to become increasingly difficult to sustain in the face of successful insurgent actions—yet time is often essential for a government to build unity of effort and legitimacy. For both the insurgent and government, time is relative and can run out as a consequence of failures or successes on either's part. Time must be an inherent part of the strategic calculation for all actors.

The political and security situation in Iraq in the fall of 2007, as described by General David Petraeus and Ambassador Ryan Crocker, is evidence the United States did not sufficiently consider these three primary dimensions in the early and mid-stages of formulating policy and strategy for Iraq. Improvements in the security situation in early 2008, however, suggest the United States is learning from this experience and is applying lessons with more positive effect today. It remains to be seen if time is available for the Iraqi national government to demonstrate sufficient unity to acquire legitimacy in the eyes of its citizens and the international community. Provided it can do so relatively quickly, a more unified international effort to assist the people of Iraq, and her government, may prevail in the manner that it did in El Salvador 26 years ago, and a "new Iraq with a constitutional, representative government that respects civil rights" may yet prevail.[63]

ENDNOTES - CHAPTER 11

1. *Joint Publication (JP) 1-02, Department of Defense Dictionary of Military and Associated Terms*, Washington, DC: Joint Chiefs of Staff, April 12, 2001, as amended October 31, 2009, p. 266.

2. Bernard B. Fall, "The Theory and Practice of Insurgency and Counterinsurgency," *Naval War College Review*, Vol. 51, Winter 1998, p. 46.

3. Carl von Clausewitz, *On War*, Michael Howard and Peter Paret, eds. and trans., Princeton, NJ: Princeton University Press, 1976, pp. 605-610. Carl von Clausewitz clearly defines war as "merely the continuation of policy by other means," p. 87.

4. Fall, p. 50.

5. Jonathan D. Tepperman, "Flash Back," *New Republic,* April 11, 2005, p. 11.

6. *Ibid.*

7. Max G. Manwaring and John T. Fishel, "Insurgency and Counterinsurgency: Toward a New Analytical Approach," *Small Wars and Insurgencies*, Vol. 3, No. 3, 1992, pp. 272-310.

8. Kinloch C. Walpole, Jr., *The Isolation of El Salvador in the International Arena*, Thesis, Gainesville, FL: The University of Florida, 1987, p. 10.

9. *Ibid.*

10. Ian F. W. Beckett, *Modern Insurgencies and Counter-Insurgencies*, London, UK: Routledge, 2001, p. 205.

11. Max G. Manwaring and Court Prisk, *A Strategic View of Insurgencies: Insights from El Salvador*, Washington, DC: McNair Papers, No. 8, May 1990, p. 3.

12. Beckett, p. 205.

13. *Ibid.*, p. 206.

14. Raymond Bonner, *Weakness and Deceipt: U.S. Policy and El Salvador*, New York: Times Books, 1984, p. 164.

15. Leslie Anne Warner *et al.*, "Money in the Bank: Lessons Learned from Past Counterinsurgency Operations," *Rand Counterinsurgency Study-Paper 4*, Arlington, VA: Rand Corporation, 2007, p. 45.

16. The ceiling on the number of U.S. military trainers in El Salvador was fixed at 55 throughout the armed conflict, according to *ibid.*, p. 45.

17. John T. Fishel, "War by Other Means? The Paradigm and its Application to Peace Operations," *The Savage Wars of Peace: Toward a New Paradigm for Peace Operations*, Boulder, CO: Westview Press, 1998, p. 4.

18. Max G. Manwaring, interview by author, Carlisle, PA, November 28, 2007.

19. For a complete explanation of the model and the techniques used to create and validate it, see Max G. Manwaring and John T. Fishel, "Insurgency and Counterinsurgency: Toward a New Analytical Approach," *Small Wars and Insurgencies*, Vol. 3, No. 3, 1992, pp. 272-310.

20. *Ibid.*, pp. 279-280.

21. *Field Manual (FM) 3-24 (MCWP 3-33.5), Counterinsurgency*, Washington, DC: U.S. Department of the Army, December 15, 2006, pp. 1-1 - 4-9.

22. Manwaring, interview by author, November 28, 2007.

23. *Joint Publication (JP) 3-07.3, Joint Doctrine for Peace Operations*, Washington, DC: Joint Chiefs of Staff, Joint Warfighting Center, 2007, p. I-6.

24. *Joint Publication (JP) 3-07, Joint Doctrine for Military Operations Other Than War*, Washington, DC: Joint Chiefs of Staff, Joint Warfighting Center, 1995, p. I-1.

25. Max G. Manwaring and Kimbra L. Fishel, "Lessons That Should Have Been Learned: Toward a Theory of Engagement for 'The Savage Wars of Peace'," *The Savage Wars of Peace: Toward a New Paradigm for Peace Operations*, Boulder, CO: Westview Press, 1998, p. 285.

26. *Ibid.*, p. 205.

27. Manwaring and Prisk, p. 13.

28. Yvon Grenier, *Emergence of Insurgency in El Salvador*, Pittsburgh, PA: University of Pittsburgh Press, 1999, p. 90.

29. Manwaring, interview by author, November 28, 2007.

30. JP 3-07.3, p. I-6.

31. *Counterinsurgency for U.S. Government Policy Makers: A Work in Progress*, Washington, DC: U.S. Department of State, October 2007, p. 13.

32. David Kilcullen, *Counterinsurgency in Iraq: Theory and Practice, 2007*, United States Government Interagency Counterinsurgency Initiative, available from *www.usgcoin.org/library/publications/CounterinsurgencyInIraq-ppp_files/frame.htm*.

33. *Ibid*.

34. Max G. Manwaring, "Italian Terrorism, 1968-1982: Strategic lessons That Should Have Been Learned," *Low Intensity Conflict & Law Enforcement*, Vol. 7, No. 1, Summer 1998, p. 128.

35. Max G. Manwaring, interview by author, Carlisle, PA, February 6, 2008.

36. Manwaring and Prisk, p. 13.

37. *Ibid*. Cited from interviews by the authors with Ambassador Thomas Pickering, former U.S. Ambassador to El Salvador, Tel Aviv, Israel, August 1987.

38. Bard O'Neill, *Insurgency and Terrorism: From Revolution to Apocalypse*, 2nd Ed., Washington, DC: Potomac Books, 2005, p. 181.

39. *Ibid*.

40. Grenier, p. 85.

41. Manwaring and Prisk, p. 16.

42. Max G. Manwaring, interview by author, Carlisle, PA. December 10, 2007,

43. Colin S. Gray, *Irregular Enemies and the Essence of Strategy: Can the American Way of War Adapt?* Carlisle, PA: Strategic Studies Institute, U.S. Army War College, March 2006, p. 26.

44. Mao Tse-Tung, *On Guerrilla Warfare*, 2d Ed., Samuel B. Griffith II, trans., Baltimore, MD: Nautical and Aviation Publishing Company of America, 1992, p. 93.

45. Manwaring, interview by author, February 6, 2008.

46. Gray, p. 27.

47. Geoffrey Blainey, *The Causes of War*, 3rd Ed., New York: The Free Press, 1988, p. 41.

48. Joseph S. Tulchin and Gary Bland, eds., *Is There a Transition to Democracy in El Salvador?* Boulder, CO: Lynne Rienner Publishers, 1992, p. 188.

49. Elisabeth Jean Wood, *Insurgent Collective Action and Civil War in El Salvador*, Cambridge, UK: Cambridge University Press, 2003, p. 257.

50. "Iraq Poll March 2007: In Graphics," *BBC News*, 19 March 2007, available from *news.bbc.co.uk/2/hi/middle_east/6451841.stm*.

51. *National Strategy for Victory in Iraq*, Washington, DC: National Security Council, November 2005, p. 1.

52. Karen DeYoung, "All Iraqi Groups Blame U.S. Invasion for Discord, Study Shows," *Washington Post*, December 19, 2007, p. 14.

53. Len Hawley and Dennis Skocz, "Advance Political-Military Planning: Laying the Foundation for Achieving Viable Peace," *The Quest for Viable Peace*, Washington, DC: United States Institute of Peace, 2005, p. 37.

54. For a perspective on the debate concerning U.S. military and economic aid to El Salvador, see the fact sheet for the Honorable Senator Edward Kennedy, *El Salvador: Pipeline of U.S. Military and Economic Aid*, Washington, DC: U.S. General Accounting Office, February 1990.

55. *Measuring Stability and Security in Iraq: December 2007 Report to Congress,* Washington, DC: U.S. Department of Defense, December 2007, p. 11.

56. *Ibid.*, p. 11.

57. The author served in the Al Anbar Province of Iraq in 2004 with the Multi-National Force-West G-3, and again in 2007 as the Commanding Officer of Battalion Landing Team 2d Battalion, 4th Marines.

58. It could be further argued that insurgency has evolved to the point it is diametrically opposed to democracy, thereby making it much more challenging to counter.

59. Clausewitz, p. 87.

60. Clausewitz, pp. 605-610.

61. Mao Tse-Tung, p. 109.

62. Manwaring, "Italian Terrorism, 1968-1982:, p. 128.

63. *National Strategy for Victory in Iraq*, p. 1.

CHAPTER 12

THE USE OF SECURITY PROFESSIONALS
IN COUNTERINSURGENCY OPERATIONS

Lieutenant Colonel Marco E. Harris
U. S. Army National Guard

From Vietnam to Panama, Afghanistan to Iraq, history demonstrates an overwhelming need to provide appropriate security as the primary factor to achieving sustainable stability in the aftermath of conflict. The consequences of not immediately establishing effective security are televised throughout the world and used to the advantage of those elements who find political and economic advantage in the resultant instability. A lack of security encourages lawlessness and plants the seeds of insurgency. Despite history's evidence, the use of law enforcement organizations to prevent or reduce the opportunity for, or the intensity and length of an insurgency has been virtually ignored by U.S. military strategists and planners. Failing to adequately recognize the unique qualities that military and civilian law enforcement or other specialized forces bring to bear on the post-conflict and insurgency environments leads to an overapplication of maneuver-centric approaches when considering the level of force to apply for restoration of security and order among indigenous populations. Such tactics create popular resentment; lessen local, domestic, and international legitimacy of the operations; and risk creating support for the insurgency. In addition, whatever the degree of security that conventional forces have established for the indigenous population is often not sustainable when the combat forces depart. This chapter discusses the lawless environment and the power vacuum frequently created by conflict; shows how this environment can fuel an insurgency; and offers insights for incorporating specialized and police capabilities into future military strategies and counterinsurgency plans.

INSURGENCY

In the emerging 21st century environment, nations with competent armed forces and capable intelligence agencies no longer fear encroachment from their neighbors and can extend security to others. Globalization, treaties, and economic well-being have fostered a relatively stable and peaceful international and domestic environment for most developed nations. The concerns of 21st security are largely about the possible collateral damage from the actions of rogue states, terrorists, and criminal elements who disregard recognized territorial and legal boundaries; and about the chaos and lawlessness of failed and failing states. Inside the borders of the latter, not only do terrorists, criminals, and political opportunists seek advantage, but fragments of the population feel disenfranchised and unjustly treated as their culture, society, and institutions fail. These factors lead to violence and other disruptive acts.[1] Conventional military forces are ill equipped to respond to these phenomena as they spread throughout the populace, particularly in urban areas. Often, despite the best intentions of the actions of a seated government or members of the international community, or perhaps as a direct result of these actions, an insurgency may take root. It is an emerging reality of the 21st century that insurgency is a preferred form of war "by those who seek to overthrow or force change of a benevolent authority," and is being pursued largely in urban areas — an environment particular ill-suited for general purpose forces.[2]

Insurgency is generally defined as "a condition of revolt against a recognized government that does not reach the proportions of an organized revolutionary government and is not recognized as belligerency."[3] Recent military doctrine has found a need to further clarify this in light of recent developments of the 21st century by indicating that "an insurgency is an organized, protracted politico-military struggle designed to weaken the control and legitimacy of an established government, occupying power, or other political authority while increasing insurgent control."[4] The same doctrine defines counterinsurgency as "military, paramilitary, political, economic, psychological, and civic actions taken by a government to defeat insurgency."[5] A recent article defined counterinsurgency even more accurately, "an integrated set of political, economic, social, and security measures intended to end and prevent the recurrence of armed violence, create and maintain stable political, economic, and social structures, and resolve the underlying causes of an insurgency in order to establish and sustain the conditions necessary for lasting stability."[6]

Insurgencies thrive particularly well in power vacuums that can typically be found following conflict, the collapse of repressive regimes, or in failing states. Often times in these circumstances perverted social institutions, governments, and political officials have contributed to the chaotic environment through their control of the population through fear and oppression, fostering feelings of mistrust, and through a void of suitable political processes. A disillusioned population is particularly vulnerable during periods of general chaos and is looking for a government that can provide for their basic needs. This period has been referred to as the "golden hour," implying it is the opportune time to act for forces of good or ill. Security is paramount to creating an environment that meets the people's expectations. Military strategies and plans too often focus on combating the insurgents instead of preventing the conditions which foster destabilizing trends and enable an insurgency. Establishing security in the short term in order to avert chaos and to prevent criminal and insurgent forces from securing a foothold in society, while concurrently restoring basic services, is vital to facilitating long-term stability. Understanding why insurgencies succeed leads to an understanding of the critical importance of getting security right.

David Galula's characterization of insurgency, although developed in the 1960s, remains relevant in the 21st century. "An insurgency is a protracted struggle conducted methodically, step by step in order to attain specific intermediate objectives leading finally to the overthrow of the existing order (China, 1927-49; Greece, 1944-50; Indochina, 1945-54; Malaya, 1948-60; Algeria, 1954-62)."[7] Galula asserts that the object of revolutionary war, or an insurgency, is the population itself. Insurgents are trying to win the population over, and the counterinsurgency is trying to sustain the people's loyalty to the established regime. It is a struggle over legitimacy and for survival. Galula concludes that these objectives are political in nature, and insurgencies are inherently protracted wars. As Galula observes, "It takes time for a small group of insurgent leaders to organize a revolutionary movement, to raise and develop armed forces, to a balance with the opponent and to overpower him."[8] Studies have shown that insurgencies on the average last 10 years;[9] these years are marked with continued internal friction caused by violence and instability. Even in the case of well-equipped and trained militaries, it is difficult to sustain public support and international approval of counterinsurgency combat activities for an extended period.

States countering insurgencies at home or abroad must recognize that defeating the insurgency is not just a military problem. As insurgent groups seek to gain legitimacy over the existing government they often and logically promote reforms and social justice for the purpose of persuading the indigenous populace and international political and civil society to support them. Over time, an insurgent group gains a practical and moral legitimacy through the use of such policies.[10] To combat insurgencies, governments and conventional armies must adapt to the challenges posed by the many political, cultural, religious, economic, moral, and social justice issues that enable an insurgency. Successfully confronting these challenges requires an increasingly secure environment.

THE LESSON OF IRAQ

The progress of the war in Iraq clearly reveals the benefits that could have been realized had the strategy and planning efforts included a more comprehensive approach to providing a stable social order following the U.S. invasion. At the end of major combat operations in Iraq, when the U.S. Army's Third Infantry Division entered the capital city of Baghdad, the Iraqi National Police had been disbanded. They blended into the populace taking with them their weapons, and more importantly, their experience and institutional knowledge of keeping order in a city the size of Baghdad. Initially, arriving U.S. forces were greeted as liberators. Shortly thereafter, U.S. Soldiers witnessed the jubilant crowds transform into rioters and looters.[11] Without the control provided by local and national law enforcement agencies — and in the absence of a U.S. security alternative — the populace burned and destroyed government buildings, stole artifacts, and carried out violent acts on citizens believed to be Ba'ath party members, or sympathetic to the former regime.

American Soldiers were exceptionally well-trained and doctrinally prepared to survive and win in the harsh conditions of conventional warfare; but they were ill prepared to conduct community policing, especially in a highly charged religious and ethnically divided environment. U.S. military and civilian leadership did not see law enforcement as a military mission and, like the Soldiers, expected to see law and order prevail. The developing disconnects were complicated because the indigenous culture is rooted in Islam and the Koran. Religion not only played a greater role in political decisions and social expectations than the U.S. decisionmakers and Soldiers grasped, but also defined in part the responsibilities of successful armies and popular expectations. The expectations of both the Americans and the Iraqi citizens were greatly disappointed.

The initial failure of the Soldiers to act, and subsequent belated actions, formed the basis for future relationships; such initial impressions are difficult to overcome, especially when they are negative. In Iraq, U.S. Soldiers who were initially photographed alongside plunderers and lawbreakers, ignoring the looting, rioting, and violence that occurred, quickly found that gaining the confidence of the average Iraqi citizen proved to be extremely difficult.[12] In a United States Institute of Peace Special Report, Robert M. Perito asserts that "Responsibility for law and order fell to coalition military forces that were neither trained nor equipped to perform police functions. U.S. soldiers complained they had not been trained to fight crime and should not be asked to make arrests."[13] The report goes on to conclude that coalition forces developed insensitivity to the violent Iraqi-on-Iraqi crime that was occurring. The negative impact of this indifferent attitude on Iraqi citizens was immeasurable, but clearly evident in the pervading Iraqi attitudes on the streets and in media reports. Since the Iraqi Police Service was unable to protect the Iraqi public and the coalition forces seemed indifferent to the welfare of the Iraqi citizens, the conditions were set for insurgency.[14]

The rift between Coalition Forces and the Iraqi people widened further when U.S decisionmakers began to react to the growing disorder. U.S. and coalition combat soldiers searching Iraqi homes appeared insensitive to common Islamic customs such as not entering a house occupied by women without a Muslim male present. This lack of cultural awareness among Coalition Forces contributed to the negative impression already taking root in the minds of many Iraqi citizens. Cultural awareness in regard to an indigenous population is now accepted as a core principle for providing legitimate security and social order so as to prevent civil disobedience and illegal activities. Cultural awareness and sensitivity to citizens' expectations is another fundamental principle of professional law enforcement operations.

An integral component of legitimacy for governance is public safety. In Iraq, that responsibility fell initially to the United States and its coalition partners following the collapse of Saddam Hussein's regime. When lawlessness took root, it resembled the symptoms of a virus, spreading from neighborhood to neighborhood, feeding on the weak and disenchanted, young and old alike. Criminal elements seeking to intimidate the populace united, using the powerful weapon of fear. Former regime enforcers used their reputations to victimize the public through further violence and extortion. What was left of the criminal justice system had been disbanded since it was wrought with government supported corruption and no appropriate substitute was provided. Public safety was nowhere to be found.[15] Islamic fundamentalists seeking to expel the infidel Americans from Islamic territory seized the opportunity to spread death and terror among the average citizens. Political opportunists took advantage of the lawlessness to acquire power. Iraqi citizens became vulnerable to anyone with a gun or a bomb strapped to their body—and susceptible to promises of security and social justice. As the golden hour slipped by, insurgency became the unwelcome bridesmaid of any U.S. supported government.

COUNTERING AN INSURGENCY

R. Scott Moore, in *The Basics of Counterinsurgency*, states "The ultimate objective of counterinsurgency strategy is lasting stability, but not one that is imposed and maintained by force or repression. Stability must provide the structures necessary to peacefully address issues that may continue to arise; those structures must be understood, institutionalized, and fully accepted by the population, who now feel they benefit from them."[16] Moore also points out that "to be successful, counterinsurgencies must be perceived as legitimate . . . legitimacy within the conflict zone occurs when populations, and their leaders, understand that the counterinsurgency results benefit them more than any alternative."[17] Hence, from an insurgent's perspective the government's legitimacy is a center of gravity, and it can be attacked by creating insecurity for the population.[18]

Moore found in his study of insurgencies that only 40 percent of counterinsurgencies were successful, and that for lasting stability, the conflict had to be resolved in all its dimensions—not just overwhelming application of military force.[19] In this strategic approach, he offers six critical tasks to be integrated for success.

1. Establish and Maintain Security: This task is broken into three subcomponents: restoring security; disarmament, demobilization, and reintegration; and maintaining security. It is a broad task that is much more encompassing than military operations. It reestablishes basic public safety and restores the confidence of the populace in the ability of government to assure security in the short run and over time. To gain trust and legitimacy, local public safety agencies and defense forces must be given training, if needed, and the opportunity to work independent of security forces. Restoring credible public safety is manpower-intensive; it requires well-trained personnel acting with situational and cultural awareness.[20]

2. Provide Humanitarian and Essential Services: This task entails rebuilding the critical infrastructure, including public transportation, utilities, communication, medical aid, and other basic quality of life services. When properly integrated, it minimizes the helplessness of the civilian population and takes the edge off the destructive effect of military operations. Hence, it enhances the effectiveness of security forces. It is often the first step in establishing political and economic development.[21]

3. Promote Effective Governance: Confidence in government from the local to the national level is required, and its consideration must be integrated into all tasks. The populace must feel that their political leadership has their interest at heart, and not that of some special group or occupying force. Effective governments create a binding social contract in which the government creates the conditions to meet basic social needs, and the citizens willingly give their allegiance and support. Such governments are not installed and need not be propped up, but earn legitimacy through serving their people's best interests.[22] The rule of law they establish supports the achievement of the other tasks.

4. Sustain Economic Development: A broken economy is often the underlying reason that ignites an insurgency. On the other hand, a strong and sustained economy helps build and maintain stability, effective governance, and long-term prosperity. Security forces are essential to creating conditions for economic development, from creating a safe environment in which to conduct day-to-day business, to augmenting the efforts of other internal and external agencies. Economic development supports the creation of jobs and normalcy. It can also falter because of fraud, corruption, and incompetence—potentially contributing to the legitimacy of an insurgency.[23]

5. Support Reconciliation: To end an insurgency, the underlying issues must be addressed and the reconciliation to reunite the population must occur, or civil order will be disrupted by continued mistrust and violence. Without reconciliation, progress in all other tasks is at risk. All parties involved in the conflict, including outside forces, must agree on how the peace or cessation of violence will be accomplished. In addition, the means to mediate local disputes, address war crimes and atrocities, and account for or resettle missing and displaced persons must be resolved. Such justice is an important

component for starting the healing process and for transitioning to sustained security and progress.[24]

6. Foster Social Change: Successful counterinsurgencies ultimately bring about political and social change. Insurgencies result from political, economic, and social weaknesses: counterinsurgencies that attempt to maintain the status quo rarely succeed. To achieve lasting stability, pre-existing conditions and attitudes must be altered. However, it does not logically follow that a democratic government should be immediately installed.[25] Appropriate social change should be integrated into all the tasks.

What the U.S. policymakers and military strategists failed to grasp in Iraq was the importance of social institutions and their impact on the fabric of public opinion. As a society emerges from conflict, it naturally looks for beneficial change and well-being. It searches for a group to provide basic security and services. Provision of services, not legitimacy, is the primary objective—but legitimacy in large part is achieved through the provision of services. A populace searching for a new stability often finds these services met by rogue elements who are seeking to gain their own legitimacy by providing for basic needs—security, shelter, food, medical aid, and economic opportunities. It matters little that the insurgents may promote instability or use intimidation. Consequently, the struggle for the population's approval becomes a war of a slightly different nature, where the battle for the hearts and minds of the citizens is less about ideology than about social accomplishments on the ground. The ideology is justified by its accomplishments. The victor in this competition gains public trust and confidence, setting the path for a nation's future political, economic, and social development. In this struggle, security is essential and must be integrated with the other tasks. Not surprisingly, the ways and means of how security is attained and sustained is paramount.[26]

COUNTERINSURGENCY CAPABILITIES

Countering an insurgency requires forces and resources to integrate and accomplish the tasks outlined above. Roles, missions, and responsibilities should be clearly stated and understood by all internal and external actors participating in the effort. Since security provides the basic foundation on which additional institutions and infrastructure are built, it is essential to get security *right* early in the process. Getting security right from the start enables the government emerging from or engaged in the conflict to take advantage of the golden hour and capitalize on the population's desire for social stability and opportunity. Getting it wrong, or getting it late, creates opportunities for insurgents, criminals, and political opportunists.

What force capabilities U.S. strategists and planners should propose to address the security requirements and the integrative nature of post-conflict operations and counterinsurgencies is an open question, but one that Iraq and Afghanistan brought to the forefront. Both suggest that conventional military forces are not necessarily the best tool to achieve long-term success in this area.

Counterinsurgency theorist David Galula states that, "conventional warfare has been thoroughly analyzed in the course of centuries—indeed for almost the extent of recorded history—and the process of battle has been sliced into distinct phases: march towards the enemy, test of the enemy's strength, exploitation of success, eventual retreat, etc."[27] Galula's argument is that in training for conventional warfare, soldiers are not challenged to deal with the issues that are characteristics of an insurgency. He asserts that "in counterinsurgency warfare, the soldier's job is to help win the support of the population, and in so doing, has to engage in practical politics."[28] Moore's codification of the six integrative tasks supports this assertion. The bravery and positive achievements of conventional forces notwithstanding, there are special skills and considerations that have proven effective in the past for countering the security issues of insurgencies. Past successes more often came at the hands of civilian and more specialized military organizations, as opposed to general purpose military forces. While military civil affairs and U.S. Agency for International Development (USAID) capabilities have been generally advocated and scrutinized, three other U.S. means need greater consideration.

U.S. SPECIAL OPERATIONS FORCES

In the United States, Special Operations Forces (SOF) are small, elite military units trained and equipped for special missions normally not part of the general purpose force mission set. While SOF units and personnel are assigned around the world, all special operations personnel, units, and Title 10 responsibilities fall under U.S. Special Operations Command (USSOCOM), one of the unified commands. USSOCOM was formed at the iniative of the U.S. Congress to ensure SOF retained its unique nature and capabilities. SOF personnel undergo rigorous selection and lengthy, specialized training, and use specialized equipment. For many, cultural awareness and immersion are inherent to their qualifications. SOF units total roughly 34,000 active and 15,000 reserve personnel in the Army, Navy, Marine Corps, and Air Force, or about 2 percent of all U.S. active and reserve forces.[29]

Special operations units conduct direct or indirect military missions focused on strategic or operational objectives in support of U.S. policy and strategy. These missions exceed the routine capabilities of conventional military forces and include unconventional warfare and foreign internal defense which bear directly on counterinsurgency capabilities, focusing on training and assistance for indigenous government agencies trying to overcome subversion and hostile internal activities.[30] U.S. special operations in the Philippines illustrate the capabilities and potential of these forces in the prospective or actual counterinsurgency environment.

The Joint Special Operations Task Force-Philippines (JSOTF-P) was created in July 2002 by the Special Operations Command Pacific. It operates "by, through and with" its Philippine Armed Forces counterparts in humanitarian, civic actions, and military advisory missions that span Moore's six tasks.[31] What security should look like in this particular environment was an inherent advisory task. As part of the military advisory role, it deployed in Liaison Coordination Elements (LCE) alongside Armed Forces Philippines (AFP) soldiers conducting counterinsurgency operations. The LCE teams and the AFP exchanged subject matter experts and conducted civil affairs projects and psychological operations. The object of the coalition operation was to conduct counterinsurgency operations against the Abu Sayyaf Group (ASG), which had been terrorizing the Philippine people for almost 20 years [32]

Through the use of civil-military assistance programs, the LCE and the AFP have constructed and repaired roads, built schools and hospitals, and established water drilling sites in an effort to improve the daily lives of the civilian populace. The AFP credits these projects with helping to separate the population from the terrorist organizations. Because of the exchange of medical subject matter expertise, a quarter of million patients have been treated by AFP personnel and LCE teams since 2002. A Commander of JSOTF-P, Colonel David Maxwell, reported that "in addition to these projects, military and information operations have created a paradigm shift within the community, denying sanctuary for terrorist elements and leaders."[33] The use of psychological operations is also having a measured effect. The PSYOP Reward for Justice Program has paid out over $10 million for information to AFP concerning the activities and location of terrorists. This information led to the neutralization of two key Abu Sayyaf Group leaders. A deputy commander of the U.S. Special Operations Command noted that "Our operation has a Philippine face on them. The people in the local areas are crediting the Philippine government for the goodness that is coming from the activity."[34] The Philippine government is winning the hearts and minds of the people and the Special Operations Forces are assisting in legitimizing the government through the use of the LCE teams, who traditionally have the mission of conducting counterinsurgency operations in theater.[35]

Unfortunately, the amount of training and resources required to create these special operations forces make them a valuable, yet scarce, resource. However, the success of the counterinsurgency efforts in the Philippines not only highlights the need for additional forces: it also demonstrates how integrating the six tasks in an unstable environment — even if a long term one — can establish government legitimacy through effective services.

THE U.S. MILITARY POLICE

U.S. military police, though not a special operations force, possess unique training and capabilities indispensable to meeting the challenges of establishing security in post-conflict environments and undermining insurgent tactics. Their training and competencies serve five basic operations: police intelligence; law and order; internment; resettlement operations; and maneuver, mobility and survivability.[36] Obviously, as part of the conventional force structure, military police have an important role on the traditional battlefield, but a part of that role is equally suitable to the post-conflict or insurgency setting. In this regard, these special capabilities contribute to restoring and maintaining public order and thereby enabling the government to create security and stability, which ultimately fosters trust and confidence in the populace.

U.S. military police are flexible and capable of transcending their strictly military role to provide the particular services required in emergency situations such as disaster relief, emergency evacuation, civil crisis, peace operations, and post-conflict operations. Like civilian law enforcement officers, military police are adept at community policing.[37] They are comfortable interacting with civilians in both domestic and international settings. Again, as with their civilian counterparts, the presence of effective military police operations creates an impression of a disciplined order and has a calming effect on distraught citizens. Such was the case with the peacekeeping and stabilization operations recently conducted in Bosnia and Kosovo, where U.S. military police joined in cooperative efforts with the UN to develop community policing initiatives with local police agencies. With over 52 percent of the military police force structure residing in the Reserve Components, and a significant number holding civilian law enforcement jobs, an added benefit for the United States is that many of these Soldiers bring their civilian policing skills and experience to the military mission.

U.S. military police are part of the conventional force structure and have clear missions as part of the general purpose forces. Yet, their unique capabilities provide significant advantages for creating and sustaining a secure environment in post-conflict or insurgency environments. These advantages extend beyond the conduct of operations in their areas of expertise, to advising and training indigenous civil and military police, and perhaps training general purpose forces serving in such environments as well. Their applicability to the emerging 21st century security environment is so profound that it rebegs the question of how much force structure should be allocated for military police.

U.S. CIVILIAN LAW ENFORCEMENT

Post-conflict insecurity and the potential for a successful insurgency can also be reduced through the effective use civilian law enforcement capabilities. A recent RAND Corporation Study commissioned by the U.S. Army War College identifies these capabilities as Special Police Units (SPU) and Transitional Law Enforcement (TLE). In regard to the latter, the transitional period is the time during which the control of security is passed to the indigenous government. It can refer to post-combat operations or the time when some lesser form of intervention winds down. Several U.S. federal agencies have law enforcement personnel that can potentially deploy to and operate on foreign soil. These agencies, in cooperation with other international law enforcement activities, can provide the following capabilities: (1) high-end qualifications to deal with organized entities such as criminals or insurgents; (2) intelligence and criminal investigation; (3) control of crowds and unruly populations; and (4) training of indigenous law enforcement. [38]

The U.S. Marshal Service (USMS) is one example of a U.S. federal agency with excellent transitional law enforcement credentials. All four of the capabilities identified above are found within its wide range of police specialties and organizational structure. Its historical legal authority to deputize nonfederal law enforcement personnel allows it to bring in large numbers of other law enforcement resources under the same legal protection enjoyed by federal marshals. [39] In addition, under the U.S. Department of Justice (DoJ), the International Criminal Investigation Training Assistance Program (ICITAP) and the Overseas Prosecutorial Development, Assistance and Training (OPDAT) program have the mandate and key capabilities to reestablish and support the rule of law globally. For example, ICITAP provides law enforcement training worldwide at all levels of the criminal justice system in a comprehensive manner. It does this through the employment of a large number of contract personnel who supplement a fairly austere full-time ICITAP staff at the DoJ. This training can be custom-made to fit the host nation requirements. [40]

Of course, ICITAP training is derived from the perspective of law enforcement in a democratic society, linking services and legitimacy back to democratic government in support of U.S. long-term interests. ICITAP is currently conducting law enforcement training in 17 countries of which Albania, East Timor, Indonesia, Nigeria, and Kosovo are representative. In Kosovo, police trained by the ICITAP are deployed throughout the newly declared independent state.[41] In partnership with ICITAP, OPDAT provides training to support the upper tier of a national criminal justice system, the judicial system. It trains prosecutors and judges in order to negate the power of intimidation used against public officials and business leaders to subvert justice.[42]

Any discussion of the use of U.S. personnel for purposes of conducting, training, or advising police in a foreign government must include reference to Title 22 restrictions. Generally, Section 2420 of the Foreign Assistance Act specifically prohibits use of U.S. funding to support external activities of this nature. However, as is often the case with prohibitions, exceptions are cited in the U.S. Code. Specifically, funding for such activities are allowed in accordance with subparagraph (b): "with respect to assistance provided to reconstitute civilian police authority and capability in the post-conflict restoration of host nation infrastructure for the purpose of supporting a nation emerging from instability, and the provisions of professional public safety training, to include training in internationally recognized standards of human rights."[43] This exclusion is critical for any reconstruction program in Iraq or Afghanistan. Equally critical, U.S. strategists and planners must recognize that in taking the necessary steps for successful nation-building, the use of civil law enforcement expertise offers one more way to counter any potential rift between the indigenous population and combat troops. The desired effects are achieved less violently and more effectively through a more precise application of specialized military and law enforcement capabilities.

CONCLUSION

Mistakes were made by U.S. policymakers, strategists, and planners in Iraq and Afghanistan. Neither effort shows an appropriate appreciation of the proper role of security and its integrative relationship with the other critical tasks highlighted by Moore's and Galula's studies of insurgency and counterinsurgency. The decision by U.S. and coalition partners to disband the Iraqi public safety institutions without a practical replacement proved harmful to the Iraqi population and coalition forces alike, greatly complicating the establishment of a legitimate government and costing many lives. Notwithstanding the decisions of policymakers, the military grossly underestimated the importance of basic security and services in post-conflict and nation-building. The liberation cast average Iraqis into far worse social conditions than they had experienced under Saddam and created opportunities for criminals and political opportunists of all types. Once these forces were unleashed, post-conflict operations took on the attributes of an insurgency. Untrained and unprepared conventional U.S. forces compounded the situation by their reliance on traditional combat power. A parallel exists in Afghanistan where apparent initial success was lost to resurgent Taliban forces resulting from the failure to grasp the integrative nature of Moore's six critical tasks. Crossing the thin line between partner and occupier could have been avoided had the United States better understood and applied Moore's six basic steps, and had the military strategists and planners grasped the relationship between post-conflict operations and insurgency.

Equally important, 21st century warfare will be triggered by policy driven belligerents who avoid conventional warfare and seek to overthrow governments through violence—

insurgencies. Then Lieutenant General David H. Petraeus grasped these emerging truths in a *Military Review* essay where he stated:

> The insurgencies in Iraq and Afghanistan were not, in truth, the wars for which we were best prepared in 2001; however, they are the wars we are fighting and they clearly are the wars we must master. America's overwhelming conventional military superiority makes it unlikely that future enemies will confront us head on. Rather, they will attack us asymmetrically, avoiding our strength—firepower, maneuver technology—and come at us and our partners the way the insurgents do in Iraq and Afghanistan. It is imperative, therefore, that we continue to learn from our experiences in those countries, both to succeed in those endeavors and to prepare for the future.[44]

Whether emerging from post-conflict situations, self-started by political opportunists, or arising from conditions in failed and failing states, insurgency is on the rise and counterinsurgency success rests on a foundation of security.

Conventional military forces are seldom able to defeat insurgencies using military means alone. Even if they could, the costs in local, international, and domestic legitimacy for applying the levels of force required might be strategically prohibitive. Hence, avoiding or curtailing instability by providing, creating, and supporting appropriate indigenous security institutions, public security becomes more paramount. Such security may be imposed to some level by general purpose forces, but it is better provided by military and civilian organizations and personnel who have particular security expertise. As with the other counterinsurgency tasks, the peculiar expertise enhances the performance of the task by virtue of training and experience because its less or noncombative nature enhances and transfers the legitimacy of the actions to the host government. In both post-conflict operations and insurgencies, military strategists and planners should make better use of SOF, military policy, and civil law enforcement capacity. This emerging truth has force structure and resource implications across the whole of government, but it leverages the golden hour and lessens costs in blood and treasure as the United States pursues its national interests in a 21st century world order.

ENDNOTES - CHAPTER 12

1. David Galula, *Counterinsurgency Warfare, Theory and Practice*, New York: Praeger, 1964, p. 8.

2. *Joint Publication (JP) 1-02, Department of Defense Dictionary of Military and Associated Terms*, Washington, DC: Joint Chiefs of Staff, April 12, 2001, as amended October 31, 2009, p. 266.

3. Philip B. Gove, ed., *Webster's Third New International Dictionary*, Springfield, MA: Merriam-Webster, 1981, p. 1173.

4. *Field Manual (FM) 3-24, Counterinsurgency*, Washington, DC: U.S. Department of the Army, December 15, 2006, p. 1-1.

5. *Ibid.*

6. R. Scott Moore, *The Basics of Counterinsurgency*, Washington, DC: U.S. Joint Forces Command, J9, Joint Urban Operations Office, n.d., p. 14, available from *smallwarsjournal.com/documents/moorecoinpaper.pdf*.

7. Galula, p. 4.

8. *Ibid.*, p. 8.

9. *Ibid.*, p. 15.

10. Moore, p. 22.

11. Robert M. Perito, *The Coalition Provisional Authority's Experience with Public Security in Iraq*, Washington, DC: United States Institute of Peace, April 2005, p. 7.

12. *Ibid.*

13. *Ibid.*

14. *Ibid.*, p. 6.

15. *Ibid.*, p. 7.

16. Moore, p. 16.

17. *Ibid.*, p. 22.

18. Montgomery McFate and Andrea V. Jackson, "The Object Beyond War: Counterinsurgency and the Four Tools of Political Competition," *Military Review*, October 2006, p. 57.

19. Moore, pp. 14-15.

20. *Ibid.*, p. 17.

21. *Ibid.*, p. 19.

22. *Ibid.*

23. *Ibid.*

24. *Ibid.*

25. *Ibid.*

26. *Ibid.*, pp. 3-9, 15, 16-17.

27. Galula, p. 84.

28. *Ibid.*, p. 95

29. Wikipedia, "United States Special Operations Command," March 20, 2008, available from *en.wikipedia.org./wiki/United_States_Special_Operations_Command*. See also *Joint Special Operations Forces Reference Manual*, 2 Ed., Hurlburt Field, FL: The Joint Special Operations University Press.

30. Major D. Jones, "Unconventional Warfare, Foreign Defense, And Why Words Matter," *Special Warfare*, Vol. 20, July-August 2006, p. 19.

31. Global Security.org, "Joint Special Operations Task Force-Philippines," available from *www.globalsecurity.org/military/agency/dod/jsotf-p.htm*.

32. Gabe Puello and Robert Smith, "JSOTF-Philippines: A Model for Counterinsurgency," *Tip of The Spear*, Vol. 18, October 2007, p. 18.

33. *Ibid.*, p. 19.

34. *Ibid.*

35. *Ibid.*

36. Robert M. Perito, *Where is the Lone Ranger When We Need Him?: America's Search For A Postconflict Stability Force,* Washington, DC: United States Institute of Peace, 2004, p. 79.

37. *Ibid.*, p. 81.

38. Terrence K. Kelly, *Options for Transitional Security Capabilities for America*, Santa Monica, CA: RAND, 2006, pp. xi, 12.

39. *Ibid.*, p. 24.

40. "ICITAP Program Descriptions," linked from the *International Criminal Investigative Training Assistance Program (ICITAP), Home Page,* available from *www.usdoj.gov/ criminal/icitap/coverMemoMereLetter.html*.

41. Perito, *Where is the Lone Ranger When We Need Him?* p. 190.

42. "Mission Statement," *Office of Overseas Prosecutorial Development, Assistance and Training (OPDAT) Strategic Plan Fiscal Year 2005-2006*, Washington, DC: U.S. Department of Justice, Office of Overseas Prosecutorial Development, Assistance, and Training, 2006, available from *www.usdoj.gov/criminal/opdat/ strategic-plan/strategic-plan.html#OPDATMissionStmt*.

43. Office of the Law Revision Counsel, U.S House of Representatives, "United States Code, Title 22, Section 2420," available from *uscode.house.gov/uscode-cgi/fastweb.exe?getdoc+uscview+t21t25+2403+0++%28 assistance%29%20%20AND%20%28%2822%29%20ADJ%20USC%29%3ACITE%20AND%20%28USC%20 w%2F10%20%282420%29%29%3ACITE%20%20%20%20%20%20%20%20%20.*

44. David H. Petraeus, "Learning Counterinsurgency: Observations from Soldiering in Iraq," *Military Review*, October 2006, p. 45.

CHAPTER 13

INFLUENCING THE FORGOTTEN HALF OF THE POPULATION IN COUNTERINSURGENCY OPERATIONS

Colonel Laura C. Loftus
U.S. Army

Muslim women's voices can help us win the war against terror by tempering their societies long-term . . . Many quasi-democracies of mostly male participants are overly influenced by extremism and do not benefit from half the population's input. In other words, the hand that rocks the cradle could also moderate the nation.

—Rachel Bryars[1]

INTRODUCTION

Stories of Iraqi Women.[2]

Following the initial euphoria after the U.S. invasion of Iraq in 2003, many Iraqi people gradually withdrew behind their sectarian and tribal divides. However, some worked across the divides to try to improve the lives of everyday Iraqis who had long suffered under the neglect of Saddam Hussein's regime. Nesreen, a woman and a doctor, was insistent upon getting the local hospital operational again. She worked with the U.S. Army to obtain critical hospital requirements, like emergency power generation and emergency medical equipment, through the Commanders' Emergency Response Program (CERP) funding. Undeterred by dangerous conditions, she traveled repeatedly to Baghdad in search of basic medical supplies and actively lobbied for needed medical equipment. Upon bringing the hospital to an operational status, Nesreen worked with neighboring U.S. Army units to facilitate medical civic action programs at the local hospital. Her status in the community was further reinforced when male city council members asked her to join the city council as a member based on her contributions to the community.

Like Nesreen, Raja was not content to sit by and simply watch developments. As U.S. forces undertook a program to construct schools, Raja sought to ensure that school projects incorporated all Iraqi children, regardless of sect, tribe, or gender. She strived to fairly distribute school supplies and to get local teachers back into classrooms. In addition, she worked through her husband to gain acceptance for the local U.S. Army unit to facilitate formation of a local women's organization.

Iraq, and indeed the rest of the world the Army operates in, is filled with women like Nesreen and Raja who have the capabilities and motivation to make significant contributions to peacemaking and peacekeeping efforts. While local Iraqi men were concerned with divisive issues such as exploiting the Sunni-Shia conflict and assailing former Ba'ath party members, these women looked for ways to bring the population together and to support all members of society. The senior coordinator of the U.S. State Department's Office of International Women's Issues also observed "a great spirit of unity among Iraqi women."[3] Nesreen's and Raja's roles suggest greater participation by women in Iraq based on a shared stake in economic and social development and may help to moderate the regional, ethnic, and religious divisions. Their activities suggest women may be a key strategic factor to consider for stability operations anywhere in the world.

It is critical for the U.S. military, and particularly the Army as a land force, to understand and appreciate the motivations and capabilities of women like Nesreen and Raja, the cultural and social constructs in which they exist, and the effects they can have on the success of military operations and U.S. policy objectives. Such understanding and appreciation leads to better and more effective strategy, planning, and tactical actions. In pursuit of these ends, this chapter first highlights the internationally recognized importance of women as peacemakers and peacekeepers, then presents an overview of actions that the U.S. Army has already undertaken which recognize the importance of women in the cultural landscape. An examination of patriarchal culture follows, which reveals factors that Army leaders need to understand about women in patriarchal societies. Next, some of the challenges that the international development community and the military face when engaging women are discussed. This chapter concludes with insights and recommendations to improve the U.S. Army's ability to relate to the moderate voices of indigenous women and to influence them in a positive manner regarding the intentions and actions the U.S. military.

WOMEN AS PEACEMAKERS AND PEACEKEEPERS

It is only fairly recently that the international community, including the United States, has recognized the importance of women as peacemakers and peacekeepers. Women's importance in these roles is directly related to the disproportionate amount of harm that both women and children experience in war. In conflicts today, civilians are increasingly targeted, resulting in civilians representing 80 to 90 percent of all casualties. Among civilian casualties, 80 to 90 percent are women and girls. Women and children are the big losers in war, but women persevere in conflict and post-conflict situations to protect families and restore normalcy.[4]

Stephanie Hampton, a human geographer, describes the actions of women facing the horrors of conflict and its immediate aftermath.

> Under extreme conditions of deprivation of the basic necessities of life and the constant threat of violence, it is often left to women to gather any remaining family and seek safety, sustenance, and shelter. When the family is secured, women's attention turns outward to the community where they organize themselves to provide schooling, medical care, and support groups for traumatized persons.[5]

Ms. Hampton asserts that women are major stakeholders in war. Women are victims, but much more significantly, they actively seek to restore normalcy and redress grievances in war's aftermath.[6]

In 2000, Secretary-General Kofi Annan, in a message for the United Nations (UN) Day for Women's Rights and International Peace revealed a similar conclusion:

But women, who know the price of conflict so well, are also often better equipped than men to prevent or resolve it. When society collapses, women play a critical role in ensuring that life goes on. When ethnic tensions cause or exacerbate conflict, women tend to build bridges rather than walls. When considering the impact and implications of war and peace, women think first of their children and their future, before themselves.[7]

In October 2000, the UN Security Council adopted Resolution 1325 (UNSCR 1325) on Women, Peace and Security, recognizing that regardless to which culture they belong, there are gender distinctive characteristics of women that can be key to making and keeping peace. These include collaboration skills; ability to work across ethnic, political, and religious lines for the common good; and willingness to use available resources for social investment.[8] Rather than categorizing women as helpless victims of conflict, this resolution acknowledges their potential and active roles in peacekeeping and peacemaking.

In 2006, the United States Institute for Peace (USIP) prepared a special report addressing the role of women in stabilization and reconstruction. This report concludes that women are the primary victims of conflict and bear a major portion of the burden of reconstruction. Women not only pursue practical reconstruction initiatives such as infrastructure repair and clean water supply, they also pursue intangibles such as repairing relationships and fostering traditions, laws, and customs. When women are placed in decisionmaking positions post-conflict, they operate in a manner that promotes good governance, insisting upon transparency and accountability to fight corruption. Recent research reveals that engaging women as peace builders both advances women's rights, a democratic ideal the U.S. Government (USG) pursues through the Department of State (DoS) and the U.S. Agency for International Development (USAID), and leads to more effective reconstruction programs, which promote a more sustainable peace.[9]

USIP acknowledges that the USG has made important progress in recognizing the importance of including women in stabilization and reconstruction operations, but asserts that there is much more to be done across the whole of government, to include the Department of Defense (DoD). The USIP report specifically recommends that the DoD develop internal capacity within the U.S. military to "recognize and address gender issues during war and in postwar reconstruction."[10] Not surprisingly, such a tasking falls most heavily on land forces, and in particular the Army.

RELEVANT ARMY DOCTRINE AND TRAINING

The U.S. military will continue its involvement with the indigenous populations of countries in crisis. As recent experience shows, this is an extremely complex and somewhat daunting challenge. Force-on-force conflict using purely kinetic effects against a known enemy seems simple and straightforward in comparison. The U.S. military has learned that post-conflict operations—stability operations—are essential to translating military success into a political victory—and culture matters in these types of operations. Despite toppling the regime, U.S. military forces on the ground were, in reality, behind from the start in Iraq. Post-conflict operations were the greater challenge. As a learning organization, the U.S. military identified a shortcoming in its capabilities to conduct

Stability, Security, Transition and Reconstruction (SSTR) and Counterinsurgency (COIN) operations, and is both implementing lessons learned during ongoing operations and seeking appropriate doctrine for the future.

Arguably, the most significant step the Army has undertaken to address these shortcomings is the publication of *Field Manual (FM) 3-24, Counterinsurgency*. Indeed, in the foreword, Lieutenant Generals David H. Petraeus, U.S. Army; and James F. Amos, U.S. Marine Corps, acknowledge it has been over 20 years since either service addressed principles and guidelines for counterinsurgency operations in a manual devoted exclusively to the subject.[11] FM 3-24 addresses the engagement of women in the following terms:

> However, in traditional societies, women are hugely influential in forming the social networks that insurgents use for support. When women support COIN efforts, families support COIN efforts. Getting the support of families is a big step toward mobilizing the local populace against the insurgency. Co-opting neutral or friendly women through targeted social and economic programs builds networks of enlightened self-interest that eventually undermine insurgents.[12]

The manual further discusses women in several chapters. In Chapter 1, which provides an overview of COIN, the essential nature of cultural knowledge is articulated, to include an observation that American ideas of normal are not universal, and different societies have different norms concerning gender. Chapter 3 addresses the critical nature of understanding the operational environment in COIN, with a specific focus on understanding the people and an emphasis on socio-cultural factors, to include society, social structure, culture, power, and authority. The manual briefly addresses considering the role of women in developing logical lines of operation for essential services in Chapter 5. However, despite this general recognition in the body of the manual and the strong paragraph in Appendix A, "A Plan for Action," outlining how hugely influential women are in COIN operations, FM 3-24 does not address women, nor how to influence them, in any great depth.[13]

As a result of its experience, the Army introduced Human Terrain Teams (HTT) in September 2007. These five-person teams are designed to work at the Brigade Combat Team level. They are unique in that they rely heavily on civilian expertise, to include anthropologists and social scientists. The intent of the teams is to provide an interpretation of the cultural landscape that will aid commanders and Soldiers in making the right decisions on the ground in COIN operations.[14] A *U.S. News and World Report* article articulates the need for these teams:

> The military has come late to appreciate the role that social connections play in Iraqi society, where divisions are not just geographic or religious but also familial and tribal. Understanding those kinds of connections, a key aim of anthropology, can be critical to forging alliances, assessing intelligence—and, military officials add, avoiding unintended consequences.[15]

An HTT operating in Afghanistan clearly grasped the implications of gender when they noticed that a large numbers of widows created by the conflict had to rely on their sons for financial support. Recognizing that these young men could easily turn to paid insurgency to fulfill this social obligation, the HTT developed a job program so that these widows could support themselves.[16] In this case, HTT actions had a positive influence by directly improving the women's dire circumstances and indirectly by discouraging potential recruits for the insurgency and creating a more favorable constituency for U.S. policy success.

WHAT THE ARMY NEEDS TO KNOW ABOUT WOMEN IN PATRIARCHAL SOCIETIES

Accounting for gender is neither obvious nor is it a traditional area of expertise within the military. Every culture is markedly different so there cannot be a one-size-fits-all approach. At the same time, this is not an issue that the military can afford to ignore, given the relative size of the female population in most nations and women's ability to influence their society publicly and privately. Iraq is a good illustrative example. Population demographics indicate that in 2006 there were 26.8 million Iraqis, with men outnumbering women by only 230,000. The ratio of males to females aged 15 to 64 was 1.02; basically the population was evenly split. Afghanistan is much the same. Of a total population of 31 million, there are 740,000 more men than women and a 1.05 ratio of males to females aged 15 to 64.[17]

Cultures and societal norms define how women wield public and private influence, but the phenomenon is nearly universal and crisis and conflict affect this power significantly. Even in very patriarchal societies, key cultural aspects highlight the power that women potentially wield, but most Westerners fail to see, or appreciate it. Such power, which manifests itself in influence on men in society, can be neutral, supportive, or actively work against U.S. military efforts. Imagine the untapped power of 13 million Iraqi women positively influencing husbands, children, and extended family regarding U.S. military actions and intentions.

Today, there is a wide range of social attitudes regarding women among patriarchal societies. Different cultures have different views on proper roles for women, what modernity implies for women, and religious interpretations of the roles and rights of women. It is these differences that make the understanding of each cultural environment that the Army operates in so critical. Engagement with women in one society may need to be very different than in another, in spite of the fact that the two societies may both be patriarchal and practice a common religion. Take, for example, the cases of Saudi Arabia and Iran.

Saudi Arabia is one of the most patriarchal societies in the world. Women are rarely seen in public, and when they are, they are in extremely conservative dress, to include a shapeless black *abaiya* (gown), *hijab* (head scarf), and *burqa* (face covering). All restaurants, public buildings, and even private homes are strictly segregated. Women are forbidden to interact with men to whom they are not related. In 2007, a Saudi gang-rape victim received a sentence of 200 lashes and 6 months in jail for being in a car with an unrelated male when they were attacked. Only 7 percent of Saudi women work, and they are strictly segregated when they do. Given the nature of modernity in the 21st century, this is unenlightened and a tremendous waste of human capital on the part of the Saudis.[18]

Contrast this with Iran; a country many assume is extremely oppressive. Iran has actually become more liberal towards women following the Islamic Revolution in 1979. This is based on a number of factors. The Iran-Iraq War (1980-88) brought women into the workforce, and they remained there. Former Iranian presidents' Rafsanjani and Khatami spearheaded a program for economic liberalization and integration into the global economy. This resulted in the development of a sizeable modern middle and working class. Although women are discouraged from public roles, they are not banned from the public sphere as they are in Saudi Arabia. The Government of Iran also recognized the importance of controlling spiraling population growth and enacted family planning at the national level, which effectively empowered women. Agitation in the 1990s by Islamic and state feminists has resulted in the removal of restrictions on education and employment, resulting in 33% of public sector employees being women in 2004. Women may serve in the parliament, and there are women's affairs offices in each government ministry. Despite all this, women are still required to wear *hijab*, and there are many onerous restrictions on their movements and public dress. However, women in Iran frame their grievances openly in Islamic terms and continue to actively work to secure greater women's rights.[19]

These two societies are both alike and unlike in regard to women. Yet, for most Americans, a veiled woman is repressed and essentially powerless. U.S. military members see such women in patriarchal societies that abound in North Africa, the Middle East, and South and East Asia—or in other terms, the AFRICOM, CENTCOM, and PACOM geographical operating areas, but never understand the true relationships. Western culture biases the military layman to evaluate women in these societies very simplistically. The layman either assumes women have no influence so they are not worth any time and effort, or there is a desire to emancipate the woman behind the veil from repression. The reality is much more complex. In most of these cultures, patriarchy places men in all the public power roles in society, to include government, religion, the military, education, and industry. Conversely, women are for the most part denied access to these public roles.[20] However, women in patriarchal societies actually exert significant influence in the home and within their networks, which include extended family and other women.

Religion is another red herring. It is easy to point to religion, specifically Islam, as the sole culprit dictating an inferior status for women in these societies. Religion does state the inferiority of women, and Middle Eastern clerics of all religious persuasion are universally conservative in regard to women's rights and roles. However, in reality patriarchal culture has perpetuated the inferior role of women to a much greater degree than religion. Many of the most egregious acts of sexism have no real basis in religion, but are the patriarchal cultures' interpretation of religion.[21] The uniform control and subordination of women perpetuated in a patriarchal society cuts across cultural and religious boundaries.[22] Yet, women do wield power within their spheres.

In very basic terms, patriarchal societies have two spheres, the public and the private. Men operate in both, while women operate predominantly only in the private sphere. The fact that women in these cultures are rarely seen in the public sphere does not mean that they are not influential in the private sphere — or that the private sphere does not affect the public one.[23] Consider the example of Bedouin women of the Negev in Israel. Men guard the land and receive visitors in the public sphere. In the private sphere, women farm and are responsible for domestic livelihood, relations with neighbors, and the marriage of daughters. These are complementary roles, each critically important, each contributing to the well-being of the family.[24]

A study of agricultural families in Afghanistan reinforces the concept of public and private spheres. Both sexes play critical roles in the functioning of the family. Women are not simply in the background: they are responsible for finances, household management, and the welfare of the family. Men make the decisions in respect to the public sphere and are responsible for community dealings and interaction outside the family. In the home, women often exert significant influence over the family, including men.[25]

In the Middle East and North Africa, private sphere networking is very powerful for women as they seek a common solidarity and consciousness. Such networking is an alternative form of power that is not observed in the public sphere. The network is not limited to the bounds of the nuclear family, but crosses family lines and extends to the greater community. Networking actually increases women's power and reduces their dependency on men. It allows them to exercise their own power and independence within their society. Through these networks, women use information as power, controlling information and using it to further their own personal and collective interests.[26] The relevance is obvious: imagine the power of these networks if women perceive U.S. military action as either positive or negative?

Another difficult concept for Americans to grasp is that Arab women do not necessarily want to threaten the existing social order. The most visible symbol of female oppression, from a Western perspective, is the required facial covering in the form of the veil. Yet many Arab women see the veil as providing both the freedom to move about in a patriarchal society as well as freedom from sexual harassment.[27] Not visible in the public sphere is an extremely strong traditional family system that Arab women highly value. This is a system with complementary sex roles; a system that provides women protection and honor. Women trade submissiveness, propriety, and honor for protection. Most Arab women want certain things, like education, health care, clean water, and basic services, but they do not want to part with the traditional family system.[28]

In the Middle East and North Africa, the Western concept of empowerment can be very dangerous for women. Empowerment, as defined by the United Nations (UN) Development Program, aims to eliminate gender inequities through targeted actions in the social and economic spheres, the civil and political rights spheres, and development.[29] In seeking Western empowerment, women can easily lose existing power and social advantages they value. Because of this, they work within the patriarchal culture and look for acceptable ways to break into the male public sphere. One of the most effective ways for women to do this is through male sanction of their activities.[30]

It is also important to understand that during conflict, women may play significant roles that are completely outside gender norms. However, in the post-conflict period patriarchal culture usually seeks to limit women again; the social roles they filled in conflict do not necessarily expand their options or influence in the public sphere with the return of normalcy.[31] On the other hand, war and conflict often introduce great social change.[32]

An additional dynamic to be considered in the post-conflict gender equation in today's world is that of extremist Islam overlaid on susceptible patriarchal societies. The politicization of Islam has resulted in a populist rejection of Western secular culture and a desire to return to a very nonsecular, pure Islamic society based on religious norms. The basic concept is that emancipated women are a reflection of an insidious Western secular culture creeping in, and women must be put back in their place.[33] Probably the best-known example of this is the brutal repression of women in Afghanistan when the Taliban took power from the Mujahedeen.

WHAT THE ARMY NEEDS TO DO

Despite the complexities of culture and gender, there are soft power possibilities that the Army can pursue to positively influence indigenous women and potentially bring more moderate voices to bear. The main objective of such activities would be to support stability operations through second order effects created by women's influence over others within the private sphere. Soft power as used here refers to nonkinetic actions focused on the women of an indigenous population.

` The U.S. Army has little or no expertise in the application of soft power in matters of gender except those learned on the ground during current operations. For many, this might beg the question of why the Army should even concern itself with this issue. The answer is quite simple. It makes strategic, operational, and tactical sense. Ongoing operations in Iraq and Afghanistan both find military personnel on the ground interacting directly with the indigenous population, long after conventional combat operations are over. As the Army has rediscovered, stability operations are among the most complex. In post-conflict operations, and in many others, the Army will find itself committed to operating environments that are nonpermissive or semipermissive during which the military will operate with few external resources, and long-term success and costs hang in the balance. It is incumbent upon the Army to tackle these environments playing its "A" game, including gender savvy.

There are overarching imperatives that the U.S. Army needs to understand when engaging women. First, there are distinct differences between humanitarian assistance, development, and military operations that affect the potential to influence women's roles. Second, a critical distinction the military should appreciate is the difference between strategic gender interests and practical gender interests. And finally, the military should not attempt to engage in the empowerment of indigenous women, but should take a supporting role as required in a broader whole of government effort.

Even though the U.S. military likes to view its missions along a spectrum of conflict, nonkinetic military actions do not fit neatly into either humanitarian aid or development operations. However, such actions do differ in purpose in different operational environments across the spectrum. Humanitarian aid or assistance is short-term immediate action to save lives and alleviate suffering, and is normally altruistic. Development activities are longer-term and are intended to address underlying socio-economic conditions.[34] Development activities are more than altruistic; there are usually political, economic, or security agendas motivating them. President George W. Bush's National Security Strategy states, "USAID's work in development joins diplomacy and defense as one of three key pieces of the nation's foreign policy apparatus."[35] Both of these activities differ from conventional combat operations. However, as Afghanistan and Iraq have demonstrated, the U.S. Army is on the ground; it must learn how to effectively work with the humanitarian and the development communities as well as with the indigenous population.

Tensions between the humanitarian, development, and military professions are inherent. All three professions work in each other's jurisdictions, sharing the same "contested aid space."[36] The military, when responding to humanitarian crises, is usually on the ground quickly with significant assets. The humanitarian community arrives simultaneously or shortly after the military, often with less immediate capacity. Humanitarians have no choice but to accept the military presence and often seek its support, but the military must also accept humanitarian organizations as independent agents that are not under military control and may have differing agendas, even while pursuing similar goals.[37] The development community — governmental, nongovernmental, and private — arrives later. At the execution level, the military should look to assist the humanitarian community and set the stage for the development community in pursuit of long-term development goals.

The term empowerment is often associated with solutions to women's issues in patriarchal societies. However, empowerment is a complex undertaking, with second and third order effects best left to other professions with a better developed appreciation of their complexity. The military does not have the indepth expertise to engage in the empowerment of women in other cultures. A useful construct for use during the development of military operations is to separate gender interests into practical and strategic. Practical gender interests are those that allow one to better one's situation within the overall system. These are such things as access to clean drinking water, medical care, and education. Strategic gender interests are those that involve a structural change to the system itself and are akin to empowerment. In terms of a patriarchal society, they may include issues of legal status, political representation in governance activities, and women's suffrage. Prior to the rise of the insurgency in 2004, Iraqi women identified practical gender interests, things essential to physical survival, as their priority. Women were interested in water, electricity, security, and income if widowed, before education or political rights, which are strategic gender interests.[38] The military may act in support of many empowerment-related activities and provide appropriate advice, but the guiding strategy and planning for empowerment should come from experts within the development community, whose focuses is on strategic gender interests at the national level.[39]

Understanding complementary efforts in contested aid space and practical versus strategic gender interests will allow the Army to operate more effectively in engaging women in stability operations. As illustrated in the following statement by Marine Master Sergeant James Allen, military units operating at the tactical level clearly understand there is the potential to positively influence men in a patriarchal society through women: "We want to empower the women to the point where they can have a positive influence on the men, when they're alone, in the home. . . ."[40] Notwithstanding the use of the word empowerment, at the tactical level leaders grasp the importance of women. Equally important, there is an evolving infrastructure above the tactical level that can and should support and guide these efforts. This infrastructure could also benefit from some refinement and further development. A critical consideration is the fact that there is minimal culture and gender expertise within the military and the closer one gets to actual execution on the ground, the further one gets away from this expertise. Hence, there is a critical requirement to share this expertise in a useable manner down to the lowest tactical level.

At the theater strategic and operational levels, combatant commands must take the military lead in efforts to facilitating positive influence among indigenous women. The concept for Joint Interagency Coordination Groups (JIACGs) at the geographic combatant command level evolved from the failure of interagency planning for post-conflict operations in Iraq. JIACGs should be a key enabler in dealing with gender issues and influence. These groups bring a wide variety of subject matter expertise to planning and execution efforts.[41] This is not to suggest that facilitating positive influence will be easy. The UN development community experienced problems in addressing gender issues in post-conflict environments and has advocated the involvement of gender advisors.[42] Arguably such expertise should be organic to the JIACGs at the combatant command level. This expertise does not have to be a specific organizational position; it can be an additional qualification or a reach-back capability. Regardless, the combatant command should provide guidance and information to subordinate units to assist efforts on the ground.

Human Terrain Teams (HTT) are another way of sharing expertise. HTTs bring culture and gender expertise right into the Brigade Combat Team with their anthropologists. HTTs should include a detailed analysis of women in their cultural intelligence preparation of the battlefield (IPB). This analysis should follow the IPB framework within FM 3-24, but with women and their issues interwoven throughout. Units with the support of their HTTs should then determine how to engage women and promote favorable influence. Additionally, as in Information Operations, women should be considered throughout every Logical Line of Operation (LLO). For example, consider the impacts of women in regard to the security LLO. If U.S. Army units can provide security for women and girls in schools, women may advocate positively for the Army and U.S. policies in the home.

Provincial Reconstruction Teams (PRT), like HTTs, is another valid attempt to operate more effectively in SSTR and COIN operations. PRTs are a civilian-military interagency effort spearheaded by the Department of State. These teams provide an interface among the U.S. Government departments and agencies, U.S. and coalition partner militaries, and provincial and local governments in Iraq and Afghanistan. Their efforts are focused on reconstruction, to include delivery of essential services and building local and regional governance capacity. PRT staffs represent a wide variety of capabilities. Different team members may prove invaluable in addressing both the practical and strategic gender interests of women. Potentially, the USAID representative, the governance team, and the bilingual culture advisor will bring new perspectives, different ideas, and more appropriate skill sets.[43] Units working in conjunction with PRTs have a much greater potential to significantly influence women in their area of operations—and should develop the potential and share the experience.

Civil affairs units and teams are another potentially critical resource for tactical level units. Civil Affairs is one military occupational specialty where education and training is better aligned for the cultural complexities the military is currently experiencing and will face in the future. Further training of civil affairs personnel in gender issues would provide an invaluable tactical and operational level resource to commanders on the ground. Such training should be incorporated into the institutional training base for each Army branch and made part of refined deployment preparation for specific regions of the world. Civil affairs planners at the operational level should be able to reach back to JIACGs within the combatant command and work directly with PRTs in theater. The hierarchical rank structure of civil affairs units lends itself to development of more specific gender knowledge at the brigade level than can be supported in the civil affairs teams operating with tactical units, making good planning and communications even more critical.

Similar to the military, the development community is awakening to the gender gap as well. Women and their needs are historically easy to overlook as the values of civil society in countries around the world generally reflect a male perspective and men's gender-expressed aspirations. Based on this, development agencies can overlook women's perspectives and under value the important human resource represented by women. As one author in the field put it, women comprise half the human race but take a secondary place in the world's cultures.[44] The ability to comprehend gender differences is generating new energy, ideas, and resources within this community. For example, the United States Institute for Peace (USIP) pamphlet, "The Role of Women in Stabilization and Reconstruction," consolidates lessons learned involving gender and development.[45] Although these lessons learned are development focused, there is also great application for the military in the pursuit of practical gender interests and for laying a proper foundation for later development.

One of the most effective ways USIP has found to engage women in a given culture is to establish connections with women's rights and issues organizations when they exist. Resources that are available to find such organizations include the DoS, USAID, the UN, and nongovernmental organizations (NGOs). Each country and region will differ in the extent to which these organizations are developed and at what level they are found. Organizations found at the national level will most likely be focused on strategic gender interests of interest to the development community.[46] Other women's organizations may exist at local levels focused on more local concerns and traditional models. Recognizing the nature and value of such organizations is important to military operations at all levels.

At the strategic level, USIP actively advocates collecting and sharing lessons learned related to gender and development across the whole of government. USIP also advocates gender training across government.[47] The DoD should be an active participant in this process, sharing the military's lessons learned and disseminating those from other government agencies within the department. What is critical at the strategic level for the U.S. military is the culling and translation of government-wide lessons learned into knowledge that the military can specifically use. In the case of the Army, this knowledge should be incorporated into the missions of the Training and Doctrine Command (TRADOC). For example, within TRADOC, such lessons learned could be militarized and immediately shared through the Center for Army Lessons Learned. In the longer term, TRADOC should integrate key gender knowledge into doctrine, institutional training and education, and combat training center scenarios.

Combatant commands must also address gender lessons learned, albeit from a somewhat different perspective. Combatant commands are largely engaged in the here and now. JIACGs should play a key role in filtering lessons learned to glean key insights and practices that are applicable to ongoing operations and archive and share others that may apply to their geographic region for possible future use.

As the military, and specifically the ground forces of the Army and Marines, have engaged indigenous local populations much more indepth manner than previously imagined, the military has recognized that U.S. forces must become much more proficient in cultural understanding and awareness. Gender education and training should be an integral part of such proficiency. However, the depth and detail of gender education and training should be tailored to the appropriate level. Indeed, the military's mission does not call for every service member to become an anthropologist or gender specialist, but it does require a degree of awareness and sensitivity, some doctrinal thought, and supportive backup. Consider this statement from U.S. Marine Corps Corporal Jennifer McNamara, "Right now, we're relationship-building, listening to these women . . . building trust."[48] The cultural subject matter expertise found in a JIACG is a long way away from Corporal McNamara on the ground, but it can guide her intuitive gender appreciation to more appropriate tactical actions. Culture and gender issues touch military units at the lowest level. To accomplish the missions of today and the future, the military must develop more knowledge on the subject and tap into more expert resources.

At the tactical level, practical gender interests hold sway. One of the most effective ways to address practical gender interests is through direct interaction and consultation with indigenous women in the area. When this is possible, it is important to understand the composition of the women in a given group. Based on the nature of a particular patriarchal society, it may be difficult to meet with a cross-section of women of different ages, social status, education levels, and urban and rural backgrounds, but generally the more diversity, the better. Once units engage directly with women, they will be able to identify practical gender interests and gain insights into strategic ones. When units initiate projects without regard for women and their interests — practical or strategic — the desired effects may not be achieved. Development literature is rife with examples of Western expectations regarding projects being completely out of touch with the realities of indigenous women. The key to overcoming this is to encourage the participation of women in the decisionmaking process.

There are four key questions which women should be asked to get a proper practical gender appreciation of a proposed project: (1) Do women desire the proposed project and will they benefit from it? (2) How can the project be improved before it is started to more adequately support the knowledge and skill level of the ultimate users? (3) Are there any potential unintended negative effects for women or others? and (4) If negative effects will occur, how can they be mitigated?[49]

While it is obvious to outsiders that local women should be part of the process when working practical gender interests, tactical units must understand it can be very difficult to secure access to women in patriarchal societies. It is a radical departure for women to break their silence in public, so even women's groups cannot always easily serve as a conduit for women to communicate their practical needs. In addition, women's organizations often do not exist at the local level. In either case, tactical leaders should continue to seek acceptable access. One of the most effective ways to bring women into the process is through male patrons. If male community leaders sanction this type of engagement, women will venture out of the private sphere to participate in the public sphere with other women.

A significant pitfall in practical gender interests is in presuming to understand the needs of the community and their related issues. Projects that appear that they will benefit women often fail to do so, or if they do result in benefits, there are likely to be negative second and third order effects that should have been earlier considered.[50] Take, for example, a situation in Iraq where a battalion focused on reopening the local hospital, including securing emergency power generation and acquiring needed basic medical equipment. About a month later after starting a local women's group, one of the women's basic complaints was the lack of female doctors to see women patients at this hospital, a shortage that could have been identified earlier by input from the women prior to reconstruction. At first blush, this seemed like an obvious strategic gender interest problem: women are not allowed to go to medical school or at least not in sufficient numbers to treat female patients. However, in this particular case, the problem was much more practical. Available women doctors had no access to childcare, so they could not leave home to treat patients at the hospital. This was a practical gender interest that could be solved once the right questions were asked and answered.[51] Army unit leaders must learn to ask the right question early on in their decisionmaking processes.

Other potential changes in military forces may help identify and address practical gender interests of women. The adoption of part of UNSCR 1325, which advocates increased roles for women in all aspects of peacekeeping, may support tactical units in efforts to engage indigenous women.[52] Just as units use military lawyers to engage judges, or military police to support police force reforms, military women serve as a practical and powerful tool with which to engage indigenous women. They can interrelate with these women in ways that are not acceptable for male military members. One could also argue that in a strategic sense, they are also new role models. In this regard, female military members may be considered as scarce and essential resources. Consequently, units without women may coordinate with those that have them for support. Of course, military women should coordinate with HTTs and civil affairs teams to determine how best to work with indigenous women and to understand long-term interagency development goals. Such activities should always complement the commander's plan for the area.

CONCLUSION

A Marine battalion commander involved in the invasion of Iraq and post-conflict operations recalls:

> We didn't give special consideration to engaging the women . . . My concern was not stepping where I shouldn't step, or dragging a woman in there that would anger the local men.[53]

The U.S. military, and indeed the whole of government, have a better understanding of patriarchal societies and the role of women today, but much remains to be learned and applied. The keys to getting it right are to understand and more fully appreciate that there is no monolithic view of women in these societies, indigenous women find value in their traditional roles and practices, these women largely exert power through the private sphere and networking, and such women can influence for better or worst U.S. success in their areas of operation.

Getting gender interests right is a military imperative. The U.S. military will continue to find itself in nonpermissive or semipermissive environments where ground forces are initially engaging the local populace with little to no hands-on support from other agencies. In these kinds of environments, it is critical to address the needs of the entire population and to not overlook the interests of women. The strategic, operational, and tactical effects the military should seek are to positively influence women who will in turn advocate in the positive within the private sphere and through their networking in regard to U.S. efforts and activities—or as a minimum, not actively oppose them. Tactical units should address practical gender interests while military commanders and planners at the operational and strategic levels should provide guidance and information in support of tactical actions, setting the conditions for tactical success. These commanders and their staffs should also provide advice to, and plan for supporting roles for the military in order to assist key interagency players address strategic gender interests. In this regard, the national vision should be the establishment of a coherent whole of government effort in a given operation that includes gender as an integrated aspect of strategy and planning.

ENDNOTES - CHAPTER 13

1. Rachel Blackmon Bryars, "Muslim Women Can Help Win the Long War," *Baltimore Examiner*, February 2, 2008, Business sec., p. 16.

2. The stories of Iraqi women are based on the author's experiences as a battalion commander in Iraq, 2003-04. The names have been changed.

3. Swanee Hunt and Cristina Posa, "Iraq's Excluded Women," *Foreign Policy*, Vol. 143, July/August 2004, p. 40.

4. Stephanie W. Hampton, "Obstacles within the International Community: The Exercise of Afghan Women's Agency for Peace in Post-Conflict Reconstruction," *Seton Hall Journal of Diplomacy and International Relations*, Winter/Spring 2004, p. 38.

5. *Ibid.*

6. *Ibid.*

7. United Nations, "Secretary-General Stresses Need to Remove Barriers to Women's Involvement," Press Release No. UNIS/SG/2513*, available from *www.unis.unvienna.org/unis/pressrels/2000/sg2513.html*.

8. *United Nations Security Council Resolution*, Res. 1325, October 31, 2000, available from *www.un.org/Docs/scres/2000/sc2000.htm*.

9. Camille Pampell Conaway, *The Role of Women in Stabilization and Reconstruction*, Stabilization and Reconstruction Series No. 3, Washington, DC: United States Institute of Peace, August 2006, pp. 1-3.

10. *Ibid.*, p. 14.

11. *Field Manual (FM) 3-24, Counterinsurgency,* Washington, DC: U.S. Department of the Army, December 2006, p. Foreword.

12. *Ibid.*, p. A-6.

13. *Ibid.*, pp. 1-15, 3-3 to 3-4, 5-14, A-6.

14. "Human Terrain Team Helps Soldiers in Iraq Understand Cultural Landscape," *US Fed News Service, Including US State News,* December 11, 2007.

15. Anna Mulrine, "The Culture Warriors: The Pentagon Deploys Social Scientists to Help Understand Iraq's 'Human Terrain'," *U.S. News & World Report,* December 10, 2007, p. 34.

16. David Rohde, "Army Enlists Anthropology in War Zones," *New York Times,* October 5, 2007.

17. *CountryWatch,* available from *www.countrywatch.com.*

18. Max Boot and Lee Wolosky, "What to Do in Riyadh," *The Weekly Standard,* available from *www.weeklystandarDCom/Content/Public/Articles/000/000/014/433sanzs.asp?pg=1.*

19. Valentine M. Moghadam, "A Tale of Two Countries: State, Society, and Gender Politics in Iran and Afghanistan," *The Muslim World,* Vol. 94, October 2004, pp. 460-463.

20. Malika Basu, "Feminist Perspective's and Gender Link in Development: The Critical Role of Women's Organizations," available from *www.ciaonet.org/wps/bam03.*

21. As 'ad Abu Khalil, "In Focus: Women in the Middle East," available from *ww.ciaonet.org/pbei/fpif/abu01.*

22. Deniz Kandiyoti, "Bargaining with Patriarchy," *Gender and Society,* Vol. 2, September 1998, p. 278.

23. Sarab Abu-Rabia Queder, "Permission to Rebel: Arab Bedouin Women's Changing Negotiation of Social Roles," *Feminist Studies,* Vol. 33, Spring 2007.

24. *Ibid.*

25. Rina Amiri, Swanee Hunt, and Jennifer Sova, "Transition within Tradition: Women's Participation in Restoring Afghanistan," *Sex Roles,* Vol. 51, September 2004, p. 284.

26. Queder.

27. *Ibid.* This article does not refer to extreme measures for covering such as those enforced by the Taliban in Afghanistan.

28. Kandiyoti, p. 283.

29. United Nations Development Program, "Practice Note on Gender Equality," November 2002, available from *www.undp.org/women/.*

30. Queder.

31. Laurie A. Brand, "Women, the State, and Political Liberalization: Middle Eastern and North African Experiences," 1998, available from *www.ciaonet.org/book/brand2/bibliography.html.*

32. Bruce D. Porter, *War and the Rise of the State: The Military Foundations of Modern Politics*, New York: Free Press, 1992. This is Porter's well-documented thesis.

33. Amiri, Hunt, and Sova, p. 285.

34. S. J. Meharg, *Helping Hands and Loaded Arms: Navigating the Military and Humanitarian Space*, Clemensport, NS: Canadian Peacekeeping Press, 2007, p. 77.

35. U.S. Agency for International Development, "USAID Primer: What We Do and How We Do It," available from *www.usaid.gov/about_usaid/primer.html*.

36. Meharg, p. 75.

37. *Ibid.*, p. 100.

38. Sherifa D. Zuhur, *Iraq, Women's Empowerment, and Public Policy*, Carlisle, PA: Strategic Studies Institute, U.S. Army War College, 2006, p. 17.

39. Sarah C. White, "Gender and Development: Working with Difference," Vivienne Jabri and Eleanor O'Gorman, eds., *Women, Culture, and International Relations*, available from *www.ciaonet.org/book/jabri/*.

40. Tony Perry, "The Conflict in Iraq: Revising Strategy; Empowering Women," *Los Angeles Times*, January 7, 2007, p. A8.

41. "Joint Interagency Coordination Group, (JIACG)," Washington, DC: U.S. Joint Forces Command, available from *www.jfcom.mil/about/fact_jiacg.htm*.

42. Hampton, p. 40.

43. Robert M. Perito, "Special Report: Provincial Reconstruction Teams in Iraq," March 2007, available from *www.usip.org/pubs/specialreports/sr185.html*.

44. Basu.

45. Conaway.

46. *Ibid.*, p. 7.

47. *Ibid.*, p. 6.

48. Perry, p. A8.

49. Basu.

50. *Ibid.*

51. This anecdote is based on the author's experiences as a battalion commander in Iraq, 2003-04.

52. "United Nations Security Council Resolution 1325 on Women, Peace and Security," October 31, 2000, available from *www.peacewomen.org/un/sc/1325.html*.

53. Hunt and Posa.

CHAPTER 14

THE BRITISH APPROACH TO COUNTERINSURGENCY:
MYTHS, REALITIES, AND STRATEGIC CHALLENGES

Colonel I. A. Rigden OBE
British Army

> The British have succeeded in counter-insurgency where others have failed because history has given them the kind of military establishment and colonial administrative experience necessary to defeat revolutionary movements.
>
> Thomas R. Mockaitis[1]

The British Military possesses a well-earned reputation for success in counterinsurgency operations gained through hard won experience following World War II. Experience has not been an easy path, and there have been successes and failures, some of which are not well recorded or remembered. Since 1945 the British armed forces have taken part in 72 military campaigns. Of these campaigns, 17 can be classified as counterinsurgency campaigns (including Afghanistan and Iraq).[2] Breaking these 17 down even further, seven can claim to be successes, one is generally regarded as a draw, five are acknowledged failures, three are limited campaigns and difficult to quantify, and two are still in progress.[3] The fact is that a counterinsurgency campaign is one of the most difficult military operations to conduct and inevitably involves a long and painful commitment.

In the numerous counterinsurgency campaigns that have been conducted by other nations since the end of World War II, very few qualify as complete successes. Measuring success in itself highlights one of the key problems in trying to assess counterinsurgency campaigns objectively. That the British can point to seven clear successes that are measurable suggests that the British approach to counterinsurgency is worthy of study. The British approach evolved through their experience of trial and error with over 200 years of Imperial policing, revolutionary warfare, and modern insurgencies around the globe. Nevertheless, the development of counterinsurgency techniques and doctrine has not always followed a coherent or considered path. It is only since 1945 that the British military have started to capture their experience effectively in doctrine, and this means that much has been ignored from the 150 years prior to this date.

Unfortunately, a number of popular myths and mind-sets have developed around British counterinsurgency based largely on what many consider to be the exemplar of the Malayan Campaign. As a result, a questionable advocacy in some quarters proposes that British doctrine is the best model, and that the British military is inherently better able to conduct counterinsurgency. Let there be no ambiguity in regard to where this author stands. The current British counterinsurgency doctrine does provide a very sound basis from which to develop a counterinsurgency campaign, but it is, as the document states, only a guideline. It is also true that the British armed forces are well-placed to fight a counterinsurgency campaign based on collective experience and mentality, but there is a danger of complacency in accepting that as the "experts" and the ones with the highest success rate, the British doctrine is complete and needs little or no modification — or that British armed forces have nothing to learn. These would indeed be dangerous assumptions in a rapidly changing world.[4] The aim of this chapter is to produce a balanced and fair assessment of the total British experience in counterinsurgency and to distill a theory that may help counter the strategic challenges of insurgency in the 21st century. Consequently, this chapter outlines the future strategic environment and answers three fundamental questions: What is the British counterinsurgency approach and how did it develop? What are the myths and realities about the development of this approach? Can a coherent theory be developed from the total British experience that can overcome the insurgency challenges of the future?

THE FUTURE

The key strategic challenge of the future is the nature of the threat. At the start of the 21st century, the physical nature of war—violence, destruction, and chaos—has changed little, but the international system has changed significantly. Communications and technology have changed the face, pace, and destructive power of war. States are still the key players within the international system, but the number and nature of nonstate actors has increased, including more rogue elements. As modern civilization rises to the next level of its evolution, there is more discontent within and among existing and emerging political structures. Strong ideologies are taking hold in some areas of the world, particularly in the Islamic world which is facing both an identity crisis and an internal ideological struggle to define its position within 21st century civilization. General Sir Rupert Smith argues that future wars will be about war among the people where the battlefield will not easily be defined, and we will see less state on state war and more internal to the state (intrastate) conflict and terrorism.[5] The current world situation gives considerable credence to this viewpoint but, as Colin Gray contends, this does not rule out state on state war, and there is every likelihood that it will continue.[6] In addition, the events of September 11, 2001 (9/11) suggest that modern insurgents have no qualms about exporting their forms of violence to a global battlefield. Hence, the magnitude and multitude of the challenges confronting state militaries makes understanding the challenge from insurgency critical.

In spite of changing power relationships among states and other intergovernmental and nongovernmental actors, international world order will still be based on some form of state-centric system in the first half of the century. The role of insurgency as a vehicle for political change is likely to remain and grow as globalization makes unequal progress in a number of realms more apparent, and challenges traditional societies. Classic intrastate insurgency will be a common feature within weak and failing states, and external interventions will ebb and flow depending on the threat to international stability and to economic prosperity as perceived at the time by the world community or key state actors. As a consequence of the ability of outside powers to intervene, more or less at will, based on their interests and willingness to expend resources and other perceived advantages, insurgencies will morph on occasion into global threats. As such, they will pose asymmetrical challenges and exploit the common advantages and disadvantages associated with the globalized world—technology, transportation, communications, economic competition, crime, and a rising civic society.

Britain's experience in counterinsurgency prior to 1998 was very much defined by the fact that Britain was the legitimate power in its former colonies or was asked to intervene through a formal treaty, friendship, or informal alliance. In most cases, the enemy was easily identifiable, and there was often only one major enemy combatant (i.e., the communist terrorists in Malaya and the Mau Mau in Kenya, Africa). In the environment of the 21st century, intrastate insurgents will be less obvious and Britain's former bonds less strong. Insurgent groups may foment global insurgency wherein insurgencies in different parts of the globe mutually support each other to change the world order or to achieve their own independent goals through collaborative actions and support. The idea of a global insurgency has not been adequately defined as of yet. An attempt to do so is offered here:

> Coordinated simultaneous conflicts involving state and non-state actors, using both regular and irregular methods at multiple locations worldwide, based on either a single coherent vision for a new world order or mutually supporting objectives that assist the participating groups towards their own goals, usually with little regard for national boundaries or international law.

The existence of a global insurgency implies a certain unity of purpose among the different groups, common campaign enablers (such as information technology, logistics, safe havens and military resources) and the possibility of achieving mass popular support. This is much more difficult to achieve than it sounds on paper. For example, al-Qaeda , as a forerunner of this form of insurgency, is trying to initiate a global Islamic insurgency to reinstate the Islamic Caliphate, using a network of Islamic terror and insurgent groups. A hybrid global insurgency is even more complex with the possibility of a marriage of convenience taking place between groups with differing ideologies or conflicting interests. This is not entirely new. For example, the strong links forged between the Irish Republican Army (IRA), the Basque Separatist Movement (ETA), and the Palestine Liberation Organization (PLO) in the 1970s created an international terrorist cabal, but the scope of cooperation and the ease of communications have changed the scale of the dynamics of such a relationship today. It has also been facilitated by criminal actors and activities. These changes in the future operating environment are the menace against which the current British approach to counterinsurgency must be measured to determine its continued applicability.

THE BRITISH APPROACH TO COUNTERINSURGENCY

The current British national approach is foremost a multiagency approach, starting with clear national interests and political direction before campaign analysis and preparation begin. It is also fair to say that, although the British military is inherently joint in its focus, the expertise associated with British counterinsurgency is largely Armycentric. This is not surprising as counterinsurgency is about interaction between people and is generally territorially focused, although this latter point is being challenged with the possible advent of a global insurgency facilitated through cyberspace.

The national level approach recognizes that the military is only one part of the overall solution, and it acknowledges that a wide range of instruments of power and methods need to be applied in order to conduct an effective campaign. The baseline doctrine publication is the British Army counterinsurgency manual, *Army Field Manual (AFM) Volume 1, Combined Part 10.*[7] The manual is organized in two distinct but interrelated parts: The first part defines insurgency and gives an excellent overview of insurgency from a limited historical and theoretical perspective. Part 2 concerns the methodology for conducting a counterinsurgency campaign. The manual is purposely laid out in this way to highlight the two protagonists' opposing viewpoints of insurgency.

British doctrine focuses on understanding both the mind of the enemy and Britain's own strengths and weaknesses so as to effectively use the latter against the insurgent. The manual defines insurgency as:

> The actions of a minority group within a state, who are intent on forcing political change by a means of a mixture of subversion, propaganda and military pressure, aiming to persuade or intimidate the broad mass of the people to accept such a change. It is an organised, armed political struggle, the goals of which might be diverse.[8]

The key ideas from this definition are that the insurgents are dissatisfied with the state or ruling power, and they want ideological change and political reform. Thus insurgencies are inherently political, and their objectives are to delegitimize the existing government and seize political power. Insurgents aim to target the broad mass of the people to make them agree with their point of view, pushing for change by persuasion, coercion, intimidation, or the application force. They use propaganda, subversion, sabotage, and direct military action in an organized way, and it is this dedication to clear objectives and organization that differentiates insurgents from terrorists, even though insurgents often use terrorism themselves at the tactical level.[9] The AFM argues that because of the insurgents' focus on the population as the centre of gravity, both the insurgent and counterinsurgency forces are in a struggle to win the "hearts and minds" of the target population.[10]

In British Army doctrine the role of counterinsurgency operations is to alter the views of those who insurgency appeals to, protect those that it targets for change, and reinforce the legitimacy of the supported government. The AFM definition of counterinsurgency is: "Those military, paramilitary, political, economic, psychological, and civic actions taken to defeat insurgency."[11] It is a simple definition, but one which recognizes the multiagency nature of counterinsurgency and the requirement to consider the use all of the elements of national power.

Current British armed forces counterinsurgency doctrine is largely an expansion of the ideas of Sir Robert Thompson and General Sir Frank Kitson based on their extensive experience in British counterinsurgency campaigns post-1945.[12] Sir Robert Thompson's ideas are really focused at the strategic and operational level, whereas General Kitson's ideas are generally seen as a practitioner's viewpoint at the operational and, more specifically, tactical level.[13] Sir Robert Thompson outlined five broad principles: (1) A clear political aim, (2) Work within the law, (3) The development of an overall plan, (4) Defeat political subversion, and (5) Secure base areas.[14] General Kitson outlined four principles: (1) Good coordinating machinery,(2) The propaganda war, (3) Effective intelligence, and (4) Operating within the law. The British counterinsurgency field manual recognizes six principles which are effectively an amalgam of Thompson's and Kitson's ideas: (1) Political primacy and political aim, (2) Coordinated government machinery, (3) Intelligence and information, (4) Separating the insurgent from his support, (5) Neutralizing the insurgent, and (6) Longer-term post-insurgency planning. These principles are supported by several key supporting concepts: namely civilian political control, working in support of the police, the rule of law, minimum force, the use of indigenous forces and "Hearts and Minds."[15] Both the principles and concepts highlight an important aspect of British doctrine. The British have traditionally used guiding principles in their doctrine rather than being overly prescriptive. Indeed, the subtitle of the British counterinsurgency manual is "Strategic and Operational Guidelines." Principles, as guidelines, allow latitude for commanders to think creatively about the task at hand while providing a clear framework to work within.

There are, however, a number of valid criticisms of British counterinsurgency doctrine. The first is that it is focused primarily on the operational and tactical levels, with only brief chapters on strategic considerations. The second is that it is too Malaya and Northern Ireland focused in its distillation of lessons learned. The third, and perhaps most relevant criticism, was raised by Dr. Ashley Jackson in a recent article in the *British Army Review*: ". . . the commendable use of British counter-insurgency experience in developing military doctrine and education needs to be more firmly tethered to broader historical context if it is to form valuable guidance for future operations."[16] His point is compelling. The British have excellent doctrine, but it tends to ignore some of the historical realities of British campaigns that are essential to understanding the pitfalls of conducting counterinsurgency operations. Inevitably, there are also a number of myths that have arisen about the British approach that have developed both within and outside the British military which need to be dispelled if the British experience is to be looked at objectively and extrapolated into useful theory.

As Thomas Mockaitis correctly points out, a coherent British approach only really came into being as a result of the lessons of the Malayan Emergency.[17] Even then it was not until 1966 (Thompson) and 1971 (Kitson) that the two most experienced and best known practitioners were able to commit the lessons of their experiences to paper. Consequently, current British doctrine is founded in only a near-term evaluation of British experience and, to some degree, its reputation is founded more on myth than the true facts behind the actual historical experience. In effect, lessons have been cherry-picked from the near-past without understanding the true context or the larger historical experience.

MYTHS

What are the myths that are inherent to the current British approach? The first myth is that the British approach to counterinsurgency is a result of a correct interpretation of experience to doctrine over time. The implication from this is that the British have become better at counterinsurgency with each campaign. This is clearly a fallacy as the passage of this knowledge was not always seamless even in modern times, and the results have been correspondingly variable throughout Britain's history. As an example, the Malayan (1948-60) and Kenyan (1952-56) campaigns are regarded as successful, but the later campaigns in Aden (1962-67), with the exception of the Radfan campaign, were a failure. Indeed, miscalculations in the early stages of the Northern Ireland campaign (1969-2007) undoubtedly set the conditions that led to a prolonged struggle.[18] This was equally true in the Imperial era where mistakes in dealing with the Mahdi in the Sudan between 1881 and 1885 and the Boers in the 2nd Anglo Boer War (1899-1902) led to the loss of the Sudan from 1885-98 and a costly 2-year guerrilla campaign in South Africa.[19] The fact is that each campaign must be planned and conducted differently to match unique conditions on the ground and in the broader strategic context.

The second myth is that the British approach is best. The British have developed a very effective approach that is worthy of study, but there are other approaches that have equally valid lessons. The French, in particular, fought colonial campaigns during the same period as the British withdrawal from empire. While they enjoyed fewer political and military successes, they produced some of the earliest and most influential counterinsurgency theory, proving somewhat the adage that defeated armies learn, while the victors continue to prepare for the last war. The works of Roger Trinquier and David Galula are of particular note. Hence, it is important to keep an open mind when considering how to deal with an insurgency.[20] In developing theory and subsequent doctrine, it is essential to study the theory and doctrine of others in order to identify principles that may be applicable to all counterinsurgency campaigns. The real lessons are that doctrine should be an application of valid theory to contemporary circumstances, and theory and doctrine are valid only as long as they account for the phenomenon of the insurgency.

The third myth is that the Malayan Emergency is the counterinsurgency exemplar. The Malayan Campaign (1948-60) was a significant success, but it was a unique event. There are some very relevant and enduring lessons in terms of understanding the nature of insurgency, the application of the multiagency approach and specific tactical techniques and procedures, but to be relevant it must be understood in context. Malaya was successful in large part because of its geo-strategic position, sharing only one border with other states (Thailand) and with easy access to a secure base in Singapore from which British forces could operate. It could be isolated, and sanctuaries more easily addressed. The jungle environment, although difficult, was mastered by the British Army, particularly the Gurkha Battalions. Some of these units had recent experience operating in the jungle from the Burma Campaign in World War II and were able to leverage their experience.[21] Separating the insurgents from the population was a long process, but the British had a significant advantage in that the insurgents were nonindigenous and had minimal internal and external support.[22] In addition, the British forces had recently learned valuable lessons from their mistakes in Palestine, particularly in terms of the requirement for an effective police force and the importance of a coordinated "hearts and minds" campaign, which enabled them to interact with the general population effectively. Internationally, the Malayan campaign was largely over-shadowed by other world events. The Chinese

Communists under Mao Tse Tung were still consolidating internally after victory over the Nationalist Chinese and provided no support to the Malayan Communists.

Perhaps of greater importance, the British recognized that Malaya was on an unstoppable path to independence, and it made no sense to hinder this process. Britain effectively undermined the Malaysian Communist Party by setting a clear political objective to grant Malaya independence by 1957.[23] In terms of direction, the Briggs Plan for Malaya was a masterpiece, but it took the personality of Field Marshal Sir Gerald Templer to turn it into reality. Furthermore, Templer had the benefit of plenipotentiary powers to execute his mission.[24] He was both High Commissioner of Malaya and Commander in Chief. Finally, the usual British problem of lack of resources was offset by the fact that the Malayan economy was growing in prosperity, and Malaya paid most of the bills. It should also be remembered that, until the Aden campaign, there was very little media coverage of British operations, and this allowed a degree of operational freedom that does not exist today. Thus, Malaya was a unique and fortuitous set of circumstances which will not likely be repeated. The concern, unfortunately, is that these unique circumstances have been used to drive how theory is derived and suggest particular doctrines that may or may not be generally applicable. Many of the lessons from Malaya are still useful, but not all of them — and the context of how they were extracted needs to be reconsidered.

The fourth myth is what is meant by the term "hearts and minds." The British have gained an excellent reputation for "hearts and minds," but this phrase is over-used and often misunderstood. "Hearts and minds" is often mistaken to mean taking a soft approach when dealing with the civilian population, but this is a misnomer. The key is changing the mindset of the target audience and, sometimes, this requires tough measures and a hard approach, i.e., mass movement of the population, curfews, and direct military action (riot control). As the mindset is being changed, small acts of support (i.e., medical and veterinary support) and the way in which government security forces interact with the population, combined with an effective information operations campaign, wins over their hearts. As Thomas Mockaitis implies, the phrase really should be "minds and hearts."[25]

The fifth myth is the use of minimum force. Minimum force is what is appropriate for the situation and can range from martial law to conventional warfighting in a counterinsurgency context. Jackson and Mockaitis point out some fairly brutal acts, by today's standards, committed by British forces which enabled them to achieve certain objectives.[26] Particular examples include rough interrogations, internment without trial, and different rules of engagement for different ethnic populations.[27] Such methodologies cannot be condoned today, but they were a significant factor in the conduct of past British campaigns. Generally, however, Jackson and Mockaitis accede that the British have consciously tried to work within the law and used the minimum amount of force necessary since the late Victorian period. What constitutes minimal force is determined by tactical circumstances and the strategic objectives, and will not necessarily be the lowest force option.

The sixth myth is that the British Army has won Britain's counterinsurgency campaigns. The British Army has been a significant factor in Britain's success but, as Jackson and Mockaitis amply illustrate, the British Army is only one of a number of security force organizations that have been responsible for the collective British success.[28]

In terms of the Army, Jackson illustrates this by describing the military forces used in colonial campaigns as the British regular army units, locally recruited colonial forces, and the indigenous population (i.e., the Iban Scouts in Malaya), all of whom were important in achieving success.[29] Jackson rightfully stresses the importance of the colonial police forces to British success. In British campaigns it has generally been the police forces that have been the primary arm of counterinsurgent actions in keeping with the modern British policy of police primacy.

THE GREATER HISTORICAL EXPERIENCE

Great Britain has far greater experience with counterinsurgency than the Malayan and Northern Ireland experiences would suggest. In two seminal books on British counterinsurgency, Thomas Mockaitis argues that the British success in counterinsurgency operations is founded in the historical legacy of Imperial policing, particularly from British experiences in the early 20th century, in Ireland (1920-22) and in British India (1919-47).[30] John Nagl partly supports this view but correctly surmises that the real roots of the development of the current approach started well before this in the 19th century.[31] Indeed, the evidence clearly shows that it is the rich experience found in the combination of the need to police the empire and the varied challenges that this involved which gave the British military a head start and a unique way to understanding how to deal with the problem of insurgency in the 20th century. It follows then that this broader history of imperial politics and limited military operations offers key insights.

Historically, as the British Empire, Great Britain's national interests can be defined as:

- Security of free trade.
- Credibility as a great world power.
- The cohesion and security of the Empire (and particularly British India).
- Security of the British Homeland.
- Enlargement of civilization and Christianity.

British strategy was therefore about physical and economic security through global leadership, a preferred trading posture, a strong navy and a minimal army, all of which enabled Britain to maintain its leadership position in the world. The British Empire was about ideas and values too; but not at the expense of the other interests. It sought to avoid major wars unless the homeland was directly threatened, or a significant threat arose to Britain's imperial possessions. As a sovereign and imperial power, Britain required armed forces that were capable of defending the homeland and of conducting expeditionary operations to protect the empire.

During the Victorian era (1837-1901), with the imperial responsibility for over 700 million people around the world, it was impossible for the people of such a small country as Great Britain to defend their global interests without the cooperation of the territories that she occupied.[32] British imperial policy thus became one of control through the indigenous populations with small operating teams in the individual countries. It was a pragmatic and sometimes naïve approach which balanced the initiative of the local commander, political and military alliances with local figures of importance, and limited resources to maintain control, stability, and the legitimacy of the Empire.

The power of the British Empire was largely the power of diplomacy and the threat of the Royal Navy, with the Army being left to sustain the status quo, a role for which they were often under-resourced. Such a policy called for a repertoire of methods for gaining local consent including: (1) Persuasion, (2) Deterrence, (3) Coercion, (4) Appeasement, and (5) Negotiation. Overall, the aim was simply to "divide and rule" the locals, thereby creating general compliance. Where this failed, military force was used, but force was always in short supply. In addition, the British policymakers and military instinctively understood that, on cessation of hostilities, both sides had to live together again which made them wish to use military action sparingly, even though sometimes military action was severe. For example, in 1901 Lord Kitchener ordered the creation of the concentration "laagers" in South Africa to cut off the Boer Commandos from their support.[33] This measure backfired when cholera struck the camps and over 20,000 men, women, and children died. Despite this, a highly effective treaty was eventually made with the Boers at Vereeniging in May 1902, which included the British paying significant reparations.[34] Within 12 years, at the outbreak of World War I, the former protagonists were fighting as allies in German East Africa and on the Western Front. That the empire survived until the second half of the 20th century and through and after the two World Wars, albeit shakily, is testimony to the success of this imperial approach.

The British Army fought over 230 campaigns in the Victorian era alone.[35] Some of these were limited wars in terms of objectives and the use of force. Others were unlimited, particularly those aiming to end a nationalist uprising. Guerrilla warfare was a fact of life in many areas such as the North West frontier of India. Insurgency is a 20th century term, but many of these earlier campaigns would now be labeled insurgencies.

It was the imperial era which gave the British Army its unique character, and this heyday of Empire produced some valuable lessons which have since evolved into modern counterinsurgency principles and doctrine. The first and foremost lesson is the principle of civilian control of the military. The primacy of civilian control was generally maintained throughout the imperial period and remains a very important factor in the conduct of British counterinsurgency campaigns. Even at the height of empire when British military commanders had almost regional/colonial plenipotentiary powers, they always served subordinate to the local civilian authority and acted on his behalf unless a state of emergency existed. In cases where the military took charge ". . . the imperial general was also a proconsul, forced to rely on his political skills as much as his operational expertise to prevail."[36] He had to look at all the problems from the point of view of his political masters, not just apply a military perspective.

The second lesson that emerges from this era is the need for operational and political pragmatism founded in cultural awareness. Spread over long lines of communication with limited manpower and resources, the British military has always had to rely on local support — indigenous political actors, forces, and logistics. Limitations in British forces and the idiosyncrasies of local leaders, forces, and culture fostered practical solutions to the problems encountered founded in an appreciation of the particular situation. The British military had to be culturally aware and often failed where it was not. Hence, British commanders had no other option than to be pragmatic when analyzing and addressing military and political issues around the world, leading to realistic points of view and, generally, cultural astuteness.

The third lesson from the Imperial experience is the value of the organizational knowledge inherent in a regimental system. The strength of the system is that lessons learned on campaign are generally carried on in regimental tradition. British regiments have long been the repository of tactical knowledge. Where the British Army (and wider military) has failed in the past is to collectively capture and retain this wisdom as an institution. Nevertheless, when faced with a task, British regiments have normally adapted well to dealing with the problem due to a historical collective memory and pragmatism born of a history of too few and too little for the task at hand. What has further facilitated this adaptation in regiments is the historical practice of delegating significant authority and responsibility to subordinate levels within the regimental organization, and particularly the empowerment of junior commanders. This imperial tradition continued in Northern Ireland where junior commanders shouldered heavy responsibility in counterinsurgency operations. Hence, one of the key points of success in British counterinsurgency is the adaptability and flexibility of its officers and soldiers, a capability born largely of the effectiveness of the regimental system.

The fourth lesson emerging from the imperial experience is founded in the historical requirement to restore an acceptable stability with minimal disruption to national interests and at low cost—a need for innovation and adaptability. Instability in any part of the empire threatened free trade and the credibility and legitimacy of British rule. With limited British manpower, constrained finances and threats from across the empire, any military action taken needed to be short, low cost in "blood and treasure," effective and long-lasting. Overstretched around the globe, the empire demanded military success at low cost, which is little different from the dilemma British armed forces find themselves in today. Modern counterinsurgencies, as in the past, require a long-term view, and the resulting campaigns are potentially expensive in "blood and treasure." Yet the lesson is clear. Even today, military forces still conduct their campaigns with insufficient forces and must rely on innovation and adaptability in leadership, planning, and tactics to succeed. As costly as fighting a modern insurgency may be, without this innovation and adaptability, the demands in blood and treasure would be greater.

THE REALITIES AND THEIR APPLICABILITY AS THE BASIS FOR COHERENT THEORY

Modern British doctrine is founded largely on post-World War II experiences, with their accompanying myths, and a historical collective regimental experience. Considered in the broader context of the total imperial experience a more comprehensive appreciation of British counterinsurgency emerges. The realities of the total British experience therefore provide a better basis for understanding the uniqueness of the British approach. A study of the existing counterinsurgency literature combined with the insights of the broader British experience suggests a more general and inclusive list of realties that better define the basis for a comprehensive theory for the 21st century. Such research reveals 17 overarching premises that validate the current British principles and reveal considerations not currently addressed in the AFM. Taken together, these 17 premises constitute a comprehensive British theory of counterinsurgency.

The 1st premise is that insurgency is war. War is a political act that requires an active decision to initiate it and a clear declaration of intent.[37] It is generally regarded as being between one or more actors within the international system which includes state actors or actors within a state. Therefore, by inference, war can be both external (among states) and internal (civil war and insurgency), or a mix of both. Hence, war is a political act, uses violence, is both offensive and defensive in nature, and can be internal or external to the state. An insurgency is internal to the state or governmental system even though the key players may be prosecuting their campaign from a safe haven outside the legal boundaries, using external support or exporting their violence against other actors within the international system. There should be no confusion: an insurgency is a war.[38] Knowing who the belligerents are and the political objectives of all relative to your own is essential to successful policy, strategy, and campaign plans.

The 2nd premise is that every insurgency is unique. The nature and context of the conflict must be thoroughly explored and understood. It takes time to fully understand the nature of the problem and to develop the lines of operation to deal with it. While broad general counterinsurgency principles may translate well across campaigns, one size does not fit all. The unique geography, history, culture, ideology, and ethnicity of a country will all affect how a campaign should be conducted. As Clausewitz so brilliantly explains: "The first, the supreme, the most far-reaching act of judgement that the statesman and commander have to make is to establish by that test the kind of war on which they are embarking; neither mistaking it for, nor trying to turn it into, something that is alien to its nature."[39] This is difficult to do in any war but in the case of an insurgency it is far more problematic. What is the true nature of the situation? Is the insurgency founded in legitimate grievances? Does it enjoy popular support? Is the existing government supportable? Is the insurgency multi-factional or unified? Is there widespread international support for the insurgency or for the counterinsurgent? The uniqueness of an insurgency is in its nature, and it takes time to assess this and develop an appropriate counterinsurgency campaign. In the absence of personal knowledge, expert advice on the region must be sought and considered before deciding on the appropriate course.

A 3rd premise is the essentiality of envisioning the long-term post-conflict end-state. As Sir Basil Liddell Hart wrote: "The object in [counterinsurgency] war is to attain a better peace—even if only from your point of view. Hence it is essential to conduct war with constant regard to the peace you desire."[40] In what is a struggle over who has the best and most achievable vision for the future, the object of the war is to achieve a better peace by compelling others to willingly accede to new conditions that define peace on terms acceptable to you. The quality of the peace will only be decided by the perception of the legitimacy of the strategy followed by engaging sufficient resources to achieve the goals and by the perception of the population of better conditions equating to peace. All planning must be done with the long term in view. Having a long-term view is one of the existing British principles of counterinsurgency.

The 4th premise is that geography matters. Geography is one of the most important factors when trying to understand the nature of an insurgency and how to conduct a counterinsurgency. Geography dictates to all belligerents and populations, affecting the mindset of each and physically defining operations. For example, land-locked countries are more likely to rely on alliances for their security and to obtain their resources from them. This also means that there are potentially more borders along which insurgents can find safe havens to prosecute their campaigns. Island countries, and countries with extensive coastlines, are more likely to depend less on their immediate neighbours and potentially become more economically powerful through trade. Insurgents may have a more restricted area in which to operate and can be more easily isolated. For counterinsurgent partners, this may also imply a significant problem in terms of logistics with limited access routes and the heavy reliance on specific ports and airfields. In the wider context of a global insurgency, the implications of geography are even more significant. Working on a broad worldwide canvas and trying to combat more than one insurgency concurrently in differing terrain adds to the complexity of developing coherent strategy and planning.

A 5th premise of a counterinsurgency theory is to not engage in a war or campaign that cannot be won at a price consistent with the political and military objectives. In the consideration or conduct of any war or campaign there may come a decision point at which the astute leader concludes the cost of success far outweighs the benefits, or success is not even possible? If a client state is on the verge of collapse and enjoys little popular support, it may be too late or too expensive to support counterinsurgency. Likewise, if there is a long-standing stalemate with equal claims to legitimacy, there is little chance of easy resolution and the costs of conducting or supporting a counterinsurgency strategy go up. No amount of military action or information operations will successfully win all the people over if the nation is truly divided. It may be that the situation must be left to resolve itself. The British experience in Palestine and Aden are clear examples of campaigns which were unwinnable and resulted ultimately in British withdrawal. Determining this decision point in the actual conduct of war is extremely difficult. Recognizing its inevitability while still in the strategy formulation or campaign planning stage is genius; acting on it is the essence of moral courage.

The 6th premise is the requirement for a clear plan. This is one of Sir Robert Thompson's five principles and is based on his experience in helping to formulate the Briggs Plan.[41] It is an essential factor for success. The plan must, however, be tailored to the peculiar and unique circumstances of the insurgency. Plans should provide a focus for all of the involved agencies, and the plans should be universally understood and accepted. Plans must clearly link to the long-term objective of an enduring peace. An excellent example of an effective plan is the British Five Front Plan for the Dhofar campaign.[42] The particular situation of Dhofar as an underdeveloped region of Oman meant that it needed economic development. The campaign end state was therefore to secure Dhofar for development and the five fronts to achieve this were :

1. To clearly identify the enemy and friendly forces by establishing an effective intelligence collection and collation system.

2. To communicate clear intent to the insurgents, the population, and the government agencies and forces.

3. To provide security by helping the Dhofaris to protect their own province by involving them in the overall provision of security.

4. To provide medical aid to the people of Dhofar in a region that had none.

5. To provide veterinary services for the cattle in the Dhofar region which are the main source of wealth.

This plan indicates an excellent understanding of the needs of the people of Dhofar set against the context of the campaign and the need to win "hearts and minds" to ensure an enduring peace. It can be easily followed and provides latitude to individual commanders as well as guidelines on how to operate. Finally, in terms of communication, it is accessible and applicable to all agencies and simple to understand. The message is also unambiguous to all audiences — local, international, and domestic.

A 7th premise of a counterinsurgency theory is that rapid adaption is inherent to success. There is always a learning stage at the beginning of each campaign that must be accounted for by organizing to learn quickly from both successes and mistakes. The belligerent who learns and adapts most quickly enjoys strategic, operational, and tactical advantages. It takes time to understand the nature of each campaign and, in the process of doing so, it is inevitable that some mistakes will be made. It is important that the potential for mistakes is minimized by a thorough assessment of the situation before deployment and a willingness to learn quickly and then adapt to the new circumstances. Once the campaign has started, the effectiveness of the method of operating must be constantly reassessed to enable the government and security forces to be proactive in regard to the population and conditions over time; and remain one step ahead of the insurgents, keeping them on the defensive. The Boyd "OODA loop" of *observe, orientate, decide,* and *act* remains the best model for describing this process.[43]

Every British campaign has a litany of mistakes made in the early stages of operations. What delineates a successful campaign is how quickly the security forces learn from their mistakes or exploit their successes before the adversary can adapt. Adaptability is an essential component of success. In the Irish Civil War of 1920-22, Mockaitis concludes that the British learned valuable lessons but too late to affect the outcome of the campaign — a victory for the Irish Republicans.[44] It is often forgotten that the Malayan Emergency did not start well. The initial approach to the insurgency was not dynamic, and a number of mistakes were made before the British realized the seriousness of the threat.[45] It was really only after the assassination of High Commissioner Sir Henry Gurney, on October 6, 1951, that Britain started to react to the situation effectively and activated the Briggs Plan.[46]

In Kenya, Africa, the first year of the campaign was the bloodiest when the British let the indigenous kikuyu-led Police conduct many of the operations without appropriate supervision.[47] The campaign was very nearly lost, but the British forces learned quickly enough to reverse the process and achieve eventual success. The learning stage suggests that it may be better to start with small measured steps until the full nature of the situation is apparent, and then make use of what has been learned to gain the advantage.

The 8th premise is that politics is the focal point. Politics and war are social phenomena. One key to countering insurgency is therefore to understand the context and nature of the social environment. It is essential to understand what the people's issues are and what can make them better. What is it that attracts people to the insurgents and how can this be ameliorated or discredited? As Sun Tzu describes it, it is not enough just to know ourselves; we must also know our adversary and what it is that has shaped them.[48]

A key element in all wars is the people, and this has been the root of British success, and sometimes failure, in counterinsurgency. People seek conditions that ensure their safety and prosperity for essentially a better life. People populate the government, man the military, and ultimately determine national will. In Western liberal society, the people empower their governments to provide for them their security and their basic needs through the democratic process. This is effectively collective survival where the people surrender some of their personal choices for the collective good.[49] In emerging or failed states, such a system may not exist or function effectively, and the people are likely to be more concerned with their simple survival.

The people, the insurgents, and the government are products of their environment and have been shaped by their unique geography, history, culture, ethnicity, and ideology, and this, in turn, shapes the unique way that they understand, conduct, and accept or respond to war. This context will determine whether they are aggressive, passive, neutral, or major or peripheral players on the stage of war. In an insurgency Clausewitz's famous trinity might be better represented diagrammatically as being placed within the overall environment and shaped by five main factors—geography, history, culture, ethnicity, and ideology (See Figure 1).

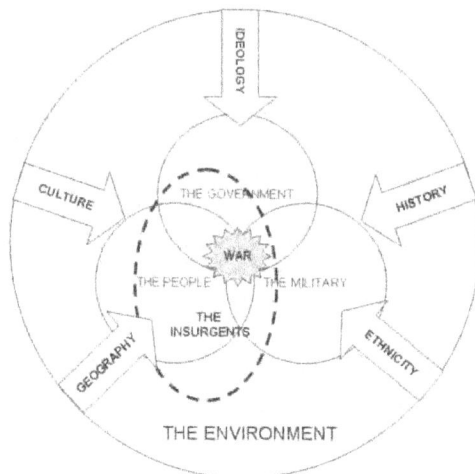

IDEOLOGY

CULTURE

HISTORY

THE GOVERNMENT

WAR

THE PEOPLE

THE MILITARY

THE INSURGENTS

GEOGRAPHY

ETHNICITY

THE ENVIRONMENT

Figure 1. The Modified Clausewitzian Trinity.[50]

In this environment, insurgents represent a separate shadow state within the state. Insurgents come from the people, and yet they are distinct because they seek to sway the general population to the legitimacy of their opposition ideology. An insurgency constructs its own alternative ideology, government, military, popular support (constituency), and administrative bureaucracy concurrently with the destructive actions (subversion, terrorism, guerrilla action) that it uses to discredit the existing government structures. The only way to combat this is to fully understand the insurgents as a political organization and use this information to target their weaknesses. The key to separating the insurgents from their popular support is ultimately political; co-opt their issues and discredit their political objectives and abilities.

220

A 9th premise of a British counterinsurgency theory is that hearts follow minds in counterinsurgency. In Hanoi in 1956, paraphrasing Mao Tse Tung, Ho Chi Minh stated that "The people are like the fish in the sea, they swim with the current."[51] In order to make the people swim in the right direction, the current of the friendly authority is the key to winning in counterinsurgency. It is essential to alter their minds to reject the insurgents' interpretation of social issues and accept the counterinsurgent government as the legitimate authority for ensuring security and social justice. When the population believes in their minds that the government best serves their interests, their hearts will follow and support the government's politics. How is this achieved?

If disputed authority is envisaged as the football at a football match, the two opposing teams are the insurgents and the indigenous government with its security forces. The observers on the sidelines are the people, other countries from the region, international agencies, and potential allies, and they can also be recruited as team members. The two teams must keep the maximum possession of the ball if they are to win the game—and preclude the other team from scoring. Each goal that is scored against the opposing team reinforces the political position and possession advantages of the ball by the scorer. Even though the opposing team starts again with possession of the ball after a goal is scored against them, they start their counteroffensive from a weaker position. A clear strategy and careful preparation are essential. Teams must understand the importance of winning and train to execute their prepared plays. Critically, winning must be achieved by learning and then adhering to the rules of the game, although the risk of using innovation and originality in interpreting these is acceptable as long as they keep to the spirit of the game—legitimacy. The team that maintains possession of the ball and uses it with the greatest amount of skill impresses not only its faithful followers but also the neutral observers. When sufficient observers—internal and external—agree a team has outscored its opponent and retained the ball sufficiently, no further observers join the losing team and the winner is affirmed. Of course, in the long run everyone loves a winner, particularly when you finally perceive them as your home team—insurgency and counterinsurgency is about affirming who is the home team.

The modified Clausewitzian model and football analogy explain classic insurgency and counterinsurgency which has two clear sides, but what about the global security environment? Do the model and analogy apply to global insurgency? The answer is yes! A global insurgency is simply a tournament, where the teams, rules, and audiences are much the same, but there are multiple and often concurrent games. Rather than tackle all of the games at once, the counterinsurgent has to play them in the appropriate sequence, and never too many at one time. The insights and experience of a winning counterinsurgent team are still valid, but they must be applied intelligently to each distinct game and field.

The 10th premise is that the requirement for a coordinated multiagency government approach is paramount to success. This is true for governments externally intervening and for existing internal governments. The overall strategy and ensuing plans must be collaborative and involve multiagencies and actors using all of the elements of national power of both the supported and supporting governments. In doing this, the activities have to be coordinated and synchronized so that they work together and not against one another. For example, security and economic development must go hand-in-hand so that security yields an economic dividend, and development is not just providing another opportunity for a target. This has been one of the key enduring tenets of the British approach and a cornerstone of every successful campaign. The best known examples are in Malaya and Northern Ireland.

The 11th premise is that it is essential to work within the rule of law. Rule of law is the visible symbol of moral justification. The aim must be to restore the civilian authority and police primacy if it does not already exist. Where it does not exist, the military must shoulder the burden until such time as the relevant civilian and police capabilities can be trained to fulfil their role. Regardless of who has the lead at a particular time, the rule of law must be both understood and demonstrated in the existing circumstances to be meaningful and fair to the local population in order to reinforce the legitimacy of the counterinsurgents. This is an existing principle of Sir Robert Thompson's theory.[52]

A 12th premise of a counterinsurgency theory is that counterinsurgents must only use the appropriate force necessary for the situation faced. The appropriate use of force is the minimum amount of force required to achieve a particular justifiable objective. This can range from full scale warfighting against an insurgent base deep in the jungle to the arrest of a single insurgent in an urban area. The British military has relied heavily on flexible Rules of Engagement (ROE) to ensure that only the minimum force necessary is used for each situation. Force must be proportionate and justified and the intent to use force clearly understood. In the British Army, operations in Northern Ireland proved this premise time and again, demonstrating that junior commanders can be empowered to make tough decisions when needed.

The 13th premise is that campaigns must be suitably resourced to be truly effective. Like all conflicts where fighting is likely, counterinsurgency campaigns are expensive in term of "blood and treasure." It is, however, the "treasure" element of this equation that is often the most lacking in counterinsurgency campaigns. Such campaigns are often the most expensive to conduct because they take longer to conclude and involve the broader costs of reconstruction and development. There is, however, a balance to be struck between resources and ingenuity. Too many physical resources can be problematic and worsen the situation by limiting innovation and confusing peripheral concerns with the real issue of minds and hearts. Counterinsurgency is manpower intensive over a potentially long period of time, and this reality needs to be considered during the early analysis of the problem.[53] However, actual resource issues are nearly always concerned with a lack of funds for the nonmilitary support to the campaign which is a critical factor in winning minds and hearts. The appropriate and realistic level of resources must be envisioned and allocated before the counterinsurgency campaign starts.

The 14th premise is that accurate and timely information and intelligence are essential to success. Insurgency and counterinsurgency both work in the same strategic environment, and the currency is information that can be used as intelligence. Conventional military campaigns also require intelligence, but the level and detail of intelligence required is much greater in counterinsurgency. A counterinsurgency campaign must win the battle for information. This is a key element in General Sir Frank Kitson's theory. [54]

A 15th premise is that the use of indigenous forces is essential to building an enduring peace for the country concerned. In all British campaigns, local indigenous forces have played an important role. They have acted as the backbone of intelligence gathering, police forces, and the local military. The importance of their use is three-fold: first, it involves them in the long-term solution in that they represent the population and therefore provide some censure over and learn to work under civil control; second, it enables the security forces to understand the nature of the conflict that they are involved in; and third, once trained and well-led, they are generally more effective in the context of the counterinsurgency environment. The long-term aim of using indigenous forces is to build up sufficient capacity for them to replace any external counterinsurgency forces. This is achieved through the process of leading, mentoring, and advising. Initially, there may be a requirement for direct leadership roles by external military professionals for the indigenous military until such time as a strong cadre of indigenous leadership has been trained to replace them. Once this has been achieved, indigenous cadre may only require oversight and the external force personnel can then switch to a mentoring role. The stage when indigenous forces are capable of standing on their own is normally synonymous with the general withdrawal of external forces and a significant improvement in the overall security situation. The British approach has then been to leave training and advisory teams in the key military and police institutions as part of the long-term commitment. This process can be represented diagrammatically (Figures 2 and 3):

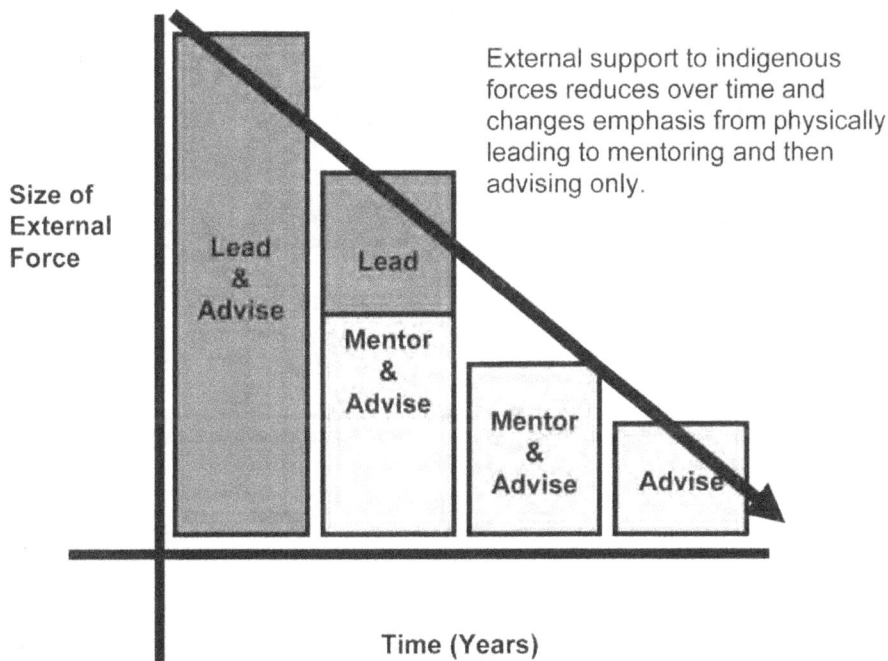

Figure 2. External Support to Indigenous Forces.

The 16th premise of counterinsurgency is that increasing constraints and less freedom of action characterize modern campaigns. The world of the 21st century is very different from 50 years ago, and both local and international expectations have changed.

The Malayan campaign and Kenya were fought largely out of the glare of the media whereas Iraq and Afghanistan have 24-hour news coverage. Conflicts in the 19th century were reported weeks later. Factors such as progress in human rights, the evolution of international law, and the advent of immediate worldwide communications have combined to create an environment in which the nature of the choices and actions of the counterinsurgents pose significant threats to the state's claim on legitimacy: these factors, among others, significantly limit freedom of action. If history is any guide, this trend will worsen as peoples', other states', and nonstate actors' expectations expand in the future. It is made worst by the fact that expectations placed on state actors are not equally applied to nonstate actors. The lesson to take from this is not to uselessly fight the march of progress, but to formulate a clear strategy that works with and around the identified constraints — or better yet, exploits them in order to achieve operational freedom.

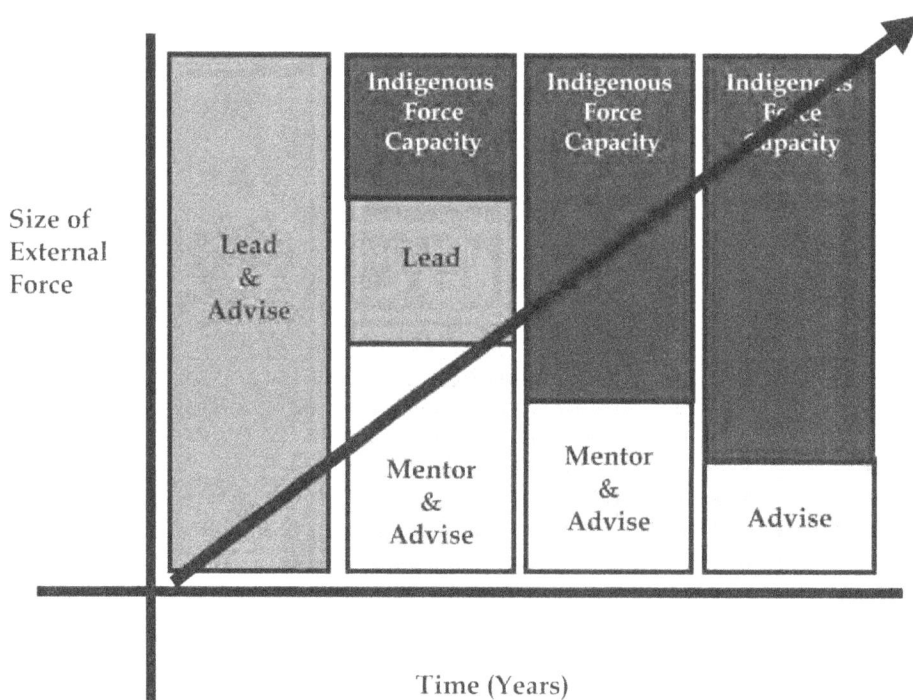

Indigenous Force Capacity grows exponentially over time commensurate with a planned reduction of external force support

Figure 3. Growth of Indigenous Forces.

The 17th, and final, premise is that negotiation is an inherent aspect of counterinsurgency. It cannot be ruled out if a long-term peace is sought. The British government and military have a long tradition of negotiating with insurgents, if it has been in British interests to do so. There are, however, three very important caveats: first, negotiations must be conditional; second, the primary aim of all negotiation is to bring the insurgents into the political process and stop violence; and, third, patience is an essential factor. Recently declassified documents show that the British government started meetings with the Provisional Irish Republican Army (PIRA) as early as 1972.[55] These meetings were not initially successful because PIRA would not agree to the stated conditions, but they continued for over 20 years until the political arm of the PIRA, Sinn Fein, achieved ascendancy within the insurgency movement, leading to the key ceasefire in 1994. Thereafter, steady progress was made towards achieving a roadmap of conditions for a permanent renunciation of violence and participation in the political process. There are a number of other important examples of similar circumstances in British history. For example, negotiations were conducted with Boer leaders during the Boer War in 1901 and 1902 and with Chinese Communists during the Malayan Emergency in 1955.[56] Needless to say, negotiations among the supporting and supported governments, allies, and other state and nonstate actors are also inherent to successful counterinsurgency.

CONCLUSIONS

The British approach to counterinsurgency is one which is notable for its successes. Unfortunately, current British counterinsurgency doctrine has evolved largely from experience post-1945, creating some myths and ignoring lessons from earlier periods. As a result, the doctrine is good but incomplete. The study of the whole of Great Britain's colonial and post-colonial counterinsurgency experience reveals new insights that are relevant to modern counterinsurgency challenges. Such a comprehensive study of the British experience results in a clearer understanding of what counterinsurgency is and the demands it places on doctrine. In examining this broader history, this chapter indentifies 17 premises that, taken together, constitute a British military theory of counterinsurgency for the 21st century. The key to the application of these premises lies in understanding that counterinsurgency is, in fact, war and victory resides in a political solution.

ENDNOTES - CHAPTER 14

1. Thomas R. Mockaitis, *British Counter-Insurgency 1919-1960*, New York: St. Martin's Press, 1990, p. 180.

2. Army Staff College Camberley, *Counter-Revolutionary Warfare Handbook*, Camberley, UK: the Royal Military Academy Sandhurst, 1988, p. Annex H, p. H1-4. This excellent précis highlights the following as COIN Campaigns: Greece (1945-46), Palestine (1945-48), Egypt (1946-56), Malaya (1948-60), Eritrea (1949), Kenya (1952-56), Cyprus (1954-58), Aden (1955, 1956-58), Muscat and Oman (1957-59), Togoland (1957), Brunei (1962), Malaysia (limited war with elements of an insurgency, 1963-69), Radfan (1964), Aden (1965-67), Northern Ireland (1969-2007), and Dhofar, Oman (1970-76).

3. Successes: Malaya, Kenya, Brunei, Malaysia, Radfan, Dhofar, and Northern Ireland. Draw: Cyprus. Partial successes: Greece (1945-46), Eritrea (1949), and Togoland (1957). Failures: Palestine (1945-48), Egypt (1946-56), Aden (1955, 1956-58, 1965-67). Extant: Afghanistan (2001-to date) and Iraq (2003-to date) are still ongoing at the time of writing.

4. Dr. Ashley Jackson, "British Counterinsurgency in History: A Useful Precedent?" *British Army Review*, Vol. 139, Spring 2006, p. 12.

5. General Sir Rupert Smith, *The Utility of Force – The Art of War in the Modern World*, London, UK: Allen Lane, The Penguin Group, 2005, p. 372.

6. Colin S. Gray, *Another Bloody Century*, London, UK: Weidenfield & Nicolson, 2005, pp. 177-185. He contends that war remains unpredictable and lists 12 hypothetical future wars variations of which could feasibly arise in the 21st century: A Sino-Russian Axis versus the United States; China versus the United States, Russia versus China; Russia versus Ukraine; Russia versus Latvia and Estonia; India versus Pakistan; the United States and/or Israel versus Iran; Greece versus Turkey; North Korea versus South Korea and the United States; the United States versus rogue states; a superpower Europe, possibly in alliance with Russia or China, versus a strategically still hegemonic United States and its Allies; and Strategic Surprise (unknowns as a prudent catch all).

7. *Army Field Manual (AFM) Volume 1, Combined Arms Operations, Counter Insurgency Operations, Strategic and Operational Guidelines - Part 10*, Army Code 71749, July 2001, p. A-1-1. This manual will be superseded in late 2009.

8. *Ibid.*

9. Frank Kitson, *Low Intensity Operations – Subversion, Insurgency and Peacekeeping*, Harrisburg, PA : Stackpole Books, 1971, p. 2. Kitson explains that one of the difficulties of defining low intensity operations is the existing terminology. He lists the British Army's classifications for irregular methods and threats as civil disturbance, insurgency, guerrilla warfare, subversion, terrorism, civil disobedience, revolutionary warfare, and insurrection. Of these, insurgents are likely to use civil disturbance, guerrilla warfare, subversion, terrorism, and civil disobedience.

10. There is no standard definition for "Hearts and Minds," but it is essentially the process of winning the popular support of the people away from the insurgents.

11. *Joint Warfare Publication 0-01.1, The United Kingdom Glossary of Joint and Multinational Terms and Definitions*, 6th Ed., London, UK: Ministry of Defence, p. C-25.

12. Sir Robert Thompson KBE, CMG, DSO, MC. A career diplomat, Thompson joined the Malayan Civil Service in 1938. He saw military service as a RAF Officer with both Chindit Operations in Burma (1943-45) during which he was awarded the DSO and the MC. After the war he returned to Malaya, where he was one of the staff who helped General Sir Harold Briggs to write the "Briggs Plan." Subsequent appointments included Permanent Secretary for Defence Malaya (1959-61) and the Head of the British Advisory Mission to Vietnam (1961-65). His best known book is *Defeating Communist Insurgency* (1966), which distils the lessons of the Malayan Emergency into five basic principles for counterinsurgency.

13. General Sir Frank Kitson GBE, KCB, MC, is best known for his three books on counterinsurgency: *Gangs and Counter-Gangs*, 1960; *Low Intensity Operations – Subversion, Insurgency and Peacekeeping*, 1971; and *Bunch of Five*, 1977. He is veteran of five counterinsurgency campaigns: Kenya, Malaya, Cyprus, Oman, and Northern Ireland.

14. Sir Robert Thompson, *Defeating Communist Insurgency; The lessons from Malaya and Vietnam*, New York, F. A. Praeger, 1966.

15. AFM Volume 1.

16. Jackson, p. 20.

17. See Mockaitis, *British Counterinsurgency 1919-1960*, pp. 8-10, for a brief description of the campaign; and p. 180, where he identifies Malaya as the turning point in the development of British counterinsurgency doctrine.

18. Rod Thornton, "Getting it Wrong: The Crucial Mistakes Made in the early Months of the British Army's Deployment to Northern Ireland (August 1969-1970)," *Journal of Strategic Studies*, Vol. 30, No. 1, February 2007. Thornton attributes the main mistakes to difficult command and control, the military commander trying to simultaneously command the Army units and the police while reporting directly to the MOD, the Provisional Irish Republican Army's (PIRA) success in luring the Army into overreacting to incidents thus effectively separating them from the people, and limited military resources (a perennial problem).

19. During the imperial era, there was very little attempt to distil the lessons of imperial policing and small wars before Colonel, later Major General, Sir Charles Callwell in 1896 with the publication of his seminal work, *Small Wars – Their Principles and Practice*.

20. Roger Trinquier, *Modern Warfare – a French View of Counterinsurgency*, Westport, CT: Praeger Security International, 2006 (1964), trans. from the French by Daniel Lee, with an introduction by Bernard B. Fall; David Gallula, *Counter-Insurgency Warfare Theory and Practice*, Westport, CT: Praeger Security International, 2006 (1964).

21. Charles Allen, *The Savage Wars of Peace–Soldiers' Voices 1945-1989*, London, UK: Penguin Books, p. 3-18. It is one of the forgotten aspects of the Malayan Campaign that the initial military defence against the Communists was down to six under strength Gurkha battalions who bore the brunt of the insurgency for the first 2 years. Despite the fact that many of the Gurkha soldiers were new recruits because of the transition from the Indian to the British Army, there was sufficient residual knowledge from Burma amongst the British officers and some of the NCOs to enable the battalions to learn quickly.

22. The Communist Terrorists (CTs) were 95 percent Chinese (the minority population). Many of their leaders had been trained by the British Special Operations Executive (SOE), Force 136, led by Colonel Freddie Spencer-Chapman DSO, and there was some good information about the leadership in the organization.

23. Ian Beckett, *The Malayan Emergency, 1948-1960*, Junior Command and Staff Course Precis, Sandhurst, UK: The Royal Military Academy Sandhurst,1986.

24. The Briggs Plan, formulated by Lieutenant General Sir Harold Briggs KCIE, KCB, DSO** Indian Army in 1951:

1. Cutting off supplies to the enemy and forcing them away from the urban areas into the deep jungle where they could be defeated by direct action.

2. Re-housing the indigenous population and giving them citizenship.

3. Defending the new villages.

4. Joint Command and Control in the form of War Executive Committees that were established from States down to Districts and included representation from the local government, military and police in each committee.

Interpreted by the author from Sir Robert Thompson, *Make for the Hills*, London, UK: Leo Cooper, 1989, pp. 92-93.

25. Mockaitis, *British Counterinsurgency 1919-1960*, p. 64. The exact provenance of the phrase "hearts and minds" is open to debate but it is generally attributed to General Sir Gerald Templer, the High

Commissioner and Commander in Chief in Malaya. In an interesting footnote, Mockaitis quotes that one of the first instances of the use of the term "minds and hearts" was actually by John Adams in a letter to H. Niles on February 13, 1818, when describing the American Revolution: "The Revolution was affected before the war commenced. The Revolution was in the minds and hearts of the people," available from *teachingamericanhistory.org/library/index.asp?document=968*. As Mockaitis concludes, it is highly unlikely that General Templer was aware of this.

26. *Ibid.* pp. 44-48.

27. Jackson, pp. 14-15.

28. *Ibid.*, p. 4.

29. *Ibid.*, p. 15.

30. Mockaitis, *British Counterinsurgency 1919-1960*. See also Thomas R. Mockaitis, *British Counterinsurgency in the Post-Imperial Era*, Armed Forces and Society Ed., New York: St. Martin's Press, 1995.

31. John A. Nagl, *Learning to Eat Soup with a Knife; Counterinsurgency Lessons from Malaya and Vietnam*, Chicago, IL: University of Chicago Press, 2005, pp. 36-39.

32. Bamber Gascoigne, "British Empire" *Encyclopedia of Great Britain*, Basingstoke, UK: Macmillan Press, 1993.

33. Thomas Pakenham, *The Boer War*, London, UK: Wiedenfield & Nicolson, 1979; London, UK: Macdonald and Company, 1982, pp. 493-495.

34. *Ibid.* At the Treaty of Vereeniging, the British agreed to pay £3 million as compensation for the destruction of farms. In addition, post the treaty, they voluntarily paid a further £2 million to loyalists and "uitlanders," the Boer term for foreigners (literally outsiders).

35. Byron Farwell, *Queen Victoria's Little Wars*, London, UK: W.W. Norton & Company, 1972. Farwell has compiled an exhaustive list of 230 campaigns at the end of his fascinating book.

36. Douglas Porch, *Wars of Empire*, Washington, DC: Smithsonian Books, 2000, p. 5.

37. Carl von Clausewitz, *On War,* Michael Howard and Peter Paret, eds. and trans., Princeton, NJ: Princeton University Press, 1989, p. 87. "War is not merely an act of policy, but a true political instrument, a continuation of political intercourse, carried on with other means."

38. For the purpose of this chapter, war is defined as a formally declared state of violence between one or more internal or external actors to resolve a political issue or difference, or in reaction to an unprovoked act of aggression against the other. Author's own definition from his U.S. Army War College paper, "Fighting for Peace."

39. Clausewitz, p. 88.

40. Sir Basil H. Liddell Hart, *Strategy*, 2d Ed., New York: Penguin Group, Meridian Publishing, 1991, p. 353.

41. Thompson was a member of the Foreign and Commonwealth Office (FCO) in Malaya, ending as the Permanent Secretary of Defence.

42. Thomas R. Mockaitis, British *Counter-Insurgency in the Post-Imperial Era*, Manchester, UK: Manchester University Press, 1995, p. 74. Mockaitis outlines the four original principles but then elaborates on the recruiting of Dhofaris into the security forces which became the third point in the plan. The plan was formulated by Lieutenant Colonel, later General, Johnny Watts of 22 SAS.

43. Robert Coram, *Boyd – The Fighter Pilot Who Changed the Art of War*, New York: Back Bay Books, Time Warner Book Group, 2002, p. 344.

44. Mockaitis, *British Counter-Insurgency 1919-1960*, p. 74.

45. *Ibid.*, p. 113.

46. Sir Robert Thompson, *Make for the Hills*, London, UK: Leo Cooper, 1989, p. 92.

47. Jackson, p. 16.

48. Sun Tzu, *The Art of War*, Trans. with introduction by Samuel B. Griffith, Oxford, UK: Oxford University Press, 1963, p. 84.

49. Attributable to the ideas of Rousseau, 1712-78, and John Hobbes, *Leviathan* (1651). In particular, see Hobbes's idea of the social contract and the link between the people, power, consent, and authority.

50. Clausewitz, p. 89.

51. The original Mao quotation is: "The guerrilla must move amongst the people as a fish swims in the sea." It is difficult to find the exact source of this quote as he uses it and similar phrases in several of his writings. It is normally attributed to his essay, "Problems of Strategy in Guerilla War against Japan," May 1938, included in his book *Six Essays on Military Affairs*, Peking, China: Foreign Languages Press, 1972.

52. Thompson.

53. For example, during the Second Anglo-Boer War, 1899-1902, the Boers had only 83,000 males of military age. The Boers had a maximum of 40,000 men in the field at any one time. Imperial Forces started with 25,000, but this figure had risen to 365,593 Imperial and 82,742 Colonial soldiers by the end of the war.

54. Kitson, *Low Intensity Operations – Subversion, Insurgency and Peacekeeping*.

55. British National Archives, "Note of a Meeting with Representatives of the Provisional IRA, 20 June 1972," British Government Minute to the Secretary of State.

56. Hansard, *Question to Secretary of State for the Colonies into the Results of the Meetings with the MCP*, November 30,1955, Vol. 546, c210W.

CHAPTER 15

FINDING AN EXIT:
DELINEATING BATTLE HANDOFF IN PHASE IV

Colonel Roger S. Marin
U.S. Army

> . . . I am here to make the case for strengthening our capacity to use "soft" power and for better integrating it with "hard" power.

> —Robert M. Gates[1]
> Secretary of Defense

Throughout its history, the U.S. military has been almost solely responsible for "Phase IV operations" largely because it is already in place upon the successful completion of its combat mission and no other entity has had the capability to assume this responsibility in a timely manner. This circumstance has become self-perpetuating as many proponents of the status quo base their argument on the fact that the military has always done it, and therefore will always be required to do it. These advocates posit that the military should stop trying to avoid the mission and instead embrace it. This argument notwithstanding, the fact remains that the expertise required to execute the majority of post-combat stability tasks resides within other agencies. Indeed, recent history has shown the current arrangement is at best grossly inefficient and at worst wholly unsuccessful. Numerous initiatives are currently underway within the U.S. Government (USG) in an attempt to "win the peace" in a more effective and efficient manner. This chapter will explain why the current approach is dysfunctional, examine the status of current initiatives, and make policy recommendations for future success in Phase IV operations.

PHASE IV OPERATIONS DEFINED

While popular usage often equates the terms "Phase IV operations," "stability operations," and "nation-building," it is useful to review the actual meanings of these concepts as they are understood by those charged with carrying them out. The Department of Defense (DoD) broadly defines stability operations as "military and civilian activities conducted across the spectrum from peace to conflict to establish or maintain order in States and regions."[2] Military support to stability, security, transition, and reconstruction (SSTR) operations is defined as "activities that support USG plans for stabilization, security, reconstruction and transition operations, which lead to sustainable peace while advancing U.S. interests."[3] Stability operations tasks include helping to rebuild indigenous institutions such as "security forces, correctional facilities, and judicial systems . . . encouraging . . . bottom-up economic activity and constructing necessary infrastructure; and developing representative governmental institutions."[4] Stability operations and reconstruction efforts are sometimes described as elements of nation-building.[5] According to James Dobbins, "Nation-building, as it is commonly referred to in the United States, involves the use of armed force as part of a broader effort to promote political and economic reforms with the objective of transforming a society emerging from conflict into one at peace with itself and its neighbors."[6]

The DoD states Phase IV (Stabilize) operations are "typically characterized by a change from sustained combat operations to stability operations" wherein the military "may be required to perform limited local governance" and "provid[e] or [assist] in the provision of basic services to the population."[7] It should be noted that Phase IV is not the only phase in which the military conducts stability operations and that the transition from one phase to the next is rarely crystal clear. Phase III (Dominate) operations, generally associated with sustained combat, are conducted to break the enemy's will and control the operational environment. In this phase, stability operations are conducted as needed to set conditions for the transition to Phase IV.[8] Phase V (Enable Civil Authority) operations are characterized by military support to legitimate civil governance in theater and include the coordination of actions of supporting or supported multinational, agency, and other organizational participants. The military end state is achieved upon completion of redeployment but combatant command involvement with nations or agencies may still be required to achieve the national strategic end state.[9]

An additional concept frequently interwoven in discussions of Phase IV operations that also merits definition here is *full spectrum operations*. The Army states that full spectrum operations consist of offensive, defensive, and stability and reconstruction operations. In this context, stability and reconstruction operations "sustain and exploit security and control over areas, populations, and resources."[10] They also "employ military capabilities to reconstruct or establish services and support civilian agencies."[11] And finally, "lead to an environment in which, in cooperation with a legitimate government, the other instruments of national power can predominate."[12]

Building on these definitional foundations, this chapter draws additional distinctions between the tasks commonly lumped under the stability operations rubrics cited above. To this end, this chapter employs the Office of the Coordinator for Reconstruction and Stabilization, Department of State's (S/CRS) post-conflict reconstruction essential task matrix (ETM), which consists of five technical sectors and 1,178 tasks, to more precisely address what is meant by Phase IV operations. The five technical sectors are Security, Governance and Participation, Humanitarian Assistance and Social Well-Being, Economic Stabilization and Infrastructure, and Justice and Reconciliation.[13]

In terms of scope, this chapter will address Phase IV operations and their included nation-building activities as opposed to nation-building activities writ large. These activities will be referred to as Phase IV operations from this point forward.

WHY CHANGE THE STATUS QUO?

One needs to look no further than the current situation in Iraq to see there is room for improvement in the U.S. approach to stability operations. The vast majority of U.S. ground forces have been virtually tied down there for 5 years with no end in sight. These forces are approaching their breaking point and will require at least $26 billion over 2 years to reset once they are finally redeployed.[14] As a result, the bulk of U.S. ground forces are and will be, for the next several years at a minimum, unavailable for any significant deployment elsewhere during what the Army's senior leadership is referring to as an on-going era of persistent conflict.[15]

Since the end of the Cold War, the United States has become involved in a new stability operation every 2 years, each of which typically lasts from 5 to 8 years.[16] As such, it is incumbent on the United States to find ways to economize on the use of its military forces to ensure they are available to respond to emerging crises. The United States has also spent much more on stability operations than on sustained combat operations since the end of the Cold War.[17] Clearly the limited resources the United States has to spend on stability operations should be allocated in a manner best suited to accomplishing the mission in the most efficient and expedient manner.

The circumstances in any Phase IV operation are unquestionably difficult and complex, and innumerable factors can be faulted when U.S. interventions are less than successful. There is also no assurance that changes to the U.S. approach to stability operations would have made any of the foregoing experiences appreciably better. However, there are some changes to U.S. policy that would seem to improve the odds for success. It stands to reason that any ability to put civilian stability operations subject matter experts in the place of military forces would at a minimum free those forces for other missions. As mentioned above, even those analysts who cite historical precedence and surrender to the idea that conditions cannot, and will not ever change acknowledge the expertise for many stability tasks resides in other agencies.[18]

The situations in Iraq and Afghanistan have spurred interest in the area of stability operations and new executive and legislative action has already occurred, but reform is only in its initial stages. The DoD should seek to reinforce and guide these actions, as outlined below, to establish a permanent and improved construct for its execution of stability operations before "stability fatigue" or the desire for a "peace dividend" at the end of the current conflicts precludes positive change from occurring and taking hold.[19]

CURRENT INITIATIVES

Department of Defense.

On November 28, 2005, the DoD published Directive 3000.05, "Military Support for Stability, Security, Transition, and Reconstruction (SSTR) Operations." This Directive provided initial guidance for this subject while acknowledging that such operations would evolve over time and that future DoD policy would further address the DoD's role. Key policy was established by the statement indicating that ". . . stability operations are a core U.S. military mission that the Department of Defense shall be prepared to conduct and support. They shall be given priority comparable to combat operations . . . ."[20] The Directive acknowledges that "Many stability operations tasks are *best performed by indigenous, foreign, or U.S. civilian professionals*. Nonetheless, U.S. military forces shall be prepared to perform all tasks necessary to *establish or maintain order* when civilians cannot do so."[21] The Directive instructs the Secretaries of the Military Departments and the Commander, U.S. Special Operations Command, to "support interagency requests for personnel and assistance to bolster the capabilities of U.S. Departments and Agencies to prepare for and conduct stability operations as appropriate . . . ."[22]

In the first report to Congress on the implementation of Directive 3000.05, the DoD notes:

> The greatest challenge to the USG's ability to conduct SSTR operations is the lack of integrated capability and capacity of civilian agencies with which the military must partner to achieve success. The U.S. Armed Forces can fill some of these gaps in civilian capacity in the short-term, but strategic success will only be possible with (1) a robust architecture for unified civil-military actions, and (2) substantially more resources devoted to making civilian U.S. Departments and Agencies operational and expeditionary.[23]

The report describes the progress that the DoD has made to restructure agencies, expand training, and synchronize efforts with other agencies, to include support for the Advanced Civilian Teams (ACT) envisioned by S/CRS.

In examining the DoD's efforts in this regard, the Government Accountability Office (GAO) found that the "DoD has developed and continues to evolve an approach to enhance its stability operations capabilities, but it has encountered challenges in identifying and addressing capability gaps and developing measures of effectiveness . . . "[24] The GAO recommends that the "DoD provide more comprehensive guidance, including a clear methodology and time frames for completion, to combatant commanders and the services on how to identify and prioritize needed capabilities and develop measures of effectiveness."[25]

Department of State.

Close on the heels of the DoD Directive, President Bush signed National Security Presidential Directive/NSPD-44, "Management of Interagency Efforts Concerning Reconstruction and Stabilization." This Directive is focused on the Department of State (DoS) and charges the Secretary of State to:

> Coordinate and lead integrated United States Government efforts, involving all U.S. Departments and Agencies with relevant capabilities, to prepare, plan for, and conduct stabilization and reconstruction activities. The Secretary of State shall coordinate such efforts with the Secretary of Defense to ensure harmonization with any planned or ongoing U.S. military operations across the spectrum of conflict.[26]

Most notably, NSPD-44 additionally makes the Secretary of State responsible for: coordinating with the DoD in the planning and implementation phases; coordinating with foreign countries, international and regional organizations, nongovernmental organizations (NGOs), and private sector entities; maximizing NGOs and international resources; and leading the U.S. development of a strong civilian response capability. Other executive departments and agencies are required to coordinate with S/CRS during budget formulation. Lastly, the Directive "does not . . . affect the authority of the Secretary of Defense or the command relationships established for the Armed Forces of the United States."[27]

According to the President's "Report to Congress on Improving Interagency Support," S/CRS will build capacity for deploying civilian officials through the establishment of a DoS Active and Standby Response Corps, engage in whole-of-government planning processes for a range of countries in transition from conflict, and provide core teams at the military operational command level in a reconstruction and stabilization crisis.[28] This report points out the continuing need for increased authorities and resources to hire nongovernment experts for crisis response, to train and equip partner military and security forces, and to build a civilian surge capacity and reserve. The civilian surge capacity includes the expansion of the Active Response Corps (ARC) of full-time first responders who can surge within a week to 30 days for up to 1 year, and the Standby Response Corps (SRC) of civilian agency employees with other ongoing responsibilities who are vetted and remain on an active roster. The Civilian Reserve Corps (CRC) program, which is in development, is to be comprised of civilians with critical expertise not actively resident in the USG and who are ready to be called as experts and advisors within 60 days for up to 2 years.[29]

The President's report also discusses the establishment of the Interagency Management System (IMS) for Reconstruction and Stabilization that will manage complex reconstruction and stabilization engagements by ensuring coordination among all United States Government stakeholders from tactical to strategic levels. The IMS consists of a crisis-specific, Washington-based Country Reconstruction and Stabilization Group (CSRG), a combatant command-integrated Integration Planning Cell (IPC), and one or more interagency field management, planning, and coordination Advance Civilian Teams (ACT) to support chiefs of mission in the field which may operate with or without military involvement.[30] The report states that "The IMS goes a long way toward improving the coordination of activities and ensuring unity of effort in reconstruction and stabilization missions."[31]

In its fiscal year 2009 budget, the DoS requested nearly $249 million for its "Civilian Stabilization Initiative," which is intended to fully fund the activities described above.[32] This is a ground-breaking request in that it marks the first time that the DoS has requested an appropriate amount of funding for its stabilization responsibilities since the President signed NSPD-44. However, previous congressionally-driven attempts to obtain lesser sums for these efforts have not fared well. For example, Senate Bill S. 613: Reconstruction and Stabilization Civilian Management Act of 2007, introduced on February 15, 2007, and seeking to authorize $80 million for S/CRS activities, was placed on the Senate Legislative Calendar on April 10, 2007, but has yet to be considered.[33]

THE PATH TO SUCCESS IN PHASE IV

To maximize the opportunities for success in future Phase IV operations, the USG should seek to implement the following policies: restrict U.S. military involvement to those conflicts absolutely vital to national security; ensure that decisive force is in place at the onset of Phase IV operations; integrate planning across the interagency at the onset of consideration of an intervention; ensure that the DoS is sufficiently funded to fully man S/CRS and all its elements; go beyond unity of effort to establish unity of command during Phase IV; and man, train, and equip military forces for the full spectrum of tasks described under the security technical sector of the S/CRS post-conflict reconstruction essential task matrix (ETM) while assisting subject matter expert agencies in becoming fully capable of assuming the balance of the tasks therein. The rationale underlying each of these recommendations is outlined in detail below.

Vital Interests and Decisive Force.

There is nothing new about the Caspar Weinberger and Colin Powell doctrines for restricting involvement in conflicts to those vital to our national interests and using decisive force to win them.[34] However, they are so fundamental to ultimate success in Phase IV that one would be remiss not to mention them here. It must also be acknowledged that the two administrations responsible for deploying military forces more frequently than ever before in U.S. history rather pointedly rejected these doctrines.[35]

Clearly, the DoD is not the ultimate decisionmaker when it comes to determining where and when military forces will be deployed.[36] Even so, the DoD does wield significant sway in the decisionmaking process. Even the richest nation in history cannot deploy its military to address all the problems of a world currently in an era of persistent conflict. U.S. resources will always be limited, and the United States must expand its use of the diplomatic and economic instruments of national power to engage a greater portion of the world's problems. The fact that the U.S. military has experienced far more frequent deployments since the end of the Cold War does not mean that this must continue to be the case in the future.

Given the U.S. military's supremacy in sustained combat against any current or currently projected adversary, the key to exploiting decisive force is to ensure it is in place at the onset of Phase IV operations. The military can become a victim of its own success when limited forces quickly prevail in sustained combat operations before sufficient forces can be amassed to establish and maintain security in Phase IV. The inability to prevent looting and a breakdown of law and order during the *golden hour* when the tide has turned and major combat operations cease, runs the risk of emboldening those who would continue to oppose the U.S. presence.[37] At this crucial point, while the local population is disorganized and resistors are off-balance, the United States must have, at a minimum, sufficient forces and supplies on hand to totally secure and meet the immediate needs of the country's capital region.[38] If the capital city cannot be rapidly brought under both control and visible order, whatever local and global credibility and legitimacy the United States possessed at the onset of the intervention will quickly erode.[39] While such erosion at the local level can serve to bolster the confidence of potential opposition forces, globally it can undermine both the domestic and the coalition will to see Phase IV efforts through to completion. Ideally, military forces should be accompanied by civil administrators, humanitarian organizations, judicial and penal experts, and sufficient funding and resources to begin the demobilization, disarmament, and reintegration of former combatants and the retraining of the police force at this critical time.[40]

To determine the size of the forces required for Phase IV operations, one must consider the size of the population and the level of security and control within the state.[41] The higher the level of residual violence and criminality, the higher the ratio of troops to population required.[42] Recent Phase IV successes in Bosnia and Kosovo, states with less post-major combat hostilities than Iraq, were accomplished with relatively high force ratios of 19 and 20 soldiers per 1,000 of population, respectively.[43] Comparatively, unsuccessful operations in Somalia and Haiti employed only five and four soldiers per 1,000 inhabitants.[44] When President Bush declared an end to major combat operations on May 1, 2003, coalition forces had about 175,000 troops on the ground, or seven per 1,000 of Iraq's population of approximately 25 million.[45] A force of 19 soldiers per 1,000 of population would have translated into 475,000 troops.

As indicated above, there are distinct advantages to employing such a clearly decisive force. The mere presence of well-equipped, capable soldiers can inhibit the ability of insurgents to organize and launch a significant fight. If an insurgency does develop, a force of this size would be large enough to maintain order; train indigenous forces; and provide the intelligence, surveillance, and reconnaissance capabilities required for counterinsurgency operations down to the small-unit level.[46] When security and control are established, a fundamental redistribution of power can occur through rapid and thorough reforms that keep the powerful and entrenched elements of the previous governing authority at bay.[47] The larger the force at the onset of Phase IV operations, the faster indigenous institutions can be reconstituted and the earlier military forces can be redeployed, reset, and made ready to execute the next operation.

Other implications of employing such an enormous force merit consideration. First, the requirement for a decisive force for Phase IV reinforces the idea that the United States should only deploy its forces when its vital interests are at stake. Second, the United States should resist unilateral interventions and assemble a larger international coalition to undertake future efforts on the scale of the regime change in Iraq. Third, the logistical realities of amassing such a force impede the speed with which the United States can employ its military power around the world. Finally, decisionmakers should pause before considering any attempt at conducting Phase IV operations in a country the size of Iran with a population of over 65 million.[48] The DoD Science Board summarizes this point in its 2004 study on *Transition to and from Hostilities*:

> . . . the military services have learned – sometimes through bitter experience – that shortchanging combat capability is much more expensive than providing the needed resources in the first place. However, this lesson has yet to be learned in the context of stabilization and reconstruction operations.[49]

Planning Integration.

As cited above, the Interagency Management System for Reconstruction and Stabilization established by the DoS, and the IMS' subordinate combatant command-integrated IPCs and ACTs in particular, provides greatly improved capability for advancing planning integration across the interagency before the next execution of Phase IV operations. At this point the DoD and the DoS should adopt the GAO's recommendations to:

> Provide implementation guidance on the mechanisms needed to facilitate and encourage interagency participation in the development of military plans, develop a process to share planning information with non-DoD agencies early in the planning process as appropriate, and orient DoD and non-DoD personnel in each agency's planning processes and capabilities.[50]

Any attempt to integrate activities across elements as diverse as those of the U.S. interagency will be faced with considerable challenges and subject to the political whims and personalities of those appointed or elected to office in the future. The DoD can catalyze this process by encouraging regular civilian agency participation in its planning and exercises.[51] Additionally, while the issue is at the forefront of the minds of its executors, the DoD and the DoS should formalize their processes for ensuring interagency integration in policy-level directives. Such codification is critical to the permanent establishment and realization of the benefits of interagency integration over the long term.

Resourcing The Department of State.

Since the publication of NSPD-44, funding for S/CRS and its stability operations initiatives has grown slowly, from $12.8 million in FY 2005 to $16.6 million in FY 2006 and to $20.1 million for FY 2007.[52] These appropriations have lagged behind presidential budget requests and have been sufficient only to permit the office to operate without providing for the creation of a capability to address a stability operations crisis. While Congress zeroed out $100 million and $75 million requests for a Conflict Response Fund for FY 2006 and FY 2007, respectively, it did authorize a $100 million transfer for each year from the DoD for services, materiel, and SSTR-related assistance.[53] In effect, the DoD transfer funded the Conflict Response Fund, which is to be used to prevent future conflicts and pay for crisis response planning and transition activities in the first four months of an intervention.[54]

Clearly S/CRS will require additional funding if it is to have the ability to plan, train, and staff a deployable cadre sufficient to fulfill the role assigned to it in NSPD-44. Even though Congress made it clear the transfer of the DoD funds was a temporary move, stakeholders believe future increases in S/CRS funding will come at the expense of decreases in DoD funding.[55] Former S/CRS director Carlos Pascual acknowledged that the multi-million dollar sum required is "a huge number in the civilian budget. [But] a tiny number when you think about the broad issues that are at stake."[56] Senator Richard Lugar, whose bill established S/CRS, believes the proposed deployable civilian corps would be a "force multiplier . . . with the authority and training to take broad operational responsibility for stability missions."[57]

The DoS expects to use the $249 million it requested for its Civilian Stabilization Initiative (CSI) to "create a civilian counterpart to the U.S. military, ready and capable to stabilize countries in the transition from war to peace."[58] The DoS conducted extensive coordination with 15 other U.S. departments, agencies, and international partners with similar desired capabilities as well as an "analysis of recent USG experiences in Haiti, East Timor, Afghanistan, and Iraq" to determine its budget request.[59] Full and continued funding of the CSI will provide for the approximately 1,100 permanent or reserve responders that the DoS expects to need to meet all its requirements in fiscal year 2009 as well as "the civilian resources required to meet stabilization challenges of the next decade and beyond."[60] When the potential impact of a DoS capability that is on site with the requisite expertise and capacity to coordinate and execute all the nonsecurity related tasks required at the onset of Phase IV operations is compared to the relatively modest sum requested to make it happen, the decision to fund S/CRS seems to be a no-brainer. Although military forces and dollars are currently stretched very thin, if necessary, the DoD should find the $249 million, requested by the DoS, in its half trillion dollar budget in a prudent effort to improve the outcome of future Phase IV operations.

Reestablishing Unity of Command.

Although *Joint Publication (JP) 3-10, Joint Security Operations in Theater*, states that "Unity of command is fundamental to effective security within the joint security area,"[61] it goes on to note that "the chief of mission is responsible for the direction, coordination, and supervision of all USG executive branch employees in that country (except those under the command of a U.S. area military commander)."[62] For a military that has always held the concept of unity of command sacrosanct, this is a significant contradiction. The military has long recognized that if there is a question as to who on the ground is ultimately in charge there will be confusion and inefficiency in attempting to accomplish the mission. This was certainly the case at the onset of Phase IV operations in Iraq when both the Coalition Provisional Authority and Multi-National Forces-Iraq operated from separate headquarters and issued separate orders that often conflicted.[63] Similarly, in Somalia, there were at one point three separate command arrangements, which resulted in at least one organization being unaware of what the others were doing.[64]

In complex Phase IV operations, "unity of command" has been replaced by "unity of effort" due to the political sensitivities of putting one cabinet department's senior leader in charge of another cabinet department.[65] This resistance must be overcome in order to reconcile the political ends with the military and civilian means so that clear attainable objectives based on a sound political vision can emerge. This can best occur when all lines of authority lead unambiguously to a single headquarters that uses combined civilian and military expertise to act as a clearing-house for decisions.[66] Stakeholders in this process have expressed strong agreement, so far in principle, that civilian agencies should lead SSTR planning and execution before and after major combat operations and that the transition to civilian leadership should occur as rapidly as possible.[67] For the sake of continuity, foreign area expertise, and keeping turbulence to a minimum, the chief of mission, if present, should be the first choice to assume the civilian lead.

The Role of the Military in Phase IV Operations.

NSPD-44 established S/CRS as the lead for U.S. stability operations and created the post-conflict ETM of individual tasks that as a whole can facilitate a country's transition from armed conflict to sustainable stability. The ETM does not assign tasks nor does it convey the capability to carry them out, but it is a compilation of what is thought to be required to be successful in Phase IV operations by several subject matter experts. As such, it is a living document subject to change based on future lessons learned. The ETM's greatest utility is in its imposition of a common language and set of missions all stakeholders can utilize to delineate roles and responsibilities in Phase IV operations.[68]

The establishment of security and control in a country emerging from conflict is the foundation upon which all other Phase IV operations rest and is clearly the sole province of the military.[69] At the same time, history has shown that the establishment of security is the most difficult task to achieve in the post-major combat environment. For these reasons, when the military prepares for the stability and reconstruction portion of its full spectrum operations, it should focus on the security tasks of the ETM and support the other sectors only in a secondary role. The DoD recognized this in its report to Congress on implementing Directive 3000.5 when it stated that "extensive development activities are best implemented by civilian experts with the support of military forces focused on security operations."[70] This is not to say that the military cannot or will not continue to be responsible for the other sectors until other agencies become capable of executing them, or that there will not continue to be overlap between the sectors even after the other agencies come on-line. The DoD recognizes this as well, noting that when "limited civilian expeditionary capacity or . . . the ambient level of violence exceeds the risk threshold acceptable to military partners . . . U.S. Armed Forces [will] continue to develop capabilities to conduct interim stabilization activities beyond the security sector."[71] Nonetheless, the military should orient itself and its limited training time and resources primarily to those tasks in the security sector.

Other reasons the military should maintain a security-focused orientation include the resulting incentive for other agencies to increase their capabilities and the reduction of problems with humanitarian operations. Inasmuch as the incentive for Iraqi and Afghani indigenous forces to take charge of their own security is retarded by the continued presence of U.S. forces, so too can civilian agencies be disinclined to make their personnel and resources available for stability exercises and operations when the military continues to shoulder the load.[72] An announcement of a DoD policy to retain exclusive responsibility for the security sector while assisting civilian agencies down a clear path to becoming fully capable of assuming the governance and participation, humanitarian assistance and social well-being, economic stabilization and infrastructure, and justice and reconciliation sector tasks would provide better encouragement to those agencies than acceding to the previous status quo.

CONCLUSION

The U.S. military goes to great lengths to anticipate, plan for, and transform itself to address change in a constant effort to remain relevant and ready to defeat any threat to national security. In order to achieve the national strategic end state in an armed conflict in a timely and efficient manner that permits the utmost flexibility and availability of the national elements of power, the United States must pursue opportunities to maximize its efficiency and economize on the use of its forces. The current situation in Iraq has opened a window of opportunity for the establishment of full and genuine civilian agency participation in Phase IV operations, the most time consuming and expensive part of military interventions. To fully exploit the opportunities for success in future Phase IV operations, the USG must restrict U.S. military involvement to those conflicts to those that are absolutely vital to national security, ensure decisive force is in place at the onset of Phase IV operations, fully integrate the interagency at the onset of its planning for an intervention, ensure full funding of S/CRS initiatives, reestablish true unity of command for each phase of the operation, and allow the military to focus on the security sector of stabilization and reconstruction tasks. Taken together, these actions will allow the military to successfully transition from the sustained combat operations of Phase III, through the stability operations of Phase IV, to redeployment in the most timely manner possible, to be better ready to take on the challenges of this era of persistent conflict. More importantly, implementation of these actions will posture the USG as a whole to more effectively and efficiently execute stability and reconstruction operations, thus winning the peace and supporting the full range of U.S. national security interests in the turbulent 21st century.

ENDNOTES - CHAPTER 15

1. U.S. Secretary of Defense Robert M. Gates, "Landon Lecture," Manhattan: Kansas State University, November 26, 2007, available from *www.defenselink.mil/speeches/speech.aspx?speechid=1199*.

2. DoDD 3000.05, *Military Support for Stability, Security, Transition and Reconstruction Operations,* Washington, DC: U.S. Department of Defense, November 28, 2005, p. 2. Available from *www.dtic.mil/whs/directives/corres/pdf/300005p.pdf*

3. *Ibid.*

4. *Ibid.*

5. Shannon A. Brown, ed., *Resourcing Stability Operations and Reconstruction: Past, Present, and Future,* Washington, DC: Industrial College of the Armed Forces, March 23, 2006, p. 9.

6. James Dobbins *et al., The Beginner's Guide to Nation-Building,* Santa Monica, CA: Rand Corporation, 2007, p. xvii.

7. *Joint Publication (JP) 5-0, Joint Operation Planning,* Washington, DC: U.S. Department of Defense, December 26, 2006, pp. IV-37; italics added.

8. *Ibid.*

9. *Ibid.*, pp. IV-37 - IV-38.

10. *Field Manual (FM) 1, The Army*, Washington, DC: U.S. Department of the Army, June 2005, p. 3-7.

11. *Ibid.*

12. *Ibid.*, p. 3-6.

13. U.S. Department of State, "Post-Conflict Reconstruction Essential Tasks," briefing slides, available from *www.state.gov/documents/organization/53464.pdf*.

14. *Replacing and Repairing Equipment Used in Iraq and Afghanistan: The Army's Reset Program*, Washington, DC: U.S. Congressional Budget Office, September 2007, p. ix.

15. The author searched the internet and found numerous quotes describing the current strategic situation as an "era of persistent conflict" by senior U.S. Army leaders such as U.S. Army Chief of Staff General George W. Casey, Jr., U.S. Secretary of the Army Pete Geren, and U.S. Army Deputy Chief of Staff G3/5/7 James J. Lovelace, available from *www.defenselink.mil/news/newsarticle.aspx?id=47751*; *www.army.mil/-speeches/2008/01/11/6972-secretary-of-the-army — -ausa-symposium-on-building-an-expeditionary-army-for-persistent-conflict/*; *findarticles.com/p/articles/mi_qa3723/is_200710/ai_n21099863*; respectively.

16. *Defense Science Board 2004 Summer Study on Transition to and from Hostilities*, Washington, DC: U.S. Department of Defense, December 2004, p. 14.

17. *Ibid.*, p. 18.

18. Lawrence A. Yates, *The US Military's Experience in Stability Operations 1789-2005*, Ft. Leavenworth, KS: Combat Studies Institute Press, 2006, p. 26.

19. Thomas S. Szayna, Derek Eaton, and Amy Richardson, *Preparing the Army for Stability Operations*, Santa Monica, CA: Rand Corporation, 2007, p. xx.

20. DoDD 3000.05, p. 2.

21. *Ibid.*, italics added.

22. *Ibid.*, p. 11.

23. *Report to Congress on the Implementation of DoD Directive 3000.05 Military Support for Stability, Security, Transition and Reconstruction (SSTR) Operations*, Washington, DC: U.S. Department of Defense, April 2007, p. I; italics added.

24. *Military Operations: Actions Needed to Improve DOD's Stability Operations Approach and Enhance Interagency Planning*, Washington, DC: U.S. General Accountability Office, May 2007, p. 3.

25. *Ibid.*, p. 4.

26. U.S. President George W. Bush, "Management of Interagency Efforts Concerning Reconstruction and Stabilization," National Security Presidential Directive/NSPD-44, Washington, DC, December 7, 2005; italics added.

27. *Ibid.*

28. U.S. President George W. Bush, *Presidential Report on Improving Interagency Support for United States 21st Century National Security Missions and Interagency Operations in Support of Stability, Security, Transition, and Reconstruction Operations*, Washington, DC: The White House, June 2007, p. 8.

29. *Ibid.*, p. 20.

30. *Ibid.*, p. 25.

31. *Ibid.*, p. 28.

32. *The Budget in Brief, Fiscal Year 2009*, Washington DC., U.S. Department of State, 2008, p. 63.

33. U.S. Congress, Senate, "S. 613: Reconstruction and Stabilization Civilian Management Act of 2007," available from *www.govtrack.us/congress/bill.xpd?bill=s110-613.*

34. U.S. Secretary of Defense Caspar W. Weinberger, "The Uses of Military Power," National Press Club, Washington, DC, November 28, 1984, available from *www.pbs.org/wgbh/pages/frontline/shows/military/force/weinberger.html*; and Colin L. Powell, "U.S. Forces: Challenges Ahead," *Foreign Affairs*, Winter 1992/93, p. 40.

35. Michael Lind, "Powell Doctrine is Set to Sway Presidents," *The Financial Times*, November 7, 2006, available from *www.newamerica.net/publications/articles/2006/powells_military_doctrine_is_set_to_sway_presidents_4287.*

36. U.S. President George W. Bush, "Bush: 'I'm the decider' on Rumsfeld," available from *www.cnn.com/2006/POLITICS/04/18/rumsfeld/.*

37. Dobbins, p. xxiv; and Hans Binnendijk and Stuart E. Johnson, eds., *Transforming for Stabilization and Reconstruction Operations*, Washington, DC: National Defense University Press, 2004, p. xiii.

38. Dobbins, p. xxiv.

39. James T. Quinlivan, "Force Requirements in Stability Operations," *Parameters*, Vol. 25, Winter 1995-96, p. 65.

40. Dobbins, p. xxiv.

41. Quinlivan, p. 60.

42. Dobbins, p. 37.

43. Binnendijk and Johnson, p. 5.

44. Dobbins, p. 38.

45. U.S. Department of Defense, "News Briefing," briefing slide, available from *www.defenselink.mil/dodcmsshare/briefingslide/59/031106-D-6570C-003.jpg*; and "Iraq Population," *Encyclopedia of the Nations*, available from *www.nationsencyclopedia.com/Asia-and-Oceania/Iraq-POPULATION.html.*

46. Dobbins, p. 37.

47. *Ibid.*, p. 41.

48. U.S. Central Intelligence Agency, "Iran," *World Factbook,* available from *https://www.cia.gov/library/ publications/the-world-factbook/geos/ir.html.*

49. *Defense Science Board 2004 Summer Study on Transition to and from Hostilities,* p. 9.

50. *Military Operations: Actions Needed to Improve DOD's Stability Operations Approach and Enhance Interagency Planning,* p. 5.

51. Szayna, p. 55.

52. *Ibid.,* p. 29.

53. *Ibid.,* p. 30.

54. *Ibid.*

55. *Ibid.*

56. Brown, p. 62.

57. U.S. Senator Richard G. Lugar, "Resourcing Stability Operations and Reconstruction: Past, Present, and Future," National Defense University, Washington, DC, March 23, 2006, available from *lugar.senate. gov/press/recorDCfm?id=253067.*

58. *The Budget in Brief, Fiscal Year 2009,* p. 63.

59. *Ibid.,* p. 64.

60. *Ibid.*

61. *Joint Publication (JP) 3-10, Joint Security Operations in Theater,* Washington, DC: U.S. Department of Defense, August 1, 2006, pp. II-1 - II-3.

62. *Ibid.,* p. GL-6.

63. Colonel Thomas Evans, U.S. Army, interview by author, Carlisle, PA, March 17, 2008.

64. Binnendijk and Johnson, p. 20.

65. Bush, *Presidental Report on Improving Interagency Support,* p. 5.

66. Binnendijk and Johnson, pp. 19-20.

67. Szayna, p. 33.

68. *Ibid,* p. 16.

69. Bush, *Presidental Report on Improving Interagency Support,* p. 13.

70. *Report to Congress on the Implementation of DoD Directive 3000.05 Military Support for Stability, Security, Transition and Reconstruction (SSTR) Operations,* p. 22.

71. *Ibid.,* p. 3.

72. Szayna, p. xvii.

CHAPTER 16

TRANSITIONING FROM WAR TO ENDURING PEACE

Colonel Michael E. Culpepper
U.S. Army

War has already revealed its new face for the 21st century with the conflicts in Iraq and Afghanistan. In this new environment, the greatest challenge for the United States is converting military victory into enduring peace. Success requires a full and coherent application of national, international, and nongovernmental efforts. Achieving the military end state through defeat of an adversary's military and the removal of the targeted regime only constitutes an interim step toward an enduring peace. The overarching strategic end state can only be achieved by the establishment of a viable, self-sustaining indigenous government. The effort to transition military victory into a strategic victory must provide for the needs of the population throughout and may prove more difficult, time consuming, and resource intensive than the major combat phase. While operations to create stability may be conducted under a variety of circumstances such as in failed or failing states, this research focuses on the challenges and functional requirements associated with achieving a lasting victory in conjunction with operations that forcibly remove an existing regime and establish a new government. This chapter reviews relevant literature and examines the nature of operations that immediately follow the major combat phase of a conflict. From this study, a synthesis is proposed for how the prevailing characteristics of these types of operations combined with the right key operational elements lead to an enduring peace.

A variety of related, overlapping, and sometimes conflicting terminology is associated with operations immediately following the major combat phase of a war or military intervention. The terms post-conflict operations, stability operations, peace operations, nation building, and counterinsurgency operations are all used, often interchangeably, in a variety of doctrinal and academic publications as labels for these operations. U.S. doctrine recognizes the criticality of success in the operations that follow the major combat phase. As an example, it now describes a six-phase model for joint operations which includes shape, deter, seize initiative, dominate, stabilize, and enable civil authority.[1] This framework (see Figure 1) reflects a significant improvement over the previous joint operations phasing model and specifically acknowledges the challenges encountered when transitioning from major combat operations to successful conflict resolution. It provides an appropriate context for the operations discussed herein. Successful transition to an enduring peace is driven by actions in all phases, but it is in the final two phases where this effort enjoys its primary focus. In this chapter, the term stabilization operations is used to describe the range of efforts encompassed by the various nuanced academic and military terms associated with stability oriented activities in a military campaign. Stabilization operations are those activities conducted in conjunction with major combat operations or military interventions to establish order and enable civil authority.

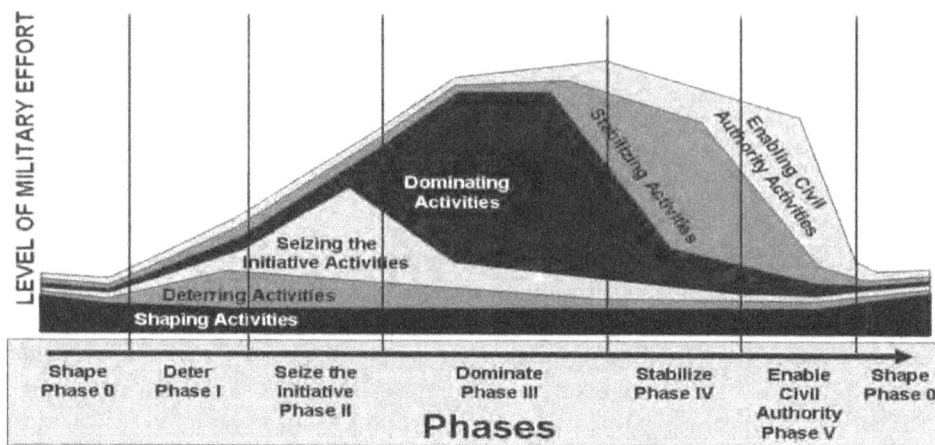

Figure 1. Notional Operational Phases versus Level of Military Effort.[2]

STRATEGIC ENVIRONMENT

The 21st century strategic environment sets the stage for stabilization operations that are more challenging than ever before. All the analysis suggests a future environment that is increasingly complex, interrelated, and characterized by a diverse array of strategic threats. U.S. Army Chief of Staff General George W. Casey, Jr., describes the current environment as an era of persistent conflict with protracted confrontation among state, nonstate, and individual actors who will increasingly use violence as a means of achieving their political and ideological objectives. He identifies six trends that are creating tension in the international community and increasing the probability of conflict. These trends are globalization, competition for energy, instability as the populations in less-developed countries grow dramatically, climate change and natural disasters, proliferation of weapons of mass destruction, and failed or failing states that can provide safe havens for terrorist groups.[3] The 2007 Army Posture Statement describes the 21st century security environment as an era of uncertainty and unpredictability that has become increasingly dangerous. This environment is characterized by a decline in the military primacy of states and a rise in nonstate extremist movements; a deterioration of adherence to international laws and norms, rise of globalization, diffusion of technology, and growing disparities among the "haves" and the "have nots" in the international order.[4] Within this shifting strategic setting, the nature of the threats to the United States is also evolving. *The National Defense Strategy of the United States* describes the relevant existing and emerging security challenges and categorizes them as traditional, irregular, catastrophic, and disruptive threats.[5] The changing characteristics of the strategic environment in the 21st century all point to increasingly complex issues and demand an appropriate corresponding shift in national security thinking.

War and the need for complementary stabilization operations are most likely to occur where there is a convergence of these dangerous trends. A substandard quality of life, inadequate social and economic opportunities, and the perceived lack of social justice create despair which increases the receptiveness of the population in a troubled state to ideologues' messages. Globalization aggravates the perception of inequities by providing such a population with greater visibility of how others are living. Technology and the free movement of information facilitate an adversary's command and control and information operations efforts and the ability of insurgents, terrorists, and criminals to move money, material, and people. This complex 21st century strategic environment provides the context for the specific operational conditions under which stabilization operations will be conducted as the United States responds to threats posed by rogue states, failing governments, or ungoverned territories.

OPERATIONAL FACTORS

Within this strategic setting, a diverse set of operational circumstances may exist for each specific stabilization effort. Stabilization operations may include among their primary challenges: a humanitarian crisis, disorder, insecurity, external intervention, infrastructure and institutional devastation, and governing legitimacy. There are numerous historical cases of stabilization operations, and, while all are different, they all share some commonality. Stabilization operations include a complex set of players and diverse social, political, and economic factors. Each operation is defined by the characteristics and capabilities in these realms.

Fundamental to success is a clear understanding of the desired end state and a full appreciation for the overt and nuanced factors of the environment in which the stabilization operation is conducted. The conduct of stabilization operations must be driven by the specific conditions of the operational environment and the strategic objectives. Comprehension of the unique set of political, social, military, and economic factors and the correct framing of the problem are arguably more complex and more essential in these types of operations than in any other. As Clausewitz stated, "The first, the supreme, the most far-reaching act of judgment that the statesman and commander have to make is to establish by that test the kind of war on which they are embarking; neither mistaking it for, nor trying to turn it into, something that is alien to its nature."[6]

The complexity of stabilization operations is increased by the diverse set of players on each side. Relevant players can be grouped into the stabilization forces, the indigenous population, and the opposition forces. Each player will have its own unique attributes, capabilities, and goals. Understanding the objectives, characteristics, and concerns of all players or parties in the conflict is critical to an appreciation of the nature of the operational environment and for the development of an effective approach. Stabilization forces collectively include those state and nonstate players pursuing stability and support for the emerging government. The opposition includes those players opposing stability and/or the emerging government. In the middle is the indigenous population, who are the focus of the actions of the external stabilization forces, the indigenous government, and the opposition forces. Stability may be a common goal for all parties, but more often instability will be seen by the opposition players as a period of opportunity to seize power or some aspects of power.

Stabilization forces include the military and nonmilitary agencies of each participating nation and the potential or emerging host nation governing entities. They may also include other organized entities within the society, such as religious, business, or political organizations that support peaceful transition. Where possible, a multinational approach to these operations may leverage a greater diversity of expertise and contribute to the perceived legitimacy of the operation in the eyes of the indigenous population and the international community. Stabilization efforts may also include external nongovernmental, private, and intergovernmental organizations. Success requires the effective integration of these military and nonmilitary capabilities. Each element of the stabilization forces has its own specific reasons for supporting stability; however they are linked by a shared desire for a stable, enduring peace that serves their interests and objectives.

The population is at the heart of the struggle for stabilization. A population includes the common man, and may include deposed political and military leaders, professional and social elites, and potential ethnic or tribal groupings. Individual members or groups may choose to be part of the opposition, they may choose to integrate in the emerging order, or they may adopt a wait and see posture before supporting anyone. A population's fundamental interests will often generally follow Abraham Maslow's hierarchy of needs. In his classic work, Maslow proposed five levels of needs that drive human behavior as reflected in Figure 2. Higher level needs are generally not important to a person until lower level needs are met.[7] What these may look like collectively for a population is open to debate, but they will often hold the key to individual motivation in stabilization operations. A people's traditions, historical standard of living, and ideological beliefs will shape their perspective for these needs. The demands and expectations of a population who have historically led an impoverished life will be much different from those of a population which has enjoyed relative prosperity. Embedded in the general population may be individuals or groups with specific ideological, tribal, nationalist, or separatist views which override typical motivations. Such differences will vary widely from situation to situation and stabilization forces must be culturally astute and should not mistake their own standards for those of the indigenous population.

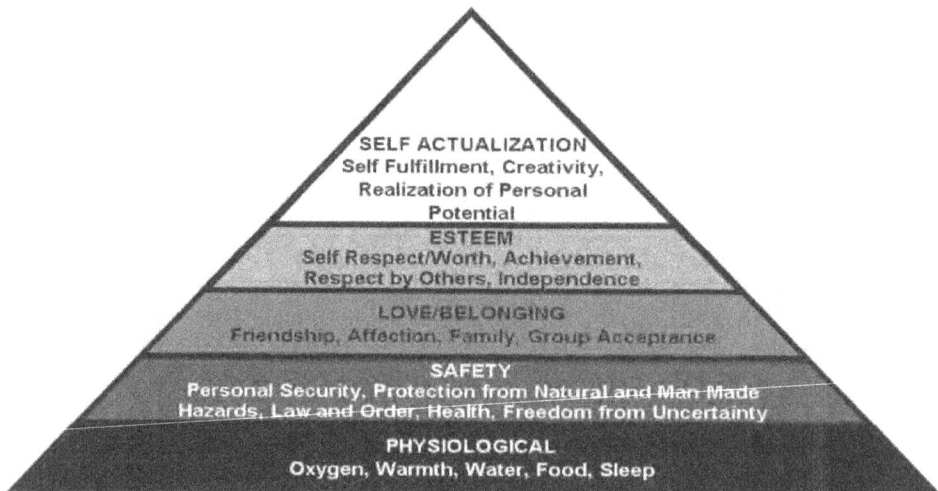

Figure 2. Maslow's Hierarchy of Needs.

Opposition to stabilization efforts can take many forms. It may include indigenous opposition to the emerging government, criminal and opportunistic factions seeking advantages in disorder, and other state and external nonstate opportunists. Each will have their own practical and political objectives and may be part of a relatively homogenous entity or part of a fractured, diverse collection of sometimes competing and sometimes complementing factions. Opportunists often have a preference for the opposition's cause, but in general they are exploiting the instability to further their own unrelated material or political objectives. The value of instability to both the opposition and opportunists provides a convergence of their interests. The opposition may have as its objective the desire to return to the previously deposed government or the establishment of a new government different from the emerging host nation government. Some may want only weak governing authorities that can be influenced, bought, or coerced in support of their own objectives. The most challenging opposition is an organized, active insurgency, but instability may also be advanced through other means such as class warfare, ethnic and tribal conflict, and economic coercion. Any opposition's primary objective is to undermine the legitimacy of the occupying force and the emerging government. They may use enticement, intimidation, terrorism, or military force to gain support or acquiescence from the people. The opposition will most often operate in a decentralized, sometimes uncoordinated fashion that complicates predictive analysis. Understanding the nature of the threats to security is critical to effectively addressing them. As in all forms of conflict, Sun Tzu's edict "know your enemy and know yourself; in a hundred battles you will never be in peril" is fully applicable.[8]

Opposition forces often enjoy many advantages over stabilization forces. They typically have the initiative and are not bound by legal constraints. When properly organized, they are inherently flexible and unencumbered by a fixed structure and overarching bureaucracy. They can choose to operate relatively cheaply in terms of manpower and material resources. It is much easier for an opposition element to advance instability than it is for the government to ensure stability. Stabilization forces must be nearly perfect in order to demonstrate effective security and stability, while the opposition needs only sporadic success to demonstrate instability and discredit the government's legitimacy.

In stabilization operations, the general population is invariably the strategic center of gravity for both stabilization forces and the opposition. David C. Gompert of the Rand Corporation advises that unlike that of conventional war between sovereigns, prolonged stabilization operations are a contest with adversaries for the trust and allegiance of the population.[9] Their support, or at a minimum acquiescence, is central to the success of both sides in the struggle. Mao estimated that if as little as 15 to 25 percent of the population support the opposition, the government would have little hope of prevailing.[10] Assuming this to be true, stabilization forces have the daunting task of gaining and maintaining support of the majority of the population, while the opposition need only gain the support of a relatively minor portion. In the end, it is the general population's view of the emerging government and their perception of security, opportunity, and governing legitimacy that will determine the outcome of any stabilization effort.

All players operate within a setting framed by the unique political and social traditions of the particular state. However, nations in which the stabilization operations are conducted will tend to share some common characteristics. For example, nations in which the United States or the international community feel compelled to intervene or pursue regime change are most likely to be failing states or rogue states. The majority of these are likely to have had authoritarian regimes. Such states are unlikely to share our values or have similar governing traditions. They are most often part of the third world where long-standing class and tribal issues have not been resolved. Such characteristics complicate acceptance of ideas such as the rule of law and social advancement as understood in the West. These characteristics shape the population's view of any emerging Western supported government. A nation with traditional aversion to foreign influences, perceptions of historical injustices at the hands of external forces, class and tribal divisions, traditionalist societies, or isolationist attitudes will provide unique and significant challenges to stabilization forces when Western style governments are advocated and supported.

Stabilization operations are almost universally described as primarily requiring nonmilitary capabilities. As David Galula reflects, revolutionary war is 80 percent political action and only 20 percent military.[11] This observation applies to the broader set of stabilization operations as well. It is also almost universally accepted that only the U.S. military will have the resources and capacity to conduct the preponderance of the stabilization effort in the early stages of a contested environment.[12] Until security conditions permit, nonmilitary and nongovernmental activities are severely restricted.

Stabilization operations are manpower intensive. Controlling territories and populations, establishing security, and restoring services require a substantial physical presence. Many estimates of manpower requirements for stabilization operations have been proposed. In his analysis of counterinsurgency warfare, Galula maintains that "no significant segment of the population can be abandoned for long — unless the population can be trusted to defend itself. This is why a ratio of force of ten or twenty to one between the counterinsurgent and the insurgent is not uncommon when an insurgency develops into guerilla warfare."[13] The U.S. Army *Field Manual (FM) 3-24, Counterinsurgency*, counters that since the focus in this type of operation is the population and not the insurgent, a more appropriate metric is the ratio of troops to inhabitants. FM 3-24 cautions that each situation is different but supports a general ratio of 20-25 troops per 1,000 inhabitants.[14] This is generally consistent with the analysis in a 2003 RAND report on major stabilization operations in the 20th century which, while identifying significant variance across operations, found ratios ranging from .2 to 100 troops per 1,000 inhabitants.[15] Specific requirements will vary based on the particular circumstances of each operation, but all generally share a demand for a high ratio of forces to ensure security and provide for the population.

In addition to the characteristics of the key players, the nature of any major combat that precedes a stabilization effort and how it concludes sets the stage for the conduct of stabilization operations. The intensity and duration of the major combat operations affects the psyche of the people and necessarily the design of the stabilization operations. The sudden absence of a governing structure may shock the nation and induce a state of disorder. The more centralized the previous government, the greater the impact will be upon its removal. Under these conditions, moving decisively to address emergency requirements and fill the void in governance is critical to success. Delays provide the opportunity for the opposition groups to organize and leverage the crisis to gain public support. The degree of development and stability in the state prior to the conflict will also dictate the degree to which indigenous capabilities may be available to support an emerging government in the aftermath.

Time is generally on the side of the belligerent with the greatest strategic patience. In a recent U.S. Army War College study, Dr. Conrad C. Crane evaluated 28 historical cases of stabilization operations with a counterinsurgency campaign and found that on average they took 11.7 years to conclude. His analysis revealed that the government has an initial window of opportunity in which it must prevail before an insurgency can establish itself. If this window is missed, the probability of success begins to favor the insurgent. His study indicated that the stabilization forces typically had about 4 years to defeat the opposition before the insurgent tended to gain the advantage. The insurgent's advantage then existed for a period of about 5 years before the trend again favored the government.[16] This analysis supports the conclusion that nations must be prepared for the early, and potentially, long-term commitment of resources in stabilization operations.

Each stabilization operation is unique to its time and circumstance. However, this uniqueness can be understood in terms of the operational factors shared by all such missions. Effective stabilization operations require a thorough appreciation of the operational characteristics comprised of the complex set of players in support of and in opposition to stability; the political, social, and economic factors; the requirement for extensive non-military capabilities; the need for substantial manpower; and a tendency toward long duration. With these specific factors in mind, the operational elements that comprise the major areas of focus for the stabilization forces can be determined and addressed.

KEY OPERATIONAL ELEMENTS

Once stabilization forces have appropriately identified the operational factors that characterize the environment and have accurately framed the nature of the problem, a coherent plan of action can be developed. Stabilization activities must focus on several interrelated sets of activities—the key operational elements. These elements form the basis of the operational design for stabilization efforts.

Much has been written about organizing constructs for stabilization operations. These include various sets of critical tasks, focus areas, lines of operation, and major mission elements. Such constructs describe the principal things that must be done in support of successful stabilization operations. James Carafano and Dana Dillon, in their writings for the Heritage Foundation, refer to the "Disease and Unrest Formula" used by World War II planners and maintain that three enabling tasks must be performed before reconstruction can be successful. This formula proposed that stabilization forces must avert humanitarian crisis, establish a legitimate government, and provide domestic security forces to support the government. Once these tasks have been completed, they maintained, post-conflict operations are essentially finished.[17] The Department of State organizes post-conflict reconstruction requirements into five essential tasks: security; governance and participation; humanitarian assistance and social well-being; economic stabilization and infrastructure; and justice and reconciliation.[18] *Joint Publication (JP) 3-07.3, Peace Operations,* also organizes around these essential tasks.[19] U.S. Army FM 3-24 describes five potential lines of operation: combat operations/civil security operations; host nation security forces; essential services; governance; and economic development.[20] The organizing constructs described above are fairly consistent with one another and reflect the basic idea that successful conflict resolution requires that the needs of the people be met and that conditions must be established to allow for the emergence of an enduring and legitimate government. These requirements can be grouped into four key operational elements: meeting survival needs; providing security; enabling social justice; and establishing effective governance.

The essence of successful stabilization operations is the necessity to gain the population's perception that the government is able to provide for their needs in both the short and long terms. These perceptions, on an individual level, are likely to follow Maslow's hierarchy with lower needs requiring immediate attention. Solutions to higher order needs will have little immediate relevance to the population until the more basic requirements are satisfied. This leads to a potentially problematic approach of focusing sequentially on survival and security, then on social, infrastructure, and governmental needs. Hostile actions will tend to drive the focus to security requirements and combat operations. While this is a critical early requirement, it can be counterproductive if pursued without appropriate consideration of other needs. Reflecting on his experience in Iraq, Major General Peter W. Chiarelli, Commander, 1st Cavalry Division, proposed that focusing too heavily on security without a concurrent commitment of an appropriate effort to enable equitable indigenous governance and the rebuilding of infrastructure may undermine the support of the populace and tarnish their perception of the emerging government and stabilization forces.[21] The interrelated nature of these elements requires that while the primacy of effort may shift through the progression of individual needs from basic survival toward prosperity and fulfillment, all requirements must be considered simultaneously and with an eye toward the strategic end state. Actions must continuously reinforce the efficacy, viability, and legitimacy of the interim occupation government first, and then the emerging indigenous government. Some requirements may have more immediate urgency, but all complement one another and must be integrated in a comprehensive approach.

In stabilization operations that are part of broader major combat operations, the military is usually the first organized entity on the scene and has the vast majority of the capabilities available to meet immediate humanitarian requirements. Survival will be the people's first priority. Therefore, the first key operational element is the provision for the basic survival needs of the population. The military's actions will begin shaping the population's perception from the beginning of major combat operations. Emergency food, water, medical care, and shelter are extremely time sensitive requirements. Timely provision of these basic survival needs has a powerful impact on the population. Failure to do so also has powerful and adverse impact. Initially, the general population will be primarily influenced by their perception of which set of players can best provide for their basic physiological needs. Success in this endeavor will profoundly impact the general population's initial view of the foreign military presence and their interpretation of military intentions as either liberation or occupation. In addition to the moral obligation to protect life and the practical efforts to win support of the population, occupying powers are also bound by specific legal responsibilities under the Geneva Convention of 1949.[22]

Inadequately addressing these requirements poses the risk of adverse perceptions in the local, international, and domestic communities. Therefore, the initial military campaign must include a plan and the resources to responsively mitigate the humanitarian crisis that is often produced in war. This requires an understanding that stabilization operations will demand greater sustainment capabilities than combat units typically possess for internal support, and to plan for and resource this requirement as an integral part of major combat operations. It also requires the ability to rapidly integrate nonmilitary relief capabilities into evolving military operations. Success in meeting survival needs is achieved when the majority of the population no longer has their basic survival as a primary concern on a day-to-day basis and they begin to focus on broader security issues.

Once basic survival needs are evident, the people will begin to shift their priorities to safety and security needs. Thus, the second key operational element is the establishment of security. Security includes the protection from crime and disorder; protection from the opposition and coercion by opportunists; and protection from other threats such as fire and health hazards that adversely impact an acceptable quality of life. While many aspects of security and reconstruction are primarily civilian functions, historical experience demonstrates that the military will have the predominant capability to conduct the initial restoration of emergency services in a contested environment. Therefore, immediate requirements must be met largely by the military until nonmilitary capabilities can be mobilized and safely employed. Security calls for a diverse set of capabilities that will require the stabilization forces on the ground to simultaneously conduct combat operations, law enforcement, border control, and other civil support functions. The line between military operations and law enforcement will be blurred. The focus of the stabilization forces must remain on the population as it pursues security functions. The people must feel secure and have the hope of a better life under the new governance without perceived violations of their personal dignity. The populace yearns for a return to normalcy. Their view of normalcy will likely be very different than that of the stabilization forces. Providing for security is particularly manpower intensive when the stabilization operation includes an organized insurgency posing military, paramilitary, terrorist, and criminal threats.

At the national level, security must also be provided against external threats. Once the sovereignty of the target nation has been compromised, stabilization forces have responsibility to protect the host nation from external threats. This includes securing the nation's borders and defending the territory against other regional states and actors. Neighboring states may perceive an opportunity to advance their interests in the defeated state. This may include resolving territorial disputes or actively supporting an opposition faction in pursuit of a government more friendly to their interests. Success in providing security is achieved when the population feels free to pursue normal routines and the indigenous security forces are capable of sustaining a secure environment against internal and external threats to security.

As survival concerns recede and a degree of security becomes evident, the people's expectations will tend to grow. Their demands for a higher quality of life will continue to rise and will increasingly focus on the pursuit of normalcy, equity, and opportunity in a functioning civil society. The people's expectations, while shaped by their culture and experience, will include a hope for improvement in their lives and some demand for justice and equitably in their society. The third key operational element is the enabling of this social justice. This will include economic opportunity, social and religious freedoms, civil services, and legal protections.

Stabilization efforts must set the conditions that allow for a return to normal labor and economic practices. Previously existing jobs need to be rapidly reestablished and relevant new jobs created. Job opportunities must provide worthwhile employment for the military age youth. Adequate employment opportunities dramatically affect the people's psyche and provide an alternative to participation in criminal activity or compensated support to the opposition. The ability to provide for oneself and family economically combats hopelessness, diminishes the appeal of opposition and ideological causes, and reduces dependency on stabilization forces.

The population will demand and begin to expect basic freedoms and fairness in their lives. Expectations may be dramatically affected by cultural and religious traditions but will increase nonetheless as survival and security concerns recede. The people's desire for order and fairness in their lives will include some culturally shaped version of basic rights and freedoms to pursue religious and social relationships of their choosing without persecution. Stabilization forces must understand the dynamics of the environment and provide for the reconciliation of newly created or long-standing tensions in order to set the conditions for emergence of equitable norms.

The people will also expect a level of basic civil services and opportunities consistent with their cultural and historical norms. This may include educational opportunity; a legal framework for resolving issues; an economic system that allows opportunity for an acceptable quality of life; and basic utilities such as electricity, water, and sewage. The rapid reestablishment of appropriate indigenous capabilities and practices and the responsive application of appropriate specialized external resources are key to progress in this effort. Stabilization forces require a comprehension of these factors and the capabilities, predominately nonmilitary, to meet societal needs. Success in enabling social justice is achieved when effective business, economic, education, social, religious, and legal opportunities are in place, and societal issues are resolved within the framework of accepted equitable practices.

As the objectives in the other operational efforts begin to be achieved, the fourth key operational element, establishment of effective governance, comes into greater play. While the social justice operational element is focused on the individual's perception about quality of life, opportunity, fairness, and self-esteem; the governance operational element is focused on the collective entities that constitute the institutions, mechanisms, and structures that provide for the operation of the nation. Legitimate, effective, and self-sustaining governance is the overarching key to successful stabilization operations. The government must provide for the needs of the population and be accepted by the people in order to be viewed as legitimate.

Governance is a civilian function, however, it is the military that is positioned to establish governance immediately following a major combat operation. The occupying force must plan for interim governance to bridge the gap until indigenous capability can evolve. Stabilization forces set the conditions to allow a viable host nation government to emerge. This may require military governance and martial law for an interim period. The goal is to transition from this to interim civilian governance by the stabilization forces and ultimately to an effective, self-determined indigenous government as rapidly as possible. This is a race against opposition forces who strive to undermine the emerging government and provide a more appealing alternative to the general population.

The interim and emerging indigenous government must have legitimacy in the eyes of the population as well as the international community. To gain the support and confidence of the population, an effective indigenous governing capability must be accepted as something other than an instrument of the occupying forces. Establishing a viable indigenous government is a time-consuming endeavor. A government that is established too rapidly in the aftermath of conquest by a foreign state will almost inevitably have its legitimacy questioned.

The population's demand for a role in the political process will vary widely depending on cultural considerations and their historical political traditions. A nation with pseudo-democratic traditions will have a population that places higher demands on self-determination. A nation with authoritarian political traditions will have a population that knows and understands little about self-determination. In fact, the concept of democratic governance may be so alien that it is viewed with apprehension, revulsion, or even fear. Religious and cultural views will temper the population's attitude about their appropriate role in governance. These factors shape how the stabilization forces implement an interim government and the characteristics of the future indigenous government.

Leveraging previously existing indigenous laws, systems, and political expertise may contribute to acceptance by the population. In cases where the existing laws and governing traditions are compatible with our values, they should be retained and enforced. Even in a situation where an oppressive government has been removed, retention of select personnel and practices will put an indigenous face on governing affairs, leverage available expertise, and provide a role for former governmental personnel who might otherwise support the opposition. Retention of portions of the previous governing system may reduce popular resistance to that which may be perceived as foreign, having been imposed by an occupying force.

Governance runs from the local to the national level. If all politics are indeed local, then governance efforts may need to be started there. The population in many developing countries may have little interest in national level governance. It is the local governance, whether formal or informal, that most impacts the population's daily lives and it is the people's connection to stabilization forces and the national level governance. This local governance may be part of an official governing hierarchy or may be tribal or religiously based. Stabilization forces must understand the nature of the environment at the local level and devote an appropriate amount of effort and resources at this level. This again requires substantial commitment of manpower to provide adequate coverage throughout the territory. Absent appropriate presence and focus by stabilization forces, opposition players will seek to fill the void at the local level.

Reconstruction is key to an enduring peace and begins with the initial restoration of emergency services and interim governance by the stabilization force. However, reconstruction will ultimately be led by the emerging indigenous government. Carafano asserts that nations are not rebuilt by other nations--they rebuild themselves once enabling conditions are set.[23] Stabilization forces enable the emerging government to get through the crisis period and into a state of viable self-governance and reconstruction. Success in establishing governance is achieved when a viable, effective, indigenous government is in place that is friendly to U.S. interests, serves the needs of its people, adheres to international norms of good governance, and is accepted as legitimate by the population.

These key operational elements constitute the major mission sets that the stabilization forces must execute. An effective stabilization operation must meet basic survival needs of the population, provide for security; enable social justice, and establish effective governance. These elements are inextricably interrelated and must be addressed as part of a coherent campaign. They cannot be divided cleanly into military and nonmilitary responsibilities, nor can they be viewed as sequential efforts. Over the course of the operation, primacy shifts from military to nonmilitary capabilities and ultimately to the host nation. As Figure 3 illustrates, the level of effort required for each operational element will shift over time based on progress and be comprised of a changing mix of military and nonmilitary capabilities. The goal is to progress as rapidly as feasible through this transition. With an understanding of these operational elements, how victory is defined is discussed next.

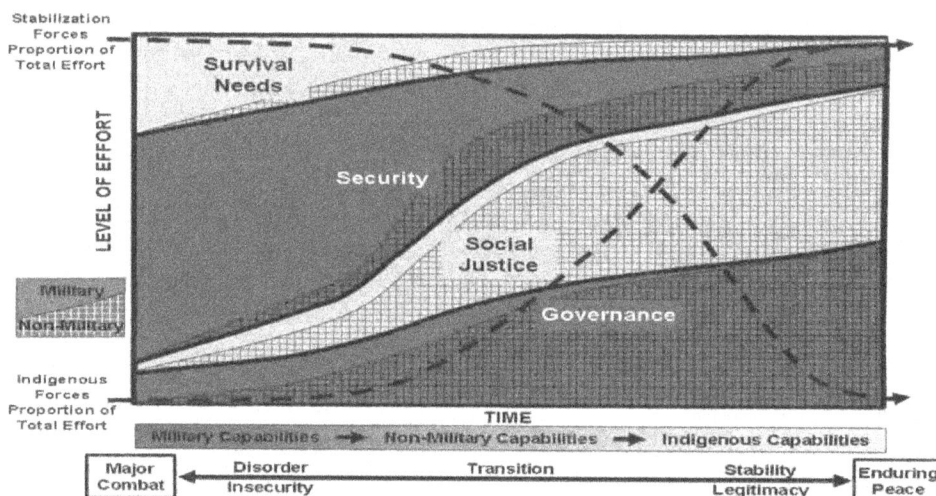

Figure 3. Level of Effort across Key Operational Elements over Time.

CONFLICT RESOLUTION

Victory is achieved when the primary challenges to stability are overcome, and secondary challenges no longer prevent effective self-governance or require substantial external military support. Establishment of a self-sustaining political, economic, social, and legal order is an inherent part of achieving successful conflict resolution. The path to victory flows through the military end state to an enduring strategic end state.

The military end state has been achieved when military capabilities no longer have primacy in the operation, and civil agencies can provide the basic governance, services, and civil order. However, the military will remain in support as long as indigenous capabilities are inadequate to fully provide for internal and external security. Military primacy transitions to civilian when security is no longer the predominant determining factor in freedom of action and when civilian capacity has been organized and mobilized. The military end state sets the conditions for achievement of the political end state.

Political objectives have not been achieved and the conflict is not resolved until a legitimate host nation government is in control, basic quality of life requirements are being met, and combative actions are not necessary for security. Jack Covey describes this end state as a viable peace where the capacity of domestic institutions to resolve conflict peacefully prevails over the power of obstructionist forces. It is characterized by an environment where conflict is resolved by a domestic political process, the security sector is reformed and subordinated to political authority, local institutions maintain the rule of law, and the formal economy outperforms the gray/black markets.[24]

IMPLICATIONS

Stabilization operations are among the most challenging and resource intensive missions a nation pursues. How a nation views this mission set and postures its national capabilities is central to the probabilities of success. This analysis of operational factors and key operational elements in stabilization operations identifies several implications including roles and responsibilities of military and nonmilitary agencies, specialized capabilities and expertise, and the feasibility of stabilization operations under certain conditions.

A successful transition to an enduring peace requires substantial nonmilitary organizations, doctrine, and authorities for security, governance, and reconstruction. Much of the current thought on these types of operations acknowledges that the required mission sets are primarily civilian responsibilities, but only the military has the capacity to conduct these operations in many circumstances. The military by default has primacy at the end of major combat operations, but lacks many of the specialized capabilities required for success. Defaulting to the military because no one else can do the mission is a haphazard approach. Therefore, if a nation's interests demand the capacity to execute these types of operations, it must develop the appropriate expeditionary capability in the military and the rest of the interagency and encourage like capabilities in non-governmental organizations. As one step in this direction, National Security Presidential Directive-44 assigns the Department of State as the lead for U.S. Government efforts to prepare, plan for, and conduct stabilization and reconstruction activities.[25] In addition, *The National Security Strategy* establishes the stabilization and reconstruction mission as a priority for the interagency and reinforces the State Department's role as the lead for the U.S. Government. It further emphasizes the priority on development of non-military capabilities to support reconstruction and stabilization efforts.[26] This is not a mission set against which U.S. Government capabilities are adequately structured and trained and while progress has been made in the last few years, the U.S. interagency capacity for major stabilization operations must continue to evolve.

Stabilization requires flexible forces that can integrate various nonstandard military and nonmilitary capabilities. Stabilization efforts must be planned for from the beginning, integrated in major combat operations, and flexibly adjusted to integrate evolving interagency and multinational capabilities as the operation unfolds. Military forces must have embedded interagency staff, advisory, planning, and execution capabilities to immediately begin addressing security, essential services, and governance shortfalls while major combat operations are ongoing. This must include integration down to tactical level units. Organizational design, doctrine, and authorities must accommodate this requirement. Globalization, population centricity, and effective opposition use of the information domain require enhanced capabilities for information operations. The focus on the population and the desired strategic end state must drive all military actions. Properly framing the problem is arguably more important in stabilization operations than in any other type of military operation. All situations will be different, and key factors will change over time. This requires flexible, adaptive leaders who are able to properly comprehend the situation upfront and continuously assess and modify the operational design as the operation evolves. Situational understanding and cultural astuteness are imperative down to the lowest levels. Leader development, training, and education must adequately address these competencies.

In some situations, the conditions in the environment may be such that the degree of devastation and domination required to gain and maintain control of the population is incompatible with our values. The culture, traditions, and historical perceptions of the indigenous population may make any externally imposed solution untenable. In these cases, it may be necessary for the conflict to spiral into further instability and civil war before an enduring, indigenously acceptable resolution is achieved. When this occurs, stabilization forces largely lose their vote in the outcome. Decisionmakers must understand the circumstances under which an optimal outcome may not be possible and the best strategy may be to not get involved.

CONCLUSION

Successfully transitioning from war to peace is an extremely complex, resource intensive, and long duration endeavor. A nation which contemplates commitment of national power for the forceful overthrow of another government must commit to the development and maintenance of sufficient capabilities to ensure the successful transition to an enduring peace. This requires expeditionary military and nonmilitary capabilities to meet immediate survival needs, establish security, set conditions for social justice, and ensure transition to legitimate, indigenous self-governance.

ENDNOTES - CHAPTER 16

1. *Joint Publication (JP) 5-0, Joint Operation Planning*, Washington, DC: U.S. Joint Chiefs of Staff, December 26, 2006, p. IV-36.

2. *Joint Publications (JP) 3-0, Joint Operations*, Washington, DC: U.S. Joint Chiefs of Staff, September 17, 2006, p. IV-26.

3. General George W. Casey, Jr., U.S. Army, Speech to National Press Club, Washington, DC, August 14, 2007.

4. Francis J. Harvey and Peter J. Schoomaker, *A Statement on the Posture of the United States Army 2007*, Posture Statement presented to the 110th Congress, 1st Session, Washington, DC: U.S. Department of the Army, 2007, pp. 1-2.

5. Donald H. Rumsfeld, *The National Defense Strategy of The United States of America*, Washington, DC: U.S. Department of Defense, March 2005, p. 2.

6. Carl Von Clausewitz, *On War*, Michael Howard and Peter Paret, trans., Princeton, NJ: Princeton University Press, 1976, p. 88.

7. Abraham H. Maslow, "A Theory of Human Motivation," *Psychological Review*, Vol. 50, 1943, pp. 370-396, available from *psychclassics.yorku.ca/Maslow/motivation.htm*.

8. Sun Tzu, *The Art of War*, Samuel B. Griffith, trans., New York: Oxford University Press, 1963, p. 84.

9. David C. Gombert, *Heads We Win: The Cognitive Side of Counterinsurgency (COIN)*, Santa Monica, CA: RAND, 2007, p. x.

10. Mao Tse-tung, *On Guerrilla Warfare*, Samuel B. Griffith, trans., New York: Praeger, 1961, p. 27.

11. David Galula, *Counterinsurgency Warfare*, Westport, CT: Praeger Security International, 1964, p. 63.

12. *Field Manual (FM) 3-0, Operations,* Washington, DC: U.S. Department of the Army, February 27, 2008, pp. 1-13.

13. *Ibid.*, p. 21.

14. *Field Manual, (FM) 3-24, Counterinsurgency,* Washington, DC: U.S. Department of the Army, December 2006, pp. 1-13.

15. James Dobbins et al., *America's Role in Nation-Building*, Santa Monica, CA: RAND, 2003, pp. 150-151.

16. Conrad C. Crane, "The Emergence and Content of New American Counterinsurgency Doctrine," briefing slides, Carlisle, PA, U.S. Army War College, September 19, 2007.

17. James Jay Carafano and Dana R. Dillon, "Winning the Peace: Principles for Post-Conflict Operations," *Backgrounder*, No. 1859, June 2005, pp. 5-6.

18. Office of the Coordinator for Reconstruction and Stabilization, *Post-Conflict Reconstruction Essential Tasks*, Washington, DC: U.S. Department of State, April 2005.

19. *Joint Publication (JP) 3-07.3, Peace Operations*, Washington DC: U.S. Joint Chiefs of Staff, December 26, 2006, pp. IV-2.

20. FM 3-24, p. 156.

21. Peter W. Chiarelli and Patrick R. Michaelis, "Winning the Peace: The Requirement for Full-Spectrum Operations," *Military Review*, October 2006, p. 13.

22. Geneva Convention (IV) Relative to the Protection of Civilian Persons in Time of War, August 12, 1949, Sec III, Art 50-56, available from *www.yale.edu/lawweb/avalon/lawofwar/geneva07.htm*.

23. James Jay Carafano, "Thinking Differently about Winning the Peace," lecture transcript, Washington, DC, Heritage Foundation, March 10, 2006, available from *www.heritage.org/Research/NationalSecurity/hl987.cfm*.

24. Jock Covey, Michael J. Dziedzic, and Leonard R. Hawley, *The Quest for Viable Peace*, Washington, DC: U.S. Institute for Peace Press, 2005, pp. 14-17.

25. George W. Bush, *NSPD-44, Management of Interagency Efforts Concerning Reconstruction and Stabilization*, Washington, DC: The White House, December 7, 2005, available from *www.fas.org/irp/offdocs/ nspd/nspd-44.html*.

26. George W. Bush, *The National Security Strategy of the United States*, Washington, DC: The White House, March 2006, pp. 43-46.

CHAPTER 17

STABILITY OPERATIONS AND GOVERNMENT: AN INHERENTLY MILITARY FUNCTION

Lieutenant Colonel Russell R. Hula
U.S. Air Force

> The writer can testify to the baleful consequences of military invasion . . . where no military government was set up and where no army commander took responsibility for the country and its inhabitants. Outside of the relative security of army posts, anarchy and civil war prevailed. . . .
>
> — Major General Barrows, Siberia 1918-20[1]

History has frequently revealed that the most complex phase in achieving peace with security comes after the formal end of fighting.[2] Since the end of major combat operations, the United States has been playing catch-up in Iraq, and to a lesser extent in Afghanistan, in an attempt to stabilize both countries and transition to viable democratic governments. Following unquestionable initial military victories, long-term success has eluded policymakers. Many argue that the United States was as ill-equipped and unprepared for the instability that followed in Iraq and Afghanistan as it was in Bosnia, Haiti, and Kosovo.[3] As a result of these recent experiences, there is a growing renaissance in thinking about stability operations. Yet, disagreement continues among policymakers, theorists, and pundits concerning who should control and conduct stability operations. Many argue that stability operations are inherently a civil issue, and it is only the dysfunctional nature of the interagency that make stability operations so challenging.[4] Others see the lead role as inherently military.[5] This chapter examines the nature of American stability operations through historical examples to determine if they are in the domain of others, or are inherently military in character.

As the United States continues to come to grips with stability operations in Iraq, policymakers are struggling with the harsh realization that Iraq is far more difficult than anticipated.[6] Even though the U.S. Government had over a year to plan and prepare for what might follow the toppling of Saddam's regime, the challenges have been both difficult and extensive.[7] U.S. responses have been improvised and poorly executed. In the war's immediate aftermath, a security vacuum led to looting which moved from government ministries, to hospitals, to schools, and finally evolved into structural anarchy.[8] Social chaos transitioned rapidly into insurgency, which further facilitated the degeneration of governance, public services, and functional infrastructure. Lacking both local and international support, the predominantly American coalition military force has as of January 11, 2008, sustained over 32,785 casualties; 3,915 deaths and 28,870 wounded, most of which occurred following the cessation of major combat operations in 2003.[9] Less time was available for stability operations planning in Afghanistan, and like Iraq, much of the stabilization effort was accomplished ad hoc.[10] Fortunately, immediately after defeating the Taliban, U.S.-led coalition forces experienced good local and international support and took fewer casualties in Afghanistan, with 472 deaths and 1,851 wounded as of January 2008.[11] While many argue that immediate stability operations have been more successful in Afghanistan, most agree that severe deficiencies in our stabilization and reconstruction processes continued to be problematic in both Afghanistan and Iraq.[12]

Most critics point to poor planning and a lack of appropriate resources as the key reasons for the difficulties seen in recent stability operations.[13] Moreover, they argue that these problems were caused by ambivalence toward who should *own* stability operations. Some believe recent military leaders focused too heavily on planning for major combat operations with the expectation of dealing with stability and reconstruction efforts later in the campaign.[14] Another view argues that meandering guidance has befuddled command and control by alternating the responsibility for stability operations among a National Security Council (NSC) Executive Committee, the Department of Defense (DoD), and the State Department (DoS), allowing no one to be properly prepared and resourced.[15] Yet another position contends the military was reluctant to consider stability operations to be a core competency, and thus, was unwilling to embrace stability operations until faced with the difficult realities on the ground.[16] While there are many reasons why stability operations have been problematic, most agree the military did not welcome the mission and the government policy was not carefully considered.

A RENAISSANCE IN STABILITY OPERATIONS THINKING

At the end of the Cold War, a renaissance in stability operations thinking began when the internal collapse of the Soviet Union released destabilizing forces around the globe.[17] A renaissance suggests a rebirth or revival and is used in this case because the development of stability operations theory and practice has an extensive history in the U.S. military. After a series of fumbled conflict resolution efforts, a more systematic and informed approach has emerged.[18]

In the past, the military and other federal agencies lacked theory and doctrine in regard to who should be responsible for resolving the issues of peacekeeping and nation-building. Consequently, in 1994, President William J. Clinton signed Presidential Decision Directive (PDD)-25 to better focus on better interagency planning and coordination.[19] Some joint publications also sought to provide guidance for conflict resolution efforts.[20] While welcomed, federal agencies believed further presidential guidance was needed.[21] As a result, President Clinton signed PDD-56 in 1997, ordering the DoD, State Department, and other agencies to create a unified program for educating and training personnel for complex interagency contingency operations.[22] Future conflict resolution efforts were to be led by a NSC Executive Committee, formed on an as-needed basis.[23] Less than 2 years later, a DoD study found that the White House and its various agencies were not following the guidance, and the NSC was not stepping forward in a leadership role.[24]

With the election of President Bush in 2001, PDD's were rescinded and replaced with National Security Presidential Directives (NSPD).[25] NSPD-1, the first of those directives, established an interagency methodology using NSC Policy Coordination Committees as the vehicle for coordination of national security policy.[26] After an apparent military success in Afghanistan and less than 2 months prior to the invasion of Iraq, President Bush signed NSPD-24, deviating from NSPD-1 guidance by putting the DoD in charge of stability operations with the establishment of the Office of Reconstruction and Humanitarian Affairs (ORHA). After events on the ground proved to be ineffective, President Bush signed NSPD-44; which acknowledges the need for unity of effort, but reversed NSPD-24 and designated the DoS as the focal point for stability operations with DoD in support.[27] At nearly the same time, the DoD released Directive (DoDD) 3000.5, *Military Support for Stability, Security, Transition, and Reconstruction (SSTR) Operations*. DoDD 3000.5 designates stability operations as a "core military mission," and while it recognizes some stability operation tasks are best performed by others, it specifies "military forces shall be prepared to perform all tasks necessary to establish or maintain order when civilians cannot do so."[28] With belated recognition, stability operations assumed a key role in successful military operations which has further stimulated interest in theory and doctrine.

Numerous contemporary authors and scholars have developed models related to the purpose and functions of stability operations. Charles Bailey has proposed applying A. H. Maslow's Hierarchy of Needs as an outline from which to develop stability operations campaign plans.[29] As one of the most researched human psychology theories, Maslow's basic premise is that human beings are motivated to satisfy needs, and lower or more basic needs must be satisfied before higher ones can be fulfilled.[30] Bailey theorized that violence and other atrocities are rooted in unfulfilled human needs and believed Maslow's physiological, safety, social, self-esteem, and self-actualization needs can be used to frame and prioritize future strategy and stability operations.[31]

While useful, Maslow's theory is based on individual motivations versus societal provisions, providing only a partial framework.[32] William Zartman has advanced a theory of state collapse based on the misplaced governmental and political character of present-day African nations.[33] He believes signposts provide warning symptoms of state failure and-states collapse when "they can no longer perform the functions required for them to pass as a state."[34] Similarly, Robert Rotberg argued nation-states exist to provide a decentralized method of delivering "political goods."[35] When a nation-state cannot provide the necessary components of a successful society and-state, which also correlate on an individual basis to Maslow's safety needs, the result is state failure.[36] An obvious relationship exists among Zartman's and Rotberg's state-collapse theories and Bailey's insights in regard to Maslow's theory of human motivation. In a more comprehensive approach, Professor William Flavin, a member of the U.S. Army War College faculty, defined the fundamentals for successful conflict termination and presented a decision matrix to help military planners track necessary functions to achieve the desired military end-state.[37] Flavin's analysis suggests that in stability operations, governments must adhere to six fundamental principles and focus on seven sectors for success. There are clear crosscutting elements and functions among all four theories, as seen in Figure 1. Flavin's decision matrix reflects a coherent synthesis of the previous three theoretical models and augments their premises with his fundamentals that he believes are necessary to achieve successful conflict termination. In doing this, Flavin provides the theory from which to develop effective doctrine for stability operations and successful conflict resolution.

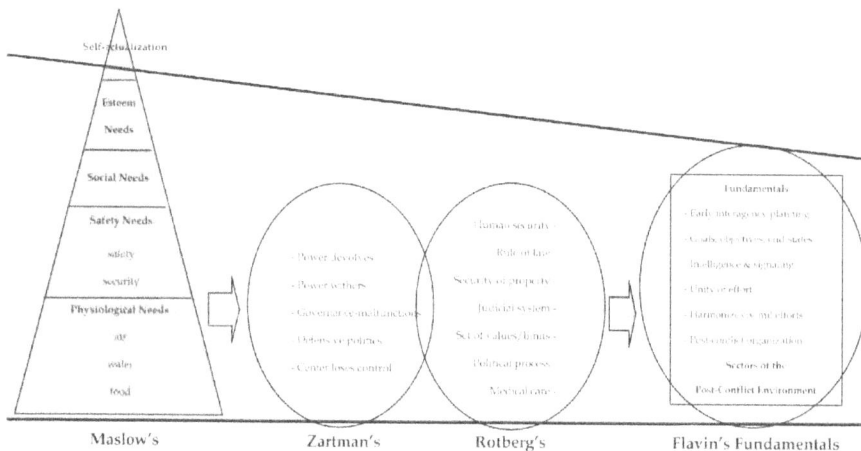

Figure 1. Relevant Theories for Stability Operations.

A number of terms and expressions are related to or used instead of stability operations. Some of the other more frequently used expressions include stability and reconstruction (S&R); stability, security, transition, and reconstruction (SSTR), Phase IV; post-conflict operations; and transition operations.[38] Stability operations can follow major combat operations or arise as part of peace operations or other interventions. The *DoD Dictionary of Military Terms* defines *stability operations* as:

> An overarching term encompassing various military missions, tasks, and activities conducted outside the United States in coordination with other instruments of national power to maintain or reestablish a safe and secure environment, provide essential governmental services, emergency infrastructure reconstruction, and humanitarian relief.[39]

Hence, the DoD definition of stability operations encompasses the meaning behind Flavin's sectors of the post-conflict environment. Consequently, his theory is a useful heuristic with which to evaluate historical case studies on stability operations so as to answer the questions of how to and who must conduct stability operations.

CASE STUDY ANALYSIS

There are four historical roles of military landpower: destruction of enemy forces, close contact, defensive occupation, and physical control and occupation.[40] Through a series of early military occupations from the Mexican War to the aftermath of the Civil War and the frontier experiences, the U.S. military gained an inherent appreciation for the value of stability operations. This experience gained formal recognition with "The Hunt Report" in 1920, which captured the occupation experiences in Germany following

World War I.[41] During the interwar period, "The Hunt Report" was followed by the initial releases of *Field Manual (FM) 27-10, Rules of Land Warfare* (1939), *Field Manual (FM) 27-5, Military Government & Civil Affairs* (1940), and the Marine Corps' *Small Wars Manual* (1940).[42] In particular, lessons learned from the Philippine War and World War I occupations were vital to the advocacy for and establishment and curriculum of the Army and Navy Schools of Military Government in 1942.[43]

Past military experience can serve as a test of Flavin's theory. While the stability operations in each conflict were unique due to a host of contextual factors, recurring themes surface when they are examined against Flavin's fundamentals for conflict termination. According to Flavin, the six keys to successful stability operations include conducting early interagency planning; establishing workable objectives, goals, and end-states; providing for adequate intelligence and signaling; ensuring unity of effort; harmonizing the civil with the military effort; and establishing the appropriate post-conflict organization.[44] Taken together, these case studies provide evidence of the inherent nature of stability operations and validate Flavin's fundamentals.

As Flavin's first premise states, "Planning for termination and post-conflict operations should begin as early as possible," with the flexibility to adjust to altering objectives and contextual factors.[45] Colonel Irwin L. Hunt concluded in his report on World War I German occupation activities, that civil affairs-military government is a specialized military function and needs to have trained personnel who can begin planning as soon as possible.[46] Thus, the U.S. Army took two essential steps to prepare for future military occupations during the interwar years.[47]   First, with information developed from U.S. Army War College committees and "The Hunt Report," two field manuals were published to provide long-needed doctrine.[48] FM 27-10 and FM 27-5 came to be known, respectively, as the Old and New Testaments of American military government during World War II.[49] Second, understanding the imminent need, the development of the framework for the American Military Government began shortly before entering World War II.[50] Significant effort and resources were devoted to identifying future requirements prior to entering World War II; but, detailed planning and force structure development for the post-surrender occupations were conducted primarily in parallel with combat operations.[51] While delays were often unavoidable due to international uncertainties, the Department of War concluded that waiting to prepare was not a good strategy to counter such enormous challenges.[52] Built from the difficult lessons of past stability operations, the U.S. Army recognized that "military government . . . is a virtually inevitable concomitant of modern warfare," thus early preparation through doctrine, organization, and training provided a solid foundation for World War II stability operations.[53]

The foremost goal in stability operations planning, according to Flavin's second premise, is to "establish an achievable end state based on clear objectives."[54] But first the National Command Authority needs to provide clear policy guidance.[55] Yet, as Flavin admits, "this is more the ideal than the reality."[56] Preceding the Spanish-American War, President William McKinley, Jr., had not identified a desired end state when he swiftly deployed additional military forces to the Philippines.[57] To make matters worse, McKinley's policy evolved throughout the conflict in what Brian M. Linn refers to as an "accidental and incremental" desired end-state.[58]   From these lessons, military leaders during World War II attempted to garner clear policies and objectives from the Secretary of War and the President. In Germany and Japan, policy was at times very broad and at other times very prolific; but always shifting due to complex international politics. The German effort was enormously complicated due a quadripartite government, of which the United States administered the American Zone of Occupation.[59] After several revisions during hostilities, the final version of the shifting policy was general in nature and left both the interpretation and application of relevant international agreements and policies to the discretion of General Lucius D. Clay, the Military Governor of Germany.[60] Reminiscent of the German experience, complex international challenges in Japan eventually created political fog and friction during the occupation. Nevertheless, in all three military occupations, a clear definition of American foreign policy was nonexistent, but was compensated for by preparation, good judgment, and a unified and agile military government.[61]

According to Flavin's third premise, "Before any conflict starts, the intelligence community must include factors affecting the termination and post-conflict operational area" in the campaign plan.[62] Unfortunately, in the Philippines, due to the speed at which President McKinley dispatched his forces, military leaders were unable to conduct early intelligence and campaign planning.[63] Consequently, only through a painful process of learning and adaptation was the U.S. Army able to determine and set the necessary conditions for a peaceful outcome in the Philippines. While the size of the regular Army was small, many U.S. senior ranking members were battle-hardened from the Civil War, Reconstruction, and Indian campaigns from which they had developed an "informal but widely accepted pacification doctrine that balanced conciliation and repression."[64] From difficult challenges such as these and others in Siberia and World War I, the U.S. military recognized as early as 1940 that the earlier experiences would be dwarfed by the enormous and multifaceted tasks the United States would face in Germany and Japan.[65] As such, planning and preparation included the analysis of the complex geostrategic factors for the two World War II theater campaigns.[66] However, their information was not always correct. For example, early interpretations of Japan as a homogenous modern society led many to mirror-image their analysis. While the homogenous trait was undeniable, the Japanese were far from being a contemporary modern culture. As General Douglas MacArthur stated, "Supposedly, the Japanese were a 20th-century civilization. In reality, they were more nearly a feudal society . . . akin to ancient Sparta," complicating occupation efforts.[67] Thus, while geostrategic analysis was important, adaptation was critical to shaping the post-surrender environment.[68]

According to Flavin's fourth premise, unity of effort is critical to stability operations success, but the current dysfunctional nature of the interagency often prevents effective preparation, planning, and focus.[69] Correspondingly, in the Philippines, policy and bureaucratic challenges were also prevalent; however, they were offset by military ingenuity and flexibility, and a focused military government effort balancing civic action and coercion.[70] Similarly, while international politics affected the organization, policies, and challenges faced by the military governments in World War II differently, not only unity of effort, but unity of command was a predominate theme. "Sound practice required the complete concentration of authority in the military governor," who was ultimately responsible and accountable for the entire complex occupation environment, and was of paramount importance.[71] The tailored, comprehensive, and unified approach to military government was integral to achieving the desired end states in the Philippines and in World War II Germany and World War II Japan.

In his fifth premise, Flavin states, "Harmonization is essential and must occur across a variety of institutions and agencies at the strategic, operational, and tactical levels, both horizontally and vertically."[72] In the past, synchronization of the extremely complex and numerous occupation functions was accomplished by leveraging the vast wealth of knowledge and expertise of the United States and its people, but centrally executed by the U.S. military. The past military did not administer the duties of military government alone. In the case of World War II, most of the American military government and civil affairs officers were civilians in peacetime, working primarily within their realm of experience.[73] Additionally, while the War Department was responsible for administering national policies, State and the other Departments of the U.S. Government were responsible for formulating their respective policies, and providing critical reach back expertise and capabilities.[74] As the experience in the Philippines indicates, "The military leader on the scene was the best agent for local pacification," and only through central direction and ownership was the military able to ensure unity of effort and harmonization.[75] That is not the same as saying civilian expertise was not integrated.

Flavin's final premise states; "Successful termination and transition into post-conflict peace operations requires an appropriate organization to ensure multinational, interagency, and international harmony."[76] In the Philippines, the policy vacuum and failure to recognize the emerging independent Filipino movement made the difficult task of organizing an expeditionary force even more complicated.[77] Cuba had been America's focus in the planning for war with Spain, not the Philippines.[78] Through an agonizing process, the organization of the military government in the Philippines emerged over time. To a great extent, the lessons learned were applied in the organizational framework and preparation for the American Military Government occupation organizations and command structures in Germany and Japan.[79] In essence, an agile military government solution enabled the U.S. military to satisfy Flavin's fundamentals for post-conflict success in the Philippines and World War II.

Flavin's theory further advocates a decision matrix with seven key sectors that must be addressed in the post-conflict environment to achieve the desired military end state: security, humanitarian assistance, human rights and social reconciliation, governance and civil administration, civil law and order, infrastructure and economic restoration, and public diplomacy/information operations.[80] The inherent nature of the post-surrender environment of the Philippines, Germany, and Japan historical examples reinforces the conviction that most in the U.S. Government have now come to accept the belief that peaceful transfer to civil government occurs through the successful fulfillment of Flavin's seven sectors, or what Rotberg referred to as "political goods."[81]

In the Philippines, through painful experiences, the U.S. Army recognized the crucial relationship between civil affairs work and the level of security, with the establishment of law and order being the most urgent priority in stability operations.[82] An entrenched Filipino insurgency followed the formal end of fighting when the political objectives of the revolutionaries and the McKinley administration diverged.[83] The breakdown of public order and services along with the loss of legitimate central authority were all compounded when the initiative was lost by the inability to provide security to the

Filipino population.[84]   However, for all of President McKinley's policy failings in the Philippines, he provided the U.S. Army with excellent guiding principles for the conduct of the provisional military government.[85]   According to President McKinley, the U.S. Army, through direction of the military governor, was directed to:

> Possess and hold the Philippines, giving to the people there peace and order and beneficent government, affording them every opportunity to prosecute their lawful pursuits, and encouraging them in thrift and industry; making them feel and know that we are good friends . . . and that they will be aided in every possible way to be a self-respecting and self-governing people . . . .[86]

As such, the U.S. Army used benevolence through every possible means, including humanitarian relief; the extension of individual liberties and rights; organizing self-government; establishment of schools, public health programs, and public works; astute propaganda; and payment for weapons.[87] However, early progress made by humanitarian efforts was often offset by a revolutionary insurgency and their terror tactics.[88]   Unlike his predecessor, Major General Elwell S. Otis, Major General Arthur MacArthur, Jr., understood the survival of the insurgency depended on the revolutionaries' capacity to control the civilian populace through intimidation and terrorism.[89]   Accordingly, MacArthur changed operations and tactics by widely dispersing his forces with increased surveillance to detect insurgents, terrorists, and supporters.[90]   Despite the fact they were often criticized for a heavy-handed approach, continuous patrols by American forces impeded insurgent efforts.[91]   Under MacArthur's leadership, the U.S. Army adapted by integrating benevolent counterinsurgency policies and methods with effective security, which in the end defeated the revolutionary movement.[92]

Viewed as the most important American precedent by interwar doctrine writers, the critical civil affairs and security best-practices from the Philippines were applied to the American School of Military Government's detailed development of training, doctrine, regulations, and capabilities for World War II occupations.[93]   In both cases, the U.S. military applied a large military security force in post-surrender Germany and Japan, to counter potential insurgencies and to solidify the psychological security of the populace absent basic needs and essential services.   The American Military Government model also prepared the framework for numerous other transition capabilities to include: establishing and mentoring civil functions and supporting institutions; establishment of public order and governance; management of public funds; public health; public relief; public works; markets; and education.[94] Furthermore, the U.S. Army developed a vast number of detailed training publications for civil services; Bank Accounting and Operations in Japan, Agriculture and Food in Japan, Field Protection of Objects of Art and Archives, and Sickness Insurance in Germany, to name a few.[95] The level of detailed preparation for the World War II occupations reflects a remarkable grasp of both the nature and magnitude of the challenges of stability operations.

Every conflict has unique and complex factors which prove problematic in achieving the desired end states. Yet, lessons learned from the Philippines, and other conflicts prior to World War II, validated the military need for and issues concerning stability operations.

Scholars such as John Gates and Brian Linn believe the success in defeating the Philippine insurgency and stabilizing the islands can be traced to a comprehensive decentralized approach. Widely dispersed U.S. commanders creatively dealt with complex essential service and security challenges, guided by the centralized framework and conduct of military government.[96] Acceptance of stability operations as a necessity of war, early preparation, and a unified and agile military government solution in World War II made it "possible to organize the civil administration of foreign territories from the outset with a view to the ultimate war and peace aims."[97] Painful experiences, yielding successful occupations, proved that a military government is a viable solution to future stability operation challenges.[98] Still, oddly the U.S. military lost its way and the reasons for this still preclude the willing embrace for what is professionally obvious.

LOSING OUR WAY

After World War II, the U.S. military misplaced and rejected the experience and knowledge from its past, thus the military government solution faded from both doctrine and practice. Three key things contributed to this dissolution. First, since its inception, the controversial nature of military government has made it equally objectionable in civilian and military communities. To civilians, the term rang unkindly, sounding too imperialistic and "vaguely unconstitutional."[99] In today's sensitive political climate, the term military government is arguably even more offensive to many of the ideological and political elites in national and international level communities. Additionally, since before the Philippine experience, military leaders have alleged that civil-military operations (CMO) and stability operations draw so heavily on personnel and resources as to affect combat efficiency.[100] Most recently, seen as "nontraditional" functions, the CMO specialty has often been viewed as a "subculture" involved in areas many commanders do not understand and consider "mission creep" as opposed to mission essential.[101]

Second, the responsibility for this essential phase of war has been ineffectively fixed with the unintended consequences of no one being capable or accountable. In an attempt to clearly define civil-military control and fix responsibilities and requirements following the occupations during World War II, the National Security Act (NSA) of 1947 created the National Security Council with the initial purpose to serve as a mechanism to coordinate political and military questions.[102] In reality, the NSA of 1947 shifted the responsibility for leading complex political-military challenges away from the military, including those integral to war, to untested bureaucratic organizations that were neither capable nor resourced for the complexity and challenges of stability operations.

Third, the U.S. military quickly adjusted its strategies, doctrine, and capabilities to those based heavily on deterrence during the Cold War.[103] As such, *Field Manual (FM) 41-10, Civil Affairs Operations*, superseded FM 27-5, and the procedural and doctrinal framework for military government slowly atrophied as the military focused on the monolithic threat of the Soviet Union.[104] As the requirement for trained military government officers in Japan and Germany dwindled with success, the training, resources, and infrastructure also contracted, leaving only a civil affairs shell with its capabilities predominantly in the reserves to play supporting roles in CMO. Despite the evidence of Vietnam, CMO has been the comprehensive term used to describe the general activities performed by a niche

269

in the military who are capable of coordination with, and providing support to civilian organizations in humanitarian, peacekeeping, and nation-building operations.[105] In the end, as these changes undid a successful doctrine and military government solution; they also helped corroborate the concept of stability operations as inherently nonmilitary and something outside the conduct of war.

IMPLICATIONS TO CURRENT AND FUTURE EFFORTS

Even with such prominent historical successes, the current U.S. military has struggled to relearn the lessons from the past. One likely reason is that the apparent parallels between the Iraq and World War II occupations have been widely criticized. Many critics believe U.S. nation-building efforts in conflicts such as Haiti, Bosnia, and Kosovo are more relevant.[106] Several of these same critics point to the early failure of the ORHA experiment in Iraq as the reason why the military should not be charged with stability operations. Yet others recognize ORHA as an "inadequate, notoriously slow-moving substitute for an interim occupation government."[107] Distinct contextual factors serve to complicate some analogies, but the aggregate historical experience validates Flavin's theory and suggests relevant doctrine. Moreover, newly emerging doctrine, capabilities, and practice provide both promise and caution for the future. Current experience, evaluated through history and context, provides three key harbingers of good and bad for the future.

First, as in the past, the U.S. Army has recently taken the lead in the interpretation of past experiences and adapting ways and means to counter current stability operations challenges. As a result of successful on-the-ground efforts, such as those by Major General Peter Chiarelli and the 1st Calvary Division in Iraq, the U.S. military again accepts that full-spectrum stability operations are a necessary phase of warfare.[108] Some of the lessons learned have recently been incorporated into the new U.S. Army *Field Manual (FM) 3-0, Operations*, which acknowledges stability operations as a core military mission and refocuses on "full-spectrum operations."[109] In correlation with Flavin's insights and the military's past experience, FM 3-0 also outlines what it calls a "whole of government approach" to "post-conflict stability sectors."[110] Yet, much remains disconcerting. The focus on the primarily civil-nature of the logical lines of operation, as outlined in FM 3-0, could encourage persistent stovepiped efforts, limited success, and interagency finger-pointing. While debatable, some critics claim the failures in Iraq were really due to the lack of planning for Phase IV of the campaign.[111] However, DoD Undersecretary for Policy Douglas Feith undertook the development of a comprehensive postwar plan, suggesting the problem was a fundamental lack of understanding of the nature of the operations.[112] According to Colonel Kevin Benson, CFLCC/J5, his staff painstakingly developed the Iraq Phase IV plan.[113] Benson says the real challenge was translating those plans into effective lines of operation while dealing with guidance and assumptions from higher echelons, deployment processes, interagency concerns, and evolving policy."[114] Further complicating the effort, General Tommy R. Franks did not advocate subordinating stability operations under his command; thus, the U.S. military purposely averted the military government solution as a template for success.[115] Recent experience again points out that without complete ownership of the problem, as was the case in the military government solution, critical components of success are overlooked or ignored.

As Major General David P. Barrows, Director of Education in the Philippines, member of the AEF Staff in 1919 Siberia, and President of the University of California, told the 1943 School of Military Government class members,

> The necessity for military government exists plainly in the character of war itself . . . For the protection of this army itself, as well as for the protection, security, and well-being of the inhabitants of the territory which it occupies, the establishment of the government, at least of some provision kind, is imperative.[116]

Second, the new Counterinsurgency FM (2007) incorporates critical instruction from past occupations.[117] Likewise, the new DoD Military Support to Stabilization, Security, Transition, and Reconstruction Operations Joint Operating Concept (2006) consolidates much of the tutelage from history including main mission elements and fundamentals of stability operations.[118] In addition, the Army's recently formed Peacekeeping and Stability Operations Institute (PKSOI) is making progress in facilitating policies, concepts, and doctrine to "address the challenging SSTRO strategic and operational issues facing the nation."[119] Organizations such as these will help prepare core military capabilities for future stability operations. However, risk exists in relation to preparation and planning for future stability operations. Unlike World War II, modern rapid decisive operations, such as were seen in Operation IRAQI FREEDOM, no longer allow the luxury for detailed and complex planning efforts during the hostilities phase.[120] In addition, the myopic nature of our nation makes it difficult to continue the current stability operations momentum once the immediate challenge fades. As Secretary Gates recently acknowledged, "On numerous occasions in the past, the [United States] concluded that the nature of man and the world had changed for the better, and turned inward, unilaterally disarming and dismantling institutions important to our national security."[121]

Third, after again recognizing the relationship between civil affairs and security, the U.S. military and International Security Assistance Force (ISAF) developed Provincial Reconstruction Teams (PRTs), which stressed governance, security, and impact development projects to "win hearts and minds" in Afghanistan.[122] Similar reconstruction teams modeled from these experiences have been developed in Iraq. Yet, PRT success has suffered from a lack of coordination and oversight. Many PRT veterans believe that the PRT program needs a concept of operations and an effective command and control structure, the very benefits the military government model provided in the past.[123] As previous military leaders came to understand so painfully, it is not only a necessary evil, it is both a humanitarian obligation and good strategy for the military to fill the *political goods* void. According to General Barrows, "It is the right and duty of a commander . . . to declare the establishment of military government, even though not directly instructed to do so by the War Department."[124] However, as mentioned before and in a reversal of roles, NSPD-44 puts the State Department in the lead, with the military merely in support for stability operations. Many in government and academia are now troubled about the consequences of such changes. After more than 2 years since the NSPD-44 policy change, the lack of State Department capabilities and Congress' reluctance to support such capabilities provides clear warning signs for the future.

CONCLUSION

Inherently military can be defined as: A function that is so intimately related to achieving the desired end-state in war as to mandate performance by the military. In American military history, stability operations have been inherently military whenever Americans have occupied others' territory. Yet following World War II, the U.S. military lost its perspective of the role and importance of this critical phase of warfare for achieving a successful peace. Iraq and Afghanistan have refocused our attention on the questions of what stability operations are and how they should be conducted. In this regard, DoDD 3000.05 reinforces the historical experience in saying, "Military forces shall be prepared to perform all tasks necessary to establish or maintain order when civilians cannot do so."[125] In the ongoing renaissance of thinking about stability operations, Flavin's fundamentals and sectors constitutes an appropriate theory for the development of 21st century doctrine. Although his theory does not directly advocate for a military government solution, its implications as well as the Congress' continuing unwillingness to substantially increase funding for other departments of government points directly at such a solution. The U.S. military's historical experience, the realities of Iraq and Afghanistan, the implications of theory for practice, and the gap between strategic objectives and resources argue for a military lead is stability operations. Since stability operations remain an inherently military function of 21st century warfare, the U.S. military must be prepared to establish a unified and agile military government.[126]

ENDNOTES - CHAPTER 17

1. Richard Van Wagenen, "The Richard W. Van Wagenen Papers," Course Materials from the 1943 class at the School of Military Government, Notes on Military Government from Major General David P. Barrows, Former Director of Education, Philippines and member of A.E.F. Staff in Siberia 1919, Charlottesville, VA, 1943, p. 3.

2. William Flavin, "Planning for Conflict Termination and Post-Conflict Success," *Parameters*, Vol. 33, Autumn 2003, p. 96.

3. Morton H. Halperin, "America Needs a New Agency to Help Failed States," *American Security Project*, Vol. 188, December 20, 2007, available from *www.americansecurityproject.org/print/188*.

4. *Ibid.*

5. Nadia Shadlow, "War and the Art of Governance," *Parameters*, Vol. 33, Autumn 2003, pp. 85-94.

6. Thomas A. Bussiere, *Post-Conflict Iraq: If You Don't Know Where You're Going . . .*, Strategy Research Project, Carlisle, PA: U.S. Army War College, March 30, 2007, p. 2.

7. Joseph J. Collins, "Planning Lessons from Afghanistan and Iraq," *Joint Forces Quarterly*, Vol. 41, 2nd Quarter 2006, p. 10.

8. John Keegan, *The Iraq War*, New York: Alfred A. Knopf, 2004, p. 207.

9. U.S. casualty statistics for Operation IRAQI FREEDOM as of January 11, 2008, available from *www.defenselink.mil/news/casualty.pdf*.

10. Collins, p. 10.

11. U.S. casualty statistics for Operation IRAQI FREEDOM.

12. Collins, p. 10.

13. *Ibid*.

14. Conrad C. Crane, "Phase IV Operations: Where Wars are Really Won," *Military Review*, May-June 2005, p. 27.

15. Halperin.

16. Peter W. Chiarelli and Patrick R. Michaelis, "Winning the Peace: The Requirement for Full-Spectrum Operations," *Military Review*, July-August 2005, pp. 4-5.

17. William P. Hamblett and Jerry G. Kline, "Interagency Cooperation: PDD-56 and Complex Contingency Operations," *Joint Force Quarterly*, Spring 2000, pp. 92-93.

18. Crane, p. 27.

19. William J. Clinton, *PDD-25: U.S. Policy on Reforming Multilateral Peace Operations*, Washington, DC: The White House, May 6, 1994, available from *www.fas.org/irp/offdocs/pdd25.htm*.

20. Hamblett and Kline, pp. 92-93.

21. *Ibid*.

22. William J. Clinton, *PDD/NSC-56: Managing Complex Contingency Operations*, Washington, DC: The White House, May 1997, available from *www.fas.org/irp/offdocs/pdd56.htm*.

23. *Ibid*.

24. Rowan Scarborough, "Study Hits White House on Peacekeeping Missions," *Washington Times*, December 6, 1999, Part A, p. A1, available from *www.fas.org/irp/offdocs/pdd/991206-pdd.htm*.

25. Steven Aftergood, "National Security Presidential Directives (NSPD), George W. Bush Administration," available from *www.fas.org/irp/offdocs/nspd/index.html*.

26. Neyla Arnas, Charles Barry, and Robert Oakley, "Harnessing the Interagency for Complex Operations," Washington, DC: National Defense University, August 2005, p. 5, available from *www.ndu.edu/CTNSP/Def_Tech/DTP%2016%20Harnessing%20the%20Interagency.pdf*.

27. George W. Bush, *NSPD-44, Management of Interagency Efforts Concerning Reconstruction and Stabilization*, Washington, DC: The White House, December 7, 2005, available from *www.fas.org/irp/offdocs/nspd/nspd-44.html*.

28. Department of Defense Directive 3000.5, *Military Support for Stability, Security, Transition, and Reconstruction (SSTR) Operations*, Washington, DC: U.S. Department of Defense, November 28, 2005.

29. Charles Bailey, "Winning the Hearts and Minds: Providing the Basic Needs First," Strategy Research Project, Carlisle, PA: US Army War College, March 18, 2005, p. 6.

30. A.H. Maslow, "A Theory of Human Motivation," *Psychological Review*, Vol. 50, 1943, pp. 370-396.

31. Bailey, pp. 7-8.

32. Maslow, pp. 370-396.

33. I. William Zartman, ed., *Collapsed States: The Disintegration and Restoration of Legitimate Authority*, Boulder, CO: Lynne Rienner Publishers, 1995, pp. 9-10.

34. *Ibid.*

35. Robert J. Rotberg, ed., *State Failure and-State Weakness in a Time of Terror*, Washington DC: Brookings Institution Press, 2003, p. 2.

36. *Ibid*, p. 90.

37. Flavin, p. 104.

38. Crane, p. 27.

39. U.S. Department of Defense, *The DoD Dictionary of Military and Associated Terms*, available from *www.dtic.mil/doctrine/jel/DoDdict/data/s/0520.html*.

40. David T. Zabecki, "Landpower in History," *Armed Forces Journal International*, Vol. 140, No. 1, August 2002, p. 40.

41. I. L. Hunt, *Report on Military Government, Report on the Activation of the Office of Civil Affairs*, Goblens, Germany: Headquarters American Forces in Germany, March 4, 1920, pp. 1-2.

42. Earl F. Ziemke, *The U.S. Army in the Occupation of Germany, 1944-1946*, Washington DC: Center of Military History, U.S. Government Printing Office, 1975, pp. 3-10.

43. The Army took the lead in developing a curriculum and training program for Military Government after the United States entered World War II. The Secretary of War, on April 2, 1942, established the School of Military Government at the University of Virginia, which eventually spread to both military installations and several other university institutions, Yale, Harvard, Pittsburgh, Chicago, Michigan, and Stanford, to satisfy the growing demand for officers with highly specialized training. See Ziemke, *The U.S. Army in the Occupation of Germany, 1944-1946*, pp. 3-19. The U.S. Marine Corps (USMC) developed the *Small Wars Manual* after lessons-learned in several interwar period conflicts in Latin America. Chapter 13 provides Military Government doctrine and techniques. See USMC, *Small Wars Manual*; reprint, Manhattan, KS: Sunflower University Press, 2004. The *Small Wars Manual* was a titled revision of the *Small Wars Operations*, 1935, which captured Marine Corps writings on the subject since 1921. The Department of the Navy also recognized the need and on June 17, 1942, detailed naval officers to the Program of Training in International Administration at Columbia University, which would eventually become the Naval School of Military Government and Administration. Schuyler C. Wallace, "The Naval School of Military Government and Administration," *Annals of the American Academy of Political and Social Science*, Vol. 231, January 1944, pp. 29-33.

44. Flavin, pp. 96-97.

45. *Ibid*, p. 97

46. Hunt, pp. 1-2.

47. Christopher T. Burgess, *U.S. Army Doctrine and Belligerent Occupation*, Monograph, Fort Leavenworth, KS: School of Advanced Military Studies, AY03-04, p. 21.

48. Ziemke, p. 4.

49. *Ibid*, p. 3.

50. *Ibid*, p. 448.

51. Crane, p. 27.

52. Hajo Holborn, *American Military Government*, Washington DC: Infantry Journal Press, 1947, p. 105.

53. Ziemke, p. 3.

54. Flavin, p. 97.

55. *Ibid*.

56. *Ibid*.

57. John M. Gates, *Schoolbooks and Krags: The U.S. Army in the Philippines, 1898-1902*, Westport, CT: Greenwood Press Inc, 1973, p. 3.

58. Brian M. Linn, *The Philippine War, 1899-1902*, Lawrence, KS: University Press of Kansas, 2000, p. 5.

59. Lucius D. Clay, *Decision in Germany*, Garden City, NY: Doubleday & Company, Inc., 1950, p. 10.

60. *Ibid*, pp. 237-238.

61. Holborn, p. 105.

62. Flavin, p. 102.

63. Linn, pp. 8-9.

64. *Ibid*.

65. Holborn, p. 2.

66. *Ibid*, pp. 1-2.

67. Douglas MacArthur, *Reminiscences*, New York: McGraw-Hill Book Company, 1964, pp. 283-284.

68. Russell Brines, *MacArthur's Japan*, New York: J.B. Lippincott Company, 1948, p. 25.

69. Flavin, p. 108.

70. Linn, p. 326.

71. Van Wagenen, p. 6.

72. Flavin, p. 105.

73. Holborn, p. 107.

74. *Ibid*, p. 108.

75. Crane, p. 31.

76. Flavin, p. 108.

77. Gates, pp. 4-5.

78. *Ibid*, p. 4.

79. Ziemke, pp. 1-6.

80. Flavin, p. 104.

81. Rotberg, p. 2.

82. Gates, p. 277.

83. Linn, pp. 11-12.

84. *Ibid*, p. 19.

85. Gates, p. 7.

86. MacArthur, p. 20.

87. Gates, pp. 270-271, 277-278.

88. *Ibid*, pp. 270-271, 278.

89. Linn, p. 18.

90. Gates, p. 271.

91. *Ibid*.

92. Linn, p. 20.

93. Van Wagenen, pp. 7-9.

94. *Ibid*.

95. *List of Publications for Training, U.S. Army FM 21-6*, Washington DC: U.S. War Department, September 1, 1944, p. 139.

96. Gates, p. 270.

97. Holborn, p. 105.

98. Troy Thomas, "Control Roaming Dogs: Governance Operations in Future Conflict," *Military Review*, January-February 2006, p. 79.

99. Ziemke, p. 12.

100. Van Wagenen, p. 9.

101. Larry Wentz, ed., *Lessons from Kosovo: The KFOR Experience*, Washington DC: CCRP, 2002, p. 503.

102. U.S. Department of State, Office of the Historian, "History of the National Security Council," available from *www.whitehouse.gov/nsc/history.html*.

103. Thomas, p. 79.

104. Ziemke, p. viii.

105. Wentz, p. 483.

106. Carolyn Lochhead, "Experts Question the Parallel to Rebuilding after WWII," *San Francisco Chronicle*, March 20, 2003 , available from *www.sfgate.com cgi-bin/article.cgi?f=/c/a/2003/03/20/MN12444.DTL*

107. Jonathan Foreman, "Disaster in Waiting: U.S. Still Bungling the Iraqi Peace," *New York Post*, May 16, 2003, available from *www.jonathanforeman.com/opeds/disaster.html*.

108. Chiarelli and Michaelis, pp. 4, 17.

109. Headquarters U.S. Army, "U.S. Army Field Manual 3-0, Operations: A Blueprint for an Uncertain Future," Road show briefing slides with scripted notes, Washington DC, The Pentagon, January 8, 2008.

110. *Ibid*.

111. Kevin C. M. Benson, "OIF Phase IV: A Planner's Reply to Brigadier Aylwin-Foster," *Military Review*, March-April 2006, p. 61.

112. Bob Woodward, *Plan of Attack*, New York: Simon and Schuster Paperbacks, 2004, p. 281.

113. Benson, p. 61.

114. *Ibid*.

115. Woodward, p. 413.

116. Van Wagenen, p. 2.

117. David H. Petraeus, James F. Amos, and John A. Nagl, *The U.S. Army and Marine Corps Counterinsurgency Field Manual*, Chicago IL: University of Chicago Press, 2007.

118. Department of Defense, *Military Support to Security, Stabilization, Transition, and Reconstruction Joint Operating Concept, Version 2.0*, Washington, DC: The Pentagon, December 2006.

119. U.S. Army War College, "Peacekeeping & Stability Operations Institute, PKSOI, Homepage," available from *www.carlisle.army.mil/pksoi/info.aspx?action=information&sideNavNum=1*.

120. Crane, p. 27.

121. Robert M. Gates, *Landon Lecture*, remarks delivered at Kansas State University, Manhattan, KS, November 26, 2007, available from *www.defenselink.mil/speeches/speech.aspx?speechid=1199*.

122. Robert M. Perito, "The U.S. Experience with Provincial Reconstruction Teams in Afghanistan," *United States Institute of Peace Special Report 152*, Washington, DC: United States Institute of Peace, October 2005, p. 1.

123. *Ibid*.

124. Van Wagenen, p. 5.

125. Department of Defence Directive 3000.05

126. Van Wagenen, p. 9.

ABOUT THE CONTRIBUTORS

JOHN E. BESSLER, a U.S. Army colonel, is currently the Division Chief in the Security, Reconstruction and Transition Division of the Peacekeeping & Stability Operations Institute, Carlisle, Pennsylvania. He previously served as an Infantry battalion commander stateside as well as Commander, Afghan Regional Security/Integration Team, Western Provinces, in Herat, Afghanistan in 2008 and 2009. He is an Operation DESERT SHIELD/DESERT STORM veteran. Colonel Bessler holds a master's degree from Central Michigan University and is a Class of 2008 graduate of the U.S. Army War College.

LORELEI E. W. COPLEN, a U.S. Army colonel, is currently the Chief, Policy and Knowledge Management division of the Peacekeeping & Stability Operations Institute, Carlisle, Pennsylvania. Her previous assignments include an aviation battalion command with the 101st Airborne (Air Assault) Division and numerous aviation operations and logistics positions throughout the U.S. and Germany. She is a veteran of the Gulf and the Iraq wars. Colonel Coplen holds a master's degree from the Eisenhower Fellowship at West Point, New York, in Organizational Leadership, and is a Class of 2008 graduate of the U.S. Army War College.

MICHAEL E. CULPEPPER is a U.S. Army colonel currently assigned as the Executive Assistant to the Director, Joint Staff. He has served in numerous infantry command and staff positions in the U.S. and overseas. He is a veteran of multiple Operation IRAQI FREEDOM tours. Colonel Culpepper is a Class of 2008 graduate of the U.S. Army War College.

GARY D. ESPINAS, a U.S. Army colonel, is currently assigned to the Office of the Secretary of Defense as an adviser to the Deputy Assistant Secretary of Defense for Russia, Ukraine, and Eurasia Policy, and serves as President of the Foreign Area Officer Association. He is a Foreign Area Officer with previous assignments in the Department of State; Headquarters, Department of the Army Staff; U.S. Embassy Moscow, Russia; and the Defense Threat Reduction Agency, Frankfurt, Germany. Originally commissioned as a field artillery officer, he is a veteran of Operations DESERT SHIELD and DESERT STORM. Colonel Espinas holds a B.A. from the University of California at Berkeley, M.A. degrees from the U.S. Army War College and Harvard University, and is a Class of 2008 graduate of the U.S. Army War College.

JAMES F. GLYNN, a lieutenant colonel in the U.S. Marine Corps, is currently the J5, Director of Theater Engagement and Plans, for Special Operations Command-Africa. Prior assignments include command of the Battalion Landing Team 2nd Battalion, 4th Marines deployed to the Al Anbar Province, Iraq, with the 15th Marine Expeditionary Unit (Special Operations Capable). Lieutenant Colonel Glynn is a career infantry officer and holds a B.S. in Mechanical Engineering from the U.S. Naval Academy, a master's degree in Military Studies from the U.S. Marine Corps Command and Staff College, and is a Class of 2008 graduate of the U.S. Army War College.

THOMAS GRAVES is a colonel in the U.S. Army and is currently assigned as the Commander, 1st Heavy Brigade Combat Team, 2nd Infantry Division at Camp Hovey, Korea. His previous assignments were as an infantryman in the U.S. Army for over 23 years. Originally commissioned from the United States Military Academy, he has commanded at multiple levels, most recently as the Commander, 1st Battalion, 36th Infantry Regiment in Friedberg, Germany. He has served in combat in Panama and Iraq including 10 months as the Deputy Brigade Commander for 2nd Brigade, 2nd Infantry Division in Ramadi, Iraq and 14 months as a battalion commander in Hit, Iraq. Colonel Graves holds a master's degree in Education from McNeese State University, is a graduate of the School of Advanced Military Studies, and is a Class of 2008 graduate of the U.S. Army War College.

MARCO E. HARRIS is a colonel in the Maryland Army National Guard and serves as the Chief of The Joint Staff, MDARNG. He holds a Bachelor's Degree from the University of Baltimore and is a Class of 2008 graduate of the U.S. Army War College.

RUSSELL R. HULA, a U.S. Air Force colonel, is currently the Operations Division Chief, Directorate of Installations and Mission Support, Headquarters Air Combat Command, Langley Air Force Base, Virginia. His previous assignments include command of a Civil Engineer Squadron at Charleston Air Force Base, South Carolina, and he twice served as a deployed Expeditionary Civil Engineer Squadron commander in Iraq and Oman supporting Operations IRAQI FREEDOM and ENDURING FREEDOM. He also served as a battle staff member aboard USSTRATCOM's Airborne Command Post (ABNCP) and Mobile Consolidated Command Center (MCCC). Colonel Hula holds an M.S. in Science from the Air Force Institute of Technology, and is a Class of 2008 graduate of the U.S. Army War College.

JAMES C. "JAIME" LAUGHREY, a U.S. Army lieutenant colonel, is currently the Senior Advisor for Intelligence, Operational Integration Division of the Peacekeeping & Stability Operations Institute, Carlisle, Pennsylvania. He previously served as the executive officer of the interagency CENTCOM Assessment Team formed by General David Petraeus in 2008-09, as a strategic analyst in the CENTCOM Commander's Advisory Group and for the Chairman of the Joint Chiefs of Staff, and in a variety of joint and Army intelligence positions both in the United States and overseas. He is a veteran of Operations IRAQI FREEDOM, ENDURING FREEDOM, DESERT SHIELD, DESERT STORM, and JOINT FORGE. Lieutenant Colonel Laughrey holds a Master's degree from the National Defense Intelligence College, and is a Class of 2008 graduate of the U.S. Army War College.

LAURA LOFTUS, a U.S. Army colonel, is currently a Special Assistant to the Supreme Allied Commander Europe/Commander U.S. European Command. She previously served in engineer units from Platoon to Brigade level and commanded a Combat Engineer battalion in the 4th Infantry Division in Iraq. During that tour, she and her Soldiers experienced first-hand the true nature and complexity of military operations in the 21st century. Colonel Loftus is a Class of 2008 graduate of the U.S. Army War College.

ROGER S. MARIN, a U.S. Army colonel, is currently the Director of the Office of Time-Dominant Operations, Analysis and Production Directorate, National Geospatial-Intelligence Agency, Bethesda, Maryland. He has served in various command and staff positions at the White House, Joint Staff, and operational and tactical units in the United States, Germany, and Panama. Colonel Marin holds a Master's degree in Strategic Intelligence from the National Defense Intelligence College and is a Class of 2008 graduate of the U.S. Army War College.

DENNIS R. J. PENN is a National Security Agency analyst. He previously served in the U.S. Navy as a linguist before joining the Agency in 1998. Mr. Penn is a Class of 2008 graduate of the U.S. Army War College.

TOM RHATICAN, a colonel in the U.S. Army Reserve, is a Group Commander in the 75th Battle Command Training Division at Fort Sheridan, Illinois. He served as the commander of an aviation task force in support of the sensitive site exploitation in Iraq in 2003. He is an attorney and has worked in private practice, the Wisconsin Legislature, and most recently for the Wisconsin Department of Veterans Affairs. Colonel Rhatican is a graduate of the University of Wisconsin School of Law and is a Class of 2008 graduate of the U.S. Army War College.

IAN A. RIGDEN, a colonel in the British Army, is currently the Assistant Head of Thematic Doctrine in The UK MOD Developments, Concepts and Doctrine Centre at Shrivenham. He served as a Gurkha Infantry battalion commander in Brunei and Afghanistan, and for a total of 7 years as a Company Commander in Hong Kong, the Falkland Islands (post-conflict), Belize, and Bosnia. He has held staff appointments in the MOD, HQ Land Forces, HQ 1st UK Armd Div and HQ MNF-I, and has been an instructor on the UK Advanced Command and Staff Course. He is a veteran of Northern Ireland, Bosnia, Afghanistan and Iraq. Colonel Rigden holds a Master's Degree in Defence Studies from King's College, London, and is a Class of 2008 graduate of the U.S. Army War College.

ROGER H. WESTERMEYER, a U.S. Air Force colonel, is currently the Director of Contracting, Ogden Air Logistics Center, Hill Air Force Base, Utah. He has served in several squadron command and higher headquarters staff positions and most recently served as Principle Assistant Responsible for Contracting-Iraq, Joint Contracting Command, Baghdad, Iraq. In this capacity, he supported the Multi-National Forces-Iraq and oversaw 15 Regional Contracting Centers executing over $6 billion annually. He holds a Bachelor's degree from the University of Kentucky, Master's degrees from the Air University and Central Missouri University, and is a Class of 2008 graduate of the U.S. Army War College.

JONATHAN P. WILCOX, a U.S. Navy commander and Medical Service Corps officer, is currently serving as Medical Plans and Operations Director and Deputy Medical Advisor at the North Atlantic Treaty Organization, Joint Forces Command Brunssum, the Netherlands. He has held various staff officer positions in the United States, Europe, and Japan. Commander Wilcox served as a Surgical Company Commander in Operation IRAQI FREEDOM and as the Medical Operations and Plans director on the International Security and Assistance Force, Kabul, Afghanistan. A board certified Aerospace Physiologist, he holds a military subspecialty in Plans, Operations and Medical Intelligence, and is a warfare qualified Fleet Marine Forces officer. Commander Wilcox holds Bachelor's and Master's Degrees from Marshall University in Huntington, West Virginia, and is a Class of 2008 graduate of the U.S. Army War College.

HARRY R. "RICH" YARGER, a retired U.S. Army colonel, is the Ministry Reform Advisor in the Security, Reconstruction and Transition Division of the Peacekeeping & Stability Operations Institute, Carlisle, Pennsylvania. Prior to joining the Institute in September 2009, he served as Professor of National Security Policy in the Department of National Security and Strategy at the U.S. Army War College where he held the Elihu Root Chair of Military Studies and taught courses in Fundamentals of Strategic Thinking; Theory of War and Strategy; National Security Policy and Strategy; Grand Strategy; Terrorism; and the Interagency. His research focuses on strategic theory, national security policy and strategy, terrorism, irregular warfare, effective governance, and the education and development of strategic level leaders. In addition to teaching positions, he served 5 years as the Chairman of the War College's Department of Distance Education. Dr. Yarger has also taught at the undergraduate level at several local colleges. His latest work is *Strategy and the National Security Professional: Strategic Thinking and Strategy Formulation in the 21st Century* (Santa Barbara, CA: Praeger Security International, July 2008). He is a Vietnam veteran and served in both Germany and Korea. He holds a Ph.D. from Temple University with fields in U.S. military history, U.S. diplomatic history, European diplomatic history, and American social history.

U.S. ARMY WAR COLLEGE

Major General Robert M. Williams
Commandant

*****

STRATEGIC STUDIES INSTITUTE

Director
Professor Douglas C. Lovelace, Jr.

Director of Research
Dr. Antulio J. Echevarria II

Editor
Dr. Harry R. (Rich) Yarger

Director of Publications
Dr. James G. Pierce

Publications Assistant
Ms. Rita A. Rummel

*****

Composition
Mrs. Jennifer E. Nevil